BEING HAL ASHBY

Screen Classics

Screen Classics is a series of critical biographies, film histories, and analytical studies focusing on neglected filmmakers and important screen artists and subjects, from the era of silent cinema to the golden age of Hollywood to the international generation of today. Books in the Screen Classics series are intended for scholars and general readers alike. The contributing authors are established figures in their respective fields. This series also serves the purpose of advancing scholarship on film personalities and themes with ties to Kentucky.

SERIES EDITOR
Patrick McGilligan

BEING HAL ASHBY

LIFE OF A HOLLYWOOD REBEL

Nick Dawson

THE UNIVERSITY PRESS OF KENTUCKY

Paperback edition 2011

Scholarly publisher for the Commonwealth,
serving Bellarmine University, Berea College, Centre
College of Kentucky, Eastern Kentucky University,
The Filson Historical Society, Georgetown College,
Kentucky Historical Society, Kentucky State University,
Morehead State University, Murray State University,
Northern Kentucky University, Transylvania University,
University of Kentucky, University of Louisville,
and Western Kentucky University.

Editorial and Sales Offices: The University Press of Kentucky
663 South Limestone Street, Lexington, Kentucky 40508-4008
www.kentuckypress.com

The Library of Congress has cataloged the hardcover edition as follows:

Dawson, Nick, 1980–
Being Hal Ashby : life of a Hollywood rebel / Nick Dawson.
p. cm. — (Screen classics)
Includes bibliographical references and index.
ISBN 978-0-8131-2538-1 (hardcover : alk. paper)
1. Ashby, Hal. 2. Motion picture producers and directors—
United States—Biography. I. Title.
PN1998.3.A7635D39 2009
791.4302'33092—dc22
[B]
2009001258

ISBN 978-0-8131-3463-5 (pbk. : alk. paper)
ISBN 978-0-8131-7334-4 (ebook)

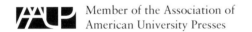

This book is printed on acid-free paper meeting
the requirements of the American National Standard
for Permanence in Paper for Printed Library Materials.

Manufactured in the United States of America.

Member of the Association of
American University Presses

For my parents, Agathe and Ken Dawson

Contents

Acknowledgments

I first became interested in Hal Ashby when I read Peter Biskind's *Easy Riders, Raging Bulls* some ten years ago. In 2002, after writing a biographical sketch of Ashby for a biography class, I joked to my tutor, Carole Angier, that I would turn it into a book. Well, the joke was on me. Carole, a brilliant biographer, proved to be the ideal mentor—pragmatic, resourceful, and generous. She shepherded me through the first year of my research, always ready with encouragement and illuminating advice. She was officially my mentor thanks to the Arts Council Writers Pool through the Royal Literary Fund and remains my mentor and great friend.

The book really began to take shape during my three months in Los Angeles. I spent the vast majority of the time consulting Hal Ashby's papers at the Margaret Herrick Library of the Academy of Motion Picture Arts and Sciences (AMPAS). Barbara Hall and her staff did an incredible job, and I am eternally grateful for the warmth of everyone there who made me feel at home for the duration of my stay. Also of great help to me during my time in Los Angeles were Snowden Becker and Brian Meacham at the AMPAS Film Archive, Caroline Sisneros and the staff of the American Film Institute library, Ned Comstock at the University of Southern California Film Library, and Todd Weiner and Mark Quigley at the University of California, Los Angeles, Film and Television Archive. And while I am acknowledging libraries, I want to thank Charles Silver at the Museum of Modern Art Film Library and the staff of the New York Public Library for the Performing Arts as well as the staffs of the British Film Institute Library, the British Library, the British Library Newspaper Library, the University of Warwick Library, and the National Library of Scotland.

My efforts to bring Ashby to life would have been futile without the contributions of Ashby's family, friends, and collaborators. The first people I interviewed were Jack and Beth Ashby, and they were most generous with their advice and guidance through the duration of the project. My heartfelt thanks go out to them and everyone else who shared their memories of Ashby with me. It was relatively late on that I made contact with Leigh MacManus, Ashby's daughter, but getting to know her added a new significance to the act of writing this book, and I now happily count her as one of my closest friends and, yes, my "American mom." In addition, special thanks go to Bill Box, Chuck Mulvehill, and Jon Voight, who opened doors to me that would otherwise have remained hidden or closed.

For providing me with rare and hard-to-find materials or expertise on the more obscure aspects of Ashby's life and work, I tip my hat to Holly Allen at Ogden High School, Thom Ernst at TV Ontario, Catherine Exton at the Bainbridge Island Historical Society, and Alison Palmer Bourke at the Independent Film Channel as well as Chris Cutri, Joyce Gallie, Jeremy Goldscheider and Richard Goldgewicht, Josh Hadley, Per B. Hansen, Heath Keane, Jerry Lembcke, Charles Lindenberg, Mary Myers, and Jim Yoakum.

I am grateful to Judith "J. B." Anderson, Jack, Beth, and Guy Ashby, Joe Baltake, Bill Box, Jeremy Goldscheider and Richard Goldgewicht, Bret Haller, Leigh McManus, Chuck Mulvehill, Larry Reynolds, Pierre Sauvage, and Jeff Wexler, for offering me the use of photographs from their personal collections, and to Ron Mandelbaum at PhotoFest in New York City and Sue Guldin at the Herrick Library, who were invaluable in helping find the remainder of the photographs reproduced in the book.

I am also grateful to the following people for granting me interviews: Judith "J. B." Anderson, Carrie Ashby, Robert Ballantyne, Joe Baltake, Maloy Baretto, Chuck Barris, Warren Beatty, Deanna Benatovich, Peter Benson, Robert Benton, Alan Bergman, Ian Bernard, A. Lee Blackman, Tom Blackwell, Bill and Gloria Box, Gianni Bozzacchi, Andrew Braunsberg, Beau Bridges, Jeff Bridges, Garrett Brown, Steve Burum, Bob Busico, Michael Butler, David Carradine, Robert Carradine, Julie Christie, Charles Clapsaddle, Gus Cooper, Guy D'Alema, Michael Dare, Andrew Davis, Lisa Day, Caleb Deschanel, Robert Downey Sr. (a prince), Charles Eastman, Pablo Ferro, James Foley, Joyce Gallie, Andy Garcia, Eva Gardos, Robert Ginty, Lee Grant, Lynn "Grif" Griffis, Janice Grow, Max Grow, James William Guercio, Betty Gumm, Eric Haller, Jerry Hellman, Simon Hinkly, Dustin Hoffman, Melodie Johnson Howe, Celia Imrie, Norman Jewison, Bob Jones, Mike Kaplan, Al Kooper, Kenneth Kleinberg, Richard La Gravenese, Prince Rupert Loewenstein, Mireille Machu, Leigh MacManus, Derek Malcolm, John Mandel, Doe Mayer, Mike Medavoy, Chuck Mulvehill, Michael O'Keefe, Rick Padilla, Alexandra Paul, Larry Reynolds, Bob Schaffel, Paul Schoeman, Dianne Schroeder Hanks, Al Schwartz, Sonya Sones, Peter Sorel, Jack Swanson, John Teton, Jon Voight, Haskell Wexler, Jeff Wexler, Rudy Wurlitzer, and Chris Young.

A large number of fellow journalists and writers gave me contact details, clippings, counsel, and encouragement. Many thanks to Peter Biskind, Jim Davidson, David Ehrenstein, Bob Fischer, Luke Ford, Darren Hughes, Jessica Hundley, Allan Hunter, Robin Lloyd Jones, Derek Malcolm, Gerald Peary, Brian Pendreigh, Stephen Rebello, Dan Sallitt, Pierre Sauvage, David Sterritt, Peter Tonguette, Sylvia Townsend, Charles Trentelman, and Linda Ruth Williams. A special thank-you goes to David Stenn for Maxine.

There were also a handful of writers who gave much, much more than I could have hoped for in terms of their editorial notes, support, and encouragement. I am deeply grateful to David Parkinson, Lee Hill, and Patrick McGilligan—dinner is on me next time.

And while I mention the writing profession, I would like to express my appreciation to Michael Bonner, Peter Bowen, Dan Jolin, Scott Macaulay, Angus McDonald, and Alan Morrison, who have all given me work when I needed it.

Additionally, my friends—despite thinking I had gone slightly crazy—were very supportive, and I must therefore give an appreciative nod to Suzi Buchner, Harry Cayton, Pete Hinstridge, Amy Lanchester, Jan Lee, Jenny Queen, Jonny Riddell, Denny Vlaeva, and Henry Volans.

Leila Salisbury and Anne Dean Watkins, my editors at the University Press of Kentucky, achieved the remarkable feat of making the process of readying the book for publication not only understandable and easy but actually enjoyable.

Very special thanks go to my parents, Agathe and Ken, and my sister, Jo. After university, I decided that rather than getting a proper job I wanted to spend the foreseeable future doing research for a book about someone very few people had heard of. My parents allowed me to come back home for long periods in order to pursue my unreasonable dream. Quite simply, without their unwavering love and support, this book would not exist.

The final acknowledgment must, of course, go to my wife, Heather. The story of our lives together is inextricably linked with this book: I met Heather when she was working at the Margaret Herrick Library; we took our lunches at the same time every day, and we kind of took things from there. Almost four years later, I can't imagine life without her, and within the context of the book, she has been my rock. A former copyeditor, she took it upon herself to go through my hefty manuscript word for word to help make it the best book it could be. She has made me a better person and unquestionably a better writer. Sweetheart, I promise the next one will be much easier.

Prologue

June 2, 1969, the morning of his first day directing, and Hal can't breathe. He has bronchitis. He can't talk. All he can do is gasp and point. The doctor comes, checks him over, and tells him he has walking pneumonia, brought on by fear.

In the seven months or so since his mentor, Norman Jewison, had told him he would be directing his first film, *The Landlord,* a nagging doubt had been eating away at him. Over the past ten years, he'd collaborated closely with Jewison, as well as such Hollywood greats as William Wyler and George Stevens, and had keenly watched how they worked. Even after a week of rehearsals, he feared he wouldn't be able to communicate properly with the actors or get them to give him what he wanted.

The rehearsals hadn't been very conventional: the cast read through the script, talked about the characters, expressed their ideas about the story. Everybody got to know each other, and it was relaxed, just how Hal liked it. Though he hadn't really addressed the problem at all, he'd hoped the week of rapping with the actors had gotten rid of that little knot inside him.

"You've got to go to bed," says the doctor.[1]

"Hell, no!" Hal manages to say between gasps and tells him to pump him full of any drug he can, to inject anything into any part of his body.[2] Just do whatever is necessary so he can go and direct.

Hal is terrified and sick, but there's a part of him that's buzzing with excitement. It's been almost fifteen years: he's made it through eight grueling years as an apprentice editor, he's worked night and day, putting his job ahead of everything, he's seen his dedication to the dream destroy two marriages, but he's won an Oscar as an editor, and now he's about to direct his first film. He's right where he wants to be: he's got a seat with his name on the back, and they're waiting for him to call "Action!"

1

Enter Hal

> I was born in Ogden, Utah. Never a Mormon. Hated school. The last of four children. Mom and Dad divorced when I was five or six. Dad killed himself when I was twelve. I struggled toward growing up, like most others, totally confused.
> —Hal Ashby

Hal Ashby's paternal grandfather, Thomas Ashby, came to America in 1870. Just twenty-one when he left his hometown of Leicester, England, he crossed the Atlantic with his eighteen-year-old fiancée, Rachael Hill. After training as a shoemaker in Lynne, Massachusetts, then the American center of quality shoemaking, he moved west in pursuit of new opportunities. He ended up in Utah, and, after unsuccessfully joining a boot and shoemaking cooperative, he settled in Ogden, where he started his own business.

Sixty miles north of Salt Lake City, Ogden was a growing town rich in potential for entrepreneurs because it was the "Junction City" of the Union and Central Pacific railway. The population was doubling every ten years, and Thomas Ashby benefited hugely from an ever-growing number of customers: by the early 1880s, he was employing eleven men and had moved to a specially constructed building with a factory in the rear and a shop in the front. His family was growing too: by 1885, Rachael had given birth to seven children (only five survived). The following year, however, she died, and Thomas married Emily Coleman, the sixteen-year-old daughter of James Coleman, one of his shoemakers. A year later, Emily bore him a son, James Thomas Ashby, but Thomas's fortunes after this did not look up.

His decision to bring his brother John into the firm and significantly expand the business coincided with a major downturn in the American economy that culminated in the Panic of 1893. Having had huge success as a maker of high-quality shoes and boots, he discovered to his great cost that luxury products were the last thing people bought when times got tough. Massively overstocked, and crippled by enormous debts, Thomas was forced to sell off $20,000 worth of goods for almost nothing. He ultimately lost his business as well as his wife, who married another man, Herbert Peterson. As the century drew to a close, Thomas left Ogden and moved to Salt Lake City.

In early 1901, the "Salt Lake News" section of the *Ogden Standard* announced: "Thomas Ashby was yesterday examined by County Physician Mayo and Dr. H. A. Anderson touching his sanity. He was found to be insane and committed to the asylum. Ashby is 53 years of age and his mental derangement was brought about by business difficulties and domestic affliction."[1] Four years later, he died in Provo, Utah, aged only fifty-five.

Raised by his mother and stepfather, Thomas's son James Ashby never really knew his father. Though the overwhelming majority of people in Ogden (and Utah as a whole) were Mormon, Herbert Peterson was a Gentile, and James grew up only nominally a member of the church. A highly sociable youth, he attended more to fraternize than because of any religious fervor but was grateful he did when he met and fell for a pretty young Ogden girl, Eileen Hetzler, at a church social function. Eileen was intelligent, strong willed, and aspirational, and in the handsome and charismatic James she saw someone with similar drive and potential. Like James, Eileen had grown up in an unconventional family setup: she was the daughter of the polygamist Ogden dentist Dr. Luther Hetzler and one of his two wives, Martha Ann Hadfield. Dr. Hetzler had died when Eileen was only three, and Martha had remarried another fervent Mormon, David Steele, subsequently showing her daughter little affection at all. Eileen was, in fact, much closer to her "Aunt Cate"—Dr. Hetzler's other widow, Catherine Tribe—with whom she remained close for many years.

On November 10, 1909, James and Eileen were married in the temple in Salt Lake City, the home of the Mormon Church. Eileen quickly became pregnant and gave birth to a boy, James Hetzler Ashby (known as "Hetz"), in December 1910. He was followed just over a year later by a baby girl, Ardith, born in February 1912. James got a job working on the Bamberger trains that took commuters to and from Ogden and

Salt Lake City, and Eileen would meet his train as it came along the Ogden Canyon, bringing him a packed lunch to eat as they walked home together.

Unlike James, Eileen had been raised as a strict orthodox Mormon, and as a condition of their marriage he had been baptized. Eileen and her family wanted James to become more involved with the church, so they convinced him to sign up to go on a mission, something usually undertaken by those without ties, young men in their late teens or early twenties, or retirees.

Unfortunately, James was sent on a proselytizing mission to South Africa, one of the most demanding missions conceivable. It was usual to go to a different state to spread the word of the church, but James had to leave his wife and children and go halfway around the world—and pay for all of it himself. Given the dangers involved in traveling to and then living in Africa, there was no guarantee that he would return. It was the biggest crisis of James and Eileen's life together so far, both financially and personally. The home that had been built especially for them at the time of their wedding was sold to pay for James's mission. Eileen and the children were relocated to a quickly assembled house built by James in David Steele's back garden, and through Steele Eileen got a job cooking in the county jail. For the next few years, she was to be the family's sole breadwinner.

On September 19, 1916, James left Ogden, his family, his friends, and everything he knew behind. During the two and a half years he was away, he traveled all the way around the world, visiting Honolulu, American Samoa (where he wrote that he "picked bananas and coconuts, and visited the natives in their huts"), Australia, Madeira, and England.[2]

In South Africa, his time was mostly spent tracting and proselytizing in Cape Town, where he was called a he-devil, attacked by prospective converts' dogs, and threatened with being shot. In his time off, however, he played tennis and baseball, caught a shark, saw penguins, scrubbed tortoises, made a whole freezer full of ice cream, and discovered the wonders of the cinema. On one occasion, he found a vantage point from which Robben Island, the Atlantic Ocean, "the Indian ocean, . . . Cape Town harbor and docks and the city of Cape Town with her suburbs" could be seen at one time, "the most beautifull [*sic*] sight I ever saw in my life."[3]

James had never left Utah before, let alone America, and his time in South Africa not only broadened his horizons immeasurably but also taught him about life's brutal realities. James and another missionary, Elder Merrill, were sent to Port Elizabeth to tract, and the pair had to make the return journey of more than four hundred miles on bicycle. If they were lucky, they slept exhausted in barns after eating scraps, but often their requests for food and shelter met with aggressive responses from wary farmers, and they had to lie in fields and ditches, able only to dream about food.

Just before James left South Africa, the Spanish influenza pandemic reached Cape Town. Within days, huge swathes of the population were stricken, and in the poorest parts of the city the dead lay in the streets, piled up on wagons to be buried in mass graves. James was fortunate not to be infected, but he nursed many of the sick and saw his fellow missionary Victor Burlando, a Mormon baby, and many more around him die. Only on Armistice Day, a few weeks later, did anyone in Cape Town smile again.

James kept a diary during the course of his mission detailing his experiences. In his final entry—dated April 19, 1919, the day he returned home—he wrote that he met a friend at the station "who took me home in his car," poignantly adding that he "spent the afternoon getting acquainted with my wife and children."[4]

On his return, James bought out the business he had previously worked for, the Uintah Dairy Company, which had a bottling plant and a milk route. Over the next ten years, he turned it into a mini empire comprising five or six routes, a neighborhood grocery store, and a roadside lunch stand. The steely determination that had gotten him through his mission, along with his innate charm, made him a natural entrepreneur.

While his business flourished, things were more difficult at home. James had missed out on crucial years of his children's development and felt distanced from Eileen. Communication during their years apart had been almost impossible: there were no telephones, and letters were sent via China and tended to turn up in bundles of twos and threes or not at all. James felt bitter about what he had been through and turned away from the church, but Eileen (who had herself become disenchanted for the same reasons) still took the children to Sunday services. They spent little time together, as James threw himself into his work and then frustrated Eileen by spending his free time playing poker with friends.

Recognizing that their marriage was in trouble, they hoped having more children might bring them closer again. So in 1925 Jack Ashby came into the world, followed four years later by his baby brother: Hal.

William Hal Ashby had, in his own words, "an interesting childhood, as those things go."[5] Born at ten minutes past midnight on September 2, 1929, he apparently weighed an enormous fourteen pounds and already had curly blond hair. Baby Hal was delivered by Eileen's brother-in-law, Dr. Wiley Cragun, at the Ashbys' family home at 3531 Washington Boulevard and then moved to the maternity hospital on Twenty-first Street. It was love at first sight for Eileen, and from that moment onward he would always be her darling baby boy. In 1960, she wrote him a letter in anticipation of his birthday, in which her continuing devotion is touchingly apparent:

> It will soon be 31 years since I first saw your dear little face. The cutest thing I ever saw. When you were 5 days old you just cried and cried day and night. I ask the nurse why you couldn't rest. She said you were colicy. But when she went out I got up and looked you over. Your poor behind was almost blistered. I changed you. Put on some old remedy I had there and informed the nurse . . . that I would change you from then on. You soon were sleeping and happy with the cutest fat hind end I ever saw.[6]

Hal and his hind end arrived the day before his father's forty-second birthday and just over two months before Eileen and James's twentieth wedding anniversary. More significantly, he was born eight weeks before the Wall Street crash that was to plunge America into the Great Depression.

Utah was one of the states worst hit by the Depression; however, the Ashbys were fortunate to escape the full impact of the crash. As Hal's father owned his own business, he was not among the many who lost their jobs, and because he owned both the Uintah Dairy Company and the grocery store, he was in a particularly strong position.

After Utah's liquor laws were relaxed in 1935, James expanded his empire by opening a drive-in beer parlor on Washington Boulevard called the Big Mug. People could drive up, drink beer for two or three hours, and then drive off again. If necessary, there were a few cots in the basement where patrons could sober up until they were fit to leave. It was a remarkably successful venture and compensated for any lean periods at the dairy or the store. At the end of the Depression, James's financial situation was comfortable enough for him and Hal to load up a wagon and take milk down to vagrants in the hobo camp on the outskirts of town.

But such father-son excursions were rare as James worked long hours at the store. Eileen, despite her devotion to little Hal, was also absent much of the time, so it was Ardith who took her younger brothers around town and to doctors' appointments and babysat whenever necessary. Because Hetz was eighteen and Ardith seventeen when Hal was born and both remained unmarried until they were in their thirties, they became like second parents to Hal and Jack. Ardith in particular did so much for them that Hal affectionately called her "Sis," as if he almost had to remind himself that she wasn't his mother.

On the occasion of Hal's third birthday, Ardith wrote a piece on her baby brother that shows the great love she felt for him. More significantly, it reveals that aspects of his personality that he would display as a director—his charm, his temper, his intrepidity, his interest in technological gadgets, and, moreover, his ability to inspire great love and loyalty in others—were already very much at the fore:

> Although Hal is now three years old I still call him my little angel from heaven. That is what he has always seemed to me. To me he is extra adorable, and of course, clever. For a child he has an extra pleasing personality. Not being backward and slightly forward he makes friends with most every one. He chatters and expresses himself so that you can't help but adore him. He has a way of flattering by telling you that you are pretty or your eyes are pretty. He is grateful for what you do for him. I love and worship him so much that I could rave on for ever, but—telling what I think of this darling little creature I forgot one or two things. First of all he has a temper. Nothing out of the ordinary, but he lets us know when he is angry or wants his way. Of course, this is natural. If he were perfect he wouldn't be such a darling.
>
> During the first weeks and months of walking we were sure he would be a great electrician when he got older. He connected

and disconnected every plug he could find and for weeks he played with an iron cord. This continued for several months, until he got so many shocks he left electric things alone.

He is still so young that it is hard to tell what he will be when he grows up. I have great hopes that he will be a good student, a leader, and have many friends.

I also wish for his advancement and that he will make something of Himself.

Love,

Hal's big sister, Ardith Ashby[7]

If Ardith was like a mother to Hal, then Hetz, in turn, was a father figure and a role model for Hal and Jack. He was a Scout leader, played the trumpet, and was a true gentleman, and accordingly Jack joined the Scouts, took up the trumpet, and grew up to be a gentleman like his brother. Hal, however, had a rebellious streak and as a boy lacked his brothers' discipline and commitment, though he would later have both in spades. He too took trumpet lessons and joined the Scouts but didn't last long with either.

Despite their differences, Jack and Hal were almost inseparable childhood companions. However, on one particular day around 1934, Jack was convinced that their fun had come to a tragic end. They were playing with a broomstick when Jack decided to throw the "spear" at a cushion on the porch swing. But just as he threw it, Hal's head popped up from behind the seat—and the "spear" hit him square in the forehead, knocking him to the ground.

Jack rushed to see what had happened to Hal and saw that there was a big gash on his forehead and that he was completely still. With great trepidation, he quickly phoned his parents at the store.

"You'd better come home," Jack gasped. "I've just killed Hal."[8]

The store was only a few blocks away, and James and Eileen rushed home in a complete panic. Fortunately, with the help of Uncle Wiley, it was discovered that Hal was merely concussed and that his gash needed only a few stitches.

For Jack and Hal, the first half of the 1930s was a happy time, filled with fun and games and the innocence of childhood. They had picnics and went on camping trips, and neither of the boys saw the signs of the problems between their parents that Ardith and Hetz had been seeing for years. On the surface, nothing seemed to be wrong. There were no arguments, and both parents always seemed to be around. But in 1935, James and Eileen got divorced.

At first, things were not much different. The divorce was dealt with quickly and amicably by both parties so that the children were not too traumatized by what was going on. Though they no longer lived with him, Jack and Hal nevertheless spent a lot of time with their father, who was still welcome at the house. They also worked for him at the store, stocking the shelves and cleaning up for extra pocket money.

The divorce seemed to be what caused the Ashbys to finally and fully split from the church. As 80–90 percent of Ogden residents were Mormons, the Ashbys being "inactive" was an issue for many people, and though they were not ostracized, they were still made to feel uncomfortable. A number of Jack and Hal's classmates at school repeated their parents' verdicts on the matter, telling the Ashby boys that they "were not on the right path."[9]

In later years, the memory that Ashby chose to share from these times was, in fact, humorous rather than sad. It concerned a trip to Salt Lake City to see the Ashbys' general practitioner, Dr. Barrett, that Hal recalled with considerable amusement:

> I went to him for a check up of some sort. All the tests were finished except for my urine specimen. Naturally I couldn't go, so Dr. B told me to go out and walk around Salt Lake, drink plenty of water, and return in an hour. It was during the summer and, as you know, there were water fountains every half block. I must have drunk from thirty of them before returning to Dr. B's office. They handed me a very small bottle, stuck me in a very small room—a room, I might add, that did not have a toilet. It was with grave misgiving that I started to pee. The misgivings were well founded; once started I couldn't stop; there was enough in me to fill five bottles the size he gave me. Needless to say, I flooded that small room. The only saving factor was a box of Kleenex. That, at least, allowed me to sop up the excess. I never told Dr. B. about that, and it must have been twenty years

> or more after that before I was able, without great difficulty, to give a urine specimen, when requested by various doctors, even if I was put in a room with ten toilets in it. Also, I have often wondered what the person thought when they emptied the waste basket in that small room and found all those soggy Kleenex tissues.[10]

On March 14, 1936, Hal's father went to Las Vegas to tie the knot with one Clarissa Little. Quite how long they'd been a couple is unclear; however, the proximity of his divorce and their wedding raises questions as to whether Clarissa was a factor in the dissolution of James and Eileen's marriage and set Ogden tongues wagging. People's allegiances were with Eileen rather than "the new woman," who many assumed had broken up a twenty-five-year marriage. Even worse, Clarissa was a Gentile. James's customers made it clear that she was not welcome at the store, and she was seldom seen about.

About this time, Eileen decided to pack up with the boys and leave Ogden. They moved a lot in the next few years while Eileen, as Jack puts it, "just bumbled around, kinda trying to find herself, . . . trying to figure out what she wanted to do."[11] First they moved fifty miles north to Logan, where Eileen set up a boardinghouse for students at the Utah State Agricultural College. They stayed there eighteen months, before moving west across the Rocky Mountains to Portland, Oregon. At the time, Hetz was working in Portland in the lumber business, and Eileen settled down there—again for a year and a half or so—putting her cooking prowess to use by opening a restaurant.

Eileen was energetic and full of ideas—which were often unconventional—and was, as Jack says, "always looking for something better." She bought bags of carrots, got Jack and Hal to clean them by putting a load in their washing machine along with a handful of scrubbing brushes, then made carrot juice and sold it, years before it became a fashionable drink. Later, Jack and Hal would laughingly call her "the original hippie."[12] She knew about food and what was good for people and made sure her children ate healthily. A number of her big business ideas revolved around food. In the late 1930s, she bought recipes for donuts and butter toffee for the sum of $200, a huge amount of money at the time. People thought she was mad, but the donuts did such good business that they easily paid back her investment.

During Eileen's restless period, Hal and Jack spent even more time together than usual because they were never anywhere long enough to properly get to know the neighborhood children. All the moving around seemed to be necessary from Eileen's perspective, but it wasn't at all easy for the boys.

To their relief, they returned to Ogden in 1939, but Eileen was still restless, and they moved five or six times within the town. Nevertheless, Hal and Jack were more grounded. They could also once again spend time with their father and, as Hal was now ten, were able to do more grown-up activities. The three of them would go into the Wasatch Mountains, pitch a tent, and spend a weekend hiking, fishing, and hunting. One of the Ashby men's traits was that they rarely had to go to the toilet, which was handy on those camping trips. (Later, when Hal spent weeks on end stuck in an editing room, determinedly focused on his task, this talent was again useful.)

Some days, Jack and Hal would borrow .22 rifles from their father, who collected guns, and go off after school to shoot at old tin cans for target practice. Other days, they grabbed their bikes and rode to a fishing hole a few miles from their home and spent the afternoon fishing or swimming. Once a week, they went to the movies. "Almost every Saturday, Hal and I went to the theaters that showed the weekly serial adventures and cowboy movies," Jack recalls.[13]

The Uintah Dairy pasteurized, bottled, and then delivered milk on seven or eight routes, and when Jack was fourteen, his father made him a delivery driver on one of the routes. The milk had to be delivered to the customers' doorsteps before sunrise, so Jack had to get up at three in the morning, and despite the hour, Hal was sometimes with him. Jack would drive the truck, and Hal would put the bottles on the doorsteps. "In the summertime we'd take the doors off the truck, and he would just jump out with the milk in his hands and run up to the porch and pick up the empty bottles and run back," Jack recalls. "It really was tough getting up that early. It really ruined our social life."[14]

Fortunately, life at home was good. Though they never had a lot of money, Eileen always made the important occasions memorable. For birthdays, she made special cakes, and Santa never let the Ashby boys down on Christmas Eve. Their father was another regular visitor at Christmas and was often invited over for dinner at other times too. In 1941, Hal did not receive individual Christmas cards from his parents, just a joint one from "Dad and Mom." Because Hal and Jack had no contact whatsoever with Clarissa, there must have been times when they almost forgot their parents were divorced at all.

On Sunday, March 22, 1942, James was due to have dinner with Eileen and the boys. Eileen thought he was unhappy with Clarissa and suspected that he wanted to end the marriage, and apparently they had even discussed the possibility of getting back together.

But he never made it to dinner.

That day, he was at the Uintah Dairy Company offices. Just before noon, he told one of his young employees, Denzil Shipley, that he was going to clean his guns, which he had not done since the end of the hunting season. At five past midday, another employee, Bernadine Anderson, heard a shot and rushed into her boss's office. By the time she got there, he was already dead, having died instantly from a shot to the head.

On the few occasions that Hal would discuss his father's death, he always said it had been a suicide; what he did not say was that he was the only person in the family who believed that. It has been said that Hal's father killed himself because he had refused to pasteurize his milk and therefore lost the dairy,[15] that he killed himself in a barn, and that Hal was the one who first discovered the body.[16] None of these stories is true: Hal's father had not lost the dairy; he had no livestock, let alone a barn; and Hal did not find his father's body.

However, determining the truth surrounding James's death is not a straightforward matter. If James was considering rekindling his relationship with Eileen and had no major business problems, there is no readily discernible motive for suicide. And that Hal alone believed his father killed himself makes suicide even less plausible. However, if one examines the sheriff's department's report, it begins to look more likely:

> Weber County Sheriff John R. Watson said today officials had decided the death of James Thomas Ashby, 54, of 3531 Washington, who died of a gunshot wound Sunday, was accidental. After an investigation, he said, officers concluded there was no need of an inquest, and none will be held unless requested by the family.
>
> Mr. Ashby died at twelve—five P.M. Sunday at the offices of the Uintah Dairy Products Co., 3667 Washington, of which he was president. Investigation revealed he had been cleaning guns

> at the time of the accident. He had cleaned two, and was working on the third when it was discharged.
>
> When police arrived, they discovered the barrel of a .32-calibre rifle clutched in one hand. The bullet had entered the head beneath the chin, and medical reports indicated death was instantaneous. Mr. Ashby was alone in his office at the time of the accident. Miss Bernadine Anderson, an employe [*sic*], was in the next room when she heard the shot. Another employe, Denzil Shipley, said he had been talking to Mr. Ashby a few minutes before. He told the youth he had not cleaned his guns since the hunting season so he decided to do it Sunday afternoon, and then have them registered, according to the sheriff.[17]

Whether or not there was an obvious motive, the circumstantial evidence all seems to point clearly to suicide. The fact that James pointedly told an employee he was cleaning his guns five minutes before he shot himself seems too measured, as if he were giving others a way of interpreting his death as accidental; and it seems highly implausible that a man so accustomed to dealing with firearms would clean a .32 rifle while it was loaded. Furthermore, the fact that he shot himself beneath his chin so the bullet entered his brain immediately causing almost instantaneous death suggests that it was a deliberate act. That his death was not fully investigated is not actually so surprising: James was a highly regarded and successful Ogden man, and delving too deeply into his death would probably have caused more grief than it was worth and been considered inappropriate and disrespectful.

The Ashbys were suffering greatly as it was. The funeral was held two days later, less than a mile from the Ashby home. It was still winter in Ogden, and snow fell as the family assembled for the service. Because of the severe bodily disfigurement, there was a closed casket and no viewing of the body. Despite his family's wishes, Jack was determined to take one final look at his father. In the swirling snow, he opened the casket and looked inside. Instead of a face, all he saw was a body with a towel wrapped around its head. "I never did see my dad . . . ," Jack recalls quietly.[18]

The impact of James's death on his family is incalculable, but it was arguably Hal who struggled most with the loss. Because of the years he was away with Eileen in Logan and Portland and the long hours James worked at the store, Hal never properly got to know his father. The one time he discussed his father's death directly with an interviewer, he said: "I was 12 years old. My father used to make me laugh a lot. He would give me a dollar for taking the soda pop bottles to the basement of the store. But we didn't know each other. And only now, in retrospect, can I see how much pain he must have been in."[19] Losing one's father and believing that he killed himself would be incredibly tough at any age, but for it to happen at twelve, when Hal was dealing with the problems of adolescence, must have made it doubly so. He was unable to discuss it with his family, so instead he bottled up the emotion, the anger, and the feeling of injustice, only ever letting it out in uncharacteristic bursts of anger or private moments of desperation.

On the rare occasions he talked to friends about his father, Hal apparently said that his father had arranged for Hal to meet him on the day he died and that when he came to find him, he discovered that he had committed suicide, abandoning him in the most permanent way possible. In the years that followed, Ashby struggled with issues about authority figures as well as fear of emotional closeness, abandonment, and betrayal. These personal demons, which massively affected every aspect of his personal life and business dealings, can be traced back to this incident.

In 1973, the photographer Richard Avedon recommended to Ashby a *New Yorker* piece called "A Story in an Almost Classical Mode" by Harold Brodkey. A rawly honest autobiographical short story about Brodkey's teenage years in the early 1940s, which were overshadowed by his parents' illness and death, it had strong echoes of Ashby's own experiences at that time. Ashby wrote to Avedon and thanked him for "turning me on to the Harold Brodkey story in September's *New Yorker.* I really enjoyed it, and found it a beautiful, thoughtful and loving story."[20] Ashby, however, never mentioned the parallels with his own life or the painful flashes of recognition that reading the story must have caused. Brodkey's work is a revisitation in middle age of the adolescent struggle with the impact of a parent's death, yet this is precisely what Ashby never did. At no stage—neither in his teens nor later on—did he ever delve deeply to examine and heal the scars caused by his father's death. That Hal Ashby "struggled toward growing up, . . . totally confused," is really no surprise.[21]

2

The Artist as a Young Man

> As a rule, the teens are when a person comes closer and closer to the realities of life, and he doesn't want this to happen, but he knows, somewhere deep inside, it must and will come. The reality he dreads most is a plain, simple fact: One day, soon now, he will have to become a responsible human being. All of his life to date has been spent in the luxury of being cared for, and now he is faced with caring for himself. He is selfish by nature, and wants desperately to retain the security he has always known. He rebels against growing up with every means available.
>
> —Hal Ashby

After Eileen brought the boys back to Ogden, Hal spent less time with Jack and began making friends, a luxury he had not had while they were moving around. He was charming and amiable and soon became widely liked. He started to express his personality through his appearance and was always up on the fashions of the day. His hair was perfectly cut and styled, and he wore peg trousers with a key chain. A dapper, handsome teenager, he looked very distinguished in his glasses, while his blond hair, blue eyes, and soft voice added an innocence to his mature sartorial style.

Following his father's death, Hal was thrust into a much more responsible role. He found himself one of the owners of the Uintah Dairy, which James had left to his four children, who, accordingly, turned it over to their mother. After the bombing of Pearl Harbor in 1941, all American boys aged seventeen or eighteen were expected to enlist. Jack left Ogden in March 1943 to join the U.S. Navy, leaving thirteen-year-old Hal, now a student at nearby Washington High School, to be the man of the house.

Hal's adventurousness and exuberance had been tempered by Jack's good sense and caution, but with Jack stationed in Guam and his father gone, there was nobody but Eileen to rein Hal in. On the milk route with Jack, there had already been signs of his rebellious streak. Hal used to check the trucks to see if any of the drivers had left anything behind. When he came across a pack of cigarettes, he'd flip one out and enjoy an illicit smoke.

Though Hal wrote Jack saying what a great time he was having in high school, the truth was that his rebelliousness stemmed from unhappiness. Many of his friends recall him dreading going home. James's death had sparked an inevitable anger and bitterness in Hal that made home life extremely difficult: he was angry at his father for leaving and at his mother because he partly blamed her, for whatever reason, for his father's suicide. Ashby's schoolmate Bob Ballantyne recalls that he referred to his parents as "that bitch" and "that son of a bitch."[1] Ballantyne's father had left when he was eight, while another schoolmate, Bob Busico, had lost his father when he was eight, and throughout his life, Hal would latch onto friends who had also gone through their formative years without fathers.

As a way of staying away from the house, Hal began to socialize more. Though he had many friends his own age, he also started hanging around with kids a few years older. The younger students were rarely accepted by the seniors, but Hal was easy to talk to, and if he liked people, he would show a genuine interest in them and make them feel valued. He also knew how to take a joke. "He was always making us laugh and had glasses as thick as coke bottles," Busico remembers. "I was always saying, 'Hal, let me borrow your glasses!' Then we wouldn't give them back and he couldn't see."[2]

Hal played basketball and football, and though he did not excel, whenever he didn't make the team, he would still be there on the bench, watching and supporting Busico and the other guys. He liked their company and enjoyed making them laugh and cheering up anybody who needed a lift. Busico was the school's star wrestler, and the crowd Ashby was socializing with was generally more sporty than academic and most interested in just having a good time.

Though Hal had the potential to be an excellent student, school was neither important nor interesting to him, and he is remembered by his classmates as someone who did the bare minimum. He didn't even care enough about school to always attend and became too well known to the truant officer for Eileen's liking.

Hal, along with Ballantyne and another friend, Clyde Brown, once decided to cut class and ended up running out of the school grounds pursued by their English teacher. The three hung out after school too, riding their bikes, shooting bows and arrows, and sometimes climbing the perimeter fence at night to take a dip in the school's old unheated swimming pool.

Hal started to go missing later and later into the evening. "I used to wander at night a lot," he once revealed in an interview, "but there were always four or five places my mother could call and find me."[3]

There was not a lot to do in a small town like Ogden, so Hal and his older friends would kill time bowling or playing pool. More often, however, they went to one another's houses, where they talked and played records. It was at this time that Hal developed a lifelong passion for music. As with anything style related, he always had his finger on the pulse, but he didn't do it to be cool; he genuinely adored music. Throughout his life, it would be a continuing joy and preoccupation, and his inspired use of music in his films would become a trademark. As a teenager, he listened to jazz and bebop, but it was ultimately rock and roll that most struck a chord with his rebellious nature.

Eileen felt that Hal's rebellious side was becoming too dominant. Though he never got into serious trouble, hanging around with an older crowd meant that he was growing up too fast for her liking and drinking beer long before the legal age of twenty-one. One day, when Hal was in the tenth grade, Eileen found a pack of cigarettes and some condoms in his pocket. She immediately called up Ardith, who was working at City Hall, and told her to come home.

"I can't," said Ardith. "I'm working."

"You have to," Eileen insisted. "It's an emergency!"[4]

During all his teen years, and for the rest of his adult life, Eileen and Hal had that difficult relationship that develops when a mother's intense love manifests itself as controlling and domineering and the child clearly wishes to escape this excessive influence. In Hal's case, he got his wish. Eileen decided what he needed was a proper education and not the miseducation in life he was getting in Ogden. At the beginning of the eleventh grade, Hal Ashby found himself far from home and at a very different kind of school.

Puget Sound Naval Academy (PSNA) was situated on Bainbridge Island, ten miles across the water from Seattle, Washington. Founded in 1938, it was a preparatory school for the U.S. Navy or Coast Guard but was often used by parents as a place for straightening out their undisciplined sons. It was remote, set in forty acres of prime land four miles from Winslow, the nearest town, and an all-male environment where discipline was always at the fore: a place with a minimum of distractions ideal for getting the best out of its pupils. The school taught not only the regular high school subjects but also naval drill, seamanship, and the rudiments of officers' behavior. Students quickly learned that no lapse in attention—whether to the subject being taught or to making one's bed—would go unnoticed. Those, like Hal, who had meandered through school and had relative freedom at home suddenly found much more demanded of them. Merits and demerits were handed out depending on pupils' performance, and if the latter outweighed the former, the imbalance could be expunged only by an hour of hard labor or drill marching per demerit.[5]

Despite having been independent and a tearaway in Ogden, Hal missed Eileen and all the comforts of home when he arrived at PSNA in the autumn of 1945. "He didn't like it at first at all," says Jack Swanson, a contemporary. "The discipline and regimentation—getting up, going to breakfast and going to lunch at a certain time—wasn't anything that he cared for."[6] After overcoming his initial frustration, however, Hal began to fit in and, as at Washington High, soon made friends and became popular.

Even more so than in Ogden, he stuck out at PSNA as somebody who was different, particularly in his appearance. "He was very neat," remembers another classmate, Gus Cooper. "He dressed more modern, like a kid from the big city."[7] "He had this crew cut and these big horn-rimmed glasses that made him look more professorial," adds Swanson. "In fact, he gave you the impression that he was a wimp at first if you didn't know him. But he was a good size, and you soon found out that he could look after himself."[8]

Swanson was at PSNA because he had previously run away from

home and, like Hal, had been sent there to get him on the straight and narrow. He ended up becoming the cadet commanding officer, with Hal as his second in command. The two roomed together and, during their time at PSNA, became close friends, though Hal was noticeably reluctant to discuss home and family. "My memory of him was that he was special in some way," says Swanson. "It's hard to explain, but he seemed to have a certain air about him that was more mature. He loved playing jokes and stuff, but he seemed older than the rest of us in some way. He was really one of those people that you never forget."[9] That ability to be serious and authoritative while also displaying a sense of fun was something that Ashby developed at PSNA and that would become invaluable to him when he was a director.

As is often the case with young people put in positions of authority, Hal took his role as a cadet officer very seriously and was as tough on the other cadets as a staff member might have been. In the mess hall, the boys ate at long tables covered in Masonite sheets. Unimpressed by the state of the tabletops, Hal once got the boys on mess duty to pick up the sheet and march out of the hall with it. For the next two hours, he made them wash and scrub it until he was satisfied with its condition. Hal also tried to toughen up the junior cadets, known as "dipes" (short for *diapers*), a name they hated. There was a boy from Seattle who, from the minute he arrived at PSNA, made it clear that he really didn't want to be there. Every week, his mother would send him a candy bar in an envelope. "Ashby had the idea that we should take this candy bar and pulverize it inside the envelope before we gave it to the kid," says Swanson. "It was like handing him a bag of sand, because we broke the candy bar into as many pieces as we could without damaging the envelope. If you couldn't stand up for yourself, if you showed the other guys you were weak, we weren't very kind. To his credit, Ashby was one of the guys who would say, 'OK, we've gone far enough,' and backed off."[10]

It was not only his peers whom Ashby was tough on. One of the principal dishes made by Blackie, the PSNA cook, was something called "fried mush." One day, Hal was eating this when he bit on something hard and almost broke one of his teeth. On inspecting the offending item, he discovered that it was the knob from Blackie's radio, which, unbeknownst to him, had fallen into the mush. Hal called Blackie into the mess hall and, in front of all the other cadets, gave him a dressing-down, about not only the offending knob but also the generally poor quality of the food. It cannot have done Hal's reputation or popularity any harm when there was a marked improvement in the standard of cooking following Blackie's very public shaming.

Another staff member Hal had a run-in with was Laird, the football coach. An ex-military man and former professional football player, Laird was, in Swanson's words, "tougher than a boiled owl, and was *hard* on us. [He] was trying to make men of us." Laird slammed into the boys too violently, and Ashby wasn't afraid to protest the coach's cruel behavior. Swanson reveals that Ashby and Laird "sort of got into it a few times. . . . One time I thought him and Ashby were actually going to get into a fistfight!"[11]

Because of the very small number of pupils at the academy, PSNA teams would invariably lose games, often by a large margin, but the one edge the boys had over their adversaries was mental and physical toughness. Gus Cooper nonchalantly recounts an incident that occurred when he was in one of the school vans on the way to PSNA's sister school, Hill Military Academy, in Portland, Oregon. "Jack Swanson was the driver, and went around the corner, and we tipped over. We were all in this van, Ashby, myself—there must have been about eight of us in there. We had to get out and push it back up, and we took off again."[12]

Fortunately, life outside the classroom at PSNA was not all rigorous drill and sporting tribulation. The boys attended dances held twice yearly to which pupils from girls' schools in nearby Seattle and Tacoma were also invited. Jack Swanson had a crush on one of the girls but couldn't get any time alone with her: "Ashby had the idea that I ought to dress up like a girl and then I could go back to Seattle with these girls when they left the academy, which I in effect did. And got into trouble for it."[13] Swanson got on the girls' bus unnoticed in his disguise but was inevitably discovered when he tried to get on the ferry back to Seattle.

Ashby became known at the academy as an adviser on matters pertaining to the opposite sex. His old Ogden friend Bob Ballantyne confesses that Ashby, despite being younger, had been more up on these things than he had: "We together learned the early ways of sex. We masturbated a couple of times together. He showed me how to get the last juices out, so it won't be dripping. It was all part of growing up."[14]

Not only was he was more clued up on certain matters than his peers, but the tall, gawky, professorial-looking Hal also unwittingly won the hearts of a Winslow shopgirl, one of the PSNA coaches' daughters, and one of the Seattle schoolgirls (who asked Swanson to put her in touch with Ashby long after Hal had left). Jack Swanson, however, recalls that the adoration of these young women was never particularly reciprocated by Hal. In the summer of 1946, he returned home to Ogden and that fall started his senior year at Washington, where he became a member of the Sigma fraternity. And it was at Washington that he would meet the first girl to have a real impact on him.

Much had changed in Ogden since his departure the previous year. The war was now over, and Jack had been back home already for six months. He had remodeled the grocery store, adding an ice-cream parlor to tailor it more to Eileen's area of expertise. Jack was also about to get married to Beth Christensen, a girl he had met in Ogden while back home for Christmas.

Strangely, Jack was not the first Ashby boy Beth had had contact with. "A bunch of us girls had a little club that we belonged to, and we had a 'girl ask boy' party," Beth recalls. "I didn't have anyone I was going with, so I said to my friends, 'Who shall I ask?' They said, 'Ask Hal Ashby, he's a neat kid.' So I called Hal Ashby and asked him to this party—and he said no! It kinda took the wind out of my sails."[15]

Hal spent much of the summer of 1946 hanging out with Jack and Beth while his mother was working at the store. "Hal was in and out," Beth recalls, "and he would ask me if I would mind pressing his trousers. He'd bring his clothes over to wash, and he'd bring the gang with him. They would sit around while they got their clothes cleaned, and I would make them some cookies."[16] After Jack and Beth got married, Hal took advantage of his elder brother's more upmarket lifestyle. Not only did he come round regularly to listen to Jack and Beth's record collection, but he twice borrowed Jack's Chrysler New Yorker, both times tearing the transmission out of it.

Over the next two years, Eileen's children all began to settle into family life. Hetz got married in June 1946, and Jack and Beth followed suit that October. Ardith, who had married in 1942, had her first child, Larry, in September 1948, and a month later Guy, Jack and Beth's first-born, made his entrance.

Despite being only seventeen, Hal was also part of this sudden rush of familial activity. A sixteen-year-old blonde at Washington called Lavon Compton had caught his eye, and he asked a mutual friend to arrange a meeting. Lavon seemed interested, so Hal was invited round to the Compton family home, and the two started dating. It was a case of opposites attracting: Hal, the troubled teenager with a rebellious streak, fell for Lavon even though—or maybe because—she was the quintessential good girl, sweet natured, dainty, and petite.

One day in February 1947, when they had been going out for three or four months, Hal and Lavon went to Eileen and told her that Lavon was pregnant and that they were going to get married. They were not old enough to wed legally in conservative Utah, but Nevada, famous for its quickie weddings, was not too far away. On March 1, 1947, Hal and Lavon drove the 250 miles from Ogden to Elko, Nevada, with Lavon's sister and brother-in-law in tow as their witnesses.

The ceremony went off without a hitch, but the marriage was difficult from the beginning. On the day they eloped, Hal and Lavon left the following note for Eileen:

> Mom,
>
> We're sorry every thing turned out this way. But maybe some day things can be made right.
>
> This $10 is on the big bill we owe you. We'll pay the rest the best we can.
>
> We'll get our things as soon as possible.
>
> Try to understand.
>
> All our love,
>
> Lavon and Hal
>
> P.S. We both love you very much and thank you for all your help.[17]

Eileen had significant reservations about the wedding but still loaned Hal and Lavon the $10 for the marriage license. However, a condition of their marriage was that Hal finish his studies back at PSNA, where there would be no further distractions. So, immediately after getting married, Hal and Lavon were separated.

It was difficult for Lavon, who not only was apart from her new husband but also had to live at home with her disapproving parents. Like Eileen, they had frowned on the union, and they were also upset that the couple had not been married in the Salt Lake City temple like good Mormons. However, it was principally Hal that Lavon's parents objected to. Much of their dislike stemmed from the fact that he was so far from the good Mormon son-in-law they had hoped for. Conversely, Hal, as Jack put it, "had nothing good to say about good old George Compton [Lavon's father]."[18]

Lavon was relieved when Hal returned to Ogden after finishing at PSNA, and they moved to a little apartment on the other side of town. The two weren't used to looking after themselves, and Hal would call Beth to ask how to cook French toast and other dishes Lavon didn't know how to make.

Hal used his experience at the Uintah Dairy to get a job at another local dairy and, as the couple couldn't afford a car, walked to work every day. However, working at the dairy made Hal's eczema flare up, so he did not keep the job for long, and Lavon's parents became very forthcoming in expressing their opinions on Hal's conduct. "They were just always after Hal to shape up, to do this or do that," remembers Jack. "It used to irritate Hal no end," adds Beth, "because they were always trying to tell him to go to church."[19]

On September 19, 1947, just two weeks after Hal's eighteenth birthday, Lavon gave birth to a beautiful baby girl, whom she named Leigh after the film star Janet Leigh. The birth of his daughter changed Hal's life radically, but instead of making him more devoted to family life, it began to raise doubts in his mind. Eileen had just bought a new home, and as Hal was now unemployed, the young family moved into a small apartment attached to the house. Hal was back home again and once again dependent on his mother—except now, not only for himself, but also for Lavon and Leigh. Despite the less than ideal circumstances of the wedding, he had embarked upon married life full of optimism, but now he felt useless and frustrated and started to reconsider his current situation.

When Lavon became pregnant, marriage was the only real option, and he did not question what he was doing because he and Lavon were in love. Yet, at the age of eighteen, suddenly he found himself married with a daughter, his freedom replaced by lifelong responsibilities. As

Jack recalls, "He just wasn't ready for marriage, wasn't ready to settle down. He didn't want to be that tied down."[20]

Hal had two choices: he could honor his marriage vows and stay, or he could leave. The latter option was selfish, but it would be a clean break, damage limitation. He knew that either way he would cause great pain, but he chose the path that he thought would be better for everybody in the long term.

While it might be tempting to speculate that Ashby left Lavon and Ogden with dreams of Hollywood, in fact he simply needed to get out. Much later, when studios were repackaging his life to be more palatable and interesting to journalists, the story of his early life metamorphosed into the following:

> A native of Ogden, Utah, Ashby was born into a typical middle-class American family. His father, a hard-working tradesman, wanted young Hal to complete high school and then join him in operating a feed and grain shop, but the son had other ideas. After being graduated from Utah State University, he joined one little theatre group after another until he found one where the management would let him direct a play. Working secretly with the actors, Ashby came up with a highly-imaginative production of George Bernard Shaw's "Androcles and the Lion" which was well received by critics, but considered a calamity by his family. Reason: Ashby dressed his actors in modern clothes and set the scene on a football field, thus alienating all the influential alumni living in his home town. There was nothing to do but leave Ogden.[21]

The claim that Hal had not only a college education but also a strong passion for drama going back to his adolescence was designed to make him fit in with other emerging directors of the time—Francis Ford Coppola, William Friedkin, Peter Bogdanovich, Bob Rafelson, Martin Scorsese—the so-called Movie Brats. They were all young, college-educated men whose passion for films stemmed from their very earliest days and whose efforts had been focused entirely on becoming filmmakers. But Hal was different. His interest in cinema was no greater than any other teenager's, he didn't go to Utah State (nor did his father own a feed and grain store), and his theater company experience (including the ludicrous *Androcles and the Lion* incident) was pure fiction.

In early 1948, only a matter of months after Leigh's birth, Hal left everything he knew in Ogden behind—his wife and child, his mother, sister, and brothers—and set off to make a fresh start.

3

Los Angeles

> Los Angeles, give me some of you! Los Angeles come to me the way I came to you, my feet over the streets, you pretty town I loved you so much, you sad flower in the sand, you pretty town.
>
> —John Fante, *Ask the Dust* (1939)

When Hal Ashby left Ogden, he knew that being responsible for a wife and child at such a young age was not what he wanted from life. He did not know what he did want, but he was confident that out there, traveling and working and *experiencing* America, he would find it. "I feel that Americans must leave their homes," he said later. "It is easier if you come from a small town because the thrust of life is outward. I feel, for example, it is harder to leave the Bronx because it is more complex than a small town."[1] In order to know oneself, Ashby felt, it is necessary to know one's country.

For a few months, Ashby drifted around, doing jobs here and there, and reading whenever he could. It was all part of the process of finding himself. Every job he did, every book he read, every town he passed through, he hoped would bring him closer to discovering what had made him know that a town like Ogden was too small to hold him. He did, however, return to Ogden every so often and would see Lavon and Leigh occasionally.

Not long after splitting up with Lavon, Ashby started dating Janice Austin, another girl he had been to high school with. He saw her on his visits to Ogden, and, according to Janice, she was very nearly the second Mrs. Hal Ashby: "He asked me to marry him, and he had bought me an engagement ring. He didn't have the money for it, and he charged it to his mom. His mom was so mad at him she made him take it back. She didn't like me very well."[2]

Eileen was understandably resistant to the idea of Ashby marrying again and told Janice that she would never accept anyone but Lavon as her daughter-in-law. Janice's father, who worked with Ardith at the waterworks, was also against the marriage, particularly when he learned that the couple's grandmothers were sisters, making them second cousins. Though marriage was no longer in the cards, Hal and Janice kept up a long-distance relationship, and Janice recalls that Ashby would write to her "every other day."[3]

Around March 1948, Lavon filed for divorce in order to be eligible for child-support payments from Ashby. The divorce came through on May 10, 1948, with a period of six months before a final judgment of divorce would be granted. Lavon was naturally granted full custody of Leigh, and Ashby was required to pay $25 every two weeks to help pay for her care. He sent an initial payment of $50, but after that nothing followed.

Fifty dollars a month was a substantial sum, and Janice recalls that she was "always getting after him to pay alimony to Lavon for the little girl, but he was having problems because he didn't have too many jobs, and he never owned a car."[4] One suspects, however, that Ashby ultimately ceased payments, not just because of financial restraints, but because of an inherent weakness in himself. He was adored by the overwhelming majority of people who got to know him, and yet, particularly in the first half of his life, he managed to alienate and hurt the very people he claimed to love the most, many of whom became greatly embittered as a result. Starting with the death of his father, Ashby's life was defined by an insistent refusal to deal with traumatic incidents and emotional conflicts. It seems he believed that if he pushed them to the very back of his mind, he could make them *un*happen. "In life, Hal was the consummate editor," says Ashby's friend, Haskell Wexler, "and some people ended up on the cutting room floor."[5]

By the summer of 1948, he found himself in Evanston, Wyoming, where he was joined by Max Grow, an old friend from Ogden. Ashby and Lavon had double dated with Grow and his future wife, who was also called Janice. Grow, who was a year older than Ashby, had hung out with him after getting out of the navy in the fall of 1947 and remembers him as enjoyable company. They had gone to dances together and once drove to Lagoon, about twenty miles south of Ogden, to see the jazz pianist and bandleader Stan Kenton. Ashby had made a special point of befriending Kenton and his band for the night, not only because he was passionate about jazz, but also because they represented an artistic lifestyle that, whether or not he was aware of it, he wanted to be a part of.

In Evanston, Ashby and Grow worked on a railroad construction job. From Weber Canyon, Utah, all the way up into Wyoming, crews of men had been refacing the old railroad bridges, and the pair joined them in Wyoming. The work was grueling and repetitive and involved chipping off the old, "rotten" concrete on the bridges and then pouring in fresh concrete.

In September, the month of Ashby's nineteenth birthday—and his daughter's first birthday—as he and Grow chipped away at the old concrete, his senses told him it was time to move on. As summer turned to fall, the cold came in early. The winter of 1948–1949 was one of the harshest that the American West ever endured, with many states experiencing record low temperatures. "When we were up on the scaffold, it started to snow," Grow recalls. "He kept saying, 'Let's go down to Los Angeles; I've got an uncle there.'"[6]

Ashby later recounted the moment he decided to go to California: "We went down to get a drink from the water barrel at 10 A.M., and we had to break the ice to get through. And I said, 'I don't know about you, but I'm going to California—livin' off the fruit of the land.'" Grow reached his breaking point soon after, when he smashed his thumb while working. After waiting three days for their pay, the pair hitchhiked south into the sunshine. "I wouldn't take any work clothes with me either," Ashby recalled. "I brought slacks and a sports jacket and resolved that these would do fine for any job I was willing to undertake."[7]

Ashby and Grow hitchhiked back down into Utah, refusing to squander their money on such things as lodgings. "Outside Provo, Utah, I slept all night by the side of the road," Ashby subsequently recalled. "The next day a deer hunter, the deer tied to the fender, gave me a ride all the way to L.A."[8] (Later, seemingly in reference to this journey, he said, "I don't own any guns and I never have. . . . It wasn't until I saw some guys kill a deer that I decided it wasn't for me.")[9]

Six hundred miles later, the hunter dropped Ashby and Grow at the intersection of Vermont Avenue and Santa Monica Boulevard on the northeast side of Los Angeles. No doubt excited to have arrived, they were brought down to earth with a bump when they discovered that Ashby's uncle—his father's half brother, William Ashby, with whom they had been planning to stay—had died two years earlier. They quickly went from being men setting out to make their fortune in the city by the sea to boys with nowhere to stay in a huge, sprawling metropolis that neither had ever been to before. They had what was left of their $40 paychecks from Evanston and nothing else.

The money seemed to disappear with alarming speed. As Ashby told it years afterward, he was trying to live off onion sandwiches but reached a point where his funds were so depleted that he bought a Powerhouse candy bar that he made last for three days. With his final dime he called his mother collect and said, "Your little boy's in California starving."[10]

Eileen responded, "Well, I never told you to go to California: you're a bright boy; I'm sure you'll think of something."[11]

Looking back on the incident, Ashby was grateful that his mother had forced him to face the repercussions of his actions. At the time, however, he was desperate and continued to solicit her help, this time in writing:

> Dear Mom,
> Well here is your little lost boy writing to you at last. I havent [*sic*] got a job yet, and I'm broke flat, but I guess everything will work out okay. I just wrote you to tell you I'm okay and to give you my address in case anything comes up.
> My address is
>
> Hal Ashby
> c/o Hi Ho Inn
> 2601 W. 6th St.
> L.A., S. Cal
>
> Well Mom, I can't think of anything to tell you, except the climate is certainly wonderful here. I'm read [*sic*] of my cold at least. I sure hope I can get a job of some kind, cause I've decided to make So. Cal. my home for life. That is if I live long enough and don't starve to death.
>
> Well Bye Bye for now Mom, and remember I always love you.
>
> Your Son
> Hal oxoxoxoxo
>
> P.S. Write when you get a chance.[12]

Ashby's calculated attempts to guilt his mother into sending money hinted at such desperation that Eileen finally gave in. He was still her baby boy—or, as he put it, "little lost boy"—and he knew that she could not hold out forever. But after a period of sending him money, Eileen decided that enough was enough.

The Hi Ho Inn was not, in fact, where he was lodging but a bar near MacArthur Park where he and Grow were regulars and had their mail sent. The two were staying in a rooming house on Fourth Avenue and Pico Boulevard, along with Herb Rose, Vern Hipwell, Ed Burton, and Dallas Fowler, a group of boys they knew from Ogden. They had come to make their fortune, seeing Los Angeles as a place where they had as good a chance as any to turn the American dream into reality.

They all recognized that getting a job, any job, was a necessity. Fortunately, with Christmas approaching, stores needed extra help. Ashby and Grow were both hired by Bullock's department store in the downtown area, working there over the holiday season and then afterward also for the January sales.

When Ashby and Grow left snowy, frozen Wyoming, they pictured Los Angeles as a city of sunshine and opportunity, at the center of which lay Hollywood. Janice Grow recalls that Ashby accompanied Grow to an open casting call at Maurice Kosloff Productions that they saw advertised in a newspaper. "Max was extremely good looking," she says. "I think they thought he could be a big heartthrob star. Don't know what Hal's ideas were."[13]

In fact, though he later admitted that he had wanted to be in the movie business because "it seemed glamorous,"[14] at the time Ashby had not yet fixed on the idea of working in Hollywood as he had never given much thought to films. He was not a child who had spent every spare moment in darkened movie houses; instead, he'd been out living life. When he went to the theater, Ashby had been more interested in serials and cowboy movies than "regular movies." "I doubt that his [Hal's] early movie experiences had any bearing on how he began his movie career," Jack says. "I never actually heard him say he wanted to work in the movie business when he grew up."[15]

After living together at Fourth and Pico for a year or so, Ashby, Grow, and the other Ogden boys went their separate ways. Grow moved to a single room elsewhere in the house, while Ashby ended up in a small

$7-a-week room in Bunker Hill. The two friends subsequently grew apart. Two or three years later, when Grow was living in Hollywood, Ashby came round with a girlfriend and drove the three of them down to Tijuana for a day trip in his convertible. That was the last time Grow saw Ashby.

Ashby went into the world knowing that his future lay out there but uncertain of what it would be. He ended up working as a salesman but was not cut out for the job. Though he had the charm, he was uneasy selling products he knew were inferior to people who didn't deserve to be shortchanged. He tried selling magazines, encyclopedias, brushes, and more besides but was always troubled by his conscience. "You were always doing a con, telling a lie," he said. "I don't like telling lies."[16]

After his move to Los Angeles, Ashby had remained in contact with Janice Austin. She thought of him as her sweetheart, though Ashby may have viewed things as slightly more casual. She came down to visit him a couple of times and recalls that on one occasion he took her for a meal at a fancy nightclub where the renowned bandleader Woody Herman was playing and even got Herman to pose with them for a picture. Not long after this, Ashby stopped replying to Janice's letters. To find out why, she drove down to Los Angeles with her mother and brother. "I remember us sitting in Pershing Square while my brother went to see Hal," she recalls. "When he came back, [I was told] Hal said he didn't want to see me. I just figured he'd met someone else."[17]

She was right, as around that time Ashby got married for the second time. Little is known about the marriage, but what is certain is that on July 25, 1949, Hal Ashby married one Maxine Marie Armstrong in Las Vegas. "[I was] married and divorced twice before I made it to twenty-one," Ashby claimed in an article he wrote for *Action* magazine.[18] If this is indeed true, then Ashby (whose twenty-first birthday was on September 2, 1950) cannot have been married to Maxine for much more than a year.

After Hal and Maxine were married, Eileen asked them to come back to Ogden. Jack and Beth had moved temporarily to Portland, Oregon, and Eileen wanted help running the store, which was now an ice-cream parlor and restaurant called Ashby's Ice Cream. Hal and Maxine moved into an apartment in Ogden and helped out at the store. It seems likely that Eileen had twisted Hal's arm to get him to come back; he had, after all, claimed that Southern California was to be his home for life.

Despite what he might have hoped he could do for Eileen, Ashby knew he could never be the dutiful son who takes over his aging mother's store. Almost inevitably, things didn't work out. Hal regretted coming back to Ogden and quarreled with Eileen. Over the years, he would repeatedly and sincerely tell her in letters how he loved her and how much her opinion meant to him, but whenever they spent prolonged periods of time together, their relationship became fraught and troubled. In the end, it was probably just a few months that Ashby and Maxine worked at the store as it quickly became obvious that it wasn't working out. The newlyweds returned to California, and Eileen sold the store soon after.

Back in Los Angeles, Ashby's marriage to Maxine fizzled out. During their time in Ogden, Maxine had had an abortion (most likely at Ashby's request), which seems to have been the beginning of the end for them. Ashby knew what he didn't want, namely, more children, but was no nearer to finding his true direction in life. "I was a kid looking for something," he said, "but I didn't know what. The movie business seemed like a terrific thing to get into."[19]

Though he went there only because it was free, it was the State Employment Office in Van Nuys that helped Ashby get his foot in the door. "I got my first job [in movies] through the State Employment Department," he recalled. "Like a jerk I went down there and told them I wanted to get into motion pictures, and that woman looked at me like 'What the hell is that?' and started going through the little index file and said, 'Well, here's something.' So I said, 'All right—I'm willing to start at the bottom.' 'Well,' she said, 'here's something at Universal with a Multilith machine. Do you know what that is?' And I said, 'No.' So she said, 'Do you know what a mimeograph machine is? Well, it's like a mimeograph machine. They don't particularly want experience.'"[20]

Ashby went to his local library to read up on the mechanics of a mimeograph (a hand-cranked copying machine) so as to be a proficient employee when he started the job a few days later. He quickly grew very comfortable at Universal, and although the job copying scripts was repetitive and undemanding, Ashby saw only opportunity around him. He says that, "like any red-blooded American,"[21] he "looked around and said, 'What's the best job around here?'"[22] In his mind, it was a director.

Ashby was very keen, and the kid in the ink-spotted smock from the copy department became well-known for his pleasing manner and willingness to learn. Starting at the bottom meant that almost everybody knew more than he did, so he talked to people whenever he could and began to learn about the possible routes to becoming a director. He initially considered training to be an assistant director, but he soon learned that there was a better route. The directors he spoke to kept repeating the same advice. "Get into editing," they told him. "With editing, everything is up there on film for you to see over and over again. You can study it and ask why you like it, and why you don't."[23]

During his time at Universal, Ashby made it his aim to learn as much as he could about editing. He befriended staff in the editing department, ran errands for them, and became their unofficial coffee boy. Editors seemed to work longer hours than everybody else, so Ashby would complete his copying and then hang out with them in the cutting rooms. He sat and watched the editors as they worked and eventually was allowed to stay on after everybody had left. By learning how to splice film together, cleaning the Moviolas and the other equipment, and even doing some tentative editing himself, he learned the basics of the trade.

Ashby developed a feel for editing and with it a passion for the process. One night when he was out drinking in Los Angeles with Bob Ballantyne, his old friend from Ogden, Ashby insisted on taking him to the building where he worked. He excitedly told Ballantyne about editing, the art and science of it, the precision required, and the creativity it allowed. "Along with describing what film editing involved he said, 'You know, you can even win an Oscar for film editing, if you're good enough,'" Ballantyne recalls. "My immediate thoughts were, 'He's dreaming.' But I said, 'Oh, really!'" Though Ashby was "wobbling from too much booze,"[24] he seemed to Ballantyne more affected by his love of editing than by the alcohol.

When telling the story of Ashby's life, people often make the assumption that he progressed smoothly through the ranks from copyboy to assistant editor, to editor, to director, as if a conveyor belt was carrying him there. This misconception was reinforced by studio biographies of Ashby, something that amused and exasperated him: "It always amazes me how they compress years of pain and frustration into two sentences."[25] The truth is that the job at Universal came to an end, and it was not an easy transition from Multilith to Moviola. In order to get work as an editor, Ashby would have to join the union and serve an eight-year apprenticeship, and to even be admitted into the union, he needed a prominent editor to vouch for him. In the end, he realized he would simply have to go back to normal, everyday work. He would bide his time and wait for his opportunity to come.

Writing about the struggle to become a success in Hollywood, Sammy Davis Jr. once remarked: "I have got jobs for dozens of other people on the fringes to keep them in contact with films. The director Hal Ashby, for instance, lived at my place for a while when he was working as a third assistant in the cutting room. He made his way up to the huge success he is today—by learning his craft from the bottom."[26] Ashby wouldn't become an assistant editor until the mid-1950s, but he and Davis became friends and companions in the early part of the decade following his return from Ogden. Throughout his career, Ashby met and befriended talented people, but in many cases—that of Davis included—Ashby knew them before they were famous. In the 1950s, he was part of a tight group of bohemian friends, almost all of whom went on to achieve success in their respective fields.

Ashby was introduced to Davis by another friend, Steve Allen, the comedian, songwriter, author, and future *Tonight Show* creator, whom he listened to in the early days of his KNX radio show and whose comic sensibility was similar to Ashby's own. At the time, Davis was still in the Will Mastin Trio alongside his father and uncle, whom he had been performing with since he was first able to walk. Ashby arguably loved musicians and their music much more than movie stars. And despite his sheltered, small-town upbringing, he never displayed the racist attitude that was so prevalent at that time. A hippie before the word was coined, Ashby looked at the person, not the skin color, and was troubled by the unenlightened minds of most Americans. One of Ashby's girlfriends from the 1950s, Gloria Flaum, remembers his concern about "discrimination and a lot of things that were going on. Hal was pretty politically motivated. I know he read the poetry of [Carl] Sandburg, and marched on a black protest march in the South."[27]

Ashby and Davis went on the road together, with "Billy Hal" (as Davis called Ashby) acting as a secretary-cum-manager. Davis struggled tremendously against the bigotry that Americans at the time thought was acceptable: onstage he was praised and applauded, but after the show he was treated as grossly inferior by the white audiences who had been enjoying his act only moments before. In the first volume of his autobiography, Davis wrote about repeatedly coming across signs outside hotels saying things such as "No Niggers—No Dogs" and "Everybody Welcome but the Nigger and the Jew,"[28] and Ashby would tell his friend Bill Box about the times he was refused entry to hotels simply because Davis, a black man, was with him. Ashby was working for Davis (though he was not with him) at the time Davis lost his eye in a horrific car accident and was one of the first by his bedside in the hospital. "He thought a great deal of Sammy," recalled Hal's third wife, Mickey. "He was close to Sammy's family; he was like one of the family, even. They were very good friends."[29]

Along with working at a button factory, several department stores, and a soda fountain (where he apparently drank more than he earned), going on the road with Davis was one of numerous jobs that he took in the 1950s just to keep the money coming in, but afterward Ashby and Sammy remained friends. During this period, Ashby met the people who would form the core of his life for the rest of the decade, the kindred spirits who would help him become the person he had always wanted to be.

Ashby's bohemian inner circle was made up of Bill Box, an aspiring cartoonist and writer, Bill Otto, who would end up in advertising, Ian Bernard, a jazz pianist and later a writer, and John Mandel, another jazz musician. Piecing together the story of their youthful exploits is something of a challenge because, as Bernard confesses, they were all smoking too much marijuana.

Shortly before he met Bill Box, Ashby was working as a secretary. He first worked for a businessman called John Brokaw who was rumored to own oil wells. Ashby not only took on secretarial and management duties for Brokaw but even painted the bathroom in his boss's West Hollywood apartment. Brokaw was neither a conventional nor a reliable boss, and once when he and Ashby were in Las Vegas on business, he was arrested for making what Box calls an "aggressive approach" to singer Lena Horne.[30] Ashby and Brokaw's partnership ended abruptly one night, when Brokaw packed up his things and left, never to be seen again.

Ashby moved on to a job at a debt-consolidation agency in Hollywood run by a man called Ray Kline who managed two rising singers, Abbey Lincoln and Pam Garner, and didn't actually want to be in the debt-consolidation business. Neither, for that matter, did Ashby, who spent as much time as he could away from his desk, socializing with his coworkers. One of Ashby's favorite colleagues was Betty Gumm, and he would happily spend long periods sitting on the floor by her desk, cracking jokes. "Hal, we've gotta work, and all you're doing is making me laugh all day," she used to tell him.[31]

Through another colleague, Bill Otto (known as "Blotto," a slang term for *drunk*), Ashby became friends with Bill Box. Box had been parking cars at a restaurant on La Cienega Boulevard, but crippling arthritis forced him to give up the job. Ashby, Otto, and the immobilized Box ended up living together in Beverly Glen, up in the Hollywood Hills.

While Box was housebound, he killed time by doodling and drawing cartoons inspired by jazz, one of the group's great shared passions. Box had always loved cartooning and saw the potential to turn his temporary incapacitation to his advantage. Along with a friend, Bill Kennedy, an aspiring singer whom he had met while parking cars, he started the Box Card Company in 1953, producing cards with bebop and hipster cartoons and slogans like "Keep Cool This Yule." Though Bernard and Mandel were playing jazz regularly at that time, Box was really the first to find a path to success, arguably providing an example for the others and further fueling their ambition. Everybody in the group helped out with the company when they could, and Ashby was part of the "night crew" who wrapped cards for Box.

While they all worked hard to reach their goals, they also had fun when they were not working. Ashby and his friends regularly went to the Coronet, a small repertory theater on La Cienega, where they watched classic Hollywood films. If they were feeling particularly flush, they would buy a good dinner, then spend the evening at Ciro's, a favorite nightclub of Hollywood's big names. Sometimes they would drive down to the Lighthouse jazz club in Hermosa Beach, and Bernard would sit in with whichever of his friends, such as West Coast luminaries Jerry Mulligan and Chet Baker, was playing that night. Ashby, Bernard, and the two Bills also regularly went to Restaurant Row on La Cienega, where there was a lounge bar with a singer every fifty yards. They frequented the Captain's Table, the Encore, the Tally Ho. "We were just exuberant youths, four or five of us out having a good time together," remembers Bernard. "We hung out at all the bars, and I had an apartment just above La Cienega, so it was very convenient. We should have all been dead probably because we were always driving with alcohol!"[32] Ashby in particular was lucky to have survived: he would drink to excess and then drive his 1949 Ford without any shock absorbers or springs.

In addition to drinking a lot, Ashby and his friends discovered marijuana when they came to Los Angeles. Or, as Bernard puts it, they collectively "grew up on weed." Ashby started smoking grass a year or so after he arrived in Los Angeles and continued to do so for almost forty years. (Some of his friends would blend his two names into one, calling him "Hashby.") Box and Bernard quit smoking marijuana a year or so later, but Bernard confesses, "We should have been fat with all the chocolate cake we ate! In those days, Ashby and the rest of us were smoking a *lot* of pot, you know? Ashby was the champion: he pretty much had a joint in his hand at all times."[33] John Mandel has happy memories of the group watching the television talent show *Rocket to Stardom* "stoned out of our heads,"[34] while Box nicknamed one of the places they lived during that period "The Happy House" because of all the pot they smoked there. Once when one of their less worldly friends came round and asked what the curious smell was, quick as a flash Ashby said, "We made some pea soup, and we burned it."[35]

Bernard stresses that the marijuana was weak compared to modern standards but admits that Ashby still overindulged: "I think he smoked weed to excess. But it wasn't a negative effect that it had on him, it just meant he got sillier and sillier. And I never, in all those years, saw Hal as a depressed person or a loner."[36] Yet while Bernard did not see his darker moments, Ashby did not manage to hide them from everybody.

Ashby and his new crowd were all fans of J. D. Salinger's *The Catcher in the Rye,* whose narrator famously does not want to discuss "where I was born, and what my lousy childhood was like and how my parents were occupied and all before they had me, and all that David Copperfield crap."[37] Ashby did not feel like going into any David Copperfield crap either, and with his group of Ogden friends having dispersed, he was relieved to have new friends who were unaware of his unhappy past.

"None of us knew *anything* about his life before we met him," Bernard recalls. "None of us knew that he'd had children, none of us knew he'd been married before—not a damn thing."[38] But Gloria started seeing the effect of Ashby's failure to deal with issues from his past: "He was very, very moody, and he could be so funny, I mean unbelievably funny. And then turn around and be every bit as moody and heavy." Gloria dated Ashby for some time and once met his mother ("a wonderful lady") when she came down to visit. After Eileen's stay, it became clear to her that his unexpected bouts of depression were rooted in unresolved problems from his troubled adolescence: "It was strange, because he could have you in stitches, but alone with him, he had a lot of dark moments. He'd become very, very upset and very down. It could be prompted by very little, because I don't think it was what was happening at the moment, I think it was stuff that he was carrying around about his father and his mother. I think that Hal had some deep feelings about his father's suicide and resentments about his mother, and I'm not sure exactly why, except that I'm sure it caused him a great deal of unhappiness."[39]

As he grew closer to his group of friends, Ashby learned that he was not the only one with a tragic incident in his past. Bill Otto's father had died young, and Otto blamed his mother for pushing him to work himself into an early grave. Clyde Wilson, a friend of Box's from his hometown of Bremerton, Washington, had come home one day to find his father had shot his mother and then turned the gun on himself. There was a kinship between the three of them, but Ashby revealed very little even to them. His persistent refusal to talk about his problems and accept help when it was offered resulted in him struggling with the demons of his past for the rest of his life. He could ignore them for periods of time, but when things went awry in his professional or personal life, it would become unbearable for him, as if the weight of the world had suddenly fallen on him.

Possibly as a way of papering over the cracks, Ashby threw himself into whatever work he was doing, trying to make money while he waited for his editing break. He was seemingly willing to pursue even the most unlikely business opportunities. He went to the Los Angeles Exhibition

Center to sell rubberized floor mats and became involved with Clyde in an equally oddball moneymaking scheme. "Clyde reveals one day that he has this furniture polish or household cleaning product," recalls Box, "and it worked really well. Somehow he had the rights to it, and Hal saw this as an opportunity. So he went to Washington state with Clyde to see if they could do something with that, but I think nothing came of that. I think he would have welcomed some kind of entrepreneurial opportunity."[40]

Ashby no doubt was frustrated to be selling household goods rather than doing something he was passionate about, but his sense of humor (he was "the champion giggler of all time," according to Bernard)[41] and enjoyment of life kept him going. "Hal had little or no cash assets but he was loaded in the humor department," says Box. "And when the mood struck him he could have you rolling on the floor."[42] Ashby had a very idiosyncratic way of looking at life, comic, but with a philosophical slant. One day in the kitchen of the house in Beverly Glen, he suddenly said, "I earn $35 a week, and where does it go? Right down this garbage disposal. If this garbage disposal were an animal, it'd be the strongest beast on the face of the earth."[43]

His enthusiasm for the arts was also infectious and revealed in him a knack for storytelling. "He was wonderful when he was talking about having seen *Guys and Dolls* or read some book and [would] retell it so wonderfully well," enthuses Box. "It was a real treat. He remembered things in great detail and was so enthusiastic about them. His monologues created little scenes and characters."[44] Ashby had an incredible memory for the things that interested him—he loved Broadway shows, bought the LPs of musicals, and knew all the words to *West Side Story*—and it was this talent that helped him bring stories so fully to life. Because listening to one of his descriptions was so enjoyable, Box says, the "book he talked about or the film he had seen might not always live up to Hal's colorful telling of it."[45] Mandel also remembers Hal's enthusiasm and his great interest not only in art but also in people: "He was great to be with. He had a tremendous curiosity about *everything* and was really interested in people. He was unlike anyone I'd ever met."[46]

A number of Ashby's friends, including Bill Otto and Ian Bernard, ended up living at the Sunset Colonial Hotel, a place that became "a center for the young Turks," according to Bernard.[47] The author John

Ridley describes the hotel as "ground zero for a bushel of fresh-off-the-bus actor and actress types . . . [who had] headed west with a lot of ideas on becoming stars . . . but not a single plan on how to reach their destination."[48] It was seedy and therefore cheap, but Ashby had friends and other like-minded dreamers all around. What's more, they knew how to have fun. When Bill Otto got married, Ashby and Bernard snuck into the groom's room on the day of the ceremony and took all the furniture out of it. "When he came home from his honeymoon to spend the night there," laughs Bernard, "there wasn't a stick of furniture in the room. Not even a bed. He wasn't that pleased."[49]

Sammy Davis Jr., now a rising star, also had an apartment at the Sunset Colonial. Ashby and Davis would hang out with actors Byron Kane and Jeff Chandler, and the four formed a club called "The Face Men of America," the name apparently referring to a certain shared sexual preference. Because Davis spent so much time on the road, he was only an occasional member of Ashby's gang but was still considered one of them. Bill Box remembers being invited along with Ashby to a party thrown by Davis after the recording of his hit song "Hey There" and seeing Sammy, one of the fastest draws in the business, showing off by twirling a pair of pistols and slamming them in their holsters. Over the years, Davis disappeared from the group as other friends became more important to him. "After he became a Rat Packer, he moved in different circles and I believe was corrupted by his own self importance," says Bernard. "Surrounded by sycophants, he forgot the 'little people.'"[50]

However, those in Ashby's circle were becoming successful too. The Box Card Company continued to thrive, and Box also started doing artwork for jazz albums put out by Mode Records. Ian Bernard cowrote and arranged the acclaimed albums *Rain or Shine* (1955) and *Moondreams* (1957) for singer Dick Haymes, with the latter release also featuring John Mandel. In the mid-1950s, Ashby himself made an appearance on a popular television show hosted by Art Linkletter called *People Are Funny,* a precursor to reality television that got its contestants to perform outrageous or zany stunts for the audience's amusement. According to Box, Ashby was given a relatively appealing task: the show sent flowers, chocolates, and other love offerings from "Your secret admirer" (i.e., Ashby) to an unsuspecting girl, and Ashby's mission was simply to bring her back to the show, which he succeeded in doing.

Bill Otto's activities in the entertainment world, however, were to prove most important for Ashby. Otto acted as assistant to production on a film called *No Place to Hide,* which was shot in Manila at the end of 1954. Won over by the director-producer-writer Josef Shaftel's big plans for the film (which were based around the exotic location and stars Marsha Hunt and David Brian), Otto invested the remainder of his inheritance in the film. Shaftel's pitch must have been particularly convincing as Otto was famously tight. "Canter's was one of our favorite places to eat, and we loved to go out to eat breakfast there," Ashby's future wife Mickey recalls, "but nine times out of ten, when the bill came [Otto] would say, 'Oh gosh, I seem to have forgotten my wallet. . . .'"[51] *No Place to Hide* would eventually be released in 1956, almost two years later, and be consigned to B-movie obscurity rather than the marquee success its makers had hoped for. Otto unfortunately lost most of his investment, but it was through his connection with Shaftel that Ashby got his chance to break into editing and start that slow rise to the top.

4

Doors Open . . .

> It is only with one's heart that one can see clearly. What is essential is invisible to the eye.
> —Antoine de Saint-Exupéry, *The Little Prince* (1943)

> I received my reward that rainy night when you decided to hire me as the fourth assistant on *The Big Country*. That, as they say, is when it all really started to happen.
> —Hal Ashby (to Robert Swink)

Before the box-office failure of *No Place to Hide* curtailed Bill Otto's relationship with Josef Shaftel, the director rushed another film into production. *The Naked Hills* (1956), shot with the working title *The Four Seasons*, was a Western, again written, directed, and produced by Shaftel, starring character actors Keenan Wynn and Jim Backus. Shooting began in the fall of 1955 at Republic, the biggest of the Poverty Row studios, and Otto brought Ashby and Bill Box along to watch.

Determined to make the most of the opportunity, Ashby volunteered to carry cans of film and soon was hired as an assistant editor. It was a B-movie job that no doubt paid almost nothing, but it was a foot in the door. Working alongside chief editor Gene Fowler Jr. (the son of screenwriter and novelist Gene Fowler), Ashby spent every available moment in the cutting room, absorbing as much of Fowler's knowledge and expertise as he could. "We shared a house, but I barely saw Hal, he worked so hard," Bill Box remembers. "He would be up before I was in the morning, off to work, and then at night come in, just grab a bite to eat and then go to bed because he was working into the night."[1]

Ashby's entry into the editing world marked the start of a period when work took precedence over everything else. At the age of twenty-six, he was now entirely focused on becoming a full-fledged editor and then realizing his ultimate dream of becoming a director. Though he would marry three more times and have many love affairs, from this point on his great passion was for his work. (Ironically, *The Naked Hills* is about a man who, for the majority of his life, lets his hunger for success jeopardize any chance of happiness that he might have with his wife and child. At the end of the film, the aging and down-on-his-luck protagonist finally realizes that it is love, not money, that he truly wanted all along.)

After this first editing job, Ashby applied to the Society of Motion Picture Film Editors, probably with Fowler's backing, in order to join the union. Editing was not a huge field, so the union was very careful about whom it allowed to join, but the timing was good, and Ashby was accepted. Thus he began the eight-year union-recognized apprenticeship that would allow him to work his way through the ranks.

By the time Ashby graduated from this arduous school of editing and became a director, his cinematic contemporaries were ten years his junior, fresh-faced film school grads with no concept of the effort he spent getting where he was. Looking back on his own experiences, he discouraged aspiring young directors from taking the editorial route: "You had to lie and cheat and do everything you could just to work. Of course, I would do editing on the side, and so forth, just to be into it and doing it. It was a tremendously debilitating thing. It is the members themselves, out of that tremendous desire to protect what they consider their livelihoods. They don't get into anything creative at all in their minds, except for a handful."[2]

Ashby described his apprenticeship as a "a trip and a half, . . . a full-out struggle," but it was well worth it for the education it gave him, not only in editing, but also in directing: "When film comes into a cutting room, it holds all the work and efforts of everyone involved up to that point. The staging, writing, acting, photography, sets, lighting, and sound. It is all there to be studied again and again and again, until you really know why it's good, or why it isn't. This doesn't tell you what's going on inside a director, or how he manages to get it from head to film, but it sure is a good way to observe the results, and the knowledge gained is invaluable."[3]

Around the same time he joined the editing union, Ashby entered into another kind of union. He was still dating Gloria Flaum when John

Mandel introduced him to a neighbor of his in Beachwood Canyon called Maloy Bartron, or Mickey to her friends. Ashby usually went for blonde, sweet, innocent types, and Mickey had short, black hair and was cute and playful with a tough edge. However, she was Ashby's age and a bohemian too, and something undeniably clicked between them.

Though they quickly fell in love, Ashby and Mickey's relationship may have begun on a professional basis. Mickey was a painter, but her art didn't make her much money, and she paid her bills working as a high-class Hollywood call girl. Mickey was an orphan who had been adopted by a couple who didn't understand her and whom she grew to resent, so coming to Los Angeles and not having to answer to anyone was a huge release for her. She was extremely sexually confident and had freely chosen to become a call girl because, as she would say, the job allowed her to sleep in every morning and work when she wanted. She had a telephone exchange where clients left messages for her, but she always had the option to say no. Her little black book contained only the names of high rollers, allegedly including Frank Sinatra, Desi Arnaz, and George Raft.

One Sunday afternoon, when Mickey and Ashby and the rest of the gang were gathered together at somebody's house, the two of them went down to have a look at Ian Bernard's new MG. It was the first time they connected, and their first "episode," as Mickey called it, was on the back seat of that very car. Mandel had suspected that they would click, and indeed Hal and Mickey quickly became a couple. Gloria, who was oblivious to the developments, was justifiably angry when she found out. According to Gloria, she and Mickey "overlapped" as she and Ashby either were still together or had only just broken up at the time. Mickey, who later became good friends with Gloria, recalls that she "went ballistic when she came home one day and found out."[4]

Despite having rushed into two short-lived marriages, Ashby was overcome by the intoxication of falling in love and proposed to Mickey almost immediately. He was deliberate, thoughtful, and considered in most other things, but when he fell in love, he surrendered to the feeling completely. "We had so much in common," says Mickey. "He had his film thing, I had my painting thing, we both loved jazz, we were both 'heads'—it all fitted in!"[5] On August 4, 1956, the couple were married in Laguna Beach, a seaside town an hour's drive down the Pacific coast from Los Angeles. They had been together for less than a month.

During the early stages of the marriage, the couple struggled financially: Ashby had insisted that Mickey give up her job as soon as they became "exclusive," but he couldn't get steady editing work. He ended up getting them both jobs at the debt-consolidation agency where he had worked previously. Because he knew Ray Kline, "we just walked into the job," Mickey remembers. "But first I had to promise not to tell people because it fell short of his own standards, and the people we knew would criticize him for it. It didn't fit into the persona that he wanted."[6] Fortunately, Ashby soon got a job as an assistant editor at Walt Disney Pictures, where most likely he worked on television rather than film projects.

Early on in the marriage, Ashby and Mickey lived with Bill Otto in Laurel Canyon, up in the Hollywood Hills. As well as being a jazz aficionado and a keen reader, Otto was an avid amateur photographer and had a darkroom in the house. He and Mickey shared a mutual admiration of each other's artistic abilities: he was a great fan of her paintings, while she got heavily into photography, quickly becoming, as she put it, a "darkroom baby."[7] Mickey was the only woman in Ashby's inner circle of friends, but she loved having the guys around and being in the company of other creative people.

While Mickey was holed up in the darkroom, Ashby was spending increasingly long hours in darkened editing rooms. He was good at becoming friends with the right people, and one job led to another. His first major studio editing job came when one of the chief editors at Disney, Ellsworth Hoagland, brought Ashby with him to United Artists. The film was director Stanley Kramer's *The Pride and the Passion* (1957), starring Cary Grant, Frank Sinatra, and Sophia Loren, and though the editing work he did was technical rather than creative, he made a positive impression while he had the chance. "He could read people well; that was why he could charm people," Mickey says.[8] During the course of the editing of *The Pride and the Passion,* Ashby not only made a lifelong friend in fellow editor Bob Lawrence, who almost thirty years later would work for Ashby on *8 Million Ways to Die,* but also made contacts at United Artists that led to his next job.

During the first few years of his marriage to Mickey, Ashby's career was progressing well, and he and Mickey were very happy. There was an ease to their relationship not only because of Ashby's laid-back personality but also because they were so well matched. He had initially swept

Mickey off her feet, but once the excitement of the romance began to lessen, she found that he was gentle, sensitive, and easygoing. Ashby was interested in Eastern mysticism, aspired to be as peaceful as one of his idols, Gandhi, and was generous to a fault. The happier he was, the more his sense of humor came to the fore, and he and Mickey had great fun together, really relishing each other's company. Ian Bernard and his wife, Judith, used to come round, and the four of them would stay up late, drinking and laughing, and often recording their conversations. They would then meet up again the next night and fall about with laughter listening to what they had said. But despite his happiness with Mickey, Ashby's demons remained. "He had a darker side which didn't come out often, but when it did it, it really did," Mickey remembers. "He'd pound his head on the wall. When he got out of it, he *really* got out of it."[9]

With his focus on his career, Ashby spent huge amounts of time working, but this did not seem to have a negative effect on his marriage. Mickey shared Ashby's love of cinema (she would later end up working as a sound-effects editor), and as an artist she understood his dedication to his craft. When Eileen came to stay with them, Ashby hardly saw her, which Mickey suspects was because "she wasn't in a position to further his career in any way. That was the way he was."[10]

This attitude won Ashby a job as fifth assistant editor on William Wyler's epic Western *The Big Country* (1958), where he worked under Bob Swink, the chief editor on every one of Wyler's films since *Detective Story* (1951). Wyler was a double Oscar winner for *Mrs. Miniver* (1942) and *The Best Years of Our Lives* (1946) and one of the most powerful directors in Hollywood. His relationship with Swink was as notable for its mutual trust and respect as for its unpredictable volatility. Wyler was known as "Forty-Take Wyler" and "Once More Wyler" because of the huge amount of film he shot, and Ashby, a noted hard worker, was hired because so many cutters were required.

Ashby once said, "My life changed when I met William Wyler and some others. Then all the doors opened, like in a movie."[11] The experience prompted a radical change in the way he thought about film, which he began to see as "the wildest, most exciting medium of all." On Ashby's very first day on *The Big Country,* one of the editors had assembled a rough cut of one reel of the film, so Wyler and his whole editing crew assembled in the projection room to look at it. Wyler stood up in front of everybody and, for the benefit of Ashby, the new boy, said, "If you have any ideas . . . any . . . no matter how wild they might seem, get them out. I, or we, might argue with you, and tell you it's a dumb idea and you are a dumb son of a bitch . . . but that doesn't matter because the heat of our anger comes only from the desire to make a good film. You must understand how we all *feel* about this film, and know in your heart that the words said in anger have nothing to do with anything personal. It will sound that way because we are driven by those strong feelings, and we don't take the time to be polite, but personal it isn't. So get those ideas out in the open and remember, the only thing any of us wants out of all this is to make a good film."[12]

This blew Ashby's mind. It was a thrill to be working with somebody of Wyler's stature but even more of one to feel so welcomed into the process. Never before had he been considered important enough to offer an opinion. In previous jobs, he had been told: "Whatever they say, don't open your mouth. Don't you say a word."[13] Wyler, however, believed in collaborative filmmaking, in which everybody was considered significant enough to contribute, and it was a working method that Ashby fell in love with and would employ himself when he became a director. He conceded that there was "a lot of yelling, hollering and swearing that went on down in those cutting rooms, but there was also about eighteen tons of love floating around there, too!"[14]

Though he would later say that he wished he had an editor he could work with as well as Wyler did with Swink, he admitted that he had "never seen *anybody* have arguments the way they had arguments."[15] Swink told him stories of the massive fallings-out they had working on *Roman Holiday* (1953), and Ashby saw incidents where their constant needling led to shouting matches and Swink throwing reels of film on the floor.

Three months or so after shooting finished, a rough cut had been assembled, and Wyler, Swink, and the editing crew gathered in Projection Room A in Goldwyn Studios to watch the twenty-eight-reel version of the film (approximately four and a half hours long). After fourteen reels, the crew took a break for dinner. As Ashby was the most junior person there, food had not been provided for him, so he stayed where he was. He waited for the crew to return and was still waiting at 11:30 P.M.

when Bob Belcher, one of the principal editors, came in and asked him why he was still there.

"I'm waiting for them to come back and we finish running the picture," replied Ashby. "They've only run the first fourteen reels."

"Oh, God," said Belcher, realizing Ashby hadn't heard what had happened. "They're not coming back."

"Why?" asked Ashby.

"Bob quit."[16]

During the meal, Wyler and Swink had been discussing the first half of the film and had a huge argument that ended with Swink walking out on the film. Nevertheless, he came in the next day and got on with the job at hand.

The flip side to Wyler's belligerence was his subversive sense of humor, which Ashby experienced firsthand. He recalled with great amusement a time when Wyler had asked his opinion on an editing matter. Ashby was rambling on somewhat, as he was prone to do, when he noticed that Wyler had an object in his hand, something like a watch fob, which he was spinning. "And as he would spin it," Ashby recalled, "you could see that it said 'Piss On You.' Needless to say, I wasn't sure how he took my thing."[17]

Though Wyler's reactions didn't always inspire confidence, the veteran director started Ashby thinking not only technically but also emotionally and creatively. As a result, Ashby felt greatly attached and committed to *Big Country*. When the film previewed in San Francisco, he was one of the few not brought along by Wyler, but he nevertheless paid his own way to attend the screening. Wyler was so impressed that Ashby was there that he had his expenses reimbursed. Everybody settled down to watch the film, and all was going well until, about an hour or so into the film, one of the reels went out of sync. It took a group of nervous editors almost ten minutes to rethread the negative and sort out the problem, by which time, as Ashby recalled, "a lot of people had come out to the popcorn stand to get candy and popcorn and so forth. And when they started the picture back up again, there was Willy running around in the lobby saying to people, 'The picture's started again, the picture's started again,' *forcing* them back into the theater! There was no question about it: he wasn't polite, he was just grabbing them and throwing them back in! It was hysterical."[18]

Ashby was learning by example all along, and seeing Wyler's passion for his films reinforced his certainty that this was where he wanted to be. Encouragingly, there were a number of editors who had gone on to direct, most famously David Lean and Robert Wise, and Ashby had only to look around him to see others who had done so. The first editor he had worked under, Gene Fowler Jr., had progressed to directing and by the end of the decade had made a clutch of films, such as *I Was a Teenage Werewolf* (1957) and *I Married a Monster from Outer Space* (1958), that were bound for classic B-movie status. One of the senior editors he had worked alongside at Walt Disney, Basil Wrangell, had combined editing with directing short films, second-unit material, television shows, and even a few features and was about to direct Cinerama's *South Seas Adventure* (1958). But there was another example even closer to home: Bob Swink.

Swink was desperate to become a director like Wyler, and the love-hate relationship between the two was greatly fueled by this desire. Wyler encouraged Swink by allowing him to shoot second unit on *Big Country* and *Friendly Persuasion* (1956) and, when he was too ill to make it to the set, had Swink oversee directorial duties on the latter for a few days. But though Wyler tantalized Swink with tidbits of directing work, he needed him as his editor and never really intended to let him go.

It wasn't just their shared dream of directing that bonded Ashby and Swink. In *Easy Riders, Raging Bulls,* Peter Biskind asserts that the absence of Ashby's father in his life from age twelve onward led him to seek out paternal substitutes, namely, Swink and, later, Norman Jewison. While there is definitely truth in this, Ashby and Swink were also particularly well-matched professional partners. In Swink, Ashby saw a master editor and mentor figure who could take him up through the system; Ashby, conversely, was the ideal pupil, a keen young man quickly becoming a skilled editor who, like Swink, was willing to work incredibly long hours to get the job done.

Ashby worked throughout the week but devoted weekends to Mickey and his friends. Ian Bernard had moved to Laguna Beach in 1956, and it was only a matter of time before Bill Box, and then Ashby and Mickey, followed. The Ashbys rented an apartment in Villa Rockledge, a beautiful cliffside house on the seafront. Both Mickey and Ashby loved it: she could paint at her leisure and soon had a little menagerie of animals made up of the strays that always seemed to gravitate toward her, and he was thrilled to be near the ocean. Bernard says the house was "a joy" to Ashby: "That's one thing I'll say, he did love the ocean. He never sat out and sunbathed, and I never saw him swim, but it was the bitch of the ocean, you know? It had a romantic implication to him."[19]

When Ashby was working on a film, he'd get up before dawn to beat the traffic and then drive up the coast to Los Angeles with the glow of the rising sun on the open road. According to Bernard, Ashby's workload and commuting "took the constitution of an eighteen-year old," but he never needed more than four hours' sleep. "He would leave before anybody was up and came back when we were all in bed," Bernard remembers. "We would leave some food out for him. I don't know how he did it."[20]

The Laguna crowd was described by Tom Blackwell as "artists, surfers, vagabonds," all getting by as best they could.[21] Blackwell was a young painter who had come from Chicago to try and make his name but was still a decade or so away from his breakthrough success as part of the photorealist movement. He enjoyed being part of this bohemian group and was a regular visitor at Ashby's seafront house. On weekends, everybody would gather together on the beach to smoke weed, drink, listen to music—Miles Davis, Art Pepper, John Coltrane—and talk about every conceivable topic. Blackwell was still wet behind the ears and latched onto Ashby, who quickly became his friend and mentor.

The aspiring artist was living on the breadline and was "so poor," Bernard says, "I think Ashby gave him clothes and some shoes. I have this weird recollection that he gave him a pair of sandals!"[22] Ashby took Blackwell under his wing and brought him along to jazz clubs, braving some of the rougher Los Angeles neighborhoods to share musical delights with the young man.

"He was the smartest man I'd ever met," says Blackwell. "Funny, as well. Without him being showy, you would know that he was the smartest guy in the room. The thing about Hal was the commanding way he spoke. He was so verbally acute, he would immediately gain your respect. He would get to the essence of things in an offhand and unforgettable way. He could summarize a scene in a way that made it so compelling, after that you could only see it his way."[23]

In his early days of editing, Ashby was already thinking a lot about directing. Blackwell recalls a car journey they took together during which they discussed Aldous Huxley's *Brave New World,* which Blackwell had just read. Over the course of the ride, the two talked about the possibility of turning it into a film, but Ashby decided it wasn't viable, that it was "way too far ahead of the zeitgeist."[24] (According to Blackwell, Ashby was always a year or so ahead of everybody else's tastes.)

Ashby continued to read widely and watch a lot of films—Hitchcock and Fellini were among his favorite directors—and whether he was making industry connections or broadening his cultural horizons, everything he did was in some way geared toward readying himself to direct. In a letter written in the early 1980s, Mickey reminded Ashby of "the days we used [to] sit around digging Basie or whom ever and throwing ideas around about making films to the music instead of vice versa."[25] She maintains that more than ten years before he started directing, Ashby already knew exactly what kinds of films he would make. "He was a very idealistic man," she says. "He wanted to make films that had a message but didn't hit people over the head with it. You know, like a subtle thing. He believed he was going to become a director; that was what he'd wanted from the very beginning."[26] Ashby was particularly influenced by Wyler because he made films marked by realism, restraint, and humor. Ashby respected Wyler because he "didn't want to be untruthful. He had very strong feelings that way, and he would make films for reasons."[27]

In around 1958, the year that Mandel broke into Hollywood with his groundbreaking jazz score to Robert Wise's *I Want to Live,* the Susan Hayward melodrama, Ashby and Bernard came up with a plan for a movie inspired by their activities with the antinuclear group SANE. *The Sound of Silence,* written by "Ian Bernard and Wm. Hal Ashby," is set in 1965, twenty years after the dropping of the atomic bomb. It centers on David Cassidy, a war correspondent obsessed with Hiroshima who begins a personal crusade to prevent further nuclear activity. The script showcases pacifist perspectives and reveals the writers' belief that art can precipitate change. The last meaningful statement in the script is from David's wife, Allyn, who tells him that as a writer he has "the ability to reach men's hearts; you can make them feel and understand. You can do a lot of good because of this. That's the way I think you should fight."[28]

Cassidy is a lot like Ashby: married with a young child and unsure whether the conventional happiness of family life can give him all he needs. Like Ashby and many of his 1970s male protagonists, he is essentially still a child, an adult whose immaturity and insecurity lurk just below the surface. He too gets angry and impassioned about events outside his control, that anger and distress coming predominantly from an inability to affect things, rather than from the wrong itself.

Ashby and Bernard were friendly with Reva Frederick, Robert Mitchum's personal assistant, and *The Sound of Silence* was written with Mitchum in mind as they felt he would be ideologically sympathetic with the film's views. Mitchum was supposedly interested, but nothing came of it, and the film was never produced.

The Sound of Silence was too personal and polemical to be entirely successful: certain characters are stereotypes, some scenarios lack realism, and the dialogue is at times clunky. Yet considering how inexperienced both writers were, the script succeeds much more than might be expected, and its powerful pacifist message was a sign of things to come.

As soon as *The Big Country* was completed, Swink moved base to Twentieth Century–Fox to begin work on George Stevens's *The Diary of Anne Frank* (1959), taking his keen-eyed protégé with him.

Stevens, like Wyler, was a veteran who had as much power and sway as any director in Hollywood and a reputation for shooting a lot of footage. In the past, Stevens had infuriated his bosses with overblown production times and lengthy editing periods, but the consistent commercial and critical success of his films made him an asset to any studio. Three of his previous four films—*Giant* (1956), *Shane* (1953), and *A Place in the Sun* (1951)—had been huge successes, and *Giant* and *A Place in the Sun* both won Stevens Best Director Academy Awards. Though Stevens didn't have the same impact on Ashby as Wyler, working alongside him nevertheless had an effect. Years later, Ashby would recount the director telling him: "In film, 25 per cent of it is in the writing, 25 per cent of it is in the shooting, 25 per cent of it is in the editing, and the last 25 per cent is what you end up with."[29]

If anything, *The Diary of Anne Frank* was a bigger operation than *The Big Country.* It was another three-hour epic, and in the Fox cutting rooms where he worked Ashby had cans of footage stacked high all around him. Sometimes it would take hours just to find one little bit of footage, but he had a superb memory for minute details in individual takes and was an invaluable help to Swink. The pair worked fourteen- or fifteen-hour days, putting editing before everything else. A secretary's memo informed the Society of Motion Picture Film Editors that "Messr.s [*sic*] Bob Swink and Hal Ashby missed the meeting this evening because it was necessary to work on our picture."[30] Out of the nine editors employed on *The Diary of Anne Frank,* it was only Ashby, the most junior, who kept working alongside his boss rather than stopping to attend a union meeting.

Ashby not only had a passion for his work but also felt a fierce loyalty to Swink. In the article "Breaking Out of the Cutting Room," he wrote affectionately about Swink's influence on him:

> When I was lucky enough to be working with Bob, he hit me with everything from the technical aspects to a philosophy of film.
>
> "Once the film is in hand," he would say, "forget about the script, throw away all of the so-called rules, and don't try and second-guess the director. Just look at the film, and let it guide you. It will turn you on all by itself, and you'll have more ideas on ways to cut it than you would ever dream possible.
>
> "And use your instincts! Don't be afraid of them! Rely on them! After all with the exception of a little knowledge, instincts are all we've got.
>
> "Also, don't be afraid of the film. You can cut it together twenty-six different ways, and if none of those works, you can always put it back into daily form, and start over."[31]

After *The Diary of Anne Frank,* Swink took Ashby with him from film to film for the rest of his apprenticeship. It meant not only a guarantee of employment but also an opportunity to observe one of the best editors around. At the start of 1959, the two were just getting started on *Spartacus* (1960) when, after just two weeks, producer-star Kirk Douglas fired director Anthony Mann. Swink and Ashby left the film when the new director, Stanley Kubrick, brought in his own editor, Ashby's friend Bob Lawrence.

Mann's firing demonstrated the precarious position of directors, who were ostensibly less important than stars with inflated egos. When Ashby became a prominent director, he avoided the spotlight as much as possible and instead concentrated on his craft and helping others as he himself had been helped.

Ashby saw at close quarters the negative effects of fame when his path crossed with the celebrated poet Robert Frost. Frost was the guest of honor at the wedding of Lelia Goldoni, star of John Cassavetes's *Shadows* (1959) and a friend of Mickey's. Ashby was photographed standing proudly next to the great man, but the story behind the picture is more revealing. Ashby and Mickey were fond of Frost's delicate, sensitive poetry but found that, in person, the man was irritable and unbearably arrogant. "He was an egomaniac!" Mickey recalls.[32]

Ashby had also seen a change in his friend Sammy Davis Jr. since he had risen to stardom. In the late 1950s, Ashby and Mickey would go for meals at Davis's house up in the hills. When Davis discovered Mickey was a painter, he commissioned her to paint his picture. Davis posed for Mickey, but she was interested in African art, and the tribal influences in her rendering of the Rat Packer were not to his liking. He had "an enormous ego," Mickey said. "He wanted a Hollywood portrait, but I didn't have it in me to do that."[33] As Davis's fame grew, he and Ashby grew apart. "One day Ashby and I were leaving the United Artists lot and Sammy stopped the car for a second," says Ian Bernard. "Having been one of our great bosom buddies, he casually said, 'We've got to get together sometime,' and Ashby and I both said, 'Yeah, sure.' He'd sort of gone off to be a great star in his own mind."[34]

Ashby felt that in order to develop, he had to broaden his horizons, both culturally and geographically. He wanted to be ready to direct important films with something to say. He needed to move to Europe.

Mickey, however, was far from enthusiastic. "I was painting," she says, "and we had this great house there up on a cliff above the ocean. As far as I was concerned we had it made, but he wanted to do this European thing."[35] She would miss her friends and being surrounded by her animals, but, carried along by Ashby's excitement, she agreed to the move. They sold everything they owned, gave up the seafront house, and bid farewell to Laguna Beach.

They went first to New York City, where they stayed with Ashby's old girlfriend Gloria and her husband. It was November 1960, and the city was covered in snow. Mickey and Gloria went out for a walk and stumbled across an apartment that they thought would be perfect for Mickey and Ashby. Mickey was much keener on the idea of moving to New York than that of changing continents, but her efforts to convince Ashby to stay were fruitless. "He wanted to go to Europe, maybe just to say he had been to Europe," she says. "I couldn't have cared less."[36]

Because he knew some film people there, Ashby chose to relocate to London. Mickey was now a sound-effects editor and had worked in television, and Ashby hoped they would both get film work through his contacts. However, they were shocked to discover on their arrival that they needed permits to work in Britain.

In an effort to salvage the situation, they bought a Volkswagen (very alien with its right-hand drive) and headed for the Continent, hoping a change of location would bring better fortune. They had little money, but in Paris they met someone who agreed to loan them his apartment for a few weeks. At the American Express office where they picked up their mail, a charismatic young man invited them to an Algerian tea-room. Because of the current tensions between Algeria and France (the Algerians were trying to gain independence from French colonial rule), it was risky to go to such places, and Ashby feared he might be arrested in a raid by the French police. "Ashby was very cautious," Mickey remembers. "It was the beginning of his career, and he sure didn't want to get into anything like that." Luckily, they spent an uninterrupted afternoon drinking tea and enjoying the establishment's "relaxed" atmosphere. "They had a lot of hash," says Mickey. "They cut open a regular cigarette and laid a chunk of hash in it, wrapped it back up and smoked it that way. Drugs kinda ran in and out of everything."[37]

Ashby and Mickey next headed for Switzerland, where they met up with Ian and Judith Bernard in Zürich for Christmas. The two couples then drove through the Alps aiming for Rome, but a blizzard halted their progress, and they had to spend New Year's Eve in a little hotel in Piacenza. At dinner, they were befriended by a group of Italians who loved Americans because they had freed them from Mussolini and fascism. The two parties saw in the start of 1961 together, toasted it with optimism, and then retired for the night. The following morning, when

Ashby checked out, he was told that the bill had been settled by the Italians from the night before. While the others were touched by this generosity, Ashby's pride was hurt. After a heated discussion, he stubbornly insisted they pay the bill again, much to Bernard's disgust.

As Mickey had feared, they struggled to adapt to life in Europe. They had fit in perfectly in Laguna Beach, but here they were seen as oddballs and hippies. Even simple things like crossing the street became confusing, as the Europeans drove on the "wrong" side of the road. Driving their little Volkswagen was disorienting and particularly difficult in Rome: on one occasion Ashby was so intimidated by the Italians' reckless driving that he froze on a roundabout by the Coliseum. Bernard had to pry him from the driver's seat and take over at the wheel.

After a few days in Rome, Ian and Judith left to go back to Laguna; Mickey enviously watched them go. As Ashby and Mickey were leaving Rome, they drove within a couple of blocks of the prison where Chet Baker was being held after a drug arrest the previous summer. The jazz icon was a friend of Mickey's, and she was desperate to see him, but Ashby refused, fearful of how the unpredictable Italian authorities might react to two strangers visiting an infamous drug addict. "When we didn't go by and stop and see Chet in prison, I really wasn't happy about that," she says. "It wasn't that risky. But Ashby was very cautious; he was at the beginning of his career and didn't want to do anything that would knock it off track."[38]

Mickey and Ashby left Italy and briefly returned to France before heading for Madrid. Because *The Pride and the Passion* had been shot in Spain, Ashby thought they might find work there. On the way, they got lost and ended up on a back road where they saw how Franco's fascist regime had reduced Spain to crippling poverty. In Madrid, too, they saw department stores covered in dust because nobody could afford to buy what was being sold. In stark contrast to the feting they had received in Italy, here they were hated because of the United States' support of Franco's government. The Spaniards did not even try to hide it. Ashby and Mickey were refused work everywhere and came away ashamed to be American. Recalling the trip, Ashby said, "The first time I ever traveled, I was disillusioned with [my] country and with what I thought we stood for."[39]

Things went from bad to worse when Mickey became very ill after eating shellfish. She returned to London, while Ashby spent two weeks in France and Spain, adding to the already considerable strain on their relationship. When he rejoined Mickey, they stayed with friends in London's comfortable Earl's Court district, but Mickey remained unwell for the duration of their trip abroad. Finally, to her great relief, Ashby agreed that it was time to head home.

While staying with one of his film friends in New York, Ashby found temporary editing work that allowed them to remain there for a few months. Mickey was instantly more at ease: every morning she would go to Grand Central Station and sit in the shadows, filling a sketchbook with drawings of travelers milling around the majestic station.

Back in Laguna, Mickey turned her sketches into paintings, and Ashby enthusiastically returned to editing. He and Swink were back at Goldwyn, cutting Phil Karlson's *The Young Doctors* back-to-back with Wyler's *The Children's Hour* (both 1961). Wyler spent quite a bit of time in the cutting room yet never cramped Swink or the other editors. This became Ashby's preferred method of working, both as an editor and as a director.

To Ashby, Wyler personified good directing. Though stylistically there are few parallels between the two, Wyler had a huge influence on how Ashby conducted himself. "I carry him around all the time when I direct," he said later, "even though I never had discussions with him about that. It all had to do with the absorption of his work and being close enough at times to really see how it happened. And it was the attitude about being able to listen to what other people had to say."[40] Ashby was always observing Wyler, right down to the tiniest details. One night, after a preview in Long Beach, Wyler and his editors returned to the Goldwyn lot to talk about the screening. During the whole discussion, Wyler was silent and just sat at his desk writing mysteriously on a pad of paper. As everyone was leaving to go home, Ashby sneaked a peek at what profound observations Wyler had jotted down. On the pad was just the word "Decisions," which Wyler had written over and over in the same spot. The incident stayed with Ashby, proof that even the most experienced minds sometimes had to go back to basics. In the 1980s, the notepads in Ashby's office were all headed with one handwritten word: "Decisions."

Ashby worked ceaselessly from his return to Laguna in spring 1961 until the end of the year, when *The Children's Hour* was released. That summer, Mickey began an affair with John Barreto, a man on the fringes of their social group. Ashby knew Barreto socially and got on well with him, but he had never identified him as a threat to his domestic happiness.

With Ashby so seldom at home, however, Mickey felt irresistibly drawn to Barreto, whom she found "magnetic, wonderful."[41] Their time in Europe had given her grave reservations about her marriage to Ashby. For the sake of his career, he had prized them away from the stability of all they knew: "My whole life was left in Laguna. I'd given up a whole lot to go on that trip. He insisted on that. It was the straw that broke *my* back."[42]

The day after Christmas, Mickey left Ashby. She was so sure she was doing the right thing that, had Barreto not convinced her to do otherwise, she would have left without an explanation. Despite her lover's intervention, she still walked out on Ashby "in a very rude way. I just left him a note on the refrigerator, like you'd leave for the milkman."[43]

In the eyes of their friends, Ashby and Mickey's relationship had become platonic. Ashby, however, had been so focused on his work that her departure was a huge shock to him. Whether he was fully conscious of it or not, he had shut her out sexually in the latter stages of their marriage, as work consumed his every waking moment. Mickey had done everything she could to get him interested again, using all her wiles and dressing up in exotic lingerie, but to no avail. (In the opinion of one of his friends, after he had "rescued" Mickey—who didn't really want or need to be rescued—Ashby found her appeal slowly lessening.)

Three days after Mickey left, a divorce complaint was drawn up against Ashby, claiming she had been subjected to "extreme cruelty" and that he had "wrongfully inflicted upon her grievous mental suffering."[44] His response was to claim that Mickey was insane and try to have her put under seventy-two-hour observation. According to Mickey, Ashby did not actually think she was mentally unstable, just "crazy for leaving him. He was on the up, and we were driving a Porsche." Barreto, on the other hand, wandered from one casual job to the next, was a heroin user, and, Mickey admits, was "practically living in his car."[45]

Ashby, however, accepted her decision and did not fight it. By the end of January, he and Mickey had been granted an interlocutory judgment of divorce. (The final judgment was not granted until May 1963.) Ashby did not contest the claims leveled at him in the complaint, although Mickey concedes they were false and made only to ensure a quick divorce. Mickey nevertheless felt guilty—and more so when Ashby generously gave her their right-hand-drive Volkswagen. "As far as I was concerned I didn't deserve anything; I had left him," Mickey says. "But he gave me that car. He was very good to me. He was a good man, a good man."[46]

She left the marriage not without the occasional backward glance. In a letter to Ashby from the early 1980s, she wrote: "Maybe I just wanted to say hello—I think I've wanted to for a long time now. Thank you for what you taught me and tried to teach me—Some dense pupil!"[47] Looking back, she says, "He was a good husband, he really was. You couldn't ask for more. I never got over feeling guilty just leaving him like I did. But that was where my heart was taking me."[48]

5

The Family Man

A baby is God's opinion that life should go on.
—Carl Sandburg, *Remembrance Rock* (1948)

Here in your hand, before your very eyes, is proof that your youngest son; the baby of your family is in fact becoming a more responsible individual.
—Hal Ashby

The Sound of Silence was written ten years after Ashby had bailed on Lavon and Leigh, and possibly marked a change in his attitude toward children. The idealistic hero, David Cassidy, has a seven-year-old son; given that the screenplay is set in 1965, he would have been born in 1958, right around the time that Ashby and Ian Bernard were writing the script. Was Ashby thinking about becoming a father again and imagining the world his child might grow up in?

Though Mickey had a daughter with John Barreto a few years after she left Ashby, she had told Ashby she did not want any children. However, she recalls that in his first few years as an apprentice editor, Ashby worked with a woman who was going through a difficult divorce and actually signed papers agreeing to be a guardian of her child. In May 1960, he did not stand in the way of Jim Montgomery, Lavon's second husband, who had raised Leigh, adopting his daughter and legally becoming her father. If the newly single Ashby felt an urge for parenthood now, he apparently wanted a fresh start at it.

In an odd coincidence, Shirley Citron was, like Mickey, an orphan, and she had always yearned for the traditional family setup she had missed out on as a child. Almost three years older than Ashby, she was a stunning blonde with long hair and gorgeous features. As Ashby's niece Meredith commented when she met her, she "even smoked sexy."[1]

According to Ashby, he and Shirley met only at the beginning of 1962, but they had both been apprentice editors at the same time, so their paths may have crossed earlier. (Shirley's only editing credit is for the film *Invasion of the Animal People* [1962]—a version of the Swedish creature feature *Rymdinvasion I Lappland* [1959] reworked with the addition of a few disjointed new scenes featuring John Carradine—which she had cut for Jerry Warren, a hack filmmaker who regularly bought and repackaged foreign films.)

Soon after they got together, Ashby wrote his mother that Shirley was pregnant. However, he was quick to explain, "The baby is not mine. Shirley was pregnant before I ever met her. Shirley was not married or even involved with anyone when she became pregnant. It was just one of those things that happen, and when it happens all you can do is make a decision. Shirley made the decision to have her baby. It was sometime later when I came along and we fell in love. I should say we discovered we loved each other."[2]

Predictably, Ashby threw himself into the romance with total abandon. He and Shirley had an instant connection, and there was an irresistible logic to their relationship: she had a child on the way and no father in sight, and Ashby finally felt ready to have a family. It was also an opportunity to rescue the woman he loved and partly atone for leaving Lavon and Leigh. Only the fact that Ashby was technically Mickey's husband stopped him from marrying Shirley immediately, but in all other ways they were man and wife.

They moved into 9878 Easton Drive, a house on a secluded lane in Benedict Canyon, away from the noise and urban sprawl of Los Angeles. Secluded and peaceful, it was an ideal place to start a family.

Ashby wrote to his mother that he was "very much in love . . . unable to find the words that could express why I feel about her as I do." Yet he acknowledged that their situations—his divorce and her pregnancy by another man—were a struggle, despite the strength of their feelings for each other: "Parts of it have been very rough; we had both our pasts. . . . But our love has been strong enough to carry us through the hardship of jealousy, fear and anything else you can think of."[3]

The birth of Shirley's daughter brought them together and made them feel positive about the path they were on. Carrie was born in Cedars of Lebanon Hospital on June 23, 1962, and christened with the surname Ashby. Though they weren't married yet, Shirley had already changed her name to Ashby, and so it was a proper family that returned to Easton Drive. A few months later, Ashby reported: "The joy of loving is fast pushing the bad things into oblivion."[4]

Though Carrie was not his own blood, Ashby called her his daughter and treated her as such. He was a dedicated father and stayed at home for the first couple of months of her life. However, he soon ran out of money and had to return to work. Once Ashby was back in the editing room with Bob Swink, cutting Byron Haskin's *Captain Sindbad* (1963), his inability to balance work and family life became apparent. After years of letting his work utterly consume him, he was unable to break the pattern. For the rest of his life, he would be a workaholic. He took photos of Carrie in August, just after starting work on *Captain Sindbad*, but three months down the line had still not developed them. Shirley, however, was understanding and in a letter to Eileen Ashby wrote: "Men need to take their time when they're doing creative things and we must be patient with them."[5]

Life on Easton Drive with Shirley, Carrie, and their two cats, Grey and Sheba, seemed to effect a change in Ashby. He had sporadically stayed in touch with his mother since leaving Ogden but was aware that from his teenage years on he had been far from an ideal son. Now that he had a family himself, he began to feel the urge to put things right. He started writing his mother every month, expressing his appreciation of her, and attempting to apologize for past wrongs. "I may treat you shabbily most of the time," he confessed, "but don't ever think for a second that I am not aware of what you are. You have given the greatest gift there is to give. You have been able to give love. Nothing is more important than that."[6]

Ashby told Eileen that her love was possibly the one constant in his life, the thing he could rely on no matter what. "I have begun to recognize your love as a kind of anchor; a solid base to living . . . to life," he wrote. "No matter what tragedies might beset me; no matter how despondent I may become; I know there is someone who wants me to be; you want me to be because I am me."[7] Previously, he had felt guilty about the inadequacy of what he had given her in return. Now, however, as he looked at Carrie, he realized that it was the role of parents to give more than they would ever receive back.

Pondering his troubled teenage years, Ashby acknowledged that he had refused his mother's help and emotionally excluded her, then never properly let her back into his life:

> Perhaps there is a point when the child reaches an age where so many new things are happening all at once; he becomes confused and frightened; it panics him. He withdraws; he starts to close things off. He wants to stop the flow of newness. In his confusion, he shuts off love, also. From this point he needs a constant pressure on the valve from somebody who has the stamina to keep loving him; despite his refusal to accept it. One day he'll get a glimmer of this love and let the valve be opened freely. Love will pour in and, in a sense, he will be born again. He will start to learn what life really is. He will accept responsibility because it is a part of loving; not because it's something forced upon him. Love will be the one basic.[8]

For Ashby, the valve had been opened by the overwhelming emotions he experienced in the role of father and husband, and his new family helped him see his family back home in Ogden in a different light. He realized that he and Jack had not seen each other in years and expressed an interest in getting to know him once again. And when Eileen sent him a picture of Leigh, along with news of her progress, he needlessly returned the picture but said that he "would be more than pleased and happy" to meet her: "I imagine it would be a little awkward at first, but I'm certain those kind of things can be overcome and I am anxious to see what kind of person she is turning out to be. One of these days, when everything is right, maybe she can come and visit in California. That is if she doesn't have some boyfriend she would be homesick for all the time she's here. We both know how that can be don't we!"[9]

It was a valiant gesture but fell far short of reconciliation. Ashby may have been ready to be a father again, but he wasn't ready to face his guilt for abandoning Leigh. It's unclear whether, in saying that he would see her "when everything is right," he was aware that that day would never come.

Nevertheless, in his newly enlightened state, he was trying to be a better person and reexamining his way of seeing things. "I was so smart," he wrote to Eileen, "it only took me about twenty-eight years to learn the fact that people are people, and should be treated as such. . . . Now, I at least try and think before I act. I try to understand how a person could feel hurt; even if I don't believe they should feel that way."[10]

Now that Ashby and Eileen were writing regularly and had a much greater understanding of each other, he invited her to visit him in Los Angeles and meet Shirley and Carrie. Eileen, however, was seventy-five, suffered from heart trouble and arthritis, and had money problems, so Ashby drove halfway to Ogden (he feared his car wouldn't make it the whole way) to meet her and took her to Los Angeles himself.

The visit was a roaring success. Not only was Eileen delighted with her new granddaughter, but she got on very well with Shirley, with whom she formed a strong bond over the next few years. In contrast to previous visits, during which Ashby barely saw her, this time they spent a lot of time together. After she left, he wrote to her, saying: "Gee, but did we enjoy you being here with us. I'll never be able to explain the good feeling I get when I see, hear, or think of you. Why don't you come again next week?"[11]

In May, Ashby's divorce from Mickey came through, and on July 31, he and Shirley legally tied the knot in a Las Vegas quickie wedding. Again, after a few more months at home, Ashby had to return to work. Because of a paucity of editing jobs, the union was being particularly vigilant about giving priority to their most senior members. As a result, Ashby had to fight to get to work on *The Best Man* (1964), a Henry Fonda movie adapted from the Gore Vidal play. Bob Swink, however, insisted on having him. Now in the final stages of his epic apprenticeship as an editor, Ashby immersed himself in his work throughout the latter part of 1963 and helped get a rough cut finished by the end of the year. Vidal, unaware that this was just a preliminary version, was upset with the results and tried to have his name taken off the film. However, when later he saw the magic Swink and Ashby had worked on the final cut, he was delighted.

Despite the hard work he did there, the editing room was for Ashby a haven, a retreat from reality that allowed him to contemplate the world and his place in it. Though he corresponded less often when he was on a film, it was with Eileen more than anyone that he shared these ruminations, even rising at 5 A.M. to write to her before work.

A generation and some forty-two years apart, Hal and Eileen Ashby nonetheless looked at the world in much the same way. He had inherited from her what he called "a continual questioning of life,"[12] and during this period it was almost as if he was in a second adolescence as he reassessed everything around him. His former belief that he knew all the answers was replaced with a realization: "That any conclusion I might reach should be considered an ultimate is absurd. This feeling, this knowing that I don't know all the answers, is a good feeling. It's good because it allows me to approach life with an open-mind."[13] He concluded: "The overall reason for life; this earth and all that goes with it . . . is a puzzle, but an extremely beautiful puzzle."[14]

Ashby's letters to Eileen from this period also reveal a concern for the direction in which America was going that would be expressed nationally over the course of the decade by the peace and civil rights movements. Ashby has always been personified as "the hippie director," not only because of his appearance, but also because there was a freedom and a joy in his films coupled with a concern for the world and a will to change things for the better: "I truly enjoy the life I live. Even with its fear, frustration, and seeming madness at times there is still the joy of just being. The joy of knowing you, of seeing—seeing, not just looking at—all the beautiful things there are in this crazy world we live in. The joy of being able to have compassion for my fellow man. To have the capacity to cry because of something that has happened to some other person is truly a blessing. Life is absurd, but its very absurdity, makes it wonderful."[15]

There was also a spiritual aspect to Ashby's soul-searching; though never a Mormon, he was nevertheless religious in a loose, modern sense. When Eileen asked him when he had given up God, he responded by saying: "I don't think anyone can just give Him up. They can renounce a conception, or idea of God, but, to my way [of] belief, to renounce God would be the same as renouncing all of life. . . . Life is much too wonderful. To dispute it, could only be a waste of time. The only thing I get angry about is when I think: Here I've been presented with this beautiful gift called Life, and someday it's to be taken from me. I'm selfish, and I want to keep it. However, I do accept that it was given, and 'give and take' is a rule that applies to all of Life."[16]

Perhaps because his father died when he was at such a vulnerable age, Ashby was painfully aware of the fact that life was short and that every opportunity should be taken, every moment savored. When discussing patience, in which Eileen was a great believer, he admitted: "If it costs me too much on the emotional ledger of my life, I refuse to . . . sit with people who have nothing in common with me just because it seems the patient thing to do. I have more important things to do with the short span of my life. Let them do what they want, but I would rather sit for an hour and communicate with a solitary leaf from a tree. To me, the leaf has more to say than some people."[17]

The beginning of 1964 was a busy time for Ashby: not only were he and Swink putting together the final cut of *The Best Man,* but the Ashby family was also moving. Fortunately, the distance was minimal, as they were taking the house at 9853 Easton Drive, just a few yards up the lane. It was smaller, but, in a letter to his mother, Ashby described it as "the nicest place I've lived in since I left home."[18]

Ashby finished his stint on *The Best Man* on the night of February 18 and began work on *The Greatest Story Ever Told* (1965) the very next morning. "I've read most of the script," he wrote to his mother, "and am truly enthused about it. What I have read is beautiful and moving, with a true feeling for the story of Christ. If the film is one-half as good as the script, it will end up as one of the finest films ever made."[19] George Stevens had shot hundreds of thousands of feet of film, making the editorial undertaking as epic as the film itself. When Ashby came on board, a crew of seven or eight editors had already been editing for a year, and he and Bob Swink, who had been assigned to cut the scenes from the Last Supper onward, were expected to be busy for a further six to eight months.

However, just two weeks after he and Ashby began, Swink was poached by William Wyler to work on his new film, *The Collector* (1965), adapted from the John Fowles novel. It was decided that Ashby should take over from his mentor, and he suddenly became a chief editor, one of four editors working under Harold Kress, the supervising editor, tirelessly assembling a film that would run four hours and twenty minutes when released. Just halfway through cutting the Last Supper, however, Ashby received an even more enticing offer from John Calley of the Filmways production company: Tony Richardson was interested in having him edit his new picture, *The Loved One*, an adaptation of Evelyn Waugh's novella.

On July 23, Ashby wrote a note to Stevens, telling him that he wanted to leave to become chief editor on *The Loved One* but that he would not do so without Stevens's permission. Stevens refused his permission, however, so Ashby said no to Calley. However, just two days later, Calley met with Ashby and asked him to begin the very next day, at a much greater salary than Stevens was paying him.

Ashby turned up at Stevens's offices with his note of resignation and decided to tell Kress rather than Stevens that he was quitting the film. Talking privately in Kress's office, he told him: "I have to leave you."

"Hal," warned Kress, "you're going to make the biggest enemy you ever had in the motion picture business."

Ashby, fearful of Stevens's reaction, asked, "Will you tell him? He might get mad and haul off."

When Kress passed on the news, Stevens responded by saying, "We just raised him from an assistant to an editor four months ago and now he's going to walk out on us?"[20]

Ashby had contravened union rules, and Stevens filed a grievance. More important, however, Ashby had broken his word, lured away by ambition and money. Five years later, Ashby wrote, "The George Stevens people were mad at me—I hope they still aren't."[21]

Though in terms of his career it made sense to quit as one of four editors working under a supervising editor to become chief editor for Richardson, Ashby felt guilty for many years. A seminar Ashby gave at the American Film Institute in 1975 was held just hours after Stevens's funeral, but because he had been immersed in his upcoming film, *Bound for Glory,* Ashby had missed the news of Stevens's death. Clearly shaken, he said that it might take him "ten or fifteen minutes to get into this thing. . . . It's a bit of a shock so if you could all just bear with me for a little bit. It's such a shock; it's the missing you know." He went on to say, "[Stevens] certainly gave a lot to all of us, that's for sure." Yet it was his guilt over *Greatest Story* ("an awful thing happened out of it") that he lingered over, his voice trailing off as he spoke.[22]

6

Norman

> Hal Ashby was, without doubt, the most committed editor I ever worked with. Over the course of my next three films, which I did with Hal, we would bond as close as brothers.
> —Norman Jewison

Had Ashby known what lay ahead, he might have thought better of his decision to work on *The Loved One;* in a letter to Ashby, the film's creative assistant, Budd Cherry, referred to its production period as "the Great Trauma of '64."[1]

In 1964, Tony Richardson was the hottest young director in town. Just a few months before *The Loved One* started shooting, his film *Tom Jones* (1963) had won four Academy Awards, including Best Picture and Best Director for Richardson, from its ten nominations. However, when MGM, with whom he had a multipicture deal, refused to reward his Oscar success with an improved contract, Richardson was determined to make them regret their decision. *The Loved One* began shooting in late July 1964 and was supposed to be done after ten weeks, but it was December before Richardson wrapped, by which time he had doubled the budget. Richardson banned producer Martin Ransohoff (whose company, Filmways, was making the picture for MGM) from the set, blew money on unnecessary location shooting, cast stars in cameos and unknowns in the lead roles, and spent huge amounts of Metro's money on Dom Pérignon and canapés and screening dailies at the exclusive Beverly Hills Hotel. Not only did he shoot an enormous amount of film (the first assembly ran to five hours), but his treatment of Evelyn Waugh's already scathingly satirical take on life and death in Beverly Hills aimed to shock. (There were allegedly three versions of the film: "rare, medium and we'll-sue.")[2]

Ashby was collateral damage in the general havoc that Richardson wreaked. After Ashby and his team had finished the first cut, Richardson took the film back to England to complete it with his usual editor. In his autobiography, Richardson wrote: "I hadn't been happy with the editors I worked with on *The Loved One* (one of them, Hal Ashby, went on to make a good career as a director) and I wanted to transfer the film back to London where I could work with Tony Gibbs."[3] He was most likely oblivious to the effects of his actions. Ashby already had a black mark against his name for the way he had left Stevens, and now the job he had risked his reputation for had been prized away from him. "It was a bad time," Ashby wrote later. "Depression and paranoia ran rampant. In short, I was on the super bummer of the year."[4]

In Ashby's eyes, it was Norman Jewison who saved his career.

At the time, Jewison was in a transitional period as a director, just as Ashby was as an editor. A Canadian expat who began his career in live television and graduated to making inoffensive comedies for Universal (including two Doris Day vehicles), he had just been brought in to take over *The Cincinnati Kid* (a movie based on Richard Jessup's poker novel), another Filmways production for MGM. The film's original director, Sam Peckinpah, had shot a riot with hundreds of extras that was not in the script and a controversial nude scene involving a black prostitute, prompting Martin Ransohoff to relieve Peckinpah of his duties after only a week. His experiences with Richardson had left Ransohoff in no mood to work with another loose cannon.

Though Jewison was an unlikely candidate for a film that was essentially a reworking of *The Hustler* (1961), with cards instead of pool, John Calley and Ransohoff desperately needed a director immediately, and he was perceived as a safe choice. Jewison accepted the job on the condition that he be given two weeks to rework the script with Terry Southern, the screenwriter on *The Loved One* and Stanley Kubrick's *Dr. Strangelove, or: How I Learned to Stop Worrying and Love the Bomb* (1964).

It was around this time that Ashby and Jewison first met. Ashby said that Calley set up a meeting between them, but Jewison recalls that he was wandering around MGM with Southern, whom Ashby had befriended on *The Loved One,* when they passed his cutting room. At the time, Ashby was still working on the first cut of *The Loved One,* and

Jewison heard him laughing at the outrageous footage. Ashby invited him in, and the two began to talk. "There was something about his sense of humor and his kindness," Jewison remembers.[5]

Ashby caught Jewison's attention early on when he proudly mentioned his apprenticeship under Bob Swink, working for Wyler and Stevens. Wyler was one of Jewison's heroes, and he and Ashby ended up talking about him for hours. Jewison began hanging out with Ashby as he cut *The Loved One,* "watching the changes, smoking a little of Hal's pot and joining him in helpless laughter. The sicker the movie got, the harder we laughed. And despite the laughter and the pot, it became obvious to me that he was meticulous and fiercely passionate about his craft." By this stage in his career, Ashby's aptitude for editing, his ability to absorb and retain information about the footage he was working on, was remarkable. "His old Moviola was surrounded by hundreds of feet of film in bins or hanging in clips from lines strung between walls," recalls Jewison, "but he knew precisely what shots were on each clip."[6]

During Ashby's dark hours after he was fired from *The Loved One,* Jewison asked him if he wanted to edit *The Cincinnati Kid.* "Oh, man, that would be great!" Ashby cried, and that was that.[7] For the rest of the 1960s, Jewison's presence in Ashby's life guaranteed him not only regular, secure work but also devoted friendship. Over the course of six films, the two would form a rare personal and professional relationship that was closer and more creatively productive than any either would experience again.

From the very start they were, as Jewison put it, "simpatico," united by a genuine love of cinema and a belief that films should make a difference in the world.[8] They shared the same political views, and both saw themselves as rebels within the system. Each represented something that the other wanted to be: Jewison was doing what Ashby had dreamed about for ten years, directing films; and Ashby had an unaffected cool that the rather straitlaced Jewison aspired to.

"Hal was always cool, man," says Jewison. "Hal was always the coolest."[9] Ashby's appearance particularly set him apart from others on the Goldwyn lot: the beatnik goatee that he had sported in the 1950s had now been replaced by a full beard, his beatnik garb and sharp shades traded in for beads, sandals, and loose-fitting Indian cotton clothes. Though his image would later be described by journalists as "hobo chic," Ashby was clean and tidy to a fault. Ian Bernard remembers: "His penchant for neatness compelled him to arrange the contents of [his] briefcase every day until everything was just so. Each item assigned to a spot. Combs, pens, notepad, etc."[10] "He wasn't unkempt at all," Jewison echoes. "He was clinically clean. Everything had to be in the right place and the editing room spotless. He hated dust."[11]

Jewison became a mentor to Ashby, and working alongside him gave Ashby a master class in how to operate as a director, starting with the way he stamped his authority on *The Cincinnati Kid*. Jewison insisted on having creative control—as he distrusted Ransohoff and all other producers—and then started making the film his way: he brought in script doctor Charles Eastman to work with Southern, scrapped Peckinpah's black-and-white footage, and announced that he would shoot in color on location in New Orleans. He also insisted that Ashby cut the film, saying he was "someone who would look at a scene and see the same possibilities in it that I saw."[12]

Jewison upset Ransohoff by shooting scenes that were not in the script, prompting the producer to send a telegram reading: "Shoot the script. Stop improvizing. You're behind schedule. Return to L.A. at once!" "If I have to come back to L.A. now, I'll leave the picture!" Jewison replied.[13] Ransohoff, who had lost $750,000 on the shutdown after Peckinpah's departure, backed down. (When they returned to Los Angeles, Jewison would hide when Ransohoff came on set, much to the amusement of the Cincinnati Kid himself, Steve McQueen.)

Ashby was instrumental in helping Jewison with a different problem, this time involving his star. McQueen was infamously selfish and insecure as an actor and was worried about acting opposite the legendary Edward G. Robinson, who was playing "the Man," whose throne McQueen's Kid is trying to win from him. Early on, McQueen asked to look at the dailies so he could see if he was "ahead" of Robinson. Jewison knew watching himself might throw off his performance, so he asked McQueen to trust his experience. However, a few weeks later Ashby cut together a short reel capturing McQueen's character that convinced the actor that his director was looking out for his best interests.

Given his track record since completing his apprenticeship, it was crucial that Ashby demonstrate his editorial prowess, and *The Cincinnati Kid* offered him ample opportunities to do so. The key sequence was the climactic card game in which the Kid plays the Man, and it was Ashby's job to make it as exciting as possible—"a gunfight with a deck of cards," as Ransohoff put it.[14] "The deeper we got into the game," Jewison says, "the more I began to feel confident that I could make it dramatic. The photography and editing were key. I counted on the creative talents of [director of photography] Phil Lathrop and Hal Ashby to help me pull it off."[15]

The film's finale is beautifully cut, slowly ramping up the tension, and Ashby pulled it off despite the problems of how to convey the passing of time in the all-night game and eye-line complications caused by the round poker table. Both the final game and the cockfight—another memorable scene, one that establishes the relationship between the Kid and predatory temptress Melba (Ann-Margret)—are cut at a brisk pace, and Ashby's decision to end the latter scene on a shot of an exhilarated, blood-hungry Ann-Margret in the audience, rather than the birds tearing each other apart, was an inspired and effective one.

Ashby had no preconceived ideas about how a film should be cut. "The film will tell you how to edit it," he said. "The film will tell you what to do in the end."[16] And just as Jewison kept Ransohoff at arm's length, Ashby let Jewison know he needed space in order to edit effectively.

"I was always very rebellious and I fought real hard," he confessed later. At one point, Jewison asked Ashby whether he should come to the editing room so that he could possibly help him "pick some takes and things." "Well, Christ, if you don't trust me," Ashby retorted, "why don't you get somebody else? You go fucking cut the picture!" They would look at the film together, he explained, when he'd finished editing it.[17]

Even after this outburst, Ashby still had to fight for his autonomy. During his years in television, Jewison had picked up the habit of snapping his fingers where he felt there should be a cut and would irritate Ashby by doing this while they were watching dailies. After three days of putting up with this, Ashby snapped his fingers just as Jewison was about to. They laughed about it, but Jewison knew never to do it again.

The importance of *The Cincinnati Kid* in both Ashby's and Jewison's careers cannot be overestimated. Jewison said the film "really kind of saved me emotionally" and called it "the one that made me feel like I had finally become a filmmaker."[18] As for Ashby, after his anguish over *The*

Loved One, working with Jewison on *The Cincinnati Kid* revitalized him: "I also got my head together at the same time. I was feelin' good, and from there on, things really happened."[19]

The Cincinnati Kid opened on October 15, 1965, to generally very positive reviews, particularly in the trades. *Variety* said: "Jewison early establishes the rightful mood for the story and he draws top performances from his entire cast. . . . His tempo is aided by the sharp editing of Hal Ashby, whose shears enable quick change of scene."[20] The *Hollywood Reporter* waxed lyrical about the film, dubbing it "thoroughly satisfying . . . in every way" and one of the best of the year, and saying that "Jewison's direction stamps him unmistakably as an important movie director, daring, imaginative, assured." Ashby's editing also drew praise for ensuring "the tempo never slackens from the opening shots, though it is never hurried or brusque."[21]

The Loved One opened the same week to a decidedly mixed reception, gaining the notoriety that Richardson no doubt had hoped for. The *Hollywood Reporter*'s reviewer feared that "its sick, sick message may be taken to heart and purse by younger audiences," while *Variety* felt it was "so way out . . . —frequently beyond all bounds of propriety in an attempt at brilliance—that its appeal probably will be restricted to circles which like their entertainment weird."[22] Critics found it more black than comic, audiences were more confused than amused, and—despite its all-star cast and MGM's high hopes—the film underperformed at the box office.

Conversely, *The Cincinnati Kid* was a big hit, earning $6 million domestically and $10 million worldwide, and guaranteeing Jewison a bright future. Ashby found himself best friends with a young(ish) director on the up who wanted to take his editor along with him. And by the time *The Cincinnati Kid* opened, filming on *The Russians Are Coming, the Russians Are Coming* was well under way.

7

Motion Picture Pioneers of America

> All of us, including Hal Ashby, although we didn't share some ideology or some political party, we did have strong feelings about what America was and what we could be, and we felt our responsibilities as artists and citizens.
> —Haskell Wexler

Back in 1963, Jewison had bought the rights to Nathaniel Benchley's *The Off-Islanders,* a novel about a Russian submarine that gets beached off the New England coast. He had engaged William Rose, the writer of *Genevieve* (1953) and *The Ladykillers* (1955), to adapt the book, but it was Christmas 1964 before Rose delivered his first draft. Jewison could not interest any of the studios in a film that they felt was, as he put it, "about a bunch of communists," but he set it up as part of his three-picture deal at the Mirisch Corporation.[1] Run by brothers Walter, Marvin, and Harold Mirisch, the company had already attracted top-line directors like Billy Wilder and William Wyler by offering them complete creative control.

Jewison and Ashby saw an opportunity to make an antiwar film that stressed the similarities between the opposing sides in the Cold War and would humanize the Russian sailors whom the Cape Cod residents mistakenly believe are invading their little island. As soon as *The Cincinnati Kid* was ready for release, Jewison went upstate to Mendocino County, California—which was doubling as Cape Cod—to begin shooting the film, now called *The Russians Are Coming, the Russians Are Coming.*

When filming began on September 9, 1965, Ashby was back in Los Angeles, and every day new footage was flown down to him. Despite what one might expect from a future director, he was happier being away from filming, as it allowed him to focus entirely on the material. "I didn't want to know what the problems were," he said. "If it took you eight hours to get this particular shot because of this and that, I didn't care; what was important was what was happening on the piece of film. You put the film together and tell the story in the certain way you feel it from the film you have."[2] They spoke on the phone every night to discuss the dailies, and even though Jewison had J. Terry Williams, his editor on the Doris Day picture *Send Me No Flowers* (1964), working alongside Ashby, it was Ashby he most depended on. "He was my rock," recalls Jewison. "He was totally supportive. Everything I shot, he loved. Whatever I did, he would fix it."[3]

The understanding Ashby and Jewison achieved in their working relationship was remarkable. "It was the most productive partnership imaginable," Ashby wrote. "From in front, Norman always gave me good film. Then, to top it off, he trusted me and my instincts. He never stood behind me in the cutting room. He let me select, and cut his film as I felt it. It was an editor's dream."[4]

On December 6, location filming on *Russians* ended, and Jewison and the company returned to Hollywood to shoot a week of interiors. Around that time, it was announced that Johnny Mandel—who a few months later won an Academy Award for Best Song for *The Sandpiper* (1965)—would write the score for *Russians*. By chance, Ashby and Mandel, both excelling in their fields, ended up working together.

As Ashby settled into his work, he found that the material posed some unique challenges. A particular problem was the inconsistency from shot to shot caused by the fickle Mendocino weather. As the production designer, Robert Boyle, remembered, there would be "six kinds of weather every day," including "absolutely dense fog, heavy rain, bright sunshine," and this made cutting scenes together difficult and allowed very little editorial leeway. Boyle recalled that in dealing with this problem, Ashby displayed "an editorial genius. He was just marvelous. He would take pieces of film from the end—sometimes the wardrobe didn't even match—but if it worked he could put it together."[5]

Ashby's main challenge, however, was how to structure the film; with five or six separate plotlines, it could have been cut together in an infinite number of ways. Ashby created version after version, turning the film inside out and then back again as he worked to find the most watchable and logical sequence of scenes. The difficulties, however, seemed only to fuel his creativity. "That was a lot of fun to edit, a lot of craziness going on," he recalled. "Whenever there's craziness going on it's always fun because you can get a little crazier, you know, and that's always a great relief. The crazier you get, the better chance you have of surviving it all."[6]

Someone who added to Ashby's fun in the editing room was Pablo Ferro. The young Cuban-born, New York–based graphic artist had made an impact with the title sequence for *Dr. Strangelove* and was now designing the opening credits for *Russians*. Ferro was immediately taken with Ashby and would become one of his most devoted and lifelong friends. "He was so easy and open," he says, adding that the same could not be said of Jewison.[7] Ferro and Ashby were peas in a pod, both approaching their work with a wide-eyed innocence and joy.

When the film was previewed, audience reactions were mixed, but the trades loved it and predicted excellent box-office returns. *Variety* called it an "outstanding cold-war comedy," saying that Jewison had handled "the varying comedy techniques with uniform success, obtaining solid performances all the way down the line."[8] The *Hollywood Reporter* also acknowledged its comic strengths ("a brilliantly funny movie, the most hilarious picture of the year") and noted: "Like all good comedy, it has for its core and springboard the hard facts of life. It strikes to the central being of the spectator, playing on his terror and unquenchable sense of the ludicrous." All involved were lauded, but Jewison—"one of the most important not only of the new, young directors, but in any class"—was specially singled out for praise. Both reviews recognized the quality of the editing in light of the challenge Ashby had faced, and the *Reporter* called it "some of the best intercutting imaginable."[9]

The Russians Are Coming, the Russians Are Coming was released on May 25, 1966, and the same day the *Washington Daily News* declared that it should be awarded the Nobel Peace Prize. Unfortunately, not everyone was so liberal minded. Following through on the film's message of tolerance, Jewison attended screenings in both Berlin and Moscow. Flying back from his triumphal visit to the Soviet Union, Jewison was greeted at the Los Angeles International Airport by a U.S. Immigration and Naturalization Service (INS) officer, who told him: "You're unacceptable." Had he not demanded to call the U.S. vice president, Hubert Humphrey—who had praised the film just weeks earlier—Jewison would have been put on a plane back to Russia or his "home," Canada, even though his job, wife, and children were all in

Los Angeles. Jewison's green card was confiscated, and he was told to report to the INS immediately. When Jewison went to try to resolve the situation, an incensed Ashby accompanied him, though he risked facing severe scrutiny himself. "If you had a problem—an emotional problem, a career problem, a drug problem—whatever your problem was, he was with you," Jewison recalls. "He was completely non-judgmental."[10]

Much to Jewison and Ashby's delight, *The Russians Are Coming* took nearly $8 million in the United States and became the fifth biggest grosser of the year. Encouraged by its success, Jewison made grand plans for the future, plans in which Ashby would play an increasingly large part. Having proved himself to be a director who could take an unconventional idea and turn it into a well-crafted, commercial film, Jewison purchased a blank-verse Western, *The Judgment of Corey,* which he planned to make with its poetic dialogue intact. Announcing that the film would start shooting in the spring of 1967, possibly with Steve McQueen starring, *Variety* felt moved to proclaim: "Critics of Hollywood, please take note, there are those trying something different here."[11]

As it turned out, that something different was not *The Judgment of Corey* but *In the Heat of the Night.*

Walter Mirisch had bought the rights to John Ball's novel about black detective Virgil Tibbs in the summer of 1965, planning to make the film quickly with one of the company's lower-profile directors. However, Stirling Silliphant's adaptation turned Tibbs's small-town murder investigation in the Deep South into a microcosmic examination of the American civil rights issue. Jewison saw it as "a plea for interracial understanding and respect" and insisted that he direct it.[12]

Robert Kennedy (whom he'd met while skiing in Sun Valley, Idaho) encouraged Jewison to make *In the Heat of the Night,* but the Mirisches saw it as incendiary material that would drive audiences away. For a start, the main character was black, so it was guaranteed to make little money in the racist South. Jewison wanted to shoot on location but was limited by the modest $2.6 million budget allotted him by Walter Mirisch. And because it was not safe for Sidney Poitier (who had recently been a target of racists while in the South), who was to play Tibbs, to film in the script's setting, Mississippi, a tiny town just above the Mason-Dixon Line—Sparta, Illinois—was chosen instead.

Ashby played a significant role in recruitment and casting on *Heat* as he was not only the picture's editor but also the "Assistant to the Producer," a role created to allow him to be as involved in as many elements of the film as possible. Impressed by the Oscar-winning camerawork of former documentarian Haskell Wexler on *Who's Afraid of Virginia Woolf?* (1966), Ashby and Jewison hired him to be the director of photography on *Heat*—despite the fact that he had never shot in color before. Ashby had met Wexler on *The Best Man,* had worked with him again on *The Loved One,* and knew he had a great eye and also shared his and Jewison's antiestablishment views.

By mid-August, Rod Steiger, Warren Oates, and Lee Grant had been cast, and filming began just over a month later in Sparta. Ashby, however, stayed in Los Angeles, casting minor roles and hiring the last remaining crew members. He'd been given the chance to edit on location but stuck by his belief that the chaos of location filming would prevent him from responding freely to the material. Nevertheless, he felt lonely and dislocated away from Jewison and the others.

One of the more enjoyable aspects of Ashby's noneditorial role was his working with Lee Grant. Grant, cast as the murdered businessman's widow, joined the Sparta company later in the shoot, and one of Ashby's tasks in Los Angeles was to help her find the right look for her character before she left for Illinois. Ashby drove Grant from store to store, offering his opinion on her hair, clothes, and shoes. He was relaxed and talkative, and in just a few days together they became friends. "He was a very straight guy, very easy to be with," Grant recalls. "He was so uncoiled that one never had a sense of his power and drive."[13]

During the two months of location filming, Ashby still had his usual phone conversations with Jewison, but he also rattled off regular memos to his colleagues. Even during the rehearsal week before shooting started, Ashby sent "The Family" a memo from "Lonesome Luke" telling them:

> a. I MISS YOU!!!
> b. The above (a.) is full out selfishness and you should also know my heart, along with every good thought from inside me, is there with you.[14]

In the same memo, Ashby included what he had found out from the coroner's office about dead bodies, providing exact details on how the corpse in the film should look as well as a sketch of a corpse with a smile on its face. His memos from this period show his playful nature and wild, infectious sense of humor. In each one, he used a different name for the recipients, from the straightforward, such as "Loves" or "The nicest people I know," to the increasingly elaborate, "Pegs of my heart," "Dayworkers of the Midwest," or "The Daring Desperates." Ashby, in turn, referred to himself as everything from "Crazyhead Hal Ashby" or "Captain / Ashby, Ret.," to "P. T. Barnum & Sons" and "The Queen of Spades."[15]

For his friends in distant Illinois, Ashby conjured up images of the (more civilized) life he was enjoying back in Los Angeles. "Dearest Motion Picture Pioneers of America," he wrote one day. "Well, another day of golfing, riding, tea and having a good time in general."[16]

His ability to home in on certain details and play on them for comic effect was particularly in evidence in a memo written the day after he visited the Pasadena Police Department to do more police-related research:

> Today dearhearts is Columbus Day. Please observe it accordingly.
>
> My knowledge of the above came about because of a still (thank God) insatiable curious nature. My across the street neighbor who I suspect as being a bit on the conservative side; Reagan for Gov. stickers on the bumpers of both cars since last Xmas yet, etc. . . . Well it seems he has a little flagpole, which I hadn't noticed, on his front lawn, and today it had the American Flag on it. Hence, I made it a point to find out what's the special occasion.
>
> Columbus, by the way, was a very, very nice man.
>
> Met with Detective Ray Bartlett yesterday and it was most entertaining. He's a registered Republican; is anti-welfare; thinks civil rights demonstrations have made the point by now and should be fini [*sic*]. Also, I had the distinct feeling he wanted to arrest me.[17]

When Jewison asked for Ashby's opinion on changing the film's title to *Between Two Trains,* Ashby initially replied seriously, but then launched into long lists of very silly alternative titles for Jewison's approval: *The Spartan Boogie Man, Uppity Jig Get Gillespie's Goat, Black and White in Color,* etc.[18]

Back in Sparta, Jewison and Wexler were having fun experimenting with the photography, the limited budget forcing them to be ultracreative and think around corners. Wexler shot handheld, played with focus, shot reflections in glass, captured a chase through the woods from the perspective of the pack of dogs, and put in the first-ever zoom shot. So much innovation made watching the dailies a treat for Ashby, who let Jewison know how he felt about their work, describing himself in one memo as "old happy (I *do* like the film) Hal."[19]

Though things were going well in Sparta, Walter Mirisch was pressuring Jewison to bring the film in on budget. Jewison had long told Ashby that they were the artists and that producers were "the enemy," moneymen who couldn't be allowed to interfere with their creativity, and Ashby now felt very strongly about this. On hearing about Mirisch's actions, he was consumed by an anger so intense it put him on the edge of desperation. In a memo to Jewison entitled "Stupidity," he vented his frustration:

> This will most certainly not be a memo of any sort. It will be closer to the ramblings of a very very angry young punk.
>
> Norman, since I talked to you this afternoon, I've become so god-damned, furiously, frustrated from anger I don't know what to do except sit here at this typewriter and rant and rave and hope I can cope with everything without blowing my cool completely.
>
> To think Walter would put this kind of pressure on you is beyond the realm of my comprehension. It is so dumb; so stupid; so far out ridiculous I could cry. I guess RUSSIANS wasn't enough to prove you are an honorable and responsible man. I swear to Christ what do you have to do[?] When I look at our dailies, and see the extra quality—I'm talking about those values which cannot be evaluated—and then I hear what you told me today I feel like going kill crazy. You really need that kind of pressure; it's so constructive. I'm sure you haven't another thing in the world on your mind. Obviously, you don't care about the picture; or

> what's the best way to tell the story. Christ, I've actually seen times when I saw something in the dailies that bothered me, and if I happened to say I was going to tell you about it somebody would inevitabley [*sic*] say: "Oh don't do that! It might upset him!" Do [you] believe how these people think?
>
> At any rate, I got some of this out of my system; for all the good it will do. I'm sure yelling like this will solve the scene. Besides, by the time you get this I'll have said the whole thing to you over the phone.
>
> If there is anyone you want me to kick in the shins or bite; please, please let me know.
>
> LOVE
>
> me
>
> oxoxoxoxoxoxoxoxoxoxoxoxo

The devotion to Jewison and the noble cause of filmmaking is very evident here, and during his months alone in Los Angeles Ashby had decided, despite his usual financial restraint, to put $100 per week of his salary back into Jewison's company, Simkoe. Ashby thought it could be used toward such things as paying for a screenwriter on an upcoming project, *The Landlord,* a novel by the black writer Kristin Hunter about a young, rich owner of a black ghetto tenement. "If you got it to spend; spend it where it will give you the most of whatever the hell you want," he wrote to Jewison. "And right now I want to spend it on something I believe in. *Me!* You! . . . And anybody else around who wants to groove the way we do. . . . Think of it? We got a too much Director (who, bye the bye is flipping me with such nice things. I must say, Norman, you really are a joy—you are many, many things and they all add up to one groovy human being. It's a good feeling to dig someone that much."[20]

In November, the company returned to Los Angeles. Once again surrounded by his friends, Ashby happily started assembling a first cut of *Heat.* "So much of this film, and the success of this film, . . . came through in the editing process with Hal Ashby," says Jewison. "What is great about the editing, and what Hal preserved in this film constantly, is those moments without any dialogue, which essentially are the best moments in a movie, regardless of what the scriptwriters tell you, because it's the human moments, the emotional moments that we hang on to."[21]

One of the most powerful of these moments comes near the beginning of the film, when Warren Oates finds Sidney Poitier alone in the station waiting room and frisks him, assuming he is the murderer simply because he is black. As the deliberately humiliating body search is conducted, a simple side-on shot shows the silent Poitier: his body is arched as he places his hands against the wall, his face barely registers any emotion, but his eyes burn with righteous anger.

During the editing of *Heat,* Ashby also managed to put his love of music to good use. He was looking at the silent footage for the opening sequence, for which Wexler had shot the train coming into Sparta with the image moving in and out of focus. As Ashby couldn't ever bear to cut silent footage endlessly, he played a song over it, "Chitlins and Candied Yams" from Ray Charles's *Ray's Moods* (1966) album: "I just laid the song in, and I'm telling you, the changes in music that went on were the changes that went on with the focus," Ashby said. "I really started to realize the whole thing. I've always gotten into the music in relation to film and what it does—just the rhythms that you have in the film at any given time and how they feed off the music."[22] This led to the idea of having Charles sing the film's theme song (both that song and the film's score were written by jazz musician Quincy Jones, a longtime friend of Charles's).

Though Ashby's career was at an all-time high, that very success was causing serious problems in his marriage. He was so engrossed in editing that he often put off going home, knowing full well that Shirley was waiting for him and his dinner had been on the table for hours. "Hey man," Jewison would tell him, "it's OK to be obsessed, but I think we should go home now." Yet Ashby found it more and more difficult and sometimes even slept in his editing room. According to Jewison, Ashby and Shirley were both flower children, "like two bohemian students. But I didn't think she was very solid. She wasn't very stable emotionally."[23]

Stable or not, Shirley was understandably unhappy about Ashby spending so much time away from her and Carrie. He often returned home to arguments or accusations, and this, in turn, made him even more inclined to stay at work, creating a vicious circle. It was far from the perfect home life that Shirley had hoped for and that Ashby had believed he could give her.

They were now living in a house on Roscomare Road, in the affluent Bel Air area, just off Mulholland Drive. It was beyond their means, but Shirley had set her heart on having a dream house to complete her idealized image of family life. The upshot, however, was that they had to take out a second mortgage, which added financial stress on top of the emotional stress that had built up in the relationship.

A further problem was that as Ashby isolated himself in the editing room, he became increasingly dependent on alcohol. He had been drinking since he was a teenager, had run with a group that smoked and drank heavily during the 1950s, and later recalled that by the mid-1960s he "was a great drinker." However, he said: "One morning I woke up and decided I was poisoning myself."[24] Ashby all but ceased drinking from this point on, only occasionally allowing himself a glass of wine or a shot of tequila with friends. However, the tendencies that made him an alcoholic—a fascination with mood-altering substances and an addictive personality—remained, manifesting themselves now in his drug use and continued workaholism.

Around the beginning of April, Ashby and Shirley separated, and he left the family home, decamping to Jewison's office, a bungalow on the Goldwyn lot. Formerly inhabited by Frank Sinatra, it had a bed and a kitchen in addition to a production office and cutting rooms. "Having that bungalow," recalls Jewison, "was the smartest thing we ever did because we were all alone, away from the suits," but now it provided a refuge for Ashby from the wreckage of his marriage.[25]

April got no better for Ashby when the Oscars rolled around on the tenth. *Russians* was nominated in four categories, with the film up for Best Actor (Alan Arkin), Best Adapted Screenplay, and Best Picture, and Ashby and J. Terry Williams shortlisted in the Best Editing category. To everybody's disappointment, the film came away without a single award, leaving Jewison and Ashby to hope that *In the Heat of the Night* might fare better in a year's time.

In mid-May, *Heat* previewed in San Francisco. Ashby and Jewison, sitting nervously at the back of the cinema, heard the audience laughing at scenes that weren't supposed to be funny. Walking out after the screening, Jewison was distraught.

"I've ruined the movie," he said.

"You're wrong, man," Ashby protested.

They ended up walking for hours through the night streets, discussing the audience's reaction. Jewison was adamant that he had botched his chance to make even a small difference in the civil rights struggle, that the film was a failure.

"You don't get it man," Ashby persisted. "The audience was really into the film. Maybe they weren't exactly sure how to react because the movie was such a new experience for them. The movie's so different."

"They laughed," Jewison said. "I can't believe they laughed so much."

"Not *at* the movie, man. *With* the movie. They were so knocked out by it, they had to react the only way they knew how in a dark theater. You have to expect some participation from an audience."

"I don't think so," said Jewison. "I've blown it."[26]

8

1968

> It was the best of times, it was the worst of times, it was the age of wisdom, it was the age of foolishness, it was the epoch of belief, it was the epoch of incredulity, it was the season of Light, it was the season of Darkness, it was the spring of hope, it was the winter of despair, we had everything before us, we had nothing before us, we were all going direct to Heaven, we were all going direct the other way.
> —Charles Dickens, *A Tale of Two Cities* (1859)

"Have you ever gone to a preview and seen a film so outstanding that you wanted to rush into the street, grab the first person you see, and shout 'Don't miss this when it comes to your favorite theatre!' Well, this is exactly how I felt when I saw *In the Heat of the Night,*" enthused Radie Harris in her *Hollywood Reporter* column. "If it isn't the big 'sleeper' of the year, I'll toss my personal crystal ball overboard into the East River."[1]

In early June, a new glow of optimism appeared in Ashby's life. *In the Heat of the Night* now seemed to be hitting just the right note with preview audiences; he and Norman Jewison were about to embark on a new film, *The Thomas Crown Affair,* in Boston; and an unusual proposition had given Ashby and Shirley a chance at reconciliation.

During the slow disintegration of their relationship, Ashby and Shirley had been in the process of trying to adopt a "hard-to-place" child, which Shirley hoped would help bring them back together. (Ashby allegedly had had a vasectomy sometime after leaving Ogden, so adoption might have been their only option.) When Ashby left, Shirley's shot at adopting went with him. However, before anybody had found out about the separation, Shirley appealed to him to help her.

"If there is one thing I'm good at," she said, "it's being a mother, and I want to follow through with the adoption! Will you play the game? Will you help me?"

For Ashby, this meant not only paying for the adoption, but also spending time getting to know the child. There was also a tacit implication that by playing "the game," Shirley and Ashby were taking a step toward mending their marriage and becoming a proper family again.

Shirley didn't press him for an immediate decision, saying simply, "Think about these things, and let me know your decision later."

Ashby's desire to be a rescuer once again took over; though he no longer found Shirley irresistible, he could not resist the opportunity to save her. Against his better judgment, he agreed to go along with her plan a few days later. "God Bless You!" Shirley cried, overjoyed.[2]

Shirley ultimately decided to adopt a mixed-race toddler originally called Baby Boy Lawrence, whom they called Steven. Steven, who became known as Teeg, was three years old when Ashby and Shirley began the adoption process in the spring of 1967. A few years earlier, Sammy Davis had adopted a mixed-race child, and now, in the wake of the Watts riots, Ashby may have seen his adoption of Steven as a politically symbolic action. Ashby and Jewison had endless conversations about the adoption, and Jewison agreed to be his guarantor and tell the authorities that Ashby and Shirley were good parents. Nonetheless, at one point Jewison sat with the two of them and asked, "Are you sure you want to do this? It's eighteen to twenty years of your life!"[3]

Throughout the making of *In the Heat of the Night,* Jewison had worked with Alan Trustman, a practicing lawyer, on his script for *The Thomas Crown Affair,* then called *The Crown Caper.* The story of Thomas Crown, a Boston banker who masterminds audacious bank robberies for kicks and is pursued, both professionally and romantically, by alluring insurance investigator Vicki Anderson, was fundamentally shallow in nature, putting style before profundity, and required leads who were classy and sexy. The role of Crown was given to Steve McQueen after the actor convinced Jewison that, despite appearances, he had the necessary sophistication, but the casting of Vicki confounded Jewison and Ashby until, just weeks before shooting began, they chose a young actress named Faye Dunaway, who had just completed filming her first feature, *Bonnie and Clyde* (1967).

With the leads in place, there was just enough time before shooting started in Boston for Jewison to take Ashby and Haskell Wexler up to Montreal to Expo '67. He wanted them to see Canadian filmmaker Chris Chapman's *A Place to Stand* (1967), in which multiple screen techniques condensed more than an hour of footage into less than twenty minutes, with a view to using multiscreen as a stylistic device in *The Thomas Crown Affair.* Jewison and Wexler had so enjoyed experimenting with the cinematography on *In the Heat of the Night,* and Ashby had so enjoyed cutting their footage, that they agreed that in *The Thomas Crown Affair* visuals would be king.

The screening of *A Place to Stand* didn't disappoint, and Ashby, Jewison, and Wexler headed to Boston plotting the use of multiscreen in *The Thomas Crown Affair;* Ashby was probably the most excited of the three and looked back on Expo '67 as "the greatest film show I had ever seen in my life."[4] While in Montreal, Ashby had bought some Cuban cigars, but on his reentry into the United States, customs officials wouldn't allow him to bring them into the country. To get rid of them, Ashby went down the customs queue, offering each person a cigar. He took devilish glee in watching Americans and Canadians alike puffing on their cigars, blowing smoke into the faces of the U.S. officials.

With each film, his partnership with Jewison led to greater responsibilities for Ashby, and on *The Thomas Crown Affair* he had an associate producer role in addition to his usual editing duties. According to Jewison, he was to act as "casting consultant, script idea man, and all-round good companion," and the job title basically allowed Ashby to work more closely with Jewison on the film from beginning to end.[5] Jewison was producing as well as directing again, and as Ashby acknowledged: "When you're really directing there's not a lot of producing you can do."[6] Ashby therefore handled whatever producing duties Jewison was too busy to fulfill. By now, the pair knew each other so well that they had a synergistic artistic and personal rapport. "I saw what a force Hal was, making Norman's creativity blossom," says Haskell Wexler. "They were a good combo, and I don't think Norman's made as good pictures since he and Hal were partners."[7]

Ashby spent little time on set and instead tinkered with the script, sorted out any problems with the day-to-day running of the production, and prepared the ground for postproduction. However, when he did venture on set, he watched closely how Jewison worked. Jewison treated his actors with kid gloves, always putting them at ease and praising them whenever possible; if he was particularly pleased with a take, he would grab McQueen and Dunaway and give them a huge bear hug. Yet despite this gentle touch, he was, according to Ashby, "more shrewd than some actors think." Jewison had a hard-edged alter ego, "Irving Christianson," who Jewison claimed produced his films. "Up in Boston we got a call from the Mirisches," Ashby recounted. "They say, 'You're a couple of days over schedule. Why don't you come back to Hollywood?' So Norman says, 'Wait a minute, I'll ask Irving.' Then he comes back and says, 'Irving wants to stay a few more days,' and hangs up."[8]

While the company was in Boston, a special preview screening of *In the Heat of the Night* was organized in the city. The film's first reviews, from *Variety* and the *Hollywood Reporter,* must have somewhat disappointed Jewison, but they were extremely pleasing to the Mirisches. Both critics saw that, aside from its racial theme, the film was essentially a flimsy potboiler. In the *Variety* critic's eyes, the standout performances by the leads helped "overcome some noteworthy flaws," Jewison's direction was "sometimes . . . pretentious," the script was "uneven," and the film as a whole was "a triumph over some of its basic parts."[9] The *Hollywood Reporter* also found Jewison's direction overly arty and thought that *Heat* "effects a feeling of greater importance by its veneer of social significance and the illusion of depth in its use of racial color." Both reviews praised Ashby's editing (though *Variety* criticized the audacious use of long shots in the chase sequence), and, significantly, both also predicted big box office for the film, with the *Reporter* saying it would "emerge one of the top boxoffice winners of the year."[10]

For Ashby and Jewison, it was difficult to decide whether critical or commercial success was more important. "We wanted to make a film that would make money, that people would see," says Haskell Wexler, "and would also express our awareness that progress was being made and that human values can supersede bigotry."[11] While the three saw themselves as artists and sought validation from their intellectual peers, good box office was arguably more crucial as it meant that large numbers of people were being exposed to and, they hoped, embracing, their message of racial tolerance. In the end, they got both. When the film was released in August, the reviews were predominantly positive and the business extraordinary: by the end of 1967, it had earned an enormous $14 million. By packaging the ideas of the civil rights movement in a detective story, they had gotten their message across to mainstream America.

As was his way, Jewison shot as much of *The Thomas Crown Affair* on location as possible, but after twelve weeks of filming in Boston, the company returned to Los Angeles to shoot interiors on the Goldwyn lot. For Ashby, this meant he would now have to face up to his situation at home. The adoption process was moving along, and Steven had been living with Shirley and Carrie since the middle of May. Shirley had sent Ashby a Father's Day card she had made with Steven and Carrie, enclosing drawings by both children, including one of "Papa Cat."

In Ashby's absence, Shirley was trying to keep the possibility of them being a family again in his mind, but as always Ashby's workaholic personality meant that he put editing and films first, to the detriment of his wife and children. His biggest frustration in life was that there weren't enough hours in the day to get his work done. "Great God but the time do fly," he wrote during the filming of *Heat*. "Each day I tell myself I'll get further ahead and we all know what really happens don't we."[12] Shirley's main frustration was that her husband was a barely present figure in the family home.

As the marriage progressed, Shirley's relative abandonment in the home led her to spend large amounts of money on herself and the house, much to Ashby's anger and frustration. Since the 1950s, Ashby had been very careful with whatever small amount he was earning, and as he moved up the ladder and his weekly paycheck got bigger, this attitude hadn't changed.

After *Thomas Crown* wrapped in late September, he took some time off to try to make sense of what was going on in his life. "It took me about six weeks to go into the cutting room," he recalled later. "I had a lot of things on my mind."[13] After carefully considering his position, he wrote an anguished letter to Shirley in which he voiced his frustrations about their current situation as well as profound doubts about his involvement in the adoption process. Clearly overwhelmed, he wrote that since Steven had arrived in their home "the emotional and financial pressures have been piled one on top of the other with an unrelenting consistency, and in such a manner, that I've finally reached the breaking point."

"Unfortunately," he continued, "it's difficult to describe the actual causes of emotional stress, let alone the results, for they seem to thrive on a cumulative basis. One thing hits you, then another, and another, and another, again and again, until it becomes a nebulous mass of churning anxiety. As a result, these feelings have reached the all consuming stage where I am unable to cope with them any longer. In fact, this thrashing about inside myself to find some sort of inner stamina to help carry me through these emotional assaults has brought me to a level of exhaustion and despair I didn't believe could exist without the advent of total insanity.

"The burden has increased by the mere fact that it's been over four years since I took more than three days off in a row, and I'm extremely aware of how tired I am because of this. However, the compulsions which drive me in this area are not new, and I'm used to working long stretches without time off. Now, the big difference comes when the little something inside me says you're pushing too hard; relax; go away; rest your mind and body; recharge them. Of course, I can't do this because the loss of income from a two or three week rest period, combined with the expense of going somewhere would be disastrous. Hell, it was a scramble to get three or four hundred dollars so I could go to Expo '67 for a few days."

Ashby had calculated that during the twelve weeks he was away in Boston, Shirley had spent almost $10,000—this at a time when she was off work getting to know Steven—and he didn't believe she would become thriftier. "If I'll just tell you what to do—you'll do it!" he wrote. "However, when I ask you to look for another, less expensive place to live, the request is ignored. When I complain about $2,000.00 per year spent on schools for two children, who aren't yet (either of them) in the first grade, then it's 'up-tight time.' It's so tight you can't even talk about it. If I ask when you plan on looking for work—again it's 'up-tight time'—and besides everything you made would have to go towards paying somebody to care for the children. Whatever happened to that independent lady who wouldn't think of asking anything from anybody?"

Ashby wanted Shirley to become financially independent, which meant ceasing to use his charge accounts and putting the house entirely in her name and having her make the payments on it herself, as he now lived in the office on the Goldwyn lot rather than at home. He also suggested that Steven should be adopted by Shirley rather than both of them. "I honestly believe this is the fair thing to do for Carrie's sake," he maintained. "As you know, Carrie isn't legally my child, and my legal adoption of Steven would really have her out on a limb if something were to happen to me—as the attorney once said—if someone were to question it. . . ."

Ashby's closing statement reveals just how extreme his feelings were about the situation: "If by the time I finish work on this film, you haven't sold the house or obtained a job of your own, or found some means of income, then let this be fair and adequate warning—I will blow everything. I will not work my life away just to have somebody drain what's left down the tubes. I'm more prepared to let all of my work during the past few years go straight down those tubes, but I'll do it of my own volition—no matter how painful it might be—and I'll find that beach somewhere in this world."[14]

Having made his feelings known, Ashby retreated into the sanctuary of the editing room and threw himself into the cutting of *The Thomas Crown Affair.* He started off with the first three reels but could not put them together satisfactorily. The plan had been to create multiscreen sequences within the film, but as this idea had been conceived only a few weeks before filming began, there had been no storyboarding, and creating a sequence from scratch proved almost impossible. Fortunately, Ashby remembered that Pablo Ferro had worked with multiscreen on a commercial and invited him to take over that part of the editing. Ferro was not only a highly creative and unconventional artist but also a welcome ally in difficult times. He faced a huge challenge as he had only two Moviola editing desks and a sketch artist to mock up the multiples he was planning, but the now iconic robbery and polo sequences he created are arguably the most stylish parts of a film in which dash and panache are everything.

Another important element in the style offensive was the music: Ashby brought in Michel Legrand (whose score for *The Umbrellas of Cherbourg* [1964] he and Jewison both greatly admired) and had him write music in response to the film. Legrand composed eighty minutes of lush orchestral music that Ashby listened to as he cut, matching the music to the image where it fit best. Legrand's collaboration with Alan and Marilyn Bergman on the film's iconic theme song, "The Windmills of Your Mind," added a further touch of style to the proceedings.

Though Ralph E. Winters (who was brought in to help finish up the film) actually edited the film's famous "chess with sex" scene, there are moments in *The Thomas Crown Affair* that were Ashby's alone: near the end, the image of McQueen and Dunaway sitting happily by their beach campfire freezes and becomes a frame in the top-left-hand corner of the screen while, in multiscreen format, we see the second robbery take place. Jewison, to whom "the editing in this picture is perhaps as stylish as the cinematography and the performances," describes this moment as "a real kind of intellectual, deeply sophisticated cinematic idea, editorially. And if someone wasn't high on marijuana, I'm sure, at the moment, that image wouldn't have even remained in the film. But that's how free we were."[15]

Ashby recalled that he was initially daunted by the prospect of editing *The Thomas Crown Affair:* "Finally one day I said, 'I'm going to go in and do it,' and I was in there for six months, seven days a week."[16] Once he'd entered the editing room, he claimed, "I didn't leave it for seven months. I mean, I literally didn't leave it. I stayed in it, I slept in it, I lived in it for seven months. I worked that hard on it."[17] That Ashby worked hard is indisputable; however, he did leave the editing room on a number of very significant occasions during that six-month period from the start of November 1967 to the end of April 1968.

Ashby spent Christmas Day and New Year's with Shirley, during which time she seemingly attempted a reconciliation. However, just two days after an intimate New Year's dinner with her, Ashby wrote to her to say he was offering her $200 per week and nothing more.

"After Christmas Eve, and dinner the other night," he wrote, "it has been especially traumatic to sit and put all that down on paper, but it seems one trauma, in the end, outweighs the other.

"I know, when you read the note, your reaction will not be pleasant. You will say it's impossible, and you won't be able to manage. Obviously, when you look at the standard of living you seem to expect to maintain, it's true, it will be most difficult to manage.

". . . Perhaps one of the points I'm trying to make out of all this is that life does change. Things don't stay the same, and we try to adapt in some way or the other, if for no other reason than survival."[18]

After writing this letter, he spent hours jotting down figures, trying to calculate what Shirley was due and what she would have to struggle for herself. In the letters he sent to her in the ensuing weeks, his tone was cool and practical, but never cruel. He was trying to be fair but felt that she had been too reliant on him.

Despite his misgivings, however, he remained a coconspirator in Steven's adoption and thus tied to Shirley in their deceit, if nothing else. During the probationary period of the adoption, Shirley told Ashby whenever someone from the Los Angeles County Bureau of Adoptions was visiting so that he could be at the house and present the image of a normal father in a normal family. It was impossible for Ashby and Shirley to completely hide their marital problems, but they never let it slip that Ashby only ever came home an hour before the social worker arrived or that he left the house just minutes after the social worker did.

On March 15, 1968, ten months after Steven's arrival, Ashby and Shirley attended an adoption hearing. Ashby was asked routinely whether he knew that, if the adoption were ratified, Steven would legally be his and that, if he and Shirley divorced, he would be obliged to provide for him. He calmly nodded yes. The Ashbys' social worker recommended that the court approve their petition for adoption, and Ashby and Shirley left that Friday afternoon as young Teeg's new parents.

Bystanders at the courthouse might have noticed that rather than leaving together to celebrate, Mr. and Mrs. Ashby went off in separate directions. While Shirley went home, Hal headed for the bank, where he discovered that one savings account, which was supposed to contain $1,100, had been emptied by Shirley a month earlier. Incensed, he immediately called his business manager and told him to cancel his weekly payments to Shirley and to stop paying her bills. When, early the next week, Shirley discovered what had happened, she tried repeatedly to contact Ashby, but he refused to speak to her. After three days of fruitless phone calls, she became desperate and went to her lawyer to seek advice. By the end of that day, March 21, Shirley had filed a divorce action against Ashby, asking for custody of and support for Steven.

Ashby claimed in court that Shirley had "committed a fraud upon him and upon the court in that she then had no intention to live with him as his wife and form a united home in which to raise the adopted child, and, on the contrary, intended to divorce [him]."[19] Ashby, in his distressed state, believed that she had used him to adopt Steven and had all along planned to divorce him as soon as the adoption came through and have Ashby support her and the two children financially without being a part of their lives. (According to Carrie, he lodged a paternity suit in an attempt to prove that she was not his daughter, but the case was thrown out.) It's questionable that Ashby had wanted a reconciliation with Shirley, but her betrayal left him stung and embittered.

Shirley denied Ashby's accusations and maintained that the withdrawal she had made represented half of a $2,200 tax refund that they had apparently agreed to split. (The previous extent of her spending of Ashby's money, and the fact that on a number of occasions following their divorce she forged Ashby's signature to fraudulently attempt to collect thousands of dollars in insurance claims, might make us view this explanation with suspicion.)

At the divorce hearing on April 4, Shirley was given custody of Carrie and Steven, Ashby was granted visitation rights, and Shirley's attempt to have a restraining order taken out against Ashby was quashed. The house was put entirely in Shirley's name, but Ashby was ordered to pay both mortgages on the house and the house's upkeep plus all utility bills, phone bills, and medical bills. He was also to pay for the family's insurance and the children's schooling (which he did for longer than he was obliged to, paying for Carrie's college education) and give Shirley $100 alimony per week. One of the few positive points for Ashby was that Shirley got their Volvo and he was allowed to keep his beloved 1964 Jaguar.

Ashby unsuccessfully tried to have his adoption of Steven annulled and on numerous occasions contested his obligation to pay for such things as the children's medical bills and Shirley's sessions with her psychiatrist. In 1970, when Steven was diagnosed as having "adjustment difficulties," Ashby wrote to Shirley refusing to pay for his psychiatric treatment:

> Perhaps I don't understand the philosophy of deceit, but somewhere in the density of your mind, you must have some idea of

> the financial burden imposed on me, while you pursue such a philosophy, as a means, to ~~try and~~ [*sic*] fulfill your own peculiar needs.
>
> As with any child, my sympathies go to Steven. I know how difficult it is for an adult to live with someone who is so expertly adroit, and talented, when it comes to lying. For a child, it must verge on the impossible. If you decide to keep Steven under the therapeutic help of [his psychiatrist], you might suggest she devote most of the time just trying to make Steven understand, and accept the fact, he was adopted by a mother who practices the art of dishonesty as a life style.[20]

Just hours after the divorce hearing, Ashby learned that Martin Luther King Jr., the leader of the civil rights movement, had been shot dead in Memphis, Tennessee. Ashby and Jewison were greatly affected by King's death, and along with Haskell Wexler, Quincy Jones, Sidney Poitier, Lena Horne, Marlon Brando, Tony Franciosa, James Baldwin, and farmworkers' union leader, César Chávez, they chartered a plane to Atlanta to attend the funeral on April 9. "It was very quiet on board that plane," Jewison remembers. "We were all overcome with a sense of hopelessness, a sense that the anger and bitterness in the country were so great, no one could save the future."[21]

That night, the group slept on a hotel floor, all overcome by the emotion of the situation. The following day, Ashby and Jewison joined the massed mourners, said to number as many as 300,000, as they escorted King's coffin to his final resting place. "I had never been that political before," says Quincy Jones, "but following the mule-drawn wagon carrying Dr. King's casket through the streets . . . in a crowd of thousands pushed me right to the edge."[22] Jones recalls that Ashby walked "confused and teary-eyed" beside him.[23] It was the belief of many that Bobby Kennedy, who marched with them at the funeral and whose own brother, President John F. Kennedy, had been assassinated five years earlier, was the only man who could bring the country together, the only man who could save America.

In observance of King's death, the Academy Awards ceremony was postponed until the day after King's funeral. Now more prescient than ever,

In the Heat of the Night was nominated in six categories, including Best Picture, with Rod Steiger (Best Actor), Stirling Silliphant (Best Adapted Screenplay), Jewison (Best Director), and Ashby among the nominees. Though Arthur Penn's *Bonnie and Clyde* and Stanley Kramer's *Guess Who's Coming to Dinner* were tipped to be the big winners (both had ten nominations), it was *In the Heat of the Night* that won the first award of the evening, Best Sound, and for the next hour or so kept on winning.

Best Editing was the tenth award to be handed out that night, and Ashby—according to Pablo Ferro's (possibly apocryphal) story—almost wasn't there to pick up his statuette. Ashby, in the editing room with Ferro working late on *The Thomas Crown Affair,* was not intending to go to the ceremony. However, Ferro managed to convince him that as they had the tickets, they might as well go. Already very late, the pair hurried to the Santa Monica Civic Auditorium, where the ceremony was being held, and were just walking into the theater when Ashby heard his name being called.

Spectators in the audience, and millions of television viewers worldwide, saw a bearded, bespectacled man in a casual jacket and turtleneck rush awkwardly down the side aisle and bustle onto the stage. However, once there, he flashed a charming smile at Dame Edith Evans, who was waiting to hand him his award, and delivered a surprisingly lucid acceptance speech. "To repeat the words of a very dear friend of mine last year when he picked up his Oscar," Ashby said (referring to Haskell Wexler), "I only hope we can use all our talents and creativity towards peace and love."[24] On a night of somber and respectful tributes, Ashby's short speech stood out as the most heartfelt: he did not thank a long list of people; he simply spoke his words, raised his statuette in acknowledgment, and walked off the stage.

Jewison missed out on Best Director, but he and Ashby were delighted to see Steiger and Silliphant win, and *In the Heat of the Night* claim the big one, Best Picture of the Year. "We all felt that the success of the movie was more than what such things tend to be," says Jewison. "It was a confirmation that America was ready for our message. That it was ready for Martin Luther King's message of hope and for Bobby Kennedy's message of reconciliation."[25]

In posed pictures taken after the ceremony, Ashby stands alongside

Edith Evans looking happy, but far from overwhelmed. During the making of *Heat,* he had joked: "Praising me can be a very dangerous thing. I become very important to myself, and sometimes go for days without so much as a 'good morning nod' to anybody because they are not worthy of same. However, I must say I do love the feeling."[26]

Although the Oscar represented the pinnacle of his career as an editor, his mind was preoccupied with his work on *Thomas Crown,* his divorce, and America's troubles. Ashby was, in fact, a little embarrassed to have won, confessing later: "The competition—particularly Dede Allen who edited *Bonnie and Clyde*—was too good. I felt my award was part of the sweep for *In the Heat of the Night.* I went so far as to try and apologize to Dede, a friend of mine and possibly the best editor in the business."[27] The whole idea of winning was also at odds with his hippie philosophy. "All awards are kind of strange," he pondered, "because if you go along with the idea of winning, what you're basically doing is hoping someone else will lose. . . . The biggest thrill I got out of it was my friends' reaction, because they seemed to be so pleased on my behalf, and I enjoyed that."[28]

His family's reaction was also ecstatic. The *Ogden Standard Examiner* quoted their proud comments, with Eileen pointing out that his Oscar was most deserved as "he has worked very, very hard at this."[29] The article, made up of information gleaned from Ashby's Ogden relatives, stated that he lived with his wife and family in Bel Air. Ashby had not told them that he had left the house in Bel Air a year before or that he and Shirley were now divorced.

9

Where It's At

> If you did not believe in God, in the importance of marriage, in the U.S. government, in the sanity of politicians, . . . in the wisdom of your elders, you automatically believed in art.
> —Ben Hecht

In the days following the Oscars, Ashby was flooded with telegrams, phone calls, and letters from friends and excited well-wishers. Haskell Wexler sent three notes, Marilyn and Alan Bergman wrote that they hoped it would be "the first of a string of those little fellows that will someday adorn your pad," and his assistant, Byron "Buzz" Brandt, wrote him a poem:

> It was a thrill working beside you
> And watching that flick come alive
> Being molded and shaped like a statue
> By tender hands, deep feeling and drive.[1]

There were even messages from luminaries like Steve McQueen ("Congratulations on your Oscar Groovy Really Groovy") and the head of the Motion Picture Association of America, Jack Valenti.[2] But the gestures that meant the most to Ashby were a phone call from William Wyler and a note from Bob Swink. Ashby was quick to acknowledge his debt to Wyler and told him, "The time I spent working with you and Bob Swink had more to do with me being 'me' than anything I can think of or imagine. You are both responsible for the planting and nurturing of those seeds which led to any aesthetic or thoughtful attitudes I now have about film, story telling, or more important—life itself."[3] His most tender sentiments, however, were reserved for Swink: "Please know your son, 'the oscar winner,' would never have been if you weren't such a damned beautiful, thoughtful, patient teacher, friend and father. How could I ever hope to express, in words, how much you have done for me. Obviously, it's an impossible task, so just know in your heart, the hours of my life spent with you are more important than any award ever could be to me."[4]

Ashby's feeling of debt to Wyler and Swink was particularly acute because of a conversation he'd had during the making of *The Thomas Crown Affair.* Jewison had suddenly turned to Ashby, with a smile, and asked him, "What do you want to do?"

"Well, I want to make films," Ashby finally replied, struggling to get the words out of his mouth. "I want to direct. That's where it's at, isn't it?"

"Right!" said Jewison. "So let's find something for you."

"It really blew my mind," Ashby wrote later. "In all the time I had known Norman, we never once touched on the subject, and here this beautiful, sensitive dude was standing there asking me about my dream."[5]

Jewison was sad at the prospect of losing his editor, but his personal relationship with Ashby took precedence over the professional one, and he was thrilled to be able to help a dear friend fulfill a long-held dream. What's more, Ashby needed to move on for the sake of his sanity.

His total focus on work to the detriment of everything else had all but destroyed his personal life, reducing his world to the cutting room. "Studio editing rooms are the most depressing places in the world," he said.[6] "I worked in those tiny rooms with those institutional green walls till I thought I'd go crazy."[7] Ashby finally admitted to himself that the strain of editing was beginning to sap his once insatiable appetite for his job. "I'd been working 17 hours a day, 7 days a week for 10 years," he said, looking back on his editing career. "I'd wake up at 3 A.M. and go to work. I'd try to leave the studio at 6 and still be there at 9. I'd got better and better at my work, meanwhile wrecking [my] marriages. Suddenly, I was tired. I'd become a film editor because everyone said it was the best training for a director. But, suddenly, I was almost 40, and I no longer had the energy to pursue it. So I stopped."[8]

To prepare Ashby for directing, Jewison kept him on as associate producer but reduced his editorial duties so he could be on set to watch and learn. To facilitate this, Ralph E. Winters was brought in to edit the final sequences of *The Thomas Crown Affair,* and Ashby took the role of supervising editor. After Martin Luther King's death, Ashby and Jewison had renewed their commitment to make socially relevant films rather than stylish but empty confections like *The Thomas Crown Affair.* They had two projects lined up, *The Landlord* and *The Confessions of Nat Turner,* the latter based on a controversial novel by William Styron about the real-life leader of a slave rebellion in the 1830s. Robert Kennedy, with whom Jewison had maintained a friendship, was enthused about their plans and sent Jewison more books that he thought might help with the research for the Nat Turner film.

However, next up was *Gaily, Gaily,* an $8 million adaptation of Ben Hecht's autobiographical novel set in the 1910s that Jewison envisioned as a lavish and intelligent period bildungsroman, America's answer to *Tom Jones.* Ashby was once again responsible for finding a composer (he chose the venerable Henry Mancini) and honing the script, while Jewison also handed over much of the casting to him. Second only to Jewison in seniority, Ashby thrived on the responsibility and visibly enjoyed the process, coming up with fun casting ideas, like having celebrity hairdresser Jay Sebring in the role of "Barber."

Queen Lil (the madam of the bordello that the young hero, Ben, mistakes for a rooming house) was to be played by Melina Mercouri, the wife of director Jules Dassin. A great admirer of Robert Kennedy, Mercouri got Jewison to arrange a meeting with him after the announcement of the California primary result on June 4. Minutes after Kennedy's victory speech, however, the president-in-waiting was assassinated.

Coming exactly two months after King's assassination, Robert Kennedy's death extinguished hope in the hearts of millions. Ashby vented his anger and desperation in a letter to his mother:

> Dearest Mom,
>
> It's two fifteen in the morning here, and I just received the tragic news that Robert Kennedy is dead. My heart is so heavy with grief that it feels as if it will burst into a million tears. How many times can our hopes and dreams be shattered by the violence that has become so very much a part of this country before the nation itself succumbs.
>
> As usual, they (our so-called leaders) are saying we are not all responsible for the senseless acts of a few, but I tell you mother

> we are all responsible, and we are all guilty, just as much as we are all part of this nation. Great God, how can they complain about our apathy in one breath, then tell us not to feel responsible or guilty if that same apathy plays some great part in creating an aura where violence becomes a way of life. What are they saying? Don't be apathetic except when convenient. Bullshit!!!
>
> I won't continue writing about all this as it pains me much too much to go on. . . . I'll write when I'm better able to control this sadness of the heart.[9]

The importance of *Gaily, Gaily* was suddenly put into perspective, but the film was about shattered innocence and the corruption of political leaders, and Jewison believed there was some contemporary relevance to his lavish period piece. He looked back on *Gaily, Gaily* as "a sprawling, complicated production," yet many of the people involved remembered it as a very enjoyable experience.[10] "We thought we were making an anti-establishment film," Jewison recalls. "It didn't work really, but we had the most fun on that film."[11]

As location shooting on *Gaily, Gaily* was beginning in Chicago, *The Thomas Crown Affair* was released. Pauline Kael, the doyenne of critics, deemed it "pretty good trash," while the review in *Variety* called it "message-free," "free of social-conscious pretensions," and "refreshingly different," claiming that, even from Jewison, the "only message in this film is: enjoy it."[12] The *Hollywood Reporter* called it "a flashy, undemanding technical achievement" that "resists the human element," and the *Los Angeles Times* agreed, dubbing it "a sleek fantasy, an essay on the importance of being disarming."[13] Ironically, a film which was uncharacteristically cynical and one-dimensional for the committed people who had made it was just the kind of shallow, escapist fare that audiences were looking for. It was one of the major earners of the summer, and brought in over $10 million during its first year at the box office.

It is unclear exactly what Ashby's duties as associate producer on *Gaily, Gaily* were, but in his "overwhelming schedule" he was helping with a documentary on the making of *Thomas Crown,* setting up an opportunity for underprivileged children to visit the set, tinkering with the script, being on hand to give Jewison advice and support, and playing a blink-and-you'll-miss-it cameo role as a drunk.[14] Over the ninety-four-day shoot, the company moved from Chicago to Milwaukee and then on to Galena, Illinois, before returning to Los Angeles to shoot interiors for two and a half months, working throughout with huge, extremely expensive sets and allegedly a daily average of more than six hundred costumed extras. "I was on the set a lot, and that was good for me," Ashby said.[15] But according to Beau Bridges, who was playing the film's protagonist, Ben Harvey, he "approached the associate producer role with 'lightness.' It was apparent to me it was not his calling."[16]

While Ashby did not necessarily take to his producer's role, Bridges remembers his enthusiasm and how good he was with people. The twenty-six-year-old son of actor Lloyd Bridges was playing his first lead role, and Ashby's support helped him greatly in dealing with the challenges he faced. An on-set photo shows the two of them laughing together, the baby-faced Bridges in his period costume of flat cap and tweed, while Ashby, thirteen years his senior, could not look any more "now" in his shades, caftan, and beads (an Oscar gift from *Gaily*'s costume designer, Ray Aghayan).

"Hal was a real renaissance man," says Bridges. "He was a kind of mentor to me. He was older, wiser, more sophisticated. At first, maybe Uncle Hal. He didn't like to be called a mentor, though, just a buddy." After *Gaily* had moved back to Los Angeles, Bridges regularly dropped by the Goldwyn lot at night to see Ashby in the Sinatra bungalow. "Mostly we just partied, and we became friends—Hal was my best friend then. I spent more time with Hal than anybody else. I still feel his influence on my life."[17]

Bridges's love interest in the film, the kindhearted prostitute Adeline, was played by nineteen-year-old Margot Kidder, a model who had been cast in her first film role after Jewison had seen her on the cover of a magazine. If Ashby's close friendship with Bridges helped him feel young, then his interactions with Kidder invigorated him in a different way. For Kidder, Ashby was something between a confidant and a father figure, although there was also a flirtation between the two that may have developed into something more. ("Lay naked on my lawn today & yesterday listening to nature type noises and getting sunburnt nipples," Kidder wrote to Ashby two years after *Gaily, Gaily*.)[18] "Margie," who would go on to famously play Lois Lane in *Superman* (1978), was unabashed in her (mainly platonic) adoration of Ashby and was endeared to his shambling, shaggy demeanor. "When you first met him," she says, "he looked like he would never be able to tie his own shoes, and . . . you worried if he was gonna cross the street."[19] While Ashby may have brought out a mothering instinct in Kidder, she also leaned on him for a kind of parental support as she struggled with her sudden fame and success and the complexities of life in general. "Find myself tuning out, shutting off my senses, becoming another mindless nonentity with the rest," she wrote to him in 1970. "Stoned a lot. A middle-aged resignation to merely functioning instead of *being*. Don't understand what's gone wrong, why I have become half dead. Hmmm. Poor Hal, seems I'm always bemoaning my plight on your shoulder. Nice shoulder to moan on. It's never as bad as I write anyway."[20]

As a thank-you present for his devotion, hard work, and friendship, Jewison gave Ashby a Jaguar, with a big red bow and an affectionate note attached. Jewison knew their special partnership was coming to an end and faced a difficult transition. "We got so close he knew what was in my head and could probably tell you what film he was going to see in the next three days before I even started the scene," Jewison says. "Therefore, our collaboration was so complete and wonderful. . . . It was a traumatic experience for me then to work with another editor because I had to find someone who kind of got inside me and was on my wavelength."[21] Ralph Winters was chosen to edit *Gaily, Gaily* after his good work on *The Thomas Crown Affair,* but his presence only underlined how valuable Ashby was to Jewison. "That was a miserable, tough picture," Winters remembered. "And I did not hit it off with Norman on that picture, but I don't know why."[22] (The relationship between the two was not helped by Winters's attempt early on to undermine Jewison's authority by asking Walter Mirisch to remove Mercouri—whom Winters thought was miscast—from the film.)

Ashby and Jewison had commissioned writer Bill Gunn to adapt *The Landlord,* and during the latter stages of shooting *Gaily, Gaily,* they received the first eighty pages of the script. Though it was a first draft and only about two-thirds complete, both Ashby and Jewison were excited about Gunn's take on the material. In the course of discussing it, Jewison offhandedly said, "Why don't you direct *Landlord?*"[23]

"You kidding?" Ashby said, unable to believe what he was hearing.[24]

Jewison shook his head. Ashby jumped up from his chair and danced frantically around the office. He was finally there.

The reason Jewison gave for having Ashby take over *The Landlord* was that a schedule conflict prevented him from doing it himself, but in fact this was just an excuse to make his friend's dearest wish come true. Jewison, however, still had to convince both the Mirisch brothers and United Artists vice president David Picker that Ashby could pull it off. He came away from negotiations with a $2 million budget—much more than a first-time director could ever have hoped for—on the condition that Jewison himself produce the film. As Ashby acknowledged, the thought in everyone's mind was, "If Ashby falls on his ass, Jewison can take over and we'll be covered."[25]

Jewison oversaw the film's finances but gave Ashby free rein in creative matters. Jewison had initially imagined the film's tone as similar to the gentle irony of *The Russians Are Coming,* but Ashby, with his edgy sense of humor, was aiming for scathing satire. In other aspects, however, he followed Jewison's lead by getting trusted friends to come on board. In *Gaily, Gaily,* Beau Bridges's portrayal of a country boy in his late teens who comes to the big city and learns the hard way how the world really works ignited a spark of recognition in Ashby; Bridges was the first person to see Gunn's script and excitedly accepted the role of Elgar Enders. Ashby also brought in production designer Bob Boyle, who had worked on *The Russians Are Coming*, and Pat Palmer, a tough young production manager and associate producer who had made himself invaluable to Jewison on *Gaily, Gaily.*

As a director, Ashby faced new responsibilities and pressures and began, as he put it, "really learning the difference between being a sounding board and using a sounding board. I couldn't just sit around the office and rap with Norman about the script, or the casting anymore. Now I found myself with the responsibility of making decisions. Final decisions. It was nervous time."[26]

Fortunately, decisions could be changed, such as his plan to stay faithful to Kristin Hunter's novel and shoot *The Landlord* in Philadelphia. Financial constraints forced Ashby to move the action to New York instead, where Mayor John V. Lindsay's permit reforms made it cheaper and easier to shoot.

Ashby felt the pressure of decisionmaking most in the casting process. He knew almost every facet of filmmaking intimately from editing, but what worried him was his ability to communicate with actors and get the best from them. To ease his nerves, he had Jewison alongside him and brought in Beau Bridges to help cast the role of Elgar's girlfriend, Lanie. After much deep thought and prolonged consideration, Ashby selected a balance of established names (Lee Grant, Pearl Bailey, Diana Sands) and promising newcomers (Lou Gossett, Marki Bey, and Douglas Grant). The presence of Grant and particularly the formidable Bailey, in her first screen role in ten years, was proof of *The Landlord*'s merit. Bailey had read the book when it was published five years earlier and decided then that she would play the plum role of Marge if it were ever made into a film; she took the part despite a simultaneous nightly commitment to perform in *Hello, Dolly!* on Broadway.

Ashby and Bridges were almost inseparable before the summer shoot in New York, united by childlike exuberance about the project. "*The Landlord* jump-started me after the huge disappointment of *Gaily, Gaily*," says Bridges. "It was a very exciting and vital time for both of us." While Ashby grew increasingly nervous about the impending shoot, Bridges became increasingly convinced of his natural abilities as a director. "He was like this huge fan," he remembers. "If you were going to tell a story, Hal was your man. He was a great audience, and absorber, and that made him a great storyteller. He was in the great tradition of storytellers. He knew what people wanted to hear, and it was effortless. I'd go over to his house, and he'd always have a bulletin board. He'd have newspaper articles, pictures, poems—a collage of what was going on in the world. It was a vital, ongoing outspeak of what was going on in his head. It was his desire to reach out to friends, coworkers, and ultimately his audiences."[27]

In the last week of May 1969, Ashby and his cast were in New York City for a week of rehearsals. A few days earlier, he had received a letter saying that his application to join the Directors Guild of America had been successful, and when he looked at his bank account, he noticed that his weekly salary had gone from the $700 he got as an editor to $1,750. There was no doubt about it: he was a director now.

10

The Director

> I always knew that when he got the chance to direct, he would prove he was a much finer director than I was.
> —Norman Jewison

Among the flood of telegrams Ashby received wishing him luck on *The Landlord* was one from a friend telling him: "The world will not be interested in the storms you encounter, but did you bring in the ship. Give it all you've got and that will suffice."[1] Ashby braved the storms of the first morning, specifically the walking pneumonia brought on by nerves. Fortunately, he was working only with Beau Bridges, and, with a lot of gasping and pointing, the two friends got through the day together. From then it just got easier, and Ashby found not only that he could, in fact, communicate well with actors but also that he enjoyed doing so.

A true hippie, Ashby believed that film was a communal art in which the best results were achieved when everybody involved contributed ideas, yet he worried that after absorbing the contributions of so many others the film might not feel like his own. However, after watching the first batch of dailies, he was reassured: "It really blew my mind when I . . . saw so much of me coming out on that screen."[2] Ashby philosophically concluded: "You don't do a film unless you want to make it, so once you have a real reason to do it, it will always be you."[3]

Ironically, while these relatively abstract worries had troubled Ashby, he seemed unfazed by much more tangible problems. Like Jewison, he was a believer in location shooting for realism, which meant filming in one of the rougher areas of New York City.

Ashby filmed in Brooklyn's then largely African American Park Slope district, where he employed a significant number of black crew members and took on many locals as extras. The company was based in Manhattan, and as the trek to Brooklyn was costing $5,000 a day,

Ashby decided to abandon the production's cumbersome trailers and instead rent apartments by the day for the cast. When Pearl Bailey and Diana Sands suddenly became neighbors, the "film people" were welcomed into the community. One woman found out that Sands loved soul food and took time off work to cook in her garden for the cast and crew, and Bailey also took to cooking on the set. At the center of everything was a now very serene Ashby. "People realized he had put his trust in them," says Bridges. "People were invited in for soup, and it was just a party."[4]

Safety was, however, still an issue, and though one policeman was posted on the set, Ashby's approach to the matter was decidedly unorthodox. "Working on the film was a real life lesson," says Bridges. "Instead of hiring a lot of police to keep the peace, Hal just hired the toughest guys in the neighborhood." The idea of turning potential enemies into friends paid off, and everybody felt safe and relaxed on set. An exception was the day they shot the scene where Beau Bridges's character, Elgar Enders, is chased down the street by a group of his tenants, led by Copee (Lou Gossett). As Bridges ran, Park Slope residents, not realizing it was part of the film, hung out their windows screaming, "Kill that white motherfucker!"[5] The scene was being shot with a long lens, so when the action finished, Bridges found himself three blocks away from Ashby and D. P. Gordon Willis. As he turned to rejoin the crew, he noticed he was slowly being surrounded by the people who had been shouting from their brownstones. Suddenly, he felt an arm around his shoulder and turned to see Gossett—his pursuer in the film—smiling at him. The two walked together back to Ashby, Willis, and the crew, just about safe.

The atmosphere that Ashby created on set was relaxed and intimate, and he added to the feeling of community by one night taking the whole cast to see Robert Downey's incendiary black comedy *Putney Swope* (1969)—even though they had a 6 A.M. start the following day. Lee Grant, who was delighted by his unconventional approach, told reporters, "Working with Hal Ashby is the cat's pajamas. He has a genuine relationship with all the actors, he establishes real friendships."[6] Pearl Bailey described Ashby's abilities by saying that he "had The Key to All of Our Locks."[7] Journalists who visited the set noted how unobtrusive Ashby was, how trusting of others to do their job well; suggestions from anybody starting with the screenwriter, Bill Gunn, all the way down to a lowly grip were welcome.

"He was so human and of the people," says Bridges. "He was a great communicator; he had his hand on the pulse. He did not direct from on high. There was no wisdom coming down from the mountaintop—it was all fun. He would mine you for gold, he would set you up so you could do your best." When Bridges's love scene with Sands wasn't going well because the pair were uncomfortable with the dialogue, Ashby quietly suggested that they improvise. "You guys know what to say," he said. "Let's just say what we'd say."[8]

When they were filming the party thrown by Marge (Pearl Bailey) for Elgar, Ashby put on a Chambers Brothers record, and everyone in the scene danced and hung out. Ashby just let the camera run, his editor's instinct telling him not to limit the possible ways the scene could be cut. Bob Boyle, a regular Hitchcock collaborator whose Hollywood career spanned four decades, watched Ashby's directorial instincts emerge: "He just *saw* the material, he was just one of those filmmakers that had a good sense of what he was doing at all times. He was a real film person."[9]

Unfortunately, due to the sheer volume of film he was shooting and his naturally relaxed pace, Ashby fell behind schedule, upsetting the Mirisches back in Los Angeles. Walter Mirisch had already complained about scenes where the actors' eyes were not clearly visible. Ashby wanted to make the ghetto scenes darker, while the scenes of Elgar's WASP family mansion, by contrast, would be bleached out. "But this is a comedy, and you've just got to see their eyes," Mirisch persisted, relenting only when he saw the scenes of the Enderses' home and finally understood Ashby's vision.[10] Ashby's comic sensibility was, in any case, unconventional, and Bridges says that he had "a bizarre, crazy sense of humor that people weren't ready for" and that he would "deal with problems that way. He would talk about the world, and he would say, 'Let's burst this fucking bubble! And let's do it with a joke.' Many of his films are profoundly tragic, but expressed with humor."[11]

When the company moved from New York to shoot the Enders house out in affluent Great Neck, Long Island, local newspapermen commented on Ashby's hippie attire, which stood out in such conservative surroundings: "A shoulder-length grey-blond, Ashby looks like a hippie who's made peace with the Establishment. He's wearing a blue shirt, an

(American) Indian medallion, dungaree jacket, grey-green jeans, sandals and sunglasses."[12] The description was totally accurate, except for one thing—Ashby had in no way made peace with "the Establishment." Jewison had always told him that producers and the studios were "the enemy." "It's not about money," he would say. "It's all about power and creative control."[13] Ashby had never forgotten that.

Jewison had so far been an absent producer on *The Landlord,* but when two weeks of bad weather and transportation problems pushed Ashby even further behind schedule, Jewison flew out to New York. Ashby had been mostly ignoring communications from the Mirisches, which he felt were distracting him from his creative task, but Jewison begged him to act more prudently.

"You gotta calm down here," he said. "You can't be too much of a rebel."

"But you said we had the power!"[14] Ashby replied. He had taken Jewison's words so seriously that, to him, the conflict was black-and-white: creative filmmakers versus mercenary producers. Over his sixteen years as a director, he never lost that mind-set.

Jewison's solution to the problem was to get Pat Palmer, who now knew Ashby's working pace, to reschedule the picture and take the pressure off Ashby, who honorably admitted, "The main reason for being behind was me." After that, things got easier, though Ashby joked that he was "not sure if the complaints were fewer, or if I just ignored them."[15] He stayed calm throughout all the schedule problems and lost his cool only once, when Lee Grant was doing a scene with a Persian cat that refused to stay on a shelf as directed. "Hal screamed at the Persian cat," says Grant. "I had never seen his temper before. We had to do too many takes because of that *fucking* cat." Eventually, Grant decided to do the scene holding the cat instead, although, as she recalls, this did not go significantly better: "I picked it up because it was scared—and then it peed all over me!"[16]

The film was eventually shot in sixty-six days and came in $400,000 over the original $2 million budget. One of the final scenes shot was not, in fact, in the script; its title was "Hal Marries Joan."

"I've been blessed with being very naive about certain things at a very late age in my life," Ashby once declared, and his marriage to Joan Marshall is a perfect example of that dominant naïveté.[17] When they got married on August 21, 1969, they had known each other for only a matter of months, but Ashby was ever the romantic ("so much so that I don't even believe what's happening sometimes") and threw caution to the wind.[18]

Marshall, a cool, classy blonde who looked strikingly similar to Lavon, was an actress five years his junior who had been on the verge of success for the past decade. Now her fine features were beginning to show the strain of a hard life: at fourteen, bulbar polio had paralyzed her vocal cords, spine, neck, and one side of her face; by twenty-four, she had left two husbands and a career as a Las Vegas showgirl behind and was living in Hollywood, an aspiring actress and a single mother of two children. In her career, luck never seemed to be with her: her big movie break was William Castle's *Homicidal* (1961), in which she played a dual male/female role (billed as Jean Arless because it was a unisex name), but the success of the film reaped no rewards for her personally; and though she landed the role of the mother in the pilot of *The Munsters* television series in 1964, she was replaced by Yvonne De Carlo when the show was picked up.

When Ashby told Jewison he was going to get married again, his response was, "Jesus, Hal, are you sure?" Jewison knew that the only thing Ashby could stay in love with was work, but he could do nothing to stop his friend from going ahead with the wedding. "I was not supportive of him marrying her," he recalls,[19] but his attempts to make Ashby see sense were futile.

There were, in any case, ample signs that Ashby was getting in over his head, as he was joining a family that was fundamentally troubled. Joan herself was emotionally fragile and had deep insecurities, her fourteen-year-old daughter, Sheri, was a tearaway banished to boarding school, and her nineteen-year-old son, Stephen, was incarcerated in a government rehabilitation center in Corona, California, for narcotics abuse.

It was not the most conventional of weddings. For a start, it took place at the F&B Ceco studio, where the ceremony was conducted by a Unitarian minister as Gordon Willis caught everything on camera. Though Joan was dressed in traditional white and clutched a bouquet, Ashby looked every inch the hippie in a white dashiki, a garland around his neck. On either side of the couple were the best man, Beau Bridges, and Jewison, who was giving Joan away, while in the tightly packed crowd behind them were Diana Sands, Marki Bey, Pablo Ferro, and United Artists (UA) boss, David Picker. The gap between Ashby and Joan was unusually large, and Ashby looked ill at ease and distracted. He fidgeted during the ceremony, his arms awkwardly akimbo and his head tilted to one side, as if he were thinking about the framing of the shot rather than the motivation of the players in the scene. When he said his vows, he sounded old and tired.

The Unitarian service stressed freedom, singularity, and loose togetherness rather than conventional marital unity and quoted the writer and poet Kahlil Gibran, who advised them to

> Give your hearts, but not into each other's
> keeping for only the hand of life can contain
> your hearts; and stand together, yet not too
> near together, for the pillars of the temple
> stand apart, and the oak tree and the cypress
> grow not in each other's shadow.[20]

After the ceremony, Ashby, Joan, Beau, and Norman joined together for a big hug, Ashby beaming, and Joan shedding a few tears. As they broke from their huddle, Ashby walked toward the camera, raised his arms to Willis, and called "Cut!"

Jewison's words of warning must have been ringing in Ashby's ears when, just after the wedding, Joan threatened to throw herself out of a hotel window. "She tried to take her own life," Jewison recalls. "She was a little neurotic, to say the least."[21] For the final days of shooting, Joan turned up on set in a wheelchair.

At the big wrap party Lee Grant organized in honor of Ashby, all the cast and crew were excitedly awaiting their director's arrival when Grant received a phone call. "She's not going to let me go," Ashby explained quietly.

"Everything depended on him coming," Grant says, exasperated at the memory of Ashby being prevented from attending his own party. "God, it pissed me off!"[22]

As *The Landlord* went into postproduction, it was a poignant time for Ashby and Jewison. With their professional association all but over, their personal ties too were soon to be severed. Unable to convince Twentieth Century–Fox to make *The Confessions of Nat Turner,* Jewison had agreed to direct the musical *Fiddler on the Roof* (1971). It was to be shot the following spring and summer in Yugoslavia, and afterward he would not return to Hollywood. Jewison had become increasingly disillusioned and finally told Ashby, "I've had enough of America. These people are killing our heroes."[23]

In their correspondence during the postproduction period of *The Landlord,* Ashby and Jewison unreservedly expressed their deep mutual respect and affection, starting their letters "Dear Heart" or "Dear Dearheart," and saying how much they loved and missed each other. Though an ocean and five thousand miles would ultimately make them grow apart, the purity and strength of their feelings toward each other never changed. "I can't think of anyone I've ever been closer to," reflects Jewison. "I'd have given my life for him."[24]

After *The Landlord* wrapped in New York, Ashby and Joan went on a brief honeymoon and then returned to Los Angeles. Having lived in the Sinatra bungalow for the past two years, he now had to find a proper home for himself and his new bride. By the time he found an apartment, they had been joined by Sheri, who had moved to a boarding school in nearby Ojai, been caught smoking, then suspended, and run away back to Los Angeles, all in the space of a month. Ashby's continued dedication to his work, despite his new familial responsibilities, was indicated by the fact that the apartment he chose in West Hollywood was only five minutes away from the Goldwyn lot.

Initially, however, Ashby stayed home and began to get to know his stepdaughter. She immediately started calling him Daddy and decided she adored him, particularly on the day he gave her a Rolling Stones concert ticket he'd originally bought for himself. While still at school in Ojai, she had written to him, saying:

> Mamma Ashby
> Papa Ashby
> Brother Love
> Baby Ashby =
>
> US ALL TOGETHER[25]

For the moment, however, the four of them could not be together, as "Brother Love" was still in Corona and not due to be released until the end of the year at the earliest. Stephen, who had yet to meet Ashby, nevertheless wrote to him regularly. Pleased that Ashby was a hippie who talked like he did, he started addressing the letters "Dear Dad" almost straight away. Once again, Ashby excelled at playing the family man as long as he stayed away from the cutting room. He visited Stephen in rehab, and the two talked about loneliness and what the future might hold for Stephen once he got clean. Ashby suggested he work for Chuck Barris, the host and creator of game shows like *The Gong Show* and *The Newlywed Game*. Barris and Ashby were good friends at the time, and a job as a contestant coordinator on *The Dating Game* was arranged for Stephen on his release.

Returning to the editing room, Ashby discovered that he had shot far more footage than he had realized and that his editor, Bill Sawyer, was swamped. Ashby brought in another editor, Edward Warschilka, and unwisely offered to edit a few sequences himself. By early November, Ashby was "spending approximately sixteen to eighteen hours per day, seven days per week in an awful little cutting room . . . trying to help put the new film together."[26] A month later he confessed, "I've been in the process of losing my mind, and trying to find it at the same time."[27]

One of Ashby's frustrations was finding someone to score the film. He had been playing Sly and the Family Stone records as a sound track to dailies and was heavily into the group's music, but when he approached Columbia Records about Stone scoring the film, the company refused, telling him: "We're in the music business and you're in the motion picture business."[28] Ashby then approached Neil Young, the ex–Buffalo Springfield singer and member of the supergroup Crosby, Stills, Nash and Young, whom Ashby and Joan had seen in concert that fall. Young and Ashby worked together for six weeks on a number of original songs and chose "Cinnamon Girl" as the film's theme. Ashby had cut the film to existing Young tracks and was waiting for the songs specially composed for the *The Landlord* when UA told him that it would require 50 percent ownership of the publishing rights to Young's music. As Young himself owned only 25 percent—his record company held the other 75 percent—the deal was suddenly in crisis. Thrown into despair, Ashby sat down at his typewriter and poured his heart out to Jewison:

My Beautiful Norman,

As of this moment, the Neil Young thing is fucked, and I have spent still another sleepless night filled with frustration, anger, and pain. Now, at 4 A.M., I'm going to attempt to explain what it is that has hung up the deal, and what my overall feelings are about the whole thing, by putting some words on paper, instead of subjecting you, and anyone else who's around, to some kind of ranting, maniacal, display of a crushed soul, right here in the office.

To be honest, I don't know anything about publishing rights, and percentages, and what have you, but I would assume, by the way everyone is acting, there's some money in it somewhere, and everybody wants a piece, including the artist who creates the whole fucking thing in the first place. . . . My heart is too much with the artist, and creative person, and it just really isn't with the money people.

I guess I shouldn't say that, as I will, if I can get a number and am able to reach Neil, ask him to give away everything to help me and our film out, as we have all worked too hard for it to end up fucked this way. So I will ask, if I can reach him, but it will be killing me inside, and I'm so very tired of that feeling. . . . Oh, Norman, if I could just find the words to let you know what's going on inside me. It just all hurts so fucking much that I can't even stop the tears from coming, while I sit here trying to write this damned note. I guess I have spent too many hours these past few weeks, sitting alone in this office, trying to cope with the pain in my life, and I feel like I'm losing, while it's gaining. It's a weird thing to sit alone in the wee hours, and hear those moans come out of my aching soul. It hurts! It hurts! Oh, Christ, it hurts!

On top of this, I become so totally aware of the inability to give anything, let alone the film, the powers of concentration which I have always been able to give before, and an overwhelming guilt falls on me, and I become even more incapacitated, until I feel as if I will really just blow apart into nothing. I don't want to let anyone down. Least of all you, my dear dear loving and loved, Norman. I just want to survive, and to keep trying in every way

I can, to make our film as good a one as possible. Please know in your heart that I will continue to try, no matter how fucked I am, if for no other reason than my love for you, and to try, in some small way, to let you (and the world) know how thankful I am just to have been lucky enough to even meet you in this trip called life, let alone have all of those good and beautiful things you give, and do, so freely. . . . In short, being loved by you has been a very groovy trip for me. I can't even imagine what my life would have been without it.

. . . From this point on, I will never again let myself be put in a position where someone, or some thing, can dictate who I must use in creating my film, and especially in an area as important as music. I know they aren't telling me who I must use, but they sure as hell are telling me who I can't use, and it all has to do with money. It doesn't have one damn thing to do with creativity. So I say fuck U.A., and fuck anybody else who feels they have to put the possibility of some remote profit in the way of my doing what I feel is the best thing for my film. Too much of my life, my heart, my blood, my pain, my tears, have been given and are now gone, for me to ever ever again be in this awful position. Let me state it very clearly: I will never again be fucked by those who find money more important than my life. It hurts too much, and I don't even want to find the strength to withstand that kind of pain. It would be a false and foolish strength, which would in the end, I'm sure, break my heart.

Please bear with me a moment while I try to explain something else that has been nibbling away at me since I was half way through the shooting, in the hope it will help explain my strong feelings about all of this. It isn't actually related, but it is. . . . Sometime, after I was into the shooting, and the initial terror and fears had gone their own natural ways just because of the fact that I finally knew I could do it, I started to have a love affair with my film and it blew my mind. It was a beautiful and groovy feeling. Then the other sad realization that they would one day take my film away, and start with that bullshit of release prints and exhibitors, and just not caring a fuck about our film, except in relation to how much money they might be able to make. In

> short, they don't care, and it started to eat away, but I fought the panic and hurt with the knowledge of knowing where they are, and why they were there, and without their money I wouldn't have a film to love. It's a reality I have learned to live with, and one I will continue to fight, in hopes they one day too will feel a little love, and maybe care a little, too. I don't know if I'll ever be able to bring any such thing about, but I am prepared to keep trying, and hoping. I only mention this because it was a strong feeling, but I was able to cope with it as such. It was one of those compromises I would make, but I knew it then, somewhere inside, my tolerance level on compromise was a low one, when it came to my creative functions in this life, and I began to prepare myself for many battles in this area, along with the possibility of not being allowed to function as a film maker at all, if my dreams and ideals got in the way of their making money. It's a price I don't want to pay, but I will if it comes to this.[29]

The Neil Young deal did indeed fall apart, and Ashby had to scramble to find his replacement, Al Kooper, a vibrant young Bob Dylan acolyte. Kooper had never scored a film before and was extremely grateful to Ashby for giving him a shot. While Ashby prepared for a May release, Kooper composed at the Chateau Marmont hotel, popping over to Goldwyn to watch the film for reference. Ashby often went along with him, and on one occasion, when the projection wasn't right, he turned around and screamed at the projectionist.

Kooper was shocked, as he had seen firsthand just how laid-back Ashby was when he had invited him along to see The Band, who were friends of Kooper's, in Long Beach. Ashby drove them there, then left his Ferrari parked illegally in the backstage parking area. When they returned to the car after the show, Ashby immediately lit a joint.

"Hal," said Kooper nervously, "there are cops all over the place and we're illegally parked here. You think it's a wise decision to walk around getting high?"

Ashby inhaled deeply and replied, "Well, what's the worst that can happen? They'll beat the shit out of us and throw us into jail."[30]

Ashby was now completely immersed in *The Landlord,* and his relationship with an increasingly fragile Joan—swept off her feet and then abandoned for his work—was rapidly deteriorating. From his letters, it is clear that even Stephen, whose only contact with them was by phone and letter, sensed the gravity of their marital problems. By the time he came out of rehab in April, Ashby and Joan's relationship was in a highly unstable phase during which they split up and got back together numerous times. Margot Kidder wrote to him, "Why, why, why, Hal, do you let yourself be other people's crutch? Is that cruel? Have you ever said *no!* to anyone in your life? It is a beautiful selfless trait, but one that tends to erode the self protective defense of IDENTITY and perhaps eventually give birth to a gnawing suspicion that one has somehow betrayed oneself. You are a man with five times as much goodness in you than most men, and a goodness that we are all taught to strive for, but it seems that that very goodness is cheating *you* of something."[31]

As *The Landlord*'s release approached, however, Ashby was unquestionably saying no to Joan and a resounding yes to the film. Instead of going home to his wife, he often worked through the night, creating numerous versions of scenes. "He could rework a scene until it was 5 A.M. and everyone was exhausted," Jewison remembers. "He would say, 'Look, it works!' I would reply, 'I don't know what you've been smoking, but it doesn't work. Maybe it's a little better . . . but it still doesn't work.'"[32] Back in the Sinatra bungalow, it was easy for Ashby to immerse himself in editing as he'd done so often before; and during the times when he and Joan had (temporarily) broken up, he just lived there. Not surprisingly, *The Landlord* was finished, after endless tweaking, only the day before its New York release.

Ashby's devotion to his work paid off—*The Landlord* was as good a film as anyone could have hoped. The editing was tight and inventive, Kooper's score had real soul, Gordon Willis's cinematography captured the worlds of poverty and affluence with a keen eye, the dialogue was smart and incisive, and the performances, particularly from Bridges, Grant, and Bailey, were a delight. Critics were positive almost without exception, and the film got raves from the *Hollywood Reporter,* the *New York Times,* the *Los Angeles Times,* and the *Village Voice;* Ashby's skill with actors, comic sensibility, cinematic style, and storytelling ability were all richly praised. Pauline Kael, who did not review it on its release, later identified it as one of the great overlooked films of the 1970s.

The Landlord had a strong personal resonance for Ashby as Elgar was strikingly similar to him: lovable, naive, angry, and confused and with an overbearing mother. Moreover, the film's opening shot of Ashby and Joan getting married mirrors the closing shot of Elgar and his girlfriend, Lanie (Marki Bey), being thrust into family life as they bring up Elgar's baby by Fanny. Ashby explained that the footage of the wedding was not only "a kind of 'dedication' to the newly-weds." The shot of Joan leaning "over to give Norman Jewison a kiss (as he gave the bride away) . . . to me it was a way of saying thanks to Norman (on film) for giving me the opportunity to direct the film in the first place."[33]

UA, buoyed by the film's stellar reviews, tried to push it to a young, hip audience with a poster campaign that showed a finger hovering over two doorbells designed to look like breasts. Already playing to a limited audience owing to its R rating (for its love scene and bad language), the misjudged campaign actually scared away audiences by characterizing *The Landlord* as coarse and crude. "They killed the movie with that terrible campaign," said Lee Grant, who earned Best Supporting Actress Oscar and Golden Globe nominations for her role, and whose sublimely funny scene with Pearl Bailey is arguably the film's high point. "They realized later what they had done and pulled those ads but by then it was too late."[34]

The Landlord ultimately took about $1.5 million at the box office, leaving Ashby disappointed that his film had failed to find its audience. Still under contract to UA through the Mirisch Company, but feeling bitter and let down, he was thinking about moving on. He was, in any case, being moved out of his bungalow and was loath to accept one of the cramped cupboards he'd been offered as his new office.

The summer was an uncertain time for Ashby, and he admitted that he was spending "the better part of my life just wondering where I am, or even if I am."[35] Jewison, Pat Palmer, and the rest of the gang were off making *Fiddler on the Roof* in Yugoslavia, and Ashby was still unsure whether his troubled relationship with Joan would sink or swim. He made a rare visit to Ogden to see his family and went on a hiking trip with Sheri, to whom he had become quite devoted. If only for her sake, he wished they could be a family again.

That did not, however, stop him from writing to Julie Newmar, the feisty actress who had played Catwoman on television and a casual acquaintance, and asking, "Do you have any idea how much I really do think of you? You are beyond a doubt the most super far out groovy lady I have ever met, and I, for some strange, weird, unknown reason, have always been frightened by the idea of trying to let you know in some way just how I do feel about you. . . . Would it bore, distress, or upset you in general, if I pursued you in a boy/girl—lady/man way?"[36]

Though *The Landlord* had underperformed financially, it had impressed the right people, and scripts were steadily coming in for his consideration. At the same time, he was developing a project at UA, working with the black author Cecil Brown on adapting his edgy novel *The Life and Loves of Mr. Jiveass Nigger,* about an age-gap, black-white, culture-clash love affair, a film that Ashby hoped to direct in Denmark, with Jewison producing. It was not, however, progressing well, as Brown had never written a screenplay before and his late delivery of a first draft, along with the controversial nature of the material, made Ashby doubt that UA would green-light the project.

During the summer of 1970, Ashby got a call from Mickey, who was now living up in Ojai and still happily married to John Barreto. She and her young daughter, Ramona, were coming down to Los Angeles with a friend who wanted to get into the movies, and she asked whether they could visit Ashby. He spent a whole day showing them around the Goldwyn lot, where he took them to a darkened soundstage and slowly brought the lights up so that, as Mickey vividly remembered, the tall cranes threw "shadows like prehistoric creatures" on the walls.[37]

When fall came, Ashby left the Goldwyn lot for good. *Mr. Jiveass* was stuck in development, but now Peter Bart, Robert Evans's right-hand man at Paramount, had a project for him. He had written to Ashby a few months earlier saying how much he loved *The Landlord,* even joking that he should change his name to Godard so that people would give his work the attention it deserved. Bart thought he'd found the perfect script for Ashby, an oddball little comedy called *Harold and Maude.*

11

Harold and Maude

> I was so loaded on that film, I could hardly walk. . . . I was lucky I didn't fall in the bay.
> —Hal Ashby

Initially, Ashby wasn't sure *Harold and Maude* was the right kind of script for him. It seemed to be set in a world of its own, and the fact that he had laughed out loud when he read the script made him doubt that it would be funny on the screen. The story was, however, right up his alley, a wildly offbeat romance between Harold, a death-obsessed twenty-year-old who repeatedly fakes his own suicide, and Maude, an irrepressible, vivacious woman a week away from her eightieth birthday. With its philosophies of nonconformism and free-spiritedness, it embodied many of Ashby's ideals, and he decided to "jump in and see what I could come up with."[1]

Harold and Maude had begun as the master's thesis of UCLA student Colin Higgins, who was working as producer Edward Lewis's pool boy. The script had so enchanted Lewis's wife, Mildred, that she got her husband to give it to Stanley Jaffe at Paramount. Peter Bart's enthusiasm had convinced Robert Evans to back the project, and the two conspired to get the film funded (on a meager $0.8 million budget) without the front office knowing what it was about. "If it doesn't work," Bart told Evans, "we'll blame it on Ashby, say he went crazy."[2]

Higgins had sold the script to Paramount with the understanding that he would direct the film, but when tests he shot proved unsatisfactory, Paramount told him he wasn't ready. When Ashby found out about this, he went to Evans and said, "Why the hell don't you just let Colin make his film? He sees it and he wants to make it."[3] Evans replied, "Hal, if you don't do it, Colin is still not going to do it; someone else will direct it."[4] Ashby committed to the film, but only with Higgins's blessing, and made Higgins his coproducer so that he could watch and learn from him on set.

Ashby's other coproducer was Chuck Mulvehill. He and Mulvehill had become close friends during postproduction on *The Landlord,* and though Mulvehill, head of production at Mirisch, was eleven years Ashby's junior, they were very much on the same wavelength. They hung out together, endlessly smoking weed and discussing movies and the problems of the world, Ashby talking at length, and with great passion, about his three major preoccupations: man's inhumanity to man, the need for understanding between people, and the human condition. "We shared a lot of philosophies," reflects Mulvehill. "He was a great teacher to me; a lot of his philosophies were good."[5]

In September 1970, when Ashby left Goldwyn to begin work on *Harold and Maude,* Mulvehill quit Mirisch to go with him. Mulvehill idolized Ashby: United Artists once printed pictures of all the directors working under their banner in *Variety,* and Mulvehill circled Ashby's picture and wrote next to it: "My Hero, Fuck The Rest!" Over the course of the 1970s, he and Ashby developed a very close relationship, and Mulvehill became one of the very few people who would see both the personal and professional sides of Ashby, a Sancho Panza to Ashby's Don Quixote who tried desperately to stop him from tilting at the studios.

When Ashby signed on with Paramount, one of their first questions was where he wanted his offices. Ashby told them he wanted a house. Now back together with Joan, he figured this way he could work and be at home with her at the same time. Paramount was bemused but agreed, and Ashby moved into a Spanish-style villa on Appian Way, high in the Hollywood hills. He was making a strong statement: he wanted to be left alone. Not only was the house sufficiently remote from the studio, but it was also situated near many of the musicians he loved—Graham Nash and Joni Mitchell, John and Michelle Phillips, Frank and Gail Zappa, Steppenwolf. On Appian Way, his neighbors were Carole King and the Mamas and the Papas' Denny Doherty.

The house, already furnished, soon became a surreal production office where director's chairs sat beside period Italian and French furniture, huge banks of editing equipment crowded a grand piano, and projection screens hung in the same rooms as chandeliers. Upstairs was the master bedroom and a billiard room complete with antique pool table where Ashby and Mulvehill spent many happy hours playing. Ashby also imposed his personality on the house by leaving his socks and underwear on the dining room table, which left one of Ashby's friends, the independent filmmaker Robert Downey, understandably puzzled. When Downey asked why he did this, Ashby said, "Don't you wish you knew where your socks and underwear were without having to look through your drawers?"[6]

"It's the best place I've ever lived," Ashby said of his new house, seemingly not noticing any conflict between his antimaterialistic hippie philosophy and living in such luxurious surroundings.[7] He honestly told people that he didn't care about money, though in one respect it clearly mattered greatly to him. Ashby was determined never to be screwed over by a studio, lawyer, or ex-wife—or even Joan, whom he was beginning to think was relying on him too much financially—but the importance of money to him in this instance was purely symbolic.

Casting *Harold and Maude* was a challenge to Ashby, but the bizarre nature of the material inspired some wild ideas for the unlikely romantic leads. For Harold, he was considering Richard Dreyfuss, Bob Balaban, and John Savage, then all promising unknowns. Also on his list were Bud Cort, who had just appeared in Robert Altman's *Brewster McCloud* (1970); John Rubenstein, for whom Higgins had written the part; and up-and-coming British pop star Elton John, whom Ashby had seen live and hoped might also do the music. He felt that Maude should ideally be European, and he had a long list made up of almost every English actress of a certain age (Dames Peggy Ashcroft and Edith Evans, Gladys Cooper, Celia Johnson, etc.) as well as Lotte Lenya, Luise Rainer, Pola Negri, and some truly left-field ideas such as Fatty Arbuckle's widow, Minta Durfree, and even Agatha Christie. Bob Evans and Jewison both thought Ruth Gordon, a diminutive seventy-five-year-old American actress and writer who had recently won a Best Supporting Actress Oscar for *Rosemary's Baby* (1968), had the vigor and enthusiasm for the part. Ashby met her in New York, but when Gordon asked if he was going to cast her, he replied, "Well, of course I want you. *Everybody* always wants Ruth Gordon. . . . But I'm flying to Europe tonight to see some actresses before I finally decide."[8]

In London, he spent his days meeting actresses and his nights partying with staff from Paramount's UK office, who introduced him to the delights of MDA, a prototype version of Ecstasy. (A decade earlier, he and Mickey had been among the first wave of people to take LSD, when it was a little-known legal drug.) While there, he also called Jewison in Zagreb, who told him later how delighted he'd been to hear his voice "filled with the old enthusiasm and spirit."[9]

Although he met with the English actress Vivian Pickles, whom he cast as Harold's mother, Ashby did not find his Maude on the London trip. When he had described Maude to Edith Evans, she said, "That doesn't sound like me, ducky. Why don't you get Ruth Gordon?"[10] Back in Los Angeles, Ashby told Gordon that she was to be his Maude and informed the illustrious Maudes he had not chosen, "After many weeks of anxiety, frustration, and self-doubt, I have, at long last, made the decision to cast Ruth Gordon." He continued, graciously, that the "other ladies of great talent, charm, and warmth" made "this particular decision . . . one of the most taxing in my lifetime to date."[11]

As Ashby began to feel the pressure of preproduction, he told his secretary, "I am, as usual, up to my ass in the picture / will cry, fall down, go crazy, and otherwise do harm to myself in general, if I have to answer—or make—another phone call."[12] He also informed her that he was locking himself away until March of the next year. He was having difficulties hiring *Landlord*'s Gordon Willis because Willis was in the East Coast cinematographers' union and *Harold and Maude* was to be shot on the West Coast. When he tried to hire Willis regardless of the unions, the West Coast union threatened wildcat strikes on all Paramount film and television productions. "I understood, I might close Paramount up," Ashby reflected. "I might be shooting but they wouldn't be shooting anything else."[13]

Paramount's perceived lack of support in this and other matters prompted Ashby to take extreme action. A month before filming, he wrote to Evans withdrawing from the film, saying, "[My] energies and creative juices have indeed finally been tapped and it would, I'm afraid, have to take its toll on the film, and *Harold and Maude* deserves better than that." He added in a memorable postscript, "I feel I could make this film about as funny as the Viet Nam war."[14] Whether he was outmaneuvering or expressing heartfelt doubt, the resulting meetings with

Evans ended in Ashby getting the budget upped to a more reasonable $1.25 million, the location changed from Los Angeles to his own choice, San Francisco, and Mulvehill promoted from production manager to producer.

His cinematographer problem was solved when Haskell Wexler recommended John Alonzo, a former documentary cameraman who had just begun working in Hollywood and with whom Ashby instantly clicked. Wexler himself helped out by videotaping screen tests with Ruth Gordon and the six potential Harolds, the tests being shot up at Ashby's house on Appian Way. Elton John had dropped out of the running (but suggested Cat Stevens, a fellow Brit, for the music), but Bud Cort, John Rubenstein, and Bob Balaban had made the final six. Ashby had no favorites, and Ruth Gordon noted: "Hal soothed each one, *genuinely* wanted each to succeed."[15] However, the two main candidates were clearly Rubenstein, Higgins's choice, and the baby-faced Cort, who was described by Bob Downey as "a bar of Camay with two eyes."[16] Cort had introduced himself to Ashby by saying "I'm playing this part."[17] After the screen test, indeed he was.

On January 3, 1971, Ashby and his cast and crew decamped to San Mateo County just outside San Francisco, and for the following two wet, overcast months they trudged from one soggy location to another. In the buildup to filming, Ashby had spent a lot of time with Bud Cort, helping him understand his character; as they were filming out of sequence, it wasn't possible for Cort to feel his way into the role, so Ashby had to shoot more footage than usual to cover himself. Cort, a former stand-up comic, was loose and improvisational, while the focused, ultraprofessional Gordon viewed the script as gospel. Not surprisingly, their acting styles were sometimes in conflict. Ashby, however, guided Cort through the difficult moments and gave him the confidence to find the character by telling him, "I know you know what you're doing. Just don't ever be afraid, because I'll always be there for you."[18]

"I was an emotional minefield," Cort recalls, "but I wanted the part, and he took a chance on me and in so doing became not only a director, but a father, a mother, a driving instructor, and a psychiatric nurse. It was a difficult part for me, but Hal was so sympathetic, so understanding. And I think back on it now, I must have driven him *crazy*, but he never ever complained, and he was there for twenty-four hours a day, six days a week."[19]

Ashby was relieved to be in Northern California, away from the Paramount suits; however, in the first few days of the shoot Ashby's production manager was woken at 1 A.M. with a complaint from Paramount's head of production, Jack Ballard. Ashby told Mulvehill to inform Paramount: "If [he] telephones this goddamn set one more time I'm not going to shoot, and if they want to have another director come up and shoot it, fine."[20]

Filming *Harold and Maude* presented many challenges, and Ashby was well served by a carefully selected crew, many of them hippies, and all of them passionate about film. Arguably, the most significant new member of Ashby's inner circle was production designer Michael Haller, a soft-spoken, highly inventive man who worked closely with Ashby on most of his subsequent films. Haller, who had recently worked on George Lucas's *THX-1138* (1971), excelled in his work on *Harold and Maude,* memorably creating Harold's Jaguar minihearse, Harold's uncle's saluting false arm, and Maude's unconventional railway-car home.

Harold's house, however, required much less effort, as the location Ashby and Haller had found, Rosecourt Mansion, was a lavishly furnished seventeen-room house with a seven-and-a-half-acre garden. With a Rembrandt hanging in the hall, the house was then on the market for $0.5 million unfurnished or $7 million furnished. Two weeks into filming, Ashby rewarded his cast and crew with a party at Rosecourt. On the night of the party, Jeff Wexler—Haskell's son, a production assistant who ran errands like buying Ashby's Sherman cigarettes—noticed that his boss was nowhere to be seen. Wexler eventually found him alone in one of the bedrooms, smoking a joint. "I want to have a party," Ashby said, "but I don't know if I want to be there."[21]

The atmosphere on the shoot was relaxed and cooperative, with Ashby setting the laid-back tone. His greying blond hair had grown long and wispy, and his beard stretched almost a foot below his chin; even in his long leather jacket and boots he resembled a serene but rather befuddled yogi. However, the unpredictable weather caused major schedule problems, so much so that on one occasion the usually unflappable Ashby lost his cool when, as Gordon recorded in her autobiography, after getting the wrong directions, "cars, campers, commissary, Cinemobile with the equipment kept passing each other and asking the gas station for directions."[22]

A month in, the production was almost a week behind schedule, and Paramount sent Peter Bart to San Francisco. Bart, who was convinced that Ashby was losing days because he was getting high, came to the set, handed Ashby a one-way ticket back to Los Angeles, and told him that if he kept on losing time he was expected to use it. (By his own account, Ashby *was* getting high, though it seemingly did not have a negative impact on his directorial abilities.) Unimpressed by Bart's stunt, Ashby stayed focused on directing the film. He had taken to playing Cat Stevens songs over the dailies and three weeks into shooting made a deal with the singer to use his music in the film.

In mid-February, despite further problems involving nearby earthquakes and an accident in which William Lucking, playing a motorcycle cop, crashed through a roadside barrier and broke his leg, Bart sent a telegram to Ashby telling him he'd seen the rushes and was "elated by film. Quality of acting is splendid. Also wish to congratulate you on bringing off real turnaround in terms of schedule. . . . Keep up the good work."[23]

One of the joys of the shoot for Ashby was his interaction with the actors. Cyril Cusack, playing Maude's friend Glaucus, made a strong impression on him. (Ashby was very distraught that he had to cut out much of Cusack's part but wrote to the Irish actor, specially praising his "singular and most special performance," and signing off, "Your most ardent fan.")[24] Ashby became particularly endeared to him when they were rehearsing a scene in which Glaucus makes an ice sculpture. As Cusack was hacking away at his ice block with a five-pronged ice pick, Ashby noticed that one of the prongs had gone into Cusack's woollen mittens. Cusack registered no emotion and kept on running the scene with Gordon and Cort as Ashby thought to himself: "Wow, that's wild: thank God it just went in the glove."

At the end of the scene, Cusack quietly said, "I believe I've stabbed myself," and took off his mitten to reveal that the ice pick had gone right through to the bone.

"Why didn't you stop right away?" Ashby asked. "That was only a rehearsal."

"Oh?" responded Cusack. "Was that only a rehearsal?"[25]

One actor Ashby wished was maybe a little *less* into his role was Bud Cort, who told him, "Hal, when we do these suicides, I want them to be so real, that the crew thinks I'm actually killing myself."[26] While filming the scene in which Harold pretends to have drowned, Cort lay face down in the heavily chlorinated water of the Rosecourt swimming pool for take after take until he could no longer keep his eyes open, and for Harold's faked hanging he nearly strangled himself by staying in the noose too long. Cort's method actor's mind-set even extended to the scene of Harold and Maude in bed together. "I'm really looking forward to getting it on with her," Cort told *New York Times* reporter Leticia Kent.[27] He said to his director, "It's only right that she and I actually have sex." "Please don't tell me this!" exclaimed Ashby.[28]

On March 13, the last day of filming, a camera jam prevented Ashby from getting his planned slow-motion shot of Harold's car going off the cliff, but he philosophically accepted the situation. The day before, he had been knocked out in a fierce windstorm and then groggily directed Ruth Gordon as she played the piano in Maude's railway compartment. Every time a take finished and Gordon stopped singing, he had rushed outside to throw up. Now he was happy to just cut his losses and go home.

Ashby returned to Los Angeles relieved to be only marginally over budget and behind schedule but exhausted and depressed. Though he rarely let any negativity he was feeling show on set, the pressure of filming had taken its toll on him. He retreated to Appian Way, where, in a downcast, paranoid state—probably exacerbated by his habitual pot smoking—he wrote to Jewison, "I have really been on the longest down bummer of my life for the past month. I guess it has a lot to do with the film. I really felt as if I was running out of time during the last two weeks of shooting, but I'm not sure now if it was not having enough time to get all my ideas on film, or if I was just running out of life time in general. At any rate, it has deteriorated to the point where I'm convinced the only reason anybody is around me is to see what they can get from me, or some such thing. I really am confused, and don't know. God knows, there isn't much to get, so why should they even bother."

"I really have missed you for such a long, long time now," he continued. "I sometimes becomes so turned around I wonder if we are still in the same world anymore."[29]

Though it is unclear when they filed for divorce, Ashby and Joan received a final judgment of dissolution of marriage on May 26, 1971. In their volatile relationship, the divorce proceedings seem not to have altered their pattern of breaking up and getting back together, and even after their divorce was finalized, their status remained unpredictable. Ashby would have brief relationships with other women, only to return to Joan. Once, after a fight, she stormed out of the house, and as she was going back along Appian Way, drove her Volkswagen off the road and forty or fifty feet down a steep incline, seemingly on purpose. Joan was unhurt, but Ashby was shaken and had to call Mulvehill, who lived only a few minutes away in Laurel Canyon, to solicit help. Ashby and Joan were reconciled, but their issues were only temporarily resolved.

After a brief period spent recovering from the strains of the shoot—reading, relaxing, and expanding his mind through the hallucinogenic powers of mescaline—Ashby returned to work on *Harold and Maude* and began setting up his next picture. He had set his heart on directing a screenplay by Joseph Gillette, *Owen Butler,* and had already pitched it to Robert Evans and interested Beau Bridges in the lead role. The project was an edgy satire in which the titular (anti)hero systematically kills a number of high-profile figures, from right-wing extremists and military men with political aspirations to Black Panthers and student leaders, and gets away with it after being investigated by a cop who condones his actions. Ashby, however, did not hold out great hopes that Paramount would fund the film and told Jewison, "The money people seem to be scared as hell of it—what with all that's going on in the good old US of A these days."[30] With its subversive humor and dubious moral stance, it was the kind of material that Ashby could have pulled off, but for the studios it was more trouble than it was worth. Accordingly, Ashby planned to make the film through a company he and Mulvehill had just set up, Dumb Fuck Films. Its brief was to cut out the middleman and allow the director to retain creative control; it was referred to always as "D.F. Films."

On *Harold and Maude,* Ashby engaged the editing team from *The Landlord,* Bill Sawyer and Edward Warschilka, and again found that he couldn't stay away from the cutting room. He desperately wanted to be rid of the responsibility but couldn't trust anybody completely with his film. All the editing was now being done at his house, and there was the added attraction of being able to cut on his new toy, a tabletop editor. After Sawyer and Warschilka had put together a first cut, Ashby took over the bulk of the work from them.

While shooting *Harold and Maude,* Ashby had been listening to Cat Stevens so frequently that the film became infused with the feel of Stevens's music. Back in Los Angeles, Ashby, Sawyer, and Warschilka had cut the film to the songs they thought worked best, but at the end of July, Ashby received a call saying that Stevens wanted to quit the film: the original plan for him to write music for the film was impossible owing to his busy schedule. Ashby flew to Paris to meet with Stevens to try and change his mind, and in the end he was able to convince him to let them use the songs they had cut in already.

A relieved Ashby returned to Los Angeles to find a telegram from Peter Bart and a bottle of champagne. Bart had seen the footage that Ashby and his editors had already finished and called it "the first half of the best movie I ever saw."[31] Paramount was now so enthusiastic that *Harold and Maude* was allotted a Christmas release so it would qualify for Oscar consideration.

In the months leading up to its previews, Ashby infuriated Evans and Bart by locking himself in on Appian Way and not answering phone calls. (He would become infamous among both friends and business colleagues for almost never returning calls.) When Paramount requested to see the film before Ashby thought it was ready, he failed to attend the screening, much to Evans's and Bart's chagrin. And when Ashby was invited to show the film at Evans's house and discuss it afterward, he went into such detail over planned changes that Evans was compelled to say that *he* felt the film was working pretty well and maybe only a few tweaks were necessary. *Love Story* (1970) actress Ali MacGraw, then Mrs. Robert Evans, loved the film but strongly felt that the love scene between Harold and Maude should be cut out. When Ashby was told the scene would have to go, he objected, saying, "That's sort of what the whole movie is about, a boy falling in love with an old woman; the sexual aspect doesn't have to be distasteful."[32] The scene was far from explicit and simply featured Harold comforting Maude, then the two kissing and falling out of shot into the bed. Ashby wanted to show the beauty of young and old flesh together, something that he knew the younger generation, the hippies, the heads, the open-minded masses, would dig, but Evans said it would repulse most audiences, so it had to go. Ashby got his way in the end by having Pablo Ferro put the offending footage into the film's trailer, much to Evans's fury and disgust.

In mid-November, *Harold and Maude* was previewed in Palo Alto, Palm Springs, and UCLA, all places with large numbers of students, a primary target audience. Ashby, Colin Higgins, and Peter Bart nervously turned up at the first screening in Palo Alto, unsure what the audience reaction would be. "At the end, more than half the audience got to its feet and applauded," Bart says. "I'd never seen that at a preview. I literally shook with excitement, then hugged Hal, who was in shock. The kids in the audience followed us outside and wanted to talk about the movie. They wouldn't quit."[33]

In between screenings, Ashby tinkered with the film, making changes depending on how the audience had reacted. On November 14, two days after the Palo Alto screening, Ashby's brother Hetz died, aged only sixty. Hetz's widow, June, wanted Ashby to come back to Ogden for the funeral, but with the next preview only a few days away, he said that he was unable to spare the time. (The last funeral he had attended in Ogden was his father's, and no doubt he did not want to dredge up memories of that dark time.) Hetz had not been a part of his life since he was a kid, and it is difficult to know what impact his death had on Ashby. Still on a high from the first screening, and consumed by a frantic need to perfect the film before the next preview, Ashby again threw himself into his work.

The response at the next two previews was equally enthusiastic (he got letters praising the film, calling it "perfect"), and at the Director's Guild screening party a few weeks later the grin on Robert Evans's face was one of a man who'd just found a gold mine. Suddenly, it looked like Ashby had a hit on his hands and from now on he, as a director and as the head of D.F. Films, would have the power to make the films he wanted to. "We felt it was going to be the best film of the year, it was going to knock 'em dead," Mulvehill recalls. "We were gonna have control over what we were gonna do."[34] The dumb fucks were not looking so dumb anymore.

"I suppose you think that's very funny, Harold," says Vivian Pickles in the opening line of *Harold and Maude*. Well, the critics certainly didn't.

Charles Champlin of the *Los Angeles Times* called the film "stylish, nutty, enjoyable and oddly provocative," Judith Crist (who had hated *The Landlord*) deemed it "an enchanting excursion into the joy of living . . . a lovely modern fairy tale," and Pauline Kael said it was "made with considerable wit and skill"—but every other film reviewer of note seemed to take great joy in brutally mauling the film.[35]

"The first review was Murf. in *Variety*," remembers Chuck Mulvehill, "and said '*Harold and Maude* is as funny as a burning orphanage.' And that was a good one. *Time* said, 'We're going to do you a favor, we'll *not* review it.'"[36] The all-important *New York Times, Hollywood Reporter,* and *New York Daily News* reviews were scathing indictments of the film's subject matter and message, though they praised Ashby's direction. Even *Playboy* was outraged, calling it "a miscalculated insult to old and young, male and female, rich and poor, none of whom is likely to identify with such cynically contrived pap."[37]

Paramount's decision to release *Harold and Maude* just three days before Christmas, when conservative values were at the fore and the cinemas were showing the year's biggest releases, was a monumental error in judgment that compounded the film's already considerable problems. Its promotion was also significantly mishandled: ignoring the glowing responses from the youth and student markets, Paramount attempted to attract a broader audience by representing it as a heartwarming film about the friendship between a young man and an old woman.

"It opened and closed in a week," says Mulvehill. "It was gone—bingo! It was so weird!"[38] Ashby, Mulvehill, and Higgins were all sore about Paramount's handling of the promotion, and Ashby particularly felt that the studio should have taken a much more provocative approach. "Jesus, I don't want to spend a year of my life making that film and not have anybody see it," he complained at an American Film Institute seminar in early January 1972.[39] By that time the film had already died at the box office.

However, Ashby had heard that in Baltimore, where a cinema owner opted not to use Paramount's publicity materials, *Harold and Maude* was doing roaring business. Those who saw it seemingly loved it—the problem was that the film had disappeared from most cinemas after only one week, killing any chance of a word-of-mouth success. "I'm proud of what is up there on the screen," Ashby told an interviewer in 1972, "and I think later the film will find an audience or at least the attention it deserves."[40]

Fittingly for a film so steeped in death, *Harold and Maude* had a Lazarus-like resurrection. It was booked by student film societies and repertory cinemas and gradually became a cult phenomenon, a movie that defined a generation and would resonate with generations to come. Over the course of the 1970s, the film played in some repertory cinemas for years at a time and was seen hundreds of times by its most ardent fans, gaining such an unlikely popularity that Paramount re-released it in 1974 and again in 1978. Over the years, it was the film that most inspired people to write to Ashby, often telling him how it had helped them through tough times with its message that one should live life to the fullest.

12

Nicholson

> [We talk about him] like we're writing a recommendation for a college scholarship.
> —Jack Nicholson (on Ashby)

In the immediate aftermath of *Harold and Maude*'s release, Ashby and Mulvehill's prospects were decidedly gloomy. "We were devastated, couldn't believe it," says Mulvehill, "and the scripts and phone calls that had been coming in just stopped. It was as though somebody had taken an ax to the phone lines. It was a really rude awakening. It was a big, big shock to Hal."[1]

But just a few months after the apparent catastrophe of *Harold and Maude,* things began looking rosier for Ashby, both personally and professionally. During the editing of *Harold and Maude,* Ashby had made Joan part of his staff at D.F. Films, and they had subsequently been reconciled romantically. They were now happily living in the house on Appian Way, with Sheri and their two cats, Booker T. and Priscilla, and hoping to find a film to make together. Though they were not being flooded with offers, those they did receive were interesting. After all, while *Harold and Maude* had alienated the majority of critics and cinemagoers, it had also sent out a message that Ashby was an accomplished filmmaker with a light touch willing to take risks and push boundaries.

In April, Ashby was approached by Michael Butler, the producer of the hit hippie musical *Hair,* who had seen *Harold and Maude* and immediately identified Ashby as the perfect director to bring his show to the screen. He invited Ashby to a performance, hoping to entice him to sign on to direct a film version in the next year or so. At the same time, Ashby was in talks with Michael Douglas about adapting Ken Kesey's seminal novel, *One Flew over the Cuckoo's Nest,* which Ashby would direct, Kesey would write, and Douglas would produce along with Mulvehill.

Kesey had yet to write the screenplay, so Ashby signed to direct a film at MGM while Kesey wrote.

Three Cornered Circle—or *No Way Out,* as it was originally titled—was a modern take on James M. Cain's classic novel *The Postman Always Rings Twice,* which in 1946 director Tay Garnett had made into one of the great noir thrillers, starring Lana Turner and James Garfield. Ashby saw potential in the script and immediately started pursuing Jack Nicholson to play the lead. Ashby and Nicholson had met about six months earlier at Bob Evans's house, where Nicholson had declared himself a fan of Ashby's work. Ashby recognized Nicholson not only as a brilliant actor and rising star but also as a savvy, all-around filmmaker who also wrote and directed and regarded every film he did as part of a carefully assembled body of work. Nicholson deliberated for six weeks while Ashby wooed him and was finally convinced more by the quality of the director than by the project itself. Ashby was thrilled and saw an opportunity to cast Michelle Phillips, the ex–Mamas and Papas singer and Nicholson's then girlfriend, in the Lana Turner role. Not only would it play on Nicholson and Phillips's real-life relationship, but it also keyed into Ashby's passion for rock and roll and his interest in blurring the boundaries between music and film. Ashby did screen tests with Nicholson and Phillips (shot by young director of photography Andrew Davis, later a highly successful director himself), but MGM, flailing financially at the time, balked at Ashby's casting idea. The studio saw Phillips as an obscure nonactress and suggested someone like Raquel Welch instead. Ashby told the MGM execs they were out of touch, Michelle Phillips *was* a big star, and how come *they* were telling him who he could or couldn't cast. "I guess they'd say their film; I say my film," Ashby reflected.[2] As the July start date neared, Ashby and MGM were still tangling over the casting decision; finally, Ashby backed out, followed by Nicholson, and the film was put into turnaround.

When *Harold and Maude* was being screened for friends and luminaries in December 1971, Ashby had twice invited Stephen Marshall to see it. Despite Stephen's regular attempts to contact Ashby, their relationship had been almost nonexistent owing to Ashby's work schedule and his feeling that—at least when he and Joan weren't together—Stephen was not his responsibility. Still, Ashby had set up Stephen with a job working for Chuck Barris, who remembers being "very glad to help with his son. He did a great job, he was a great kid."[3] Stephen made friends at his job, dreamed of making films like Ashby, and tried to stay clean, though he still took mescaline and acid. Eventually, he left his job with Barris, and on July 21, 1972, only two years after his release from rehab, he died of an overdose, aged just twenty-two.

Though Ashby paid for the funeral and burial, Stephen's death appeared to mark the end of any romantic association between Ashby and Joan. Guilt ridden over his failure as a father figure to Stephen, Ashby finally realized that he was simply not cut out for the responsibilities of family life. Whether he was conscious of it or not, Stephen's death was linked for him with his father's suicide: not only had he abandoned Stephen as his father had abandoned him, but Stephen's death reinforced the idea that being part of a family unavoidably lead to traumatic loss. After five failed attempts, he resolved never to marry again.

Talking about his frustration over the way *Harold and Maude* was handled, Ashby once said: "When you've devoted a year-and-a-half to something, you watch and fret over it as you would over a child."[4] He loved his films like children, children he would devote himself to completely for eighteen months and then set free into the world. His childhood—in which his parents' divorce was followed by a period of moving around with his mother, his father's suicide, Jack leaving for war, and then he himself being sent to the naval academy—had created a staccato rhythm in his life that he could not change. His romantic passions were fervent and genuine, but they burned so strongly they couldn't last. After Joan, his relationships generally lasted only as long as his films did, and because Ashby unconsciously compartmentalized his life, the start and finish of a film would often coincide with the start and finish of a romance. Mulvehill, whom Ashby relied on to soften the blow for girls he was about to break up with, observed the pattern that developed: "One relationship usually ended because another was building. He wanted close relationships, but when they got close he didn't want them. It was all about responsibility, and he was all about work."[5]

Ashby had sworn off marriage but hadn't lost any of his romanticism. He loved women, loved having them around, and whenever one moved out of the house on Appian Way, it was often only days before another moved in. Deanna Benatovich, the first of the women to live with him after Joan, arrived in Los Angeles with nowhere to stay and ended up next door to Ashby on Appian Way, in the house where Denny Doherty lived. As the room she was staying in was actually Doherty's, he found her a linen delivery van.

"I now had a truck and was busy making it a home so I could live in it," Benatovich remembers. "I was a little hippy with long hair. I was in my truck outside making drapes . . . when the mysterious neighbor who I had only heard about came out near sunset and asked me if I would like to get high. We did and just hit it off and were up all night talking. We had so much in common and were on the same wavelength I felt an immediate empathy with him. At dawn I went back to my room as I had a rule then to never sleep with someone I just met. The next night Hal came out again to invite me in. I was confused because Hal was not that attractive but quickly that didn't matter as I got to know him better. We ended up making love in the window box with the lights of L.A. before us. I wish I could remember exactly what he said now, but it was something like 'I want you to move in. I want to have you here. I want us to be together.' He was so cute, he showed me some empty drawers I could use and made room in his armoire for my clothes. That was it. I was in love. He was so cool and he loved me too."[6]

Benatovich moved in with Ashby only hours later and quickly became a part of his life, reading scripts and going to screenings with him, even playing pool with him and Mulvehill. Benatovich loved movies almost as much as Ashby but had not seen *Harold and Maude*. One day, Ashby dropped her off at a cinema where it was showing. "I was blown away," says Benatovich. "It was such a great movie, I was floored that I was living with this great mind. I had found a soul mate. We could read each other's minds."[7]

"I read so many scripts and so much of it is useless," Ashby had told an interviewer earlier that year. "If you don't like something from the beginning you're hardly going to like it much better six months later."[8] Strangely, however, *The Last Detail*—which had been sent to Ashby at D.F. in the fall of 1971 and the reader's report had dismissed as "lengthy and unimaginative"—suddenly became very appealing.[9]

Coincidentally, during preproduction on *Three Cornered Circle*, Nicholson had told Ashby about *The Last Detail*, his upcoming film at Columbia. Ashby would have been keen to direct it, but the winter shooting date clashed with postproduction on *Three Cornered Circle*. But when both Ashby and Nicholson pulled out of their deals at MGM, Nicholson mentioned *The Last Detail* again and suggested, "Why don't we try and move you over and get you to do this?" "That would be great," said Ashby.[10]

The Last Detail was a gritty, obscenity-strewn drama about two navy lifers, "Badass" Buddusky and "Mule" Mulhall, transporting a naive young prisoner, Larry Meadows, to the brig after he commits a petty theft. "I loved the script and I had got to know Jack well enough so that we both knew we wanted to work together," Ashby said later. "When the opportunity to direct *The Last Detail* came up, I jumped at it. The script is full of a very honest kind of humor about developing human relations and a certain wry insight into people just doing their jobs."[11] Producer Gerry Ayres had bought the rights to Darryl Ponicsan's novel back in 1969 but struggled to get it made because of Columbia's fears about the bad language in the script by Robert Towne, then Hollywood's most sought-after script doctor. Towne, however, refused to tone down his script, and the project remained in limbo until the bankable Nicholson got involved.

Ayres backed Nicholson's recommendation to bring Ashby on board. "He's intelligent, sensitive, capable," said Ayres of Ashby. "How many Hollywood directors do you know who you can say those things about?"[12] Keen to accurately depict the navy, Ashby and Ayres read navy publications and interviewed current and ex-servicemen, who helped them correct minor inaccuracies in the script, which they deemed otherwise extremely realistic. Ayres hoped to gain the navy's approval, but when he sent the screenplay to its Information Office, the response he got was that the film would "have no plot left by the time you altered your script sufficiently to get our cooperation."[13]

The film's start and end locations were the Norfolk, Virginia, naval base and the brig at Portsmouth, New Hampshire, and without navy cooperation Ashby would have nowhere to shoot these scenes. Fortunately, the Canadian Navy was willing to help. In mid-August, Ashby and his casting director, Lynn Stalmaster, traveled to Toronto to look at a naval base they were being offered and meet with actors. The base suited their needs perfectly, and Ashby met a promising young actress (and *Harold and Maude* fan), Carol Kane, whom he cast in a small role. Overall, the trip was a resounding success—except that when Stalmaster arrived back in Los Angeles, Ashby was not with him.

"Hal, you've got to *dress* to get through Immigration," Jewison had always told him when they traveled together.[14] Jewison would smarten up when he flew, and refused to walk beside Ashby with his beads, sandals, long beard, and the distinct smell of pot lingering on him. But at Toronto International Airport, ignoring Jewison's advice finally caught up with Ashby. He was carrying only a small amount of marijuana, but his claim that it was just "herbs" failed to save him from being arrested. Mulvehill got Columbia's lawyers to post his bail and flew out to Toronto himself to bring him home. Ashby, with Jewison's words no doubt ringing in his ears, complained bitterly about his treatment, especially when, on his arrival at Los Angeles International Airport, he was hauled off the plane and searched yet again.

Columbia was understandably annoyed by the incident but gave Ashby a reprieve after Nicholson came out strongly in support of him. Ashby, however, realized that he needed to make some changes if he wanted the studios to consider him employable. While he would still be a vegetarian, write letters supporting environmental bills, promote peace and love, and smoke dope, he resolved to distance himself from his hippie image. A few years before, when traveling with black filmmaker Carlton Moss to give a guest lecture at Fisk University in Nashville, Tennessee, Ashby had to change flights in Dallas; the Texan airport officials took one look at him and refused to let him on the plane. He knew he couldn't afford to let anything like that happen again.

Six months on, a Columbia attorney represented him in court; the offense was pardoned and, two years later, struck from the record. But just days after the incident, Ashby did something much more significant. "I remember the night he woke me up in the middle of the night and he had shaved his beard," says Benatovich. "It was so strange to see his face without it."[15] The beard grew back, but from then on, he kept it short.

With Nicholson set to play Buddusky, casting of *The Last Detail* focused mainly on the parts of Mule and Meadows. Robert Towne and Nicholson were old friends (Towne wrote the script with Nicholson in mind), and both were also close with Rupert Crosse, an accomplished African American actor who had received an Oscar nomination for Best

Supporting Actor for his role in the Steve McQueen vehicle *The Reivers* (1969). Nicholson was excited about sharing the screen with Crosse, whom he felt would be perfect as Mule.

That left Meadows. Bud Cort came to Appian Way and begged for the part, but Ashby knew he wasn't right. In the script, Meadows was small, the kind of guy who gets trampled on by everybody, but Ashby thought this was a hackneyed take on the character. When Stalmaster gave Ashby a final selection of actors, the two that stood out were Randy Quaid, who had appeared in Peter Bogdanovich's *The Last Picture Show* (1971), and John Travolta, an actor who had so far done only commercials. "Hal had all these pictures of boys pinned up on a board," says Benatovich. "He asked me who I thought would be good and I looked at all these attractive types. Then I saw Randy and I knew it was him, and Hal said he thought so too. Randy was like a big penguin; everybody wanted to mother him."[16] Randy Quaid had just the offbeat, vulnerable quality that Ashby wanted, and at an imposing six foot two he looked suitably awkward next to Nicholson, one of the shortest leading men in Hollywood. Ashby couldn't guarantee that Quaid was the best actor out of the bunch but trusted his instincts that he was the right choice.

The Last Detail was a clear step up for Ashby: he had his biggest budget ($2.6 million) and salary ($95,000) yet and was working with Jack Nicholson. He enthusiastically entered preproduction, spending ten days on Catalina Island finessing the script with Towne and working with Nicholson on his part.

A shadow was cast over the proceedings, however, when Rupert Crosse went missing after discovering he had terminal cancer. In an almost unprecedented move, Ashby put production back a week to give Crosse time to come to terms with the news and decide if he was well enough to be in the film. To everybody's sadness, Crosse had to decline and, with only a matter of days left till production, Ashby and Stalmaster scrambled to find his replacement.

"The last phone calls I got from Rupert were from Jamaica, his home," Ashby said. "He'd rave, 'The water here is so good!' He would laugh and made me laugh. What was I to do, say, 'Rupert, you're dying, don't laugh'? I had to laugh with him."[17] In March 1973, just a month after production on *The Last Detail* finished, Crosse passed away.

13

The Last Detail

> He had a sense of truth, and what was a real moment. He didn't like to watch moments that were not real, and he was willing to let—to a fault sometimes—things go wherever he felt they should as long as they stayed real.
> —Robert Towne (on Hal Ashby)

Because Ashby and his cast and crew were shooting in Toronto at the time, they voted by absentee ballot in the U.S. presidential election on November 7, 1972. Richard Nixon's image had appeared on a television screen in *The Landlord* and in a deified picture on the office wall of Harold's Uncle Victor, in both cases embodying for Ashby all that was wrong with the country. Though he was rarely vocal about it, Ashby was highly politicized and in the past two years had written numerous letters to Washington to lobby for several environmental acts, help Hopi Indians, stop the clear-cutting of forests, and push for the abolition of the death penalty and the withdrawal of U.S. troops from Vietnam. He cast his vote for Nixon's opponent, Democratic senator George McGovern, who was campaigning as the "peace" candidate. (He also voted for the proposed environmental measures and the relaxation of laws on obscenity and marijuana.)

For the rest of the year, Ashby and the company stayed in Canada, where the rain, snow, and freezing temperatures of a Toronto winter made California seem a world away. Despite the cold, they felt fortunate to be far from the depression many felt back home when Nixon won a landslide victory, taking 60 percent of the popular vote.

Ashby had decided to shoot the film chronologically, as this would help the inexperienced Quaid and Otis Young, the actor who had replaced Rupert Crosse, ease their way into the characters. Toronto doubled as Norfolk, but with this exception, Ashby's company made the same journey Buddusky and Mulhall took as they gave Meadows a taste of the good life before his internment, traveling from Virginia up the East Coast to New Hampshire, and taking in Washington, D.C., New York, and Boston on the way.

Quaid, in his first major film role, found himself thrust into a surreal new world. "The first night I arrived for *The Last Detail,*" he recalls, "I went to Hal's hotel room, and someone came in with a huge garbage bag filled with grass, saying, 'I got the supply for the movie!'"[1] Quaid was concerned about making a good impression in his first scene: "I remember I was very nervous, and I had my eyes twitching, my eyeballs rolling, and my lips quivering, and my head shaking, and my hands trembling, and had my inner monologue working, and I was really acting. We did a take, and Hal came over to me, and put a hand on my shoulder, and leaned down and said, 'Randy, we don't have to do the whole movie in the first scene.' It had a very calming effect on me, and I was able to do the part with the confidence he always instilled in me."[2]

Ashby kept a close eye on Quaid but allowed him to develop into the role, just as Meadows grows in confidence and comes out of his shell over the course of the film. "Randy, I loved him because he was very outgoing," Ashby said, "and as an actor the man is a genius. I've never worked with anybody in my life like him."[3]

Michael Chapman, the first-time director of photography who was shooting *The Last Detail,* was another up-and-comer whom Ashby had taken a chance on. It was no secret that Chapman was not Ashby's first choice—he had tried to get Haskell Wexler, Nestor Almendros, and Gordon Willis—but Chapman had been Willis's camera operator on *The Landlord* and had served an apprenticeship with him much as Ashby had with Bob Swink. Chapman and Ashby formulated a specific look for the film, using natural lighting to bring a stark realism and immediacy to the action.

Chapman's documentary-style photography was perfectly in tune with the tight, deliberate script by Robert Towne, whose emotionally spare writing featured characters who were not immediately likable. Ashby was making a politically charged film (it was overtly antimilitary, with clear anti–Vietnam War undercurrents), but unlike his previous films, in which he attacked social and political targets with broad humor based on stereotypes, here the people whose actions and beliefs he was questioning were his main characters.

Talking about Towne's protagonists, Ashby said, "There's no way I could ever relate to what they're doing with their lives. But I would never take cheap shots at them. I felt sorry for them and tried to get to know them through their plights."[4] His experiences at Puget Sound Naval Academy, and the ideologies he had acquired since then, made him naturally prejudiced against hardened navy lifers like Buddusky and Mulhall, but his attempts to understand and sympathize with them brought him closer to the material and arguably took him to a higher level as a director. *The Last Detail* was, as Gerry Ayres described it in a letter to Ashby, "an off-handedly humorous handling of what is to all other intents a serious business," finding the absurd and darkly funny in an essentially depressing situation.[5] Because of his respect for Towne's writing, Ashby held back from his natural impulse to treat the script as a rough blueprint, saying that he "would not go for improv on Bob's scripts because his scripts are so damn good."[6] The one notable exception was in a scene where the sailors are hanging out with some hippie girls. When one of the girls, played by Nancy Allen, compliments Buddusky on his uniform, Nicholson ad-libbed, "They are cute, aren't they? You know what I like about it? One of my favorite things about this uniform is the way it makes your dick look, eh?"

Ashby loved working with Nicholson; however, in the first few days of the shoot, he worried that his acting was a little too large. "But I didn't get into anything with him, because I wanted to see it on film first," Ashby said. "It just felt too big, but when I looked at it, it wasn't. I've never seen anything like it. It was just a natural thing, and it never happens too big for film."[7] Though Nicholson's instincts were sound, he didn't rely on them, instead working hard to ensure that he knew and understood Billy "Badass" Buddusky inside out. Unbidden by his director, he made each take minutely different from the ones before; he was giving his own personal interpretation of the character and giving Ashby leeway in the editing room. Nicholson's awareness as a screen actor was acute, and he would ask Ashby to let him look through the viewfinder as a shot was being set up so he knew the parameters of the scene and how much freedom he had within the frame. "Hal is the first director to let me go, to let me find my own level," Nicholson enthused. "I'm playing this character Billy on two, three, four different levels, all at the same time. And that is the difference between college and pro football."[8]

Because the film was so much about machismo and masculinity, there were only a handful of minor female roles, such as the prostitute, played by Carol Kane. Another actress with a small supporting role was Kathleen Miller, a pretty twenty-eight-year-old who was making her film debut after a number of years on the New York theatrical scene. She and Ashby fell for each other while they were shooting in Toronto, and, after a week together, Miller says, "We decided we didn't want to be apart, so I jumped into it."[9] Miller was the daughter of Aaron Miller, who for years had run the television arm of Paramount, and she had grown up in Los Angeles with Cary Grant turning up at her tenth birthday party and Candice Bergen as one of her best friends. Ashby and Miller decided that she would move in with him in Los Angeles, so when the company traveled to Virginia and then snaked back up the East Coast, she went with them.

The production had been barred from filming on a U.S. naval base, but no one could stop shooting *outside* one. In Norfolk, Ashby audaciously shot a scene outside the gates of the base in order to fool people into thinking the footage from Toronto was filmed there too. He was due to shoot some scenes on a train in nearby Richmond, but the railroad equipment he had wanted was not available there, so it had to be moved from Atlanta, Georgia, at great cost, much to the annoyance of the Columbia executives.

When the trains arrived, there were more problems. Ashby had an eight-page scene to film of Nicholson, Young, and Quaid on the train, starting with them getting on at the station. However, the train had been left in the yards instead. With only that day to get the scene in the can, Ashby was then told that he had to be finished by 2 P.M., and as he prepared to start shooting he discovered that the train was painfully slow.

"Jesus Christ, can't we go any faster?" asked Ashby. "This train's really slow."

"We're in the yard," he was told. "We can't go any more than seven miles an hour."

Observant viewers noted the train's sluggish pace in that scene, but for the most part Ashby's assumption that people's focus would be on Nicholson and company proved well-founded. "It's crazy," he said, recalling the incident. "So what you do is let things go that you wouldn't ordinarily let go and you say, 'Fuck it, it's a film. . . .'"[10]

After five days in Washington, D.C., and another five in New York, where Ashby shot after hours at the Rockefeller Center ice rink (using Gerry Ayres and Pablo Ferro among the extras), the company moved on to Boston, the final destination on their whistle-stop tour. The city's Suffolk County jail doubled as the brig at Portsmouth, and, because it was still operational, the cast and crew had to be locked inside for the two days they shot there, allowed to move around only with special passes. As Columbia complained about the budget and urged Ashby to finish quickly, he shot the final scenes in the desolate wastes of Deer Island, across the bay from downtown Boston. A reporter visiting Ashby as he filmed the last shots on freezing Deer Island asked him to talk about the film. "I'm cold," was all he could manage to say.[11]

The day after the film wrapped, Ashby had his editor send along what he had cut together so far. He was feeling very positive about the way the shoot had gone but was shocked to see the first sections of the assemblage. Ashby felt he had no option but to fire the editor, recalling, "I really almost got ill. I mean, I didn't know what the hell his point of view was at all, other than trying to use every piece of film I shot."[12] The young editor, all too aware of his director's reputation as a master cutter, had tried to second-guess what Ashby would have done. In his downcast state, Ashby feared he would have to edit the film himself, despondently thinking: "Holy Christ, here I'm going to have another fucking year of my life in this room."[13]

Fortunately, Gerry Ayres suggested he bring in Robert C. Jones, the editor Ayres had used on his last film, *Cisco Pike* (1972). Jones, the son of director and former editor Harmon Jones, had been nominated as Best Editor for *Guess Who's Coming to Dinner* (1967) the year Ashby won his Oscar. ("That was one reason I hated him right off the bat!" Jones jokes.) Jones was wary of working for Ashby, as he'd heard "horror stories" about him working "ungodly hours" and also that "he edited at his house so you couldn't escape."[14] Jones, however, was probably the quickest editor in the business—exactly the person Ashby needed—and he cautiously agreed to cut the film.

While Jones got started, Ashby turned his attention to other projects. In mid-February, he flew out to Ken Kesey's ranch in Eugene, Oregon, to work with him on the *One Flew over the Cuckoo's Nest* screenplay for a few weeks as the film's producers, Michael Douglas and Saul Zaentz, wanted the film ready to shoot in July. During the filming of *The Last Detail,* Ashby had been in communication with Peter Sellers, who had seen *Harold and Maude* and was very keen to work with Ashby. Sellers had sent him a number of scripts, including *Arigato,* based on Richard Condon's comic novel about a wine heist. Ashby got Terry Southern to help with the script, while Southern himself was pushing for Ashby to direct *Merlin,* his Arthurian project that Mick Jagger was tentatively considering.

In order to get his head around *The Last Detail,* Jones had put the film back into rushes, and just six weeks after starting he had a first cut ready. Ashby said later that the four-hour first cut was "the best the picture ever was" and even thought it releasable in that form.[15] He found Jones's editing a revelation and was totally in awe of his ability to choose the right takes, cut together pieces of film that didn't match, be creative with the material, and do all this *quickly.* He was slightly envious of his new editor's skills but as a director was delighted to have Jones working for him. Although he still spent a lot of time in the editing room, Ashby had finally found an editor he trusted completely and felt able to leave Jones to his work.

In May, he went to New York to hold auditions for the supporting roles in *Cuckoo's Nest* and saw a raft of young actors, including Danny DeVito, James Woods, F. Murray Abraham, and William Devane, as well as some less classically trained actors such as Meatloaf and John Belushi. He also saw, and passed on, Ronny Cox, Burt Young, and Lane Smith, all of whom he would end up working with later.

Ashby was in close communication with Kesey, a real kindred spirit, who was growing worried about the producers' response to his take on the film. Kesey wrote to Ashby:

> There are a lot of thoughts, speculations, fantasies that flit about my ravelled heap of a head, that I must keep out of my adaptation because such thoughts, I have discerned, upset our colleagues. Yet since these thoughts seem to be potentially pertanate [*sic*] to

> our project I intend to pen them to you alone, kinda like Memos From Selznik [*sic*] only these will be Ruminations to Ashby.
>
> Like let us say that I am one of them straight-foreward-spoken [*sic*] types, the sort that says I may not know what Art I like but can you dance to it? Does it move me to move? Or just move me, in a banal, worthless Norman Rockwell trick? Take the flick of Woodstock. Everybody knew it was a great and holy scene that went down and so were aptly moved by the flick. Norman Rockwell movement, though. Whereas Altamont was a horse of a darker color and is still up in the air, thus pertinant [*sic*], because we are still up in the air. Nobody knows whether what went down was Good, Bad or Pure Hellish. Not yet. But they do know you could dance to it, had to dance to it, like a barefooty boy prancing across a Jooly [*sic*] highway uncomfortably hot. I'd like to make Cuckoo's Nest that kind of uncomfortable.[16]

Producer Saul Zaentz, who needed a mainstream success after the recent failure of his last investment in a Broadway show, was particularly displeased with Kesey's approach. "I fear for our project," Kesey wrote to Ashby. "Not that it won't happen but that it will happen out from under our crazed but gentle auspices." Kesey proposed that he, Ashby, and the film's director of photography and production designer—Haskell Wexler and Mike Haller—take a road trip in a rented Winnebago to the locations where they would be shooting. Kesey, who had never written a screenplay before, also hoped the trip would alleviate the writer's block he was suffering from. "When I'm clear on this thing," he wrote later, "I'm articulate and it snaps into focus as a syncopated fugue of images and emotions that convey the meaning of madness. But when I become unclear, as I have been for weeks now, all I see is a rock-and-roll light show with a rickety plot." Kesey was adamant that the film had "to *be* madness communicating, not a film about madness. If we don't attempt with our full intention we fail at the outset. We might play it safe and bring in a calculated work of critical and financial success but we will still have failed."[17]

Ashby wanted Jack Nicholson for McMurphy, the lead in *Cuckoo's Nest,* but Douglas and Zaentz claimed the actor was asking too much money. When they continued to express dissatisfaction with Kesey's screenplay and offered the writer a disadvantageous contract, Ashby and Kesey regretfully withdrew from the project. "I worked on that for a whole year or more and they wouldn't cast Jack Nicholson in the part," Ashby said later, "so I took a walk. That's the truth. They made up excuses."[18] (In a cruel irony, Nicholson was later cast by Ashby's replacement, Milos Forman, and the film, released in 1975, became only the second ever to sweep the five main categories at the Academy Awards. Nevertheless, Ashby was disappointed by the film, managing to say only "Milos did his best. . . .")[19]

With *Cuckoo's Nest* gone, Ashby focused on the other projects he had in the pipeline. Leaving Jones and his assistant editors to finish *The Last Detail,* Ashby flew to London to spend ten days with Peter Sellers and discuss not only *Arigato* but another novel Sellers wanted to bring to the big screen, Jerzy Kosinski's *Being There.* "When I read *Being There,* I was crazy about it," Sellers said. "I had just seen *Harold and Maude,* which I thought was sensational, so I rushed a copy of the book to Ashby."[20]

Ashby had been in London only a day when he got a phone call from a panicked Bob Jones. Columbia, annoyed by Ashby's disinclination to return phone calls and his perceived tardiness in delivering a final cut of *The Last Detail,* had decided enough was enough. Jones and Robert Towne were in Ashby's house on Appian Way working on the film's structure when the head of Columbia's editing department called to say that a studio representative was coming to take the film. Jones refused to accept this, and a string of phone calls followed until he was talking to John Veitch, head of production.

"You don't have any choice," Veitch said. "We're taking it."

"I do have a choice," Jones retorted. "I have the key to the house. I'm locking it up, and sending everybody home. If you want to take it, you're breaking and entering."[21]

On hearing what had happened, Ashby called Columbia and managed to appease the powers that be. It was not only the duration of the editing process that was making them nervous: the film featured an unprecedented amount of bad language that they could not monitor or control as long as the film was being cut on Appian Way. The studio was also in major financial trouble, having recorded a loss of $84 million between 1971 and 1973, and was desperate for films with as much commercial appeal as possible.

Ashby returned to Los Angeles intrigued by Sellers's pitch for *Being There,* a modern parable about a childlike gardener who unwittingly becomes a political heavyweight. Sellers's career, however, was in a slump, and neither he nor Ashby was in a position to raise enough money to make the film. "I guess I didn't have the strength then or something," Ashby reflected later. "I couldn't get the damn thing set up."[22] That left Sellers pinning his hopes on *Arigato,* and Ashby was committed enough to the project to turn down Michael Butler's offer to direct the movie version of *Hair.* He may have regretted this decision when his misgivings over *Arigato*'s script compelled him to back out of the film and he suddenly found himself with nothing on the horizon.

By August, a final cut of *The Last Detail* had been completed and submitted to the Motion Picture Association of America (MPAA). The MPAA gave it an R rating but, significantly, did not feel any cuts were necessary. In fact, as Gerry Ayres told Columbia's new president, the former agent David Begelman, the MPAA thought it the "finest picture of the year without contest."[23] Despite such an endorsement from so conservative an organization, Columbia was unhappy with the film and asked for twenty-six lines with the word "fuck" in them to be cut.

Ashby and Towne were understandably resistant. During a meeting at Columbia, Towne explained that within the structure of the armed services, the protagonists were rendered essentially impotent, that all they could do was complain and swear. However, the Columbia executives were concerned only with the number of obscenities and explained that, while they did not want to emasculate the film, they had to do something about the "very, very strong" language. "We want you to do something about it," they said. "We want you to help us with it, because we feel we can reach a broader mass audience that way."

"Wait a minute," said Ashby, "you're telling me that if the word 'fuck' is used eighty times in the film and if we cut it down to forty times, we're going to reach a broader audience?"

"Exactly."

"I don't even know what the hell you're talking about," Ashby replied, "because I guarantee you now that the first time somebody opens his mouth and says 'fuck,' there's going to be 10 people who get up and leave the theater. But if we do it and that just becomes part of it, maybe people can actually have some fun with the picture, because that's the way these guys talk."[24]

Ashby managed to convince Columbia to let him preview *The Last Detail* as it was so that the public's reaction could be gauged. "So we previewed it in San Francisco," Ashby said, "and I don't think even 10 people got up and left."[25] Buoyed by this success, and finally realizing what a good film it had on its hands, Columbia decided to give the film a limited release to qualify for Oscar consideration—without any cuts. The plan was then to have a wide release in the spring of the following year when, the studio hoped, its Oscar buzz would generate optimum interest and ticket sales.

On November 9, 1973, just eight days before her eighty-sixth birthday, Eileen Ashby died at her home in Ogden. Hal flew in for the funeral, held three days later, but looked awkward and out of place among the other mourners as he sat at the back of the chapel. "He just wasn't conventional," his brother Jack said, recalling that he turned up for the funeral "in the clothes that he had with him. He said, 'I've never had a suit, never worn one, and I couldn't be buying one just for the funeral.'"[26]

Ashby had been so engrossed in his work and his troubled personal life that he only occasionally contacted his mother during the last years of her life. His homecoming trip to Ogden in 1970 came eighteen months later than promised, and he didn't even attend Hetz's funeral. Though he sent money every month to help pay for Eileen's care, it was partly to assuage the guilt he felt about not writing or calling. He was afraid she would ask how his life was and didn't want to admit to another failing or failed marriage, so he had cut himself off from her. As Eileen struggled with crippling arthritis, failing sight, and heart problems, all she wanted was some proof that she was still in her little boy's thoughts.

"You have had 5 marriages," she wrote to him in 1969, "yet you have never called me even one day before the marriage to let me know you were being married. And never, never am I told of the divorces.

"I know I am not very bright. I don't even pretend to be. I have always given all the love and service that any mother could give.

"Actually I am much too old to take into my heart new wives and new grandchildren and in a very few years to find that wife and children have been divorced and another wife and family soon takes their place. Your actions are not exactly new to me. Many of them are honest exact duplicates of your father. He knew I would not quarrel with him just as you know I am not going to come to Calif. and criticize you."[27]

Because Eileen could no longer travel to see Hal, as she had done until the late 1960s, the physical distance between them had turned into an emotional divide. Once, just a year or so before she died, Ashby decided to drive up to Ogden to see her as he had something he wanted to tell her. The trip was lonely and surreal: he spent the first night sleeping in his car in Zion National Park in southern Utah and woke to find a troupe of girl guides peering into his car. When he reached Ogden, he decided not to visit Eileen immediately. Instead, he checked into a motel across the street from her house and just sat in his room watching the light in her window. The next morning, he got into his car and drove back home.

In one of Eileen's last letters to Hal, she expressed regret over the way all his marriages had gone but stressed, "I am very proud of you in regard to the way you have climbed in the picture business. You must have a large portion of the Ashby genius. I know of at least 6 geniuses in the Ashby family. But I have only known one Hal." The letter ends, "I feel like I have never really known you since you were a young boy."[28]

While *The Landlord* and *Harold and Maude* shared a certain playful, rebellious spirit, *The Last Detail,* with its stark realism and emotional sparseness, did not seem much like "a Hal Ashby film." Yet by moving beyond the broad humor of his earlier films and attempting to empathize with characters he didn't naturally connect with, Ashby had matured greatly as a filmmaker.

His directing has been criticized for being light-handed, but Towne's script was so densely written that it allowed little space for a director's ego to intrude, and the directorial restraint, in fact, feels just right. Ashby appears in a cameo, as a man sitting at the bar watching with obvious pleasure as Nicholson plays darts, and the scene is an apt analogy for his approach to directing. Whenever possible, he let his actors go, guiding them only when necessary. The results were sensational, and Nicholson and Quaid both richly deserved the Oscar nominations they received for Best Actor and Supporting Actor, respectively.

When *The Last Detail* got its one-week, Los Angeles–only release, it garnered rave reviews, and Academy members came in almost unprecedented numbers to see it. Nicholson, Quaid, Towne, and Ashby were the main recipients of the critics' plaudits: Nicholson's performance confirmed him as a genuine star, Quaid was dubbed a hot prospect, Towne was Hollywood's new Shakespeare, and Ashby (in the words of Andrew Sarris) with his "sensitive, precise direction" had "burst into the major leagues."[29] Michael Haller's production design and Michael Chapman's cinematography, which combined to create the film's austere, wintry look, Jones's tight editing, and Ashby's old friend Johnny Mandel's cleverly ironic use of military music all drew praise as well. Considering the excellent word of mouth and high level of interest in the film, Columbia missed a trick by withdrawing the film after its limited run. Two months later, when *The Last Detail* was released nationwide, it once again got excellent reviews. It took a respectable $4 million at the box office, but everyone knew it could have earned much more.

14

Shampoo

> Hal had a temperament that I guess was almost Buddha-like in some ways. He literally made you think better in his presence. It wasn't always so much what he said, but he had such a calming influence, and particularly with two people like Warren and I were, who were prone to be volatile.
> —Robert Towne

> Warren treated him like any other member of the crew. But Hal had to stay around; it was like his bargain with the devil because it was going to be a big hit.
> —Lee Grant

The Last Detail consolidated Ashby's growing friendship with Jack Nicholson, and he became part of the actor's inner circle, going with him to Lakers' games, and hanging out at his house on Mulholland Drive. He got to know Nicholson's new girlfriend, Anjelica Huston, and many of his friends, including record producer Lou Adler, writer Rudy Wurlitzer, and, most notably, Warren Beatty.

One night in the fall of 1973, Beatty told Ashby about *Shampoo,* a project he and Robert Towne had been working on six or seven years earlier about the exploits of a womanizing hairdresser in Beverly Hills. Both Towne and Beatty had written versions, and they had fallen out over whose ideas were better, but Beatty was now keen to resurrect the project and make it his next film. At Beatty's invitation, Ashby read both scripts and concluded that a combination of the two could produce a very good film. He was savvy enough to know that working with stars like Nicholson and Beatty could only raise his profile and help his career. "Warren was a giant star," says Jerome Hellman, who would later make *Coming Home* with Ashby, "and Hal looked up to and cherished his friendship with Warren. I think for him to do *Shampoo* was like a validation, because complicated as Hal was, and as quixotic as he was, he didn't want to fail, he wanted to be on the A-list."[1]

Despite resistance from Towne, who inexplicably felt that Ashby did not sufficiently respect his scripts, Beatty brought in Ashby to direct *Shampoo*. Beatty had found a home for the film at Columbia, which recognized Beatty as a star who could deliver the megahit it desperately needed. The next step was to put together a shooting script combining Beatty's and Towne's screenplays. The two men had huge respect for each other, but their relationship resembled a volatile marriage, fraught with jealousy and suspicion. When Ashby and Beatty first went to work on *Shampoo*'s script, Ashby wrote a note to his secretary, saying, "I'm going to be working with Warren for next few days. Taking no phone calls. . . . *Don't* tell [Robert Towne] I'm working with Warren—(Don't tell anyone I'm working with Warren)."[2] After a few days alone with Beatty in his suite at the Beverly Wilshire Hotel, during which they constructed what Ashby called "a long rough composite kind of script," Ashby brought in Towne to hone and pare down what they had collated together.[3]

In the intensive ten-day period it took to write *Shampoo,* the demons of Beatty and Towne's friendship emerged as they wrestled for control and Ashby played referee. Towne says the writing sessions were fueled by "adrenaline and rage," with the pair most often referring to each other as "motherfucker" and Towne shouting at Beatty, "You cunt. . . . You're just being a cunt. . . . That's more cunt stuff."[4] "We had a very volatile time, I remember," says Towne, "and Hal was in the middle, and thank God he was. We'd talk about it, and then I'd go into the next room and write ferociously and come out. We were all a little thrown by the surprising quality of the work, and the speed."[5] Beatty also ultimately felt extremely positive about the results of the claustrophobic writing session, calling it "the most creative 10 days of my life, probably."[6]

In its first drafts, written in the late 1960s, *Shampoo* had a contemporary setting, but during the rewrites it became a period film set on the eve of the 1968 presidential election. Bridging several genres, it was a sex comedy that drew inspiration from Thomas Wycherly's play *The Country Wife* (1675) and (apparently) Beatty's own bed-hopping antics, but it was also a thoughtful backward look at America's recent history, reflecting Beatty's newly politicized mentality. The lack of strong female roles (the main cause of Beatty and Towne's previous falling out) had been resolved by giving Beatty's character, lothario hairdresser George Roundy, an ex-lover, Jackie, and a girlfriend, Jill. In a provocative bit of casting, they would be played by two of Beatty's real-life exes, Julie Christie and Goldie Hawn, respectively.

Ashby was to get $125,000 plus 7.5 percent of net profits for directing and was given a budget of $4.5 million (of which $2 million was "above the line," i.e., for the marquee actors' salaries). Beatty, who invested $1 million of his own money in the film, had initially considered directing but decided to take the role of "creative producer" instead. The initial implications of this were that he had already brought on board Christie and Hawn as well as Carrie Fisher, the seventeen-year-old daughter of Debbie Reynolds and Eddie Fisher. Fisher was playing Lorna, the sexually precocious daughter of Felicia Karpf, one of George's many client-lovers.

Ashby began casting the remaining roles by bringing in his friend Lee Grant to play needy Beverly Hills housewife Felicia. *Shampoo* was his first Los Angeles–based film as director, so he entertained himself by coming up with the people who, for him, personified the city and, particularly, Hollywood. For the role of Lester Karpf, Felicia's businessman husband whom George both cuckolds and lobbies to invest in his salon, Ashby shortlisted agent and producer Freddie Fields, director Gene Saks, and Columbia head honcho David Begelman, before opting for Broadway actor Jack Warden. He cast producer Tony Bill as Johnny Pope, the film director who is chasing Jill, after considering Paramount boss Robert Evans, director Richard Donner, and a then unknown Harrison Ford for the role. He also gave bit parts to two other producers, Brad Dexter and William Castle, the latter the man behind *Homicidal,* the film that had nearly launched Joan Marshall (as Jean Arless) to stardom. Marshall herself appeared in one of the beauty salon scenes, as did Kathleen Miller, who played Anjanette, the client who is memorably introduced when George is blow-drying her hair, her head nestling suggestively in his groin. "I did *Shampoo* while I was living with Hal," says Miller. "I wanted to do the part Goldie did, but they wanted stars. I guess I pushed Hal too much, it wasn't fair of me. When I did *Shampoo* I felt everyone thought I got it because of Hal."[7]

As Ashby began to assemble his crew, it became clear that Beatty regarded Ashby as *his* director more than *the* director. Ashby wanted Haskell Wexler as his director of photography, but Beatty vetoed this idea because of Wexler's reputation for being difficult to work with. Ashby's favored production designer, Michael Haller, didn't make the cut either. Beatty instead brought in Laszlo Kovacs and Richard Sylbert as cinematographer and production designer because he had worked with them before and knew their abilities. In fact, with the exception of Bob Jones, whose editorial brilliance Ashby refused to give up, the entire crew of *Shampoo* was made up of "Warren's people."

"Warren is the kind of person who, once he makes up his mind to do something, . . . is hysterically committed to it," said Towne. "He's like a sergeant blowing his whistle and going over the top and leading the troops into the machine guns."[8] When filming commenced on March 11, 1974, Beatty converted his dressing room into a makeshift apartment so that he could spend eighteen hours a day working on the film without ever going home.

The shoot, scheduled for a tight fifty-eight days, was tough on everyone. Goldie Hawn was unhappy with the simplistic personality of her character, Jill, and Julie Christie agreed with her that they probably should have swapped roles. And though Christie and Beatty's breakup a year earlier had been amicable, the closely autobiographical nature of their story line strained their working relationship; once he reportedly made her wait all day to do a scene, then made her do thirty-eight takes, stopping only when *he* was happy with it.

Beatty also alienated Lee Grant by telling her she had the wrong expression on her face. "Well, I got a migraine and went home for two days," Grant recalls, "and when I came back I told . . . Hal Ashby that I couldn't work like that and I had to quit."[9] Ashby's response was just to say OK, as he didn't want to force Grant to stay on the film. "He never got exercised about it," Grant says. "I felt like he was on my side."[10] Just as she was walking out, Beatty conceded that he might have been wrong.

Grant's feelings were shared by many on the set as Beatty had an alienating obsession with getting the film done to his specifications. "I was not happy with Warren," remembers Goldie Hawn. "He was so uncomfortable during the whole movie, he looked so troubled, always frowning—he was running the whole show."[11]

Beatty's need to be in control was particularly problematic for Ashby. Speaking at an American Film Institute seminar just months after completing *Shampoo,* Ashby's uncertain, stumbling account of working with Beatty hinted at just how frustrated he became: "It wasn't as difficult—many times it wasn't easy—it was very difficult because I was working with an actor who was the producer of the film and we spent a little bit of time trying to differentiate between that, never with much success—you really can't because you're talking about a lot of things when you're doing a film. I really believe that films are a communal endeavor. I'm the director of the film; I know I'm the director of the film. I know that when I say, 'Turn it on, turn it off,' that that's when they're going to turn it on and turn it off."[12]

Ashby faced a repeat of Arthur Penn's struggles on *Bonnie and Clyde*—on which Beatty had also been a "creative producer"—as he dealt with Beatty's compulsion to make the movie his way. "I had been with the project for many years and had specific ideas about what I wanted to do," Beatty says. "I liked to be free to come up with foolish ideas and see that they were foolish afterwards." Talking about Ashby's later collaboration with Jerry Hellman on *Coming Home,* Beatty admits that Hellman was a better producer for Ashby: "He was less intrusive than I am. Well, I'm not intrusive, I'm *active.*"[13]

On set, Ashby was as quiet and gentle as he had been on previous films. "Hal was a very sweet and softspoken person," says Peter Sorel, the still photographer on *Shampoo,* "never raised his voice even when a highpowered screenwriter and our star/producer were rather louder about their directorial input. I thought he was a man of infinite patience."[14] Beatty called Ashby "the nicest, kindest man," but that very kindness, which in the past had been an asset, here became a weakness.[15]

In the first few days, when Beatty asked what a shot was going to look like, Ashby said, "Hey, come look through the camera."

"It won't embarrass you?" Beatty asked.

"What's going to embarrass me?" said Ashby.[16]

Though Ashby didn't see this as any different from when he had let Nicholson do the same, Beatty took it as an invitation to infringe on Ashby's turf. As shooting progressed, a pattern emerged: Beatty would get his takes first (eight or ten, on average), and when he was happy, he'd ask Ashby whether *he* wanted the actors to go again. And then Towne, who had his own power struggle with Beatty, would put his oar in too. The film was a collaboration between three very creative minds, but Beatty admits, "Robert and I were not in total agreement, and Hal and I were not in total agreement."[17] "We'd get three different directions," says Goldie Hawn, "one from the director, one from Bob, and one from Warren. There were times when we'd say, 'Guys, get together, can one person give me a note?' So it became difficult."[18]

When Beatty talked about *Shampoo* in interviews, he always presented himself as "the filmmaker"; in his eyes, Ashby was just another crew member. Beatty and Towne often went off on their own to discuss scenes, then came back to tell Ashby how they wanted things done. Though he was isolated when he wasn't needed, when Ashby was shooting a scene, he was given literally no space, as Towne would crouch next to the camera on one side while Beatty leaned over his shoulder on the other. If either wasn't satisfied with a take, the actors would go again.

Once, in a state of desperation, Ashby went to production designer Richard Sylbert and told him, "I can't take it anymore. These guys won't let me alone."

"He hated it," Sylbert recalled, "because we'd have meetings, and we'd go, 'All right, Hal, this is what we're gonna do.' We beat the shit out of him, had him boxed in. . . . They'd make him reshoot, do takes he didn't want to do, coverage he felt he didn't need. But generally he was smart enough to just go with the flow. He was the best person they could have hired, because Ashby's feelings about people were very good. He was a sweetheart of a man, and a wonderful director. To do that movie, you couldn't be mean, you couldn't do an Altman."[19]

Ashby, with his ingrained dislike of producers, found himself being bulldozed by his producer but could not haul him off the set this time because he was also the film's star. He was all about collective creativity, but the deal had always been that everybody knew that he was the head of the collective. "Hal was like an office boy on that," says Haskell Wexler, who visited Ashby on the set, "and he wasn't used to being that way. Warren chewed Hal up and spit him out."[20] When Haskell's son, Jeff, saw Ashby near the end of the shoot, he remembers him as "not being there at all" and Beatty doing most of the directing. "This is not fun," Ashby told him. "He was in exile on that film," Jeff says, "but a self-imposed exile."[21]

For Ashby, the world of the film wasn't much more hospitable than that of the set, and he struggled to feel sympathy for Towne's shallow and self-absorbed characters. He described Beatty's alter ego, George, as "a lame" and had nothing in common with the moneyed, idle, and apathetic Felicia and Lester Karpf.[22] Even so, he fought the tendency to portray them as caricatures: "They're not people I spend time with, but they're people I've looked at and felt badly for. So I spent a lot of time being very kind to those people. The other way's easy. To make fun of people is easy. Life isn't that easy."[23]

Ashby saw an opportunity in *Shampoo* to underline the characters' social and moral corruption by showing how it was reflected in American politics. He had his assistants find television footage of Nixon's speeches and those of his vice president, Spiro Agnew, and picked out the most ironic clips he could find. Though the film is set on election day, politics are barely discussed, and no one is seen voting, so what is said by politicians on televisions in the background provides the core of the film's political thrust. In one scene, Nixon talks in his first speech as president about "bringing the country together." At the same moment, Lester says to George, "Maybe Nixon will be better. What's the difference? They're all a bunch of jerks." He then adds, "You can lose it all, you know, no matter who you are." A few months after the film wrapped, Nixon resigned in the wake of Watergate. Beatty admitted to an interviewer, "The Nixon-Agnew scenes get much larger laughs than I had intended, because of what has happened since. I didn't really plan it that way."[24] Ashby, however, had planned it that way. The Nixon jibes were just a continuation of what he had done in *The Landlord* and *Harold and Maude* and also *The Last Detail,* in which a hippie incredulously asks Mulhall what he could possibly like about Nixon. For Ashby, Nixon's resignation only confirmed what he had known all along.

In Ashby's rare off-hours, he looked to distract himself from his frustrations on set. Though he was seemingly still with Kathleen Miller during the making of the film, Deanna Benatovich remembers: "He would come by my place in Malibu sometimes and spend the night. When I asked him if we were getting back together I must have scared him and he stopped coming by. Hal didn't sleep very much and would frequently be up all night watching movies. He used to joke that they were paying him so much that he was being paid to watch movies and even make love to me."[25]

Ashby also found that having allies around him raised his spirits, and he welcomed visits from Bob Jones, Haskell and Jeff Wexler, and Tom Blackwell, his friend from the Laguna days who was now a successful artist in New York. Blackwell, who had maintained sporadic contact with Ashby over the years, saw him on a trip to the West Coast with his wife, Linda, and wrote afterward about his relief: "I always go through paranoid trips where I think you don't want to see me, but then when I do see you, it's the same old Hal. It's really funny too, because when I knew you in Laguna you were still struggling to get somewhere and I was just a kid trying to be an artist. Deadly serious, of course, but nowhere. I guess the thing that sticks is that we both hung on and made it in our own way, we're both still growing and it didn't ruin us as people. I guess I've known so many people who copped out and settled for less than what they could do, and it means a lot to see what you're doing. *The Last Detail* was a hell of a movie."[26]

Blackwell was not the only person to think *The Last Detail* was a hell of a movie; the awards season, which took place during the *Shampoo* shoot, confirmed just how highly regarded the film was. Nicholson won Best Actor awards from the National Society of Film Critics and the New York Film Critics Circle as well as at the Cannes Film Festival and the British Academy Awards, where Towne also won. Randy Quaid and Nicholson were nominated at the Golden Globes but both lost, and Quaid, Nicholson, and Towne all came away empty-handed at the Oscars. This was a particular disappointment to Nicholson, who said, "I like the idea of winning at Cannes with *The Last Detail,* but not getting our own Academy Award hurt real bad. I did it in that movie, that was my best role. How often does one like that come along?"[27]

Because Ashby believed that film was a communal art, he'd never had his Best Editing Oscar for *In the Heat of the Night* engraved with his name, feeling everyone involved in the film had actually won it. He was galled when Nicholson was snubbed by the Academy so righted the wrong by giving his dear friend his own Oscar, which Ashby felt he truly deserved.

Despite what transpired on set, at the end of the *Shampoo* shoot Beatty was singing Ashby's praises, highlighting his intelligence and sensitivity as a director. Speaking today, Beatty says that Ashby's direction was the reason his performance in the film was so good, and his admiration for

Ashby is clear: "The word that comes to mind with Hal is 'modest.' His attitude was modest, his way of shooting was modest. Whenever Hal ventured himself on a choice in making the movie, I always felt he was right. Hal was never a person to speak crazily. I don't remember ever feeling that Hal was wrong about much of anything. He wouldn't speak until he knew what he thought, and then he would say it in the most encouraging way. I would call him a strong director—he wanted to put actors on the screen, not put himself on the screen. He had a great sense of humor, had great subtlety, and got the best out of people."[28]

Shampoo wrapped on June 12, and Ashby, keen to get away from the film for a while, started thinking about his next project. His agent, Mike Medavoy, had two possible projects for him to direct: *North Dallas Forty,* a hard-boiled drama about the high-octane lives of professional American football players, at Paramount, and an adaptation of Isaac Asimov's *Caves of Steel,* at Columbia. Actress Ellen Burstyn, whose stock was high after the huge success of *The Exorcist* (1973), contacted Ashby about directing *Alice Doesn't Live Here Anymore* (1974), a script by a first-time writer called Robert Getchell. Burstyn later told Ashby, "I was torn between you and Marty Scorsese, and finally decided on Marty because of a certain hard edge in *Mean Streets* [1973] that I thought would balance a certain softness in the *Alice* script."[29] Ashby was announced as the director of *North Dallas Forty* but pulled out of the deal (the film, directed by Ted Kotcheff, was released in 1979), and soon after Michael Butler called to tell him that the offer to direct *Hair* was still on the table.

Things fell quickly into place, and by early July a deal was set up through Peter Bart to make the film at Paramount, with Colin Higgins and Michael Haller signed as screenwriter and production designer, respectively. As Bob Jones was busy editing *Shampoo,* Ashby decided to go to England with Butler to work on ideas for *Hair.* But he wasn't leaving just *Shampoo* behind; he was also leaving Kathleen Miller.

Ashby's relationship with Miller had become increasingly strained, in part because of the disparity between their careers; while Ashby was directing high-profile films (in which he gave her walk-on parts), she was working only occasionally, on television shows like *Kojak* and *Cannon,* and would sporadically put her energies into a novel or a screenplay, with even less success. She was fast approaching thirty and had no illusions that Ashby was going to marry her. When he flew off to England for a few months, both knew it was the end of the relationship.

Owing to the continuing success of the stage version of *Hair,* Butler was a rich man, and his newly acquired wealth allowed him to play at being the country gentleman. He had bought Warfield Hall, in the Berkshire village of Warfield, a sizable manor house near enough to London that its fifteen bedrooms were regularly occupied by people from "the scene" but distant enough to give its occupants a break from the bustle of the city. Butler was an active polo player, and enjoyed trips to London, but spent much of the summer with Ashby just relaxing and talking.

"I really loved Hal—I thought he was a terrific guy," says Butler. "I considered him a very close friend; I liked spending time with him, liked being with him in any way possible. We just hung out together. I found him very calm. A very kind individual, very warm, very interesting. He would describe to me his philosophy about how he did things. Yes, he was quiet, but he was very easy with me in terms of talking."[30] Over the course of a placid summer, Ashby and Butler smoked dope and discussed their vision of *Hair,* agreeing that it should retain as much of the philosophy and feel of the original as possible.

However, not long after his return to Los Angeles, Ashby had a change of heart about *Hair.* "All I know is that I was up at my home in Montecido," says Butler, "and I got a call from Peter Bart that Hal had pulled out of the film. I took off like a shot and came down to LA because this was a terrible blow. I actually got busted on my trip coming down for smoking a joint and so I wound up spending some time in jail."[31] After their summer together, Butler felt betrayed when Ashby abandoned the project and disappointed that he had not found out from Ashby himself. He suspected that Ashby was "worried sick about the scope of the film project. Hal's movies had always been small pictures. By that, I mean small situations involving few people. Almost any musical, but particularly *Hair,* involves large casts. It's more like directing an army."[32]

In the fall of 1974, Ashby worked with Bob Jones on the editing of *Shampoo.* He was disappointed that the music he had planned to include—Jefferson Airplane, the Byrds, Buffalo Springfield—was not in the film. Initially, *Shampoo* had been full of songs from 1968, but through a combination of Beatty's dislike of Ashby's musical choices and Columbia's budgetary restraints, most tracks were cut.

Ultimately, it was Paul Simon who composed the film's haunting, wispily ethereal score—approximately three minutes of music spread thinly over the duration of the film. "Christ, I've never done a picture before where I didn't bring the theme in till reel five, almost halfway through the film," said Ashby. "It was only used four or five times. All we wanted was just the suggestion of a theme. In other words, what I think we were doing was going anti-score."[33]

Everyone who knew Ashby knew that he was an avid music lover, and not a likely advocate of "anti-score," and that this was yet another example of Beatty's control over *Shampoo*. The film wasn't edited to Ashby's wishes either, as Beatty explains: "We had some small disagreements on the final editing of the movie. I was very happy with the final result, but in general I think Hal was more inclined to go for a more relaxed pace."[34]

Ashby, however, looked to the future and focused on positives. Since his return to Los Angeles, he had been dating actress Dyan Cannon, and, in a strangely fortunate turn of events, his former agent, Mike Medavoy, had become the head of West Coast production at United Artists (UA). Earlier that year, Medavoy had set up a two-picture development deal for Ashby at Universal, and he now put together a similar deal at UA. The only project specified in Ashby's UA agreement was *Beyond the Mountain* (a.k.a. *Zebulon*), a Western written by Jack Nicholson's friend Rudy Wurlitzer. Originally written for Sam Peckinpah (for whom Wurlitzer had previously penned the 1973 *Pat Garrett and Billy the Kid*), it intrigued Ashby because it showed the Indians' perspective and eschewed the stereotype of the West as an arena for the symbolic battle between good and evil. Ashby once told Wurlitzer, "I've never regretted saying 'no' to anything—it always led to something better."[35] Sadly for Wurlitzer, Ashby also passed on *Beyond the Mountain* when it failed to fill UA with sufficient confidence. But saying no did indeed lead to something better.

In early 1975, Ashby and Beatty began previewing *Shampoo*. After a poor response from a conservative Santa Barbara audience, Beatty remembers that David Begelman and he "drove back to Los Angeles together, and he gave me a nice little pat on the knee while he was driving and said, 'Look, they can't all work. On to the next!' But the next night we showed the movie in Beverly Hills and it was as good a reaction as you could ever want."[36] After that screening (held at the Directors Guild building), Bob Rafelson declared himself "ecstatic" and told Ashby, "You are Brilliant."[37] Ashby noticed at the screening that the directors' wives, however, looked very uncomfortable. "All of them were getting up-tight," he said. "They thought we were presenting Hollywood. It wasn't that at all. One person said to me afterwards that his wife said, 'I know what that asshole [Beatty] is out doing all the time.' And we weren't even presenting Hollywood people."[38]

Though Judith Crist and Pauline Kael both declared the film a masterpiece, most critics gave it only lukewarm reviews. They were troubled by its uncomfortable mix of sociopolitical satire and brazen sexuality and were disappointed that the coming together of such a starry cast and talented creative team had not produced something more impressive. The film's mixed critical reception was illustrated in its coverage in the *New York Times,* where it received a very poor review from Walter Goodman but was called the best comedy of the year so far by the paper's chief critic, Vincent Canby, just a few months later. Whatever its flaws or merits, *Shampoo* got people talking, and its coarse language and sexual content had audiences flocking to see it. When asked about what was behind the controversial scene in which Julie Christie ducks under a restaurant table to give Warren Beatty a blow job, Robert Towne quipped, "At this point—probably $30 million of film rental."[39]

Fans of the film debated just how closely Beatty's character was based on the man playing him, but none considered possible parallels with *Shampoo*'s unassuming director. George is one of Ashby's long line of young heroes (or antiheroes) bemused by life, yet in him there is a crucial difference: the quintessential Ashby hero is a quester and a questioner who fights to find his place in the world despite the fact that he does not fit in and, indeed, because of it—but George is the opposite. He wanders through life passively accepting the status quo, always saying that everything is "great" when we know it is not. As Jill tells him, "You never stop moving, you never go anywhere."

Towne's constant rewriting during the *Shampoo* shoot had prevented him from working on an epilogue set in the present day that he and Beatty felt would provide a fitting ending to the film. An epilogue was being considered even up to the last day of dubbing, but the ironic (if unsurprising) truth was that Beatty's and Towne's ideas for it were completely different as the two had radically different visions of the course their characters' lives would take. Luckily, for once Beatty's and Towne's failure to agree allowed Ashby to get what he wanted, which was to end the film as the script had it, with Beatty's George on a hill, watching as Jackie, the only woman he had ever truly loved, leaves to run away with Lester. It not only appealed to Ashby's romantic sensibility but also echoed the final scene of *Harold and Maude,* where the hero also looks down on the world from on high (in that case, the top of a cliff) after losing *his* one true love.

In short, though *Shampoo* was not nearly as much of a Hal Ashby film as it might have been, it at least had a Hal Ashby ending. "I prefer that kind of thing," Ashby said. "I like to leave a little bit of an enigma there about exactly what it is because I think that's what makes it not a totally down kind of an ending."[40] In both Towne's and Beatty's epilogues, the characters continued on the wrong paths; the way Ashby left it, his compassionate ambiguity at least allowed us to feel hope for their futures.

15

Glory Bound

> Find out who is causing the Trouble here in this old World—remove the Power from their hands—place it in the hands of those who aint Greedy—and you can roll over and go to sleep.
>
> —passage underlined by Ashby in his copy of Woody Guthrie's *Woody Sez* (1975)

When Oscar time came around, Columbia put Ashby forward as a candidate for Best Director, but he wasn't nominated. *Shampoo* received four Academy Award nominations in all, for Beatty and Towne's script, Richard Sylbert's art direction, and Jack Warden's and Lee Grant's performances, but Grant was the only one to return home with a smile on Oscar night. Though Ashby was delighted for Grant, he felt a degree of detachment when it came to the film and said, "That's not my picture, that's Warren's picture."[1] However, he was still relatively happy with *Shampoo,* saying, "There are always things that will gnaw at me, but I'm not walking around holding my head in my hands."[2]

Ironically, the film Ashby was least invested in as a director was his biggest hit by far: *Shampoo* performed astronomically at the box office, where its saucy sensationalism rapidly earned it $22 million and made it Columbia's most successful film of all time. As a result, Ashby was no longer associated with worthy small-scale pictures that underachieved financially but came to be seen instead as a director who could deliver big films with mass appeal.

Both his "creative collaborators" on *Shampoo* were keen to work with him again: Robert Towne wanted Ashby to direct *Personal Best,* a script about female athletes that Ashby ultimately convinced Towne to direct himself (the film was released in 1982), while Beatty says, "We always talked about the things he was doing [and] I was always hoping we'd do another film together."[3] A decade later, Beatty asked Ashby to direct *Dick Tracy,* an offer Ashby turned down because he felt the comic book characters were too one-dimensional (Beatty himself wound up directing the film in 1990), and right after *Shampoo* he was trying to interest Ashby in another sexually explosive project, an adaptation of Erica Jong's *Fear of Flying.* According to *You'll Never Eat Lunch in This Town Again,* a book by the film's prospective producer, Julia Phillips, Beatty wanted to turn Jong's novel into a porn film "with see-through dildos and vibrators."[4] (Beatty, however, says Phillips's contentions were pure fabrication.) Ashby feared that the movie would be too glib, and even though Dyan Cannon wanted to be in it, he passed. His reasons for doing so were disputed by those involved: according to Jong, Ashby was "driven away by Julia's craziness," while Phillips claimed Ashby got tired of Columbia execs "dicking around" and not making up their mind whether they wanted him.[5]

It was easy enough to say no to *Fear of Flying* as offers were now flooding in. Producer Richard Roth wanted Ashby to do either *Sheltering Sky* (1990) or *Havana* (1990), Barbra Streisand offered him *A Star Is Born* (1976), he was being considered as a potential director for *Network* (1976), and he was linked to *The Great Brink's Robbery* (1976) with Dustin Hoffman, whom Ashby was very keen to work with after the two had become friends. Though all these films eventually got made, Ashby was not the director of any of them.

Ultimately, Ashby narrowed the list down to two possible projects: *I Never Promised You a Rose Garden,* a novel about a suicidal teenage girl in a psychiatric hospital, and *Bound for Glory,* the memoir by the Dust Bowl troubadour Woody Guthrie. Ashby was drawn to *Rose Garden* but feared that with Milos Forman's *One Flew over the Cuckoo's Nest* due to come out later that year, it would be seen as an attempt to jump on the "funny farm film" bandwagon. The Woody Guthrie project, however, had excited him even before he saw the script.

Ashby had first heard about *Bound for Glory* during discussions at United Artists (UA) about his next project. Published in 1943, the book had since spawned numerous unsatisfactory screenplays, mostly written by friends of Guthrie's who were too close to the subject matter to have the proper perspective. The film's producers, former UA production chief Robert Blumofe and the late Guthrie's agent and friend Harold

Leventhal, brought in Robert Getchell to write a new script. Getchell, riding high on the success of *Alice Doesn't Live Here Anymore,* was a young writer with a fresh take on the material and focused his script on a four-year period of Guthrie's life (1936–1939) rather than the three decades covered in the book. *Bound for Glory* was first offered to Arthur Penn—who had directed Guthrie's son, Arlo, in *Alice's Restaurant* (1969)—but Penn turned it down. Getchell and Blumofe had in any case wanted Ashby over Penn. With his leftist ideologies and deep compassion for his characters, he was a natural choice—and his new cachet in Hollywood didn't hurt either. "He's always been known as a good director," Getchell noted, "and since *Shampoo* as a good, *powerful* director."[6]

Ashby had long been intrigued by Woody Guthrie, an iconic American figure who had become much more widely known after Bob Dylan (one of Ashby's musical heroes) cited him as a major influence. Guthrie was a wanderer, a restless man who had left his wife and children behind to travel the country, singing songs and trying to change the world. ("I understand Woody Guthrie very well," Ashby admitted.)[7] In his writing and songs, Guthrie focused on individuals and their struggles, yet he always added a potent political subtext, much as Ashby did in his movies. "His radicalism stems from his desire to be in contact with the people," Ashby said. "I make my films about people."[8]

"He loved that sense of freedom that Woody Guthrie had, never tied down to anything," says Mireille "Mimi" Machu, Ashby's girlfriend at the time. "He loved to roam."[9] Ashby had met Machu (also known as I. J. Jefferson) at the wrap party for *Chinatown* (1974), which she had been invited to by her ex-boyfriend, Jack Nicholson. When she caught sight of Ashby, she thought, "That's the best-looking person in the room," and then was delighted to discover that he was the director of *Harold and Maude,* which she had fallen in love with when she saw it in Paris. Ashby and Machu hit it off immediately, but he wasn't single at the time, and it wasn't until a year later, in early 1975, that the two got together. Ashby was in preproduction on *Bound for Glory,* and they hung out a lot when Machu was house-sitting at Nicholson's pad on Mulholland. "He had the best sense of humor in this town, and we laughed a lot together," says Machu. "He really loved people. He loved to watch game shows and see people win. He loved to see people's lives changed for the better." Machu was attracted to him because of the desire he brought out in her to look after him, how he treated her as an equal, how he made her feel happy and involved in everything—and because he was "a great kisser."[10] Nicholson gave their relationship his blessing and even invited them to stay with him and Michael Douglas for a week in Oregon, where they were filming *One Flew over the Cuckoo's Nest.* (During their visit, there was an unfortunate incident in which Nicholson's dog, Big Boy, ate Ashby's front teeth when his bridge fell out.)

Not long after Ashby had committed to do *Bound for Glory* for UA, budgetary concerns became an unexpected factor as the estimated cost of $4 million was higher than the studio had expected. For a film with no stars attached yet, spending such a figure constituted quite a gamble. Ashby brought in Chuck Mulvehill, who had been in the wilderness since *The Last Detail,* and had him work out a budget for *Owen Butler* as well as *Bound for Glory* so that if the Guthrie film was considered too expensive, he'd have a cheaper fallback option. (Mulvehill's return to the fold was marked in the film by an in-joke: the pastor whom Woody asks about work is standing next to a church sign saying "C. Mulvehill.") In the end, however, Mike Medavoy and UA decided that the Guthrie epic, the prestige picture, was the film that deserved to be made.

Ashby was adamant that *Bound for Glory* would not be a hagiography, but he worried about the reaction from die-hard fans who were already skeptical about Hollywood trying to tell Guthrie's story. It was the first time that Ashby had dealt with factual material, and he said, "Doing a film about a real person drove me crazy at first, trying to be faithful, until I decided I should just do a story about the character."[11] He nevertheless did extensive research on Guthrie, migrant workers, the hobo life, and the Dust Bowl; read John Steinbeck's factual account of migrant life in California, *Their Blood Is Strong* (1938); put up Depression-era pictures on his wall; and looked at the material that had been collected by Twentieth Century–Fox for John Ford's 1940 adaptation of Steinbeck's *The Grapes of Wrath* (1939). He also read Guthrie's diary and letters from the relevant period and integrated historical incidents not mentioned in *Bound for Glory* into the script as well as some of his own memories of traveling around after leaving Ogden. He watched films from the 1930s and documentaries about the period and also all the Preston Sturges films that he could find. Ashby was a huge fan of Sturges—most famous for *The Lady Eve* and *Sullivan's Travels* (both

1941)—a social satirist who focused on the human elements of comedy, created brilliantly observed characters, and brought out the best in his actors.

Ashby worked closely with Robert Getchell, but Robert Downey felt that Ashby himself should have written the screenplay. "There wasn't anybody in the '70s who made so many great humanist films, yet didn't write them," Downey says. "It was as if Ashby had written them, though; that was how it felt to him." Downey recalls that Ashby used to show him ideas he had written down on scraps of paper and ask, "What should I do with all of these?"[12]

For the moment, however, Ashby's main concern was finding his Guthrie. As he had been a short, wiry man, Dustin Hoffman and Jack Nicholson were obvious choices, but Nicholson opted to make *The Missouri Breaks* (1976) with Marlon Brando instead, and Hoffman, a dedicated method actor, demanded six months to learn the guitar. Robert DeNiro and Al Pacino were considered, but both had already committed to other projects. Johnny Cash, Kris Kristoffersen, Glen Campbell, James Taylor, Art Garfunkel, and Arlo Guthrie all expressed interest in playing the role, but Ashby was looking for an actor, not a musician. (Bob Dylan was sent the script as a courtesy; he declined the part but offered to direct the film.)

David Carradine, then best known for the *Kung Fu* television series, heard about *Bound for Glory* from Barbara Seagull Hershey, his ex-wife, and immediately called his manager to get an audition. Ashby initially laughed at the idea, but when Carradine's manager insisted, "David is Woody Guthrie!" and explained he had long coveted the role, he gave him a chance. "Hal didn't want me," says Carradine, "but I went in and knocked him flat."[13] Carradine turned up with his guitar and played songs and told stories and jokes for the whole afternoon.

Much as Ashby liked Carradine, he looked nothing like Guthrie and was far too tall. "He told me that if I were six years younger and six inches shorter, he would hire me right on the spot," Carradine recalls of his second meeting with Ashby. "I told him I'd do the part with my knees bent."[14] Six weeks after their first meeting, Ashby had offered the role to Richard Dreyfuss, but Dreyfuss had asked for more money; and the folk singer Tim Buckley, whom director Henry Jaglom had suggested to Ashby, had tragically died of a drug overdose. So Ashby called in Carradine and had Haskell Wexler shoot a screen test. Ashby had moved from Appian Way (after the house had become too full of editing equipment) out to Malibu Colony and now lived with Machu and Sean, her ten-year-old son by Sonny Bono, right on the beach. Carradine also lived in Malibu and used to run along the beach past Ashby's house every day, refusing to let Ashby forget him. "One time he leaned out the window and said, 'Hey, why don't you come in and say hello?'" Carradine recalls. "I hung out with him a lot as a result, and I realized, 'If I just keep running past Hal's house, I'll get the part.'"[15] Ashby later recalled it was Warren Beatty who pointed out that Carradine had "the right 'I don't give a fuck' attitude" that he was looking for.[16] Ashby knew that he was not making a documentary, that nobody would look like Guthrie and be able to act *and* sing, and that Carradine having the spirit of Woody Guthrie was more than enough.

Medavoy and the other UA brass were far from convinced as Carradine was a television actor with a reputation for being difficult to work with and not the big name they were hoping for. Out of respect for Ashby, they agreed to at least look at Carradine's screen test; as Getchell puts it, they "came to jeer and stayed to cheer."[17] Apparently, after only thirty seconds of the test, Ashby's decision to cast Carradine was fully endorsed.

Ashby wanted *Bound for Glory* to be as authentic as possible, so he sent Carradine off to Oklahoma, where Guthrie had grown up, to work on his Okie accent and learn to play the fiddle. To further the authenticity, Ashby wanted unknown faces in other roles: character actor Ronny Cox was hired to play Guthrie's sidekick, Ozark Bule (a composite of a number of Guthrie's friends, including Will Geer), and Ashby audaciously gave acclaimed Broadway actress Melinda Dillon her film debut in a dual role, playing both Guthrie's wife, Mary, and singer Memphis Sue. He also brought in Randy Quaid at the last minute to play union rep Luther Johnson, another composite character.

Unlike on *Shampoo,* Ashby was now surrounded by friends. Not only was Mulvehill back as his production manager, but he had both Wexlers, Haskell and his son Jeff, working on the film. Ashby had wanted Jeff as his sound mixer on *The Last Detail* and *Shampoo,* but union problems had twice prevented it. This time, Ashby made a stand and insisted that Jeff work for him, union rules or no. In the end, Ashby agreed that a union sound mixer would be employed as well, as long as Jeff did the work. For Haskell and Hal, it was the first time they had worked together since Ashby had become a director, and it was particularly fitting that this should be the film that reunited them: not only had Haskell previously been asked to direct *Bound for Glory,* but he had also known Guthrie when they were both in the merchant marine. Bob Jones would edit, but that wasn't his only role on the film, as he had recently started writing as well. He had given Ashby an original treatment; Ashby didn't particularly like it, but he nevertheless employed Jones to write an adaptation of Saul Bellow's *Henderson the Rain King,* a property he had just acquired. Impressed with his script, Ashby asked him to help with rewrites on *Bound for Glory* on top of his editing duties.

Possibly the most crucial member of Ashby's crew on *Bound for Glory* was production designer Mike Haller. On a period piece like this, there was a huge amount of work to be done, beginning with finding the right locations. Haller drove thousands of miles through Texas, Oklahoma, New Mexico, and Arizona, looking for dusty, barren landscapes, but found that places like Pampa, Texas, where Guthrie had lived in the 1930s, were now far too green and modern. Finally, Haller remembered visiting an area near Sacramento, California, that had the right sparse look and found the towns of Stockton and Isleton, which would become the film's bases for the remainder of the year.

In mid-August 1975, Ashby began shooting in Stockton, the very place where William Wyler had shot *The Big Country* almost twenty years earlier. The locations seemed trapped in time and were perfect for *Bound for Glory.* The tendency of period films was not to have skyline shots, as this required locations that were not blighted by modern buildings, telephone antennas, or television aerials, but Ashby had told Haller that he didn't want shots angled downward. "I wanted everything to be at eye-level," said Ashby. "[But] it's difficult to say, 'Let's go outside and start shooting 1937.'"[18]

The film's look was also crucial in evoking the feel of the period. Ashby, Haller, and Haskell Wexler had initially conceived *Bound for Glory* as a black-and-white film because of all the photos of the Depression that they had surrounded themselves with. But as this was commercially unfeasible, they decided instead on a bleached-out, monochromatic look that still had the warmth and life of color. Haller and Wexler set about getting rid of all strong, saturated hues: blue jeans and overalls had to be hand-dyed gray, painters were on hand at all times to tone down the colors of billboards or signs, and Fuller's earth, rubbish, and tumbleweed were blown into shots to give the requisite dusty look.

Wexler infuriated directors with his slow pace and headstrong attitude, yet Ashby loved working side by side with his friend. "Haskell's crazy," he said affectionately. "He likes to take a lot of chances." Wexler was used to being creatively inhibited by his directors, but Ashby told him, "All you have to do is tell me that you're going to try something. I'm not going to jump up and down. If it works, great, and if it doesn't work it doesn't work."[19] Wexler had recently shot a commercial with Garrett Brown, the cameraman who had developed the Steadicam, a revolutionary device that stopped the camera from shaking, allowing for shots that were previously inconceivable. When Wexler mentioned Brown's invention, Ashby immediately said, "Sure, do you wanna try that?"[20]

The Steadicam was used for a number of shots in the film, the most memorable of which was in the migrant camp Mike Haller built in Isleton, filled with nine hundred extras. The camera swooped down on a crane and then followed Carradine through an endless crowd of migrants when it reached ground level. On the very first attempt, the camera moved slowly and elegantly, and the take continued for so long that one of the extras thought it must be over and started telling Carradine about a car he was trying to sell. "Say, buddy, lemme tell you bout that Plymouth . . . ," he began. Carradine ignored him, but he persisted, "No, really, what we talked about, I think I can get it for you."[21] Ashby kept filming, hoping the extra would stop, but finally called "Cut!" The take had to be scrapped, but after three more, he got one that was perfect. "Just watching it was some kind of trip," he said.[22] When the shot was screened at dailies two days later, it got a standing ovation.

A week or so into September, Ashby was already a few days behind schedule. The company was moving around constantly, locations were awash with extras who were usually sitting around waiting, and, according to Blumofe, the whole operation was "like planning a war."[23] It certainly was a battle for Ashby, who had a large budget and a cast and crew of almost unprecedented size; the pressure of this, coupled with the huge physical strain of shooting, was taking its toll on him. "I got depressed when I found we'd been shooting for 39 days and had covered 14 pages of the script," he said. "We made up time later when every one felt good about the film. But we did go over the budget and I had a tantrum."[24]

Ashby's biggest headache was the trains. After the problems on *The Last Detail,* he swore he would never work with trains again, but his excitement about *Bound for Glory* had made him forget all that. Guthrie was well known for riding the rails, so the trains were an integral part of his character. Haller, another veteran of *The Last Detail,* tried to preempt any problems by studying freight train schedules. However, he recalled, "We'd . . . sit there with our print-outs thinking everything was fine . . . and the expected train just wouldn't be there. A main-liner would show up instead . . . and our freight train would chug in three hours late and backwards. We'd lose half a day in shooting before it could be turned around."[25] On one occasion, while they were waiting to get a shot of a train approaching, it came at them from the opposite direction. Rather than just turning the camera around, Wexler switched it off. "Bob Downey could have made a whole film on what you've just cost us," Ashby told him.[26] It was no exaggeration: the shoot was costing up to $50,000 a day, and over the course of filming many days were lost because of train problems.

Ashby was fortunate, however, not to lose his leading man to the trains. Carradine, who was extremely fit after his martial arts training on *Kung Fu,* was predominantly doing his own stunts in the film. He had ridden the rails himself as a young man, so when he jumped on to the train, Ashby said, "It looks too easy."

"OK," replied Carradine, "I'll try and make it look harder."

This time, Carradine reached out and pretended he couldn't quite keep up with the freight carriage, but by mistake brushed the rail with his hand, throwing himself off balance. "It just pulled me right off my feet and I sort of went under the train, actually," says Carradine. "There's a close-up shot of it where you see my head going down, and the moment it goes down the truck goes right over it, and it would have taken my head right off."

Seeing the near-fatal effect of his request, an ashen Ashby said, "OK, that's it, no more stunts. You can't do your own stunts anymore."

"Hal, it's already happened," Carradine retorted calmly, adding with a smile, "and anyway, it's your fault!"[27]

Recalling his problems with the trains, Ashby said, "I thought I would go crazy."[28] The film was getting further and further behind schedule, and the trains and the huge crowd scenes left Ashby stressed and exhausted. Possibly to keep his energy up, he started to use cocaine. Once, when Carradine was in Ashby's trailer, he turned over a copy of the *Los Angeles Times* and found several lines of the drug.

"Do you do a lot of this stuff?" asked Carradine.

"As much as I can," Ashby replied.[29]

Unfortunately, the coke only increased Ashby's stress and gave him unpredictable mood swings. Haskell Wexler's slow pace was just one of numerous factors that had put the film so far behind schedule, but in his unstable mind frame Ashby decided to sack him and refused to give a reason. "Then he started to scream and stomp," says Wexler. "I went to Hal and I said, 'You're not the Hal Ashby I love and respect. You're the Hal Ashby who's doing something to himself up his nose, and I'm not going to accept it.' I really chewed him off for being a doper."[30] The fight was left unresolved that night, but despite being fired, Wexler turned up the next morning, and both acted like nothing had happened.

Ashby recognized that his cocaine use was a problem and took steps to remedy the situation. "I started using coke in 1975, at the point when it became epidemic in Hollywood," Ashby said a few years later. "I stopped pretty quickly. I was making *Bound for Glory* and I became short-tempered. I'd get cross with Haskell Wexler for things that weren't his fault. It's not my nature to be curt and quick-tempered. I saw what was happening and stopped using it."[31]

"We all had our dark periods on drugs," says Robert Downey. "And nobody was telling us to be careful with the stuff." However, Ashby's real drug of choice, and the only one he used regularly, was not coke but weed. "I couldn't keep up with him on marijuana," Downey says. "Hal would smoke marijuana like it was a cigarette—there was a permanent crease in his lip." Downey, himself known for his hedonism, was smoking grass with Ashby in Malibu Colony one night when Ashby said, "Let's go down to the water."

"I can't even leave my chair," said Downey, paralyzed by the pot.

"Do you want me to go down there," offered Ashby, considerately, "and I'll tell you what happens?"[32]

Despite his reputation for being difficult, Carradine was on his best behavior during *Bound for Glory* and later called Ashby the best director he had ever worked with. Still reeling from his recent breakup with Barbara Hershey, at the start of filming he was, by his own account, "virtually suicidal" but felt that he "should finish this great film before . . . [doing] anything about it, and then see."[33] His moods were unpredictable, and he could go from being charming and talkative to being nonverbal for days on end. Ashby knew that Carradine related to Woody enough not to need too much guidance but still found ways to support his actor. "Hal would be right beside the camera," says Carradine, "and I used to actually play my dialogue to him rather than to whoever I was talking to because I'd get this feedback from him. Hal's basic element in his directing was that he would watch while you were working and seemed to be looking at you like you were an absolutely phenomenal actor, like 'God, that's so great.' And that made you feel like it *was,* and it moved you up a notch."[34]

To make him feel fully included in the filmmaking process, Ashby invited Carradine to watch the rushes with him every day. On top of the large amount of film Ashby was shooting, there was, Carradine says, "all this extra footage that Haskell would shoot every day because he'd go out and shoot with his own camera and shoot trains going by and migrant workers and stuff like that, and there was lots of it." With 6 A.M. starts most days, Carradine decided one night that he'd had enough and was getting up to go when he heard Ashby's voice behind him gently say, "Oh, givin' up, are you?" "So I sat through just about three hours of dailies every night for nineteen weeks," says Carradine, "and saw every foot of film that was shot."[35]

Only once, when some migrant workers marched past, did Carradine play to his rebellious image. "David started marching with them," Ashby recalled. "By the time we found him, he was two miles away; and he had held up shooting for three hours."[36] Blumofe was angry with Carradine, whose stunt had cost them time and money.

"Aw, come on," Carradine said. "It's what Woody would have done."[37]

Blumofe let a smile creep across his face because it was exactly what Guthrie would have done. Many of Guthrie's living relatives, including his first two wives, Mary and Marjorie, and most of his children, visited the set during filming and expressed their approval of how the film was being made. Carradine, whom they had felt was unusual casting, received the ultimate compliment when Guthrie's son Joady declared, "He's got Woody's vibes."[38] Guthrie collaborator Pete Seeger also came to see filming and was impressed "by Ashby's attention to detail and determination to get the authentic picture."[39]

In December, the company returned home to Los Angeles for the final weeks of filming, but it was early January 1976 before it wrapped, almost six weeks later than scheduled: the shoot had lasted nearly five months, and the budget had ballooned from $4.4 to $7.6 million. Ashby was relieved filming was over but continued to suffer from the rigors of the shoot. In Allensworth, there had been a disastrous attempt to re-create a dust storm (one of the film's crucial set pieces) by blowing dust and dirt through metal tubes. Though during the storm Woody declares, "A little dust won't hurt," everyone became ill, coughing and spluttering, and Ashby got into another fight with Haskell Wexler when the cinematographer added the potentially harmful Fuller's earth to the mixture to give the dust the right color. Ashby, whose lungs were weak from years of smoking, suffered the most. He became asthmatic from the dust and developed a harsh, rasping cough and then pneumonia; even after the film had wrapped, the cough refused to go away.

Ashby always shot a lot of film, but in postproduction he discovered that he had shot twice as much as usual, close to 150 hours of footage. The house up on Appian Way was so full of film that Ashby had to move his music editor into the garage in order to give everyone else room to work.

As Bob Jones worked on a first cut, Ashby turned his mind to future projects. High on his list was *The Hawkline Monster,* a gothic Western by the cult author Richard Brautigan, for which Brautigan himself had written a treatment at Ashby's request. Also in play was Jones's script of *Henderson the Rain King.* Ashby put the idea of doing *Henderson* to Mike Medavoy, who told him, "As much as I think this is terrific material, I'm afraid of it as a movie. I'd like to see it but I'm afraid I don't think we would want to make it."[40] Ashby had planned to have Jack Nicholson play Henderson, the middle-aged American who travels to Africa, and he was also in the frame for *Hawkline,* a bizarre story about two gunmen hired by enigmatic identical twin sisters to kill the "monster" in their cellar. In early 1976, Ashby announced that he would shoot *Hawkline,* but not until the following summer, as he was not yet happy with Brautigan's script.

When Ashby finally decided on a follow-up to *Bound for Glory,* it surprised everybody. MGM—which at the time was still suing Ashby for quitting *Three Cornered Circle*—had offered him an adaptation of Mildred Cram's whimsical novella *Forever,* a property the studio had been trying to make since 1940. Ashby could have a period of recuperation as filming would begin in the spring of 1977, but apart from this—and the fact that he would be paid $350,000 for his directorial duties, almost double his salary on *Bound for Glory*—there was little appealing about either the deal or the film itself. As on *Three Cornered Circle,* MGM would have approval over Ashby's casting, and *Forever,* a fifty-eight-page story of love and reincarnation, was infamous for being so insubstantial that it was nigh impossible to adapt for the screen. It was almost devoid of dialogue and so dated that only the basic concept could have survived in a credible film. Predictably, Ashby pulled out of the deal.

He had been tempted away by *Straight Time,* which Dustin Hoffman wanted him to direct. Hoffman and Ashby were friends and were always on the lookout for possible collaborations. "He was an emotional creature; he worked with what moved him. We were kin," says Hoffman.[41] *Straight Time* was a semiautobiographical novel by ex-con Edward Bunker (who later played Mr. Blue in *Reservoir Dogs* [1992]) that Hoffman had bought back in 1972. He had initially planned to direct as well as act, but at the last minute thought better of it, so Ashby was drafted, bringing Mike Haller and Bob Jones with him.

However, Ashby's cough from the dust storm worsened until he had to be hospitalized. With production imminent, First Artists, the company bankrolling *Straight Time,* refused to wait for Ashby to recover. (The film was eventually directed by Ulu Grosbard and released in 1978.) Though this was a blow, Ashby's health concerns were much graver as the doctors feared he had lung cancer. It was a huge scare for Ashby, who stopped smoking his Shermans and started fasting to purify his system. Fortunately, his cough was not a symptom of cancer but one of dust inhalation. He was put on medication, which he took for years afterward.

The scare also coincided with the end of his relationship with Machu. He was jealous of her exes, particularly Sonny Bono, and found it difficult having Sean around, whom he said was a constant reminder of her former lover. "Hal wasn't meant to live with everyone," says Machu. "He didn't know how to deal with kids. We were crazy about each other, but we had different needs." They began having screaming fights, and on one occasion, Machu threw an ashtray at Ashby's big Advent television, putting a dent in it. For Ashby, who loved his technological gadgets, this was the last straw. He told Machu it was over and shouted, "You leave!" "No, you leave!" Machu screamed back.

As Machu was recovering from a recent operation, Ashby agreed to move out and let her stay until Sean's school term had ended. His next-door neighbor, director John Frankenheimer, tried to keep tabs on her for Ashby, who was worried about what she might do. Ashby offered Machu a Mercedes, a trademark gift he gave to departing exes. "The Mercedes was the kiss of death for a relationship," says Haskell Wexler. "I would always ask him, 'Did she get a 350 or a 312?'"[42] Machu, however, turned down the car and instead took with her only some ridged dishes, which she knew Ashby didn't want as he had complained that one couldn't eat pancakes off them. In the end, she left earlier than agreed when Ashby offered her $1,000 as an incentive; his business manager, Larry Reynolds, escorted her off the premises, ensuring she left without harming Ashby's prized possessions, his typewriter and baby grand piano. Though Machu admits the breakup was "not very pleasant," the two stayed friends and later worked together at Lorimar, where Ashby employed her as an editorial consultant and script reader.[43]

The split was a recognizable symptom of Ashby's postproduction depression. "He would get into terrible funks, usually at the end of a picture," says Chuck Mulvehill. "He was losing the film, a thing he could control. Then he would be in the bedroom for weeks at a time. He would only come out at night when he went tomcatting."[44] As one woman left, another would always arrive; during the summer of 1976, he was out with Buddy Joe Hooker, the stuntman on all his movies, when they met Dianne Schroeder, a friend of Hooker's. "He was in a truck with Buddy Joe in a rural area of Agoura," Dianne recalls. "They were coming off a beekeeper's property, and he had fallen in a creek! And when I was introduced to him, he acted like he wasn't wet at all. I wish I'd had my camera—it was hilarious."[45] Later, Ashby, Hooker, and Schroeder all went out to dinner together, and she heard about Ashby's health problems. As she had a background in health and fitness, Schroeder offered to help Ashby, and they established a working relationship that soon developed into something more.

Though a number of his friends described her as the only woman who ever understood Ashby, Schroeder maintains that while her relationship with him did have a romantic element to it, she was never one of his long line of girlfriends. "We had an extremely close, loving friendship, and I had complete respect for him as a person and an artist," she says. "I am very proud to have known him, that there was mutual respect and mutual love. If you look at the list of women he was with, or had affairs with, I do not feel I am part of that list. There was romance involved, but I feel it was somewhat of a guarded relationship because I was much younger, and he felt protective of me. The main part of it was friendship."[46]

After their romance ended, Schroeder and Ashby nevertheless remained extremely close. "Hal allowed people to keep on loving him after a love affair was over," Schroeder continues. "He was not into loving in a superficial way. On a spiritual level, he was very sensitive, enlightened, and kind. He knew who really cared about him, and he let them be in his life."[47]

David Carradine says the four-hour first cut of *Bound for Glory* was the best version of the film. However, releasing it in that form would have been commercial suicide and was never considered by either Ashby or UA. Throughout the summer, Ashby screened the film for actors, journalists, studio execs, and friends and fine-tuned the cut for the next screening on the basis of their reactions. The feedback was hugely positive, and many people, including the Guthrie family themselves, were overwhelmed by the film and its rousing evocation of Guthrie and a bygone America. Alan Arkin, Peter Falk, and Jeff Bridges were all huge fans, and Jack Nicholson attended almost all the screenings and gave Ashby helpful suggestions for cuts. *Bound for Glory* was supposed to premiere at the Toronto Film Festival in September, but Ashby decided the film still wasn't ready to be seen by a paying audience, stressing that it was "a work print" that "still needs polish."[48] By October, he had a 135-minute version that he was pleased with, but in an unprecedented move, Mike Medavoy requested that the film be made *longer* and that certain scenes he had enjoyed in earlier versions be reinstated. Ashby—who had told Carradine previously, "If I shorten it up, maybe an extra hundred thousand people will see it"—was happy to oblige him but wondered what impact this would have on the film's box-office success.[49]

Bound for Glory was the biggest film of Ashby's career so far, in terms of length, budget, scope, and ambition, a period epic in the great Hollywood tradition. For a filmmaker who had previously focused on the present and the recent past, Ashby displayed an uncanny ability to bring the past to life. Yet this skill arose from already-apparent strengths: attention to detail, an affectionate understanding of his characters, and an ability to elicit vivid performances from his actors. A paean to the common man and his struggle, the film was just as relevant to 1976 and the struggles of César Chávez as it was to the times it portrayed. Though it had gone hugely over budget, every dollar spent could be seen up on the screen: Haskell Wexler's cinematography looked stunning, the footage of the migrants, capturing their humanity in simple, revealing shots, adding greatly to the emotional impact of the film; and Mike Haller's work matched, if not eclipsed, Wexler's achievements as the film is filled with period cars, trucks, shops, houses, and whole towns (including the migrant camp Haller built) that combine to genuinely evoke the 1930s.

For Ashby, *Bound for Glory* was also a film with great personal meaning. At the start of the film, one of Woody's friends describes California as a place where seeds will sprout the day after they have been planted, a promised land that has "everything a man needs." This is how Ashby saw California when he himself was on the road, struggling to get by, and the twenty-odd years he had spent there since had not shaken his idealistic belief that this was the only place to be.

"If I feel close to any of my screen characters," Ashby said later, "it's Woody Guthrie in *Bound for Glory*. We're alike and I put all my own remembrances in that film—of being out of work, of living off a Powerhouse candy bar for three days, of feeling more responsibility to your work than your family."[50]

Writing about *Bound for Glory* just before its release, the critic Joseph McBride called it "a majestic film, the most ambitious film made in the United States since *The Godfather Part II*, and one of those rare pictures which are made with lavish resources, meticulous care, and concern for epic breadth that characterize the way the great Hollywood movies used to be made."[51] UA was equally excited, and opened the film in early December in light of its significant Oscar potential. It received an excellent critical reaction: the praise for Ashby and Wexler was almost universal, and Carradine, who appears in every scene in the film, was also highly lauded, his *Kung Fu* tag long forgotten. The film's detractors all had semi-informed ideas of what *Bound for Glory* should have been, of how Woody Guthrie should have been depicted. "I learned a long time ago," Ashby said, "that anybody who really knows a lot about Woody Guthrie, I'll never make it for them, I cannot win."[52]

But in a more significant sense, Ashby had won. While *Shampoo* had changed the way he was perceived by Hollywood, *Bound for Glory* altered the way critics looked at him. "Ashby interests me," wrote *Village Voice* critic and auteur theory proponent Andrew Sarris, "but I have not completely figured out his style."[53] Ashby had previously been viewed by many critics as a journeyman director and certainly not an auteur, but *Bound for Glory* forced a reappraisal of his career, and suddenly he was being compared to the men he had served his apprenticeship under, William Wyler and George Stevens. Asked about what connected his films, Ashby said, "There's no story line or anything like that running through my pictures, but I try to do films that deal with human relations, with people relating to one another."[54] McBride, however, noticed the confused young (and increasingly not-so-young) men who were the protagonists of his films, observing "a strong sense in all five [of Ashby's] films of the necessity to break through a stifling code of traditional morality into a more open and spontaneous way of dealing with the world's hypocrisy and injustice."[55] It seemed that, finally, Ashby was starting to get the recognition he deserved.

16

Coming Home

Once I was a soldier
And I fought on foreign sands for you
Once I was a hunter
And I brought home fresh meat for you
Once I was a lover
And I searched behind your eyes for you
And soon there'll be another
To tell you I was just a lie
—Tim Buckley, "Once I Was" (1967)

He was a one-of-a-kinder. The most creatively *disorganized* director I've ever worked for. Hal's knack was to create organized mayhem. I mean, he thought it out, but he waited for magic.
—Bruce Dern

Around the same period that Ashby cut his ties with *Straight Time,* director John Schlesinger pulled out of *Coming Home.* The film had been in the works since 1973, when Jane Fonda, inspired by a meeting with Ron Kovic, author of *Born on the Fourth of July,* had asked her friend Nancy Dowd to write a script about a paraplegic Vietnam veteran. When Dowd's script was deemed unfilmable, the creative team behind *Midnight Cowboy* (1969)—writer Waldo Salt, producer Jerome Hellman, and director Schlesinger—came on board and secured a development deal at United Artists (UA). Hellman and Salt did huge amounts of research to create a realistic picture of a paraplegic vet's life, but only ten days after Salt delivered his script, Schlesinger announced he wasn't going to direct the film. "The exact way he expressed it," says Hellman, "was that as a 'baroque English faggot,' he wasn't the right person to sit in the VA [Veterans Administration] hospital and talk to these guys about their urine bags."[1]

Schlesinger felt he was too much of an outsider to comment on the Vietnam War and its impact, and Hellman and Fonda realized they needed a counterculture director. Ashby was an obvious choice. Fonda knew him from political fund-raisers, and in 1973 Hellman had written him a fan letter praising *The Last Detail*'s "simplicity, directness and . . . absence of tricks."[2] Bob Rafelson was also considered for the job, but after Salt, Fonda, and Hellman had spoken to both, they agreed Ashby was the clear choice.

Ashby quickly made the film his own by hiring Chuck Mulvehill, Mike Haller, and Jeff and Haskell Wexler (who had made a Vietnam documentary, *Introduction to the Enemy* [1974], with Fonda) and casting the major roles. UA, under Mike Medavoy, was keen to offset the film's risky subject matter and improve its box-office prospects by casting a big-name actor as the paraplegic, Luke Martin. Medavoy suggested Sylvester Stallone (Hollywood's newest star after the phenomenal success of *Rocky* [1976]) or Al Pacino, but Ashby put forward Jack Nicholson, saying, "It would be very hard for me to imagine any male role that he couldn't do." Fonda, who was producing the film, was to play Sally Hyde, the soldier's wife who falls for Luke, and Jon Voight and Bruce Dern were up for the part of her hawkish husband, Bob. Voight approached Ashby and told him, "Believe me, I will do anything in this picture. I would be glad to play the captain, but I would prefer Luke."[3] When Nicholson decided that, after *One Flew over the Cuckoo's Nest*, he didn't want to spend any more time in claustrophobic hospitals, Ashby cast Voight as Luke, and Dern as Bob Hyde.

Voight seemed perfect for the part as he not only felt a strong affinity for the character but also had been an active anti-Vietnam campaigner. But Medavoy, who already had major reservations about the project, was not pleased with the choice and told Ashby outright: "No way. . . . The man has no sex appeal." He even offered to add a million dollars to the budget so that they could get a bona fide star. Ashby, backed by both Hellman (whose previous film with Voight had been the hugely successful *Midnight Cowboy*) and Fonda, stood strong. "Unfortunately," Ashby recalled, "I'd already made up my mind."[4]

One of the reasons Ashby backed Voight so strongly was his clear dedication to the role. Even before he was given the part of Luke, he started doing research and talking to vets, and as soon as he was cast, he bought a wheelchair and joined the Long Beach Raiders wheelchair basketball team, the paraplegics not only teaching him to play but also becoming his close friends. After weeks of hanging out with them and discussing every conceivable aspect of their lives, he almost believed he was a paraplegic too. If one of his feet fell off his wheelchair, he would reach down with his hands and put it back up again. In interviews, he referred to the paraplegics used as extras in *Coming Home* as "the other paras," as if he were one of them.[5] He attended the cast party in a wheelchair and, even after shooting had finished, kept one at his house in case the other paras came round and wanted to shoot hoops with him like old times.

Ashby had enjoyed the research process on *Bound for Glory* immensely and, with Dianne Schroeder as his research assistant, set about learning all he could about Vietnam and America in the late 1960s. Schroeder put together eleven huge volumes of articles on Vietnam and paraplegia, along with hundreds of photos of 'Nam soldiers, underground antiwar publications, and transcripts of Vietnam documentaries. *Coming Home,* like *Shampoo,* was set in 1968, and Ashby took the opportunity to revisit all the music he had not been allowed to use in Beatty's film. He had Schroeder put every song he liked from the latter period of the decade onto six cassettes and then played the tapes around the clock. He had photographs of Vietnam pinned up on the walls of his work room and borrowed a number of films from the Vietnam Veterans against the War. The idea was "to be like a sponge and absorb everything."[6]

Another part of Ashby's research involved shooting "rap sessions" at Jon Voight's house, where paraplegics talked about everything from first dates to their children to their darkest moments. He ended up with about eleven hours of footage and was so taken with it that at one stage he planned to insert parts of it into the fictional narrative of *Coming Home.*

During much of the Vietnam War, Ashby had been obsessively involved in his work (and distracted by his tumultuous private life), and he now felt guilty for not having participated sufficiently in the antiwar movement. "I was active in as many things as I was able to deal with," he reflected, "none of them being enough."[7] Ashby declared that America, and Hollywood, "should not forget that period in our history, that we cannot just say life goes on."[8] However, he also realized that *Coming Home* could be more than simply an indictment of the Vietnam War and decry the very principle of war itself.

With *Bound for Glory* all but finished, Ashby began working with Salt and Hellman on a rewrite of *Coming Home,* tailoring it to his own sensibilities. (Haskell Wexler had expressed concern over Salt's script, telling Ashby he had "made great films out of lousy scripts before" but was worried about a script that he felt was "dependent on cheap sex" and "could only work if there were a true mature love developed between Luke and Sally.")[9] Hellman was a neighbor of Ashby's in Malibu Colony, and the three met daily at Hellman's house, but Salt, who was used to collaborating with Schlesinger, proved difficult to work with. Progress was painfully slow, and with six weeks to go before the film's start date, they had only thirty-seven pages of the new script. One day in November, Salt left a meeting early, saying he wasn't feeling well. Ashby and Hellman worked on alone, and an hour later they received a call to say that while driving home, Salt had suffered a massive coronary.

Fonda, who had long been in the wilderness after acquiring her "Hanoi Jane" tag, was a hot property in Hollywood once again and was filming *Coming Home* in the brief interval between Ted Kotcheff's *Fun with Dick and Jane* (1977) and Alan J. Pakula's *Comes a Horseman* (1978). This meant that Ashby had to be ready to start shooting at the beginning of January. Ashby needed a writer to finish the shooting script, but the problem as he saw it was that writers tended to bring with them oversized egos and that he "ran the very real risk of having the baby thrown out with the bathwater."[10]

The answer was to get a writer who wasn't a writer: Bob Jones. Ashby had found his creative contributions on *Bound for Glory* very helpful, and he was a quick, inventive thinker who had, in Hellman's words, "an editor's eye and a writer's talent."[11] All Salt's notes on plot ideas, biographical studies of the characters, transcripts of countless interviews, notes on paraplegia, and early drafts and redrafts of the screenplay—a huge mountain of paper—were passed on to Jones so that he could finish what Salt had started.

"I miss you all very much and ache to be part of this important and final preparatory period," Fonda wrote to her *Coming Home* colleagues.

"But I'll arrive in fine shape and am already raring to go. I have very good feelings about the working situation. You have all braved some heavy storms with such equanimity."[12] What she didn't know was that, despite the positive noises Hellman was making to calm a concerned UA, they were still a very long way from having a finished script. When the truth came out, she admitted to wondering "if, in the face of such setbacks, victory could be pulled from the jaws of defeat."[13]

Just before shooting began, she asked Ashby, "Have you ever started a film knowing no more about what we're going to do than this?"

"No," he replied.

She looked at him and said simply, "I hope it works."[14]

Though Fonda was nervous, Ashby was undaunted. Getting input from everyone and doing it all on the fly was his chosen working method anyway. As Hellman said, "He's a very fluid filmmaker. He's a man who is always very open to discovery, to surprise. He loves that spontaneous part of the process."[15] Ashby went so far as to say the film might even benefit from not being rigidly preplanned: "I felt that because we're dealing with personal relationships in the film, the very fact that we were in limbo in certain areas would enhance it—we would be able to get deeper into the characters by not having the scenes worked out in advance; we might even discover things we wouldn't normally look for. So I felt pretty good about that, even though I knew it was going to be hard."[16]

On January 3, 1977, five weeks after Salt's heart attack, filming began. "We started shooting before we were ready," Ashby recalled. "We had three or four scripts, an ending that didn't work and the first 30 or 40 pages weren't any good."[17] To make matters worse, UA, whose budget for the film had already nearly doubled from $2.5 to $4.85 million, was getting jumpy. Because of the film's controversial themes, the studio had already offset the risk by putting Ashby and the other principal cast and crew members on deferred salaries, paying them a lesser fee plus a percentage of the film's profits. If the film was a box-office success, they would be rich, but if it bombed, they'd get 3 percent of nothing.

Principal photography began with a composite of Salt's and Jones's work acting as the shooting script, but two days in Ashby realized it wasn't working. "I saw where Jon was coming from with his character," he explained, "so I just threw the first script out."[18] Voight's intense connection with his character became the guiding influence, and Ashby let him do whatever felt right. Voight was grounded by the presence of the fifty paraplegics on set, and he and Ashby were aware that this was probably more their film than anybody else's.

During the first two weeks of shooting, Ashby worked on the script with Rudy Wurlitzer, a much-needed outside influence. The two of them hung out quite a bit anyway and often strolled on the beach, discussing basketball, politics, and Ashby's problems with the studios. Describing his reaction when he saw a pretty girl walking along the shore in Malibu, Ashby once told Wurlitzer, "I feel like this big bear—I just want to grab her!" To make their working arrangements more convenient, Wurlitzer actually moved in with Ashby for this period. "I haven't worked with a director who was so open with the writing process," says Wurlitzer. "He had this ability to be seamless in how he worked with a writer. Everything he did was a collaboration—he had no ego. The work was really fun because there was real give and take and he was really generous. He got the best out of you. That was one of the marks of his work, how well he got on with writers."[19] For Ashby, however, this was a grueling period, with his rewrite sessions coming on top of a full day's work; he recalled, "I would come home at about eleven at night, and we'd work till about four in the morning, and I'd get to work at six. We just wrote all night."[20]

The actors participated in the rewriting process as well, and on weekends during filming, Ashby would get together with Fonda, Voight, and Dern and tape their improvisations, allowing them to create spontaneous and honest versions of existing scenes that Jones then worked into the shooting script. Every night he would discuss with his cast the scenes they were to shoot the following day and work out with them the optimum approach to a scene. As long as Ashby knew the purpose for a scene and that purpose was retained, he was happy for the actors to be free and creative within that framework. As he put it, "Even though I'm that unstructured, I *am* structured."[21]

Despite his dedication and attachment to his character, Voight became hugely despondent at the results of his efforts. At the end of a day's shooting early on, he turned to Ashby and said, "I quit. I'm not good enough to do this part. Get Al Pacino or somebody."[22] Ashby told him that he believed in him and that they would work through any problems together, and fortunately this plea made Voight rethink his decision.

Voight may have been feeling the pressure of his first major Hollywood leading role since *Deliverance* (1972) five years earlier, but Ashby's restrained approach to directing seemed to settle him. In one scene early on in shooting, Voight kept blowing his lines. After five or six takes, the camera broke, and Voight felt responsible for even that. Ashby came and sat down next to him and lightened the mood by making a few jokes.

"We could be here all day doing this thing," Voight said.[23]

"What's the difference?" Ashby replied. "We're having a good time, aren't we? Good company? What a nice time. It's great that we're together, we're all making a movie. I don't care if we stay here all afternoon. This is it. Can't be better."[24]

Immediately, Voight felt at ease. "I knew I would have the time to do it, and I knew that he liked what I was doing for some reason," he says. "It was just a *nice* feeling with Hal, that he was so accepting of everything. And in that atmosphere, I finally got it!"[25]

The opening scene of the film, where paraplegic vets discuss the war, has a haunting introductory shot of Luke just sitting quietly and listening that Voight played as a reflection of Ashby's own gently watchful nature. He assimilated other aspects of his director's personality as well in his portrayal of Luke. He had Ashby's beaming, spontaneous laugh and, with the same beard and shaggy blond hair, almost looked like his baby brother. Voight loved watching the dailies with Ashby because no matter how heavy the material was, Ashby would be talking to the characters up on the screen and have everyone in stitches. "He wouldn't let anybody else take themselves too seriously," says Voight. "I was very alert during the piece to Hal's sense of humor because it really fitted. It was a sense of humor that came from deep pain and could guide you through horrors. And all the guys in the ward had it. I can see Hal's humor in almost every scene, and it was the catalyst of Hal's humor and personality that made me do certain things. My character in *Coming Home* was in some way an interpretation of Hal's internal drama and grace, in the face of all that pain."[26]

Voight's instinctive, emotional approach to acting, however, was very different from that of Fonda, who always knew her lines perfectly, and Ashby had to help the two find a working balance. Voight felt his lines in an early scene were far too polemical, and he stayed up one night worrying about the scene he was going to shoot the following day. "I decided it was all or nothing," says Voight. "I felt the movie wouldn't work if it stayed as it was."

When he arrived on set and joined Ashby and Fonda for a read through, he was so nervous his legs were shaking. As they were running lines, Voight came to a page and a half of dialogue about the VA and suddenly said, "You see these words on these pages. . . . I can't say these words."

Fonda folded her arms, in a huff, and said, "Well, what do you propose we do?"

Ashby sat there silently, doing nothing but watching Voight and Fonda as if it were in fact Luke and Sally who were trying to resolve a situation.

"You see these words on these pages," Voight repeated. "I can't say these words—but you can."

"And what will you say?" Fonda asked.

"I'll say 'You're attractive when you're angry, Bender'—or something like that. . . ."

Fonda initially expressed her concern over her ability to learn all the new dialogue, but Ashby quietly pointed out that they had two hours before they needed to shoot the scene.

As Fonda left, Ashby turned to Voight and said, "Well, that was easy."

Voight, who had been terrified, was astonished at how calm Ashby had remained when both of them knew that the success of the film hung in the balance.

"It was amazing," Voight says. "I was a desperate wreck. If this didn't work, I had no second plan; if they didn't accept this, I was gone."[27]

When the scene was shot a few hours later, Fonda knew her lines, and the change in speaker had eliminated the polemicism, replacing it with an honesty and immediacy that really rang true.

Because of the film's subject matter, and also because of Fonda's reputation, the U.S. Army, the U.S. Navy, the national guard, the marines, and, most crucially, the VA had refused to cooperate in its making. After previous attempts to get help from the U.S. armed forces on *The Russians Are Coming* and *The Last Detail,* these refusals were not a surprise to Ashby. The VA called the as-yet-unproduced film exploitative and dishonest, and its chief medical officer wrote to Chuck Mulvehill saying that the script showed "veterans as weak and purposeless, with no admirable qualities, embittered against their country, addicted to alcohol and marijuana, and as unbelievably foulmouthed and devoid of conventional morality in sexual matters."[28] The most immediate upshot of this was that Ashby's plan to film the hospital scenes in the VA's Long Beach Spinal Cord Facility had to be abandoned. They were shot instead at Rancho Los Amigos, a civilian hospital for spinal cord injuries in Downey, a small town southeast of Los Angeles. All the paraplegics and quadriplegics in the facility were used as extras and supporting cast, while only Voight and one other actor, Willie Tyler, "played" paraplegics. By using real people rather than actors, Ashby created a visually powerful condemnation of the Vietnam War: "As a filmmaker, what more graphic thing could I have than that paraplegic ward. You hardly have to use any words."[29]

Ashby and his crew may have feared that the six weeks at the hospital would be difficult and depressing, but it turned out to be the most rewarding portion of the shoot. "They're actually more up than we are," said Ashby of the patients. "Once they've made the decision to go on living, they become very positive thinking people."[30] Fonda quickly became a hit with the paraplegics, regardless of what they might have felt about her before. She was kind, considerate, and knowledgeable about their condition, and they recognized that she was the driving force behind the first film to tell their story. And as Voight said, "A lot of the guys disagreed with her politically, but they sure were attracted to her sexually."[31]

With not only his usual gang around him but also this buoyantly optimistic bunch of extras, Ashby thrived on set. He noted, "It's one of the only times I can think of where I've been around 50 or 60 people for six weeks at a time and liked every one of them."[32] During the month and a half of twelve- and fourteen-hour days, many of the cast and crew developed close relationships with the quadri- and paraplegics and had their eyes opened to the problems and complexities of their everyday existence. From early on, crew members would help patients from their chairs to their beds and spoon-feed them as they ate lunch together.

Voight's approach to his role was to *be* Luke Martin as much as possible: he stayed in his wheelchair for three weeks of filming and some nights would stay over at Rancho Los Amigos. He became one of the bunch, and his spirits dipped after the shoot in Downey ended: "When I left the hospital, I actually missed it, because that's where all my buddies were, that's where the juices were really cooking. All the little things that happened on the periphery, they were all exciting to me. I just loved to walk into a scene with five or six of the guys—they were so terrific, always contributing so much, that when I got on my own I thought 'Where are my buddies? I can't talk to these *walkers!* I got nothin' to say!'"[33]

Away from Rancho Los Amigos, staying in character was not so effortless for Voight. Fonda and Haskell Wexler both thought he was playing Luke too soft, but Ashby trusted Voight's instincts. Ashby and Fonda did not always see eye to eye on matters of interpretation—the way a character would act or the meaning of a particular line—but he always heard her out. He welcomed suggestions from all quarters, and Haskell Wexler says that everyone working on *Coming Home* "felt as if they had participated in the making of the film—even if they really hadn't—because that was the atmosphere that he fostered."[34]

Robert Carradine, David's youngest brother, remembers how protective Ashby was of his film and his actors. Before his first scene, a picnic scene with Fonda, Voight, and Penelope Milford (who was playing Fonda's best friend), Carradine recalls that he was "very intimidated and *really* uncomfortable." Noticing this, Ashby had the actors talk through what might have happened just before the scene started; Voight decided they would have been smoking dope, so Ashby and Voight had a smoke to set the mood. By the time they had fully "prepared" for the scene, Ashby said that they had lost the right light for the shot and shooting would have to wrap for the day, thus granting Carradine a reprieve. The next day Carradine's nerves had settled, and he gave a strong performance that he puts down to Ashby's ability to "peel off layers of reluctance, reluctance to completely give."[35]

Though Ashby was a picture of calm, he was pushing himself to the limit, working all the hours in the day to make the film as good as it could be. His efforts, however, were lost on UA. During the period when he was rewriting with Rudy Wurlitzer, he came home to find a script report on *Coming Home:* "The first two goddamn paragraphs were about how I had miscast the film, how I'd made this horrible mistake—and it didn't matter what the hell I did with the screenplay, because it wouldn't work anyway." Mike Medavoy and the other UA execs were due to visit the set the following day, and as he worked through the night, Ashby became increasingly angry. In the morning, he phoned Hellman and told him, "Call Mike Medavoy's office and tell them if they come on the set, I go off the set."[36]

The culmination of Luke and Sally's romance came in the scene where they made love for the first time. From the start, everyone had wanted to represent the reality of paraplegics' lives and felt that this scene should be no exception. An artist's model was used as a body double, and when Fonda saw the footage, she was upset. Both she and Ashby knew paraplegics could sometimes get erections, even prolonged ones, but Fonda had wanted Luke and Sally's lovemaking to involve oral rather than penetrative sex. Ashby, however, had used the body double in such a way as to suggest the latter. "Aha," Fonda thought, "when it comes to shooting my close-ups, I won't move, so he won't be able to cut it in." With only Ashby and Haskell Wexler there and sheets draped over the bed to ensure privacy, Fonda shot her scene and was fully focused on what she was doing when Voight whispered, "Jane, Hal's yelling at you." Suddenly, Fonda heard Ashby saying, "Ride him, goddammit!"[37]

Wexler continued shooting the scene, but Fonda froze, refusing to comply with Ashby's wishes. He continued to shout, "Move your body, goddammit!" but Fonda would not. "Finally, he gave up and stormed off the set," Fonda remembers. "I felt bad. I'd never seen Hal mad; he was usually so mellow."[38] When Fonda saw the way Ashby had cut the scene, however, she was pleased with the results. His editing implied that Luke gave Sally orgasmic oral sex, and it was a great, sensual advert for the sensitivity and sexual prowess of paraplegics. (Fonda later said that Ron Kovic told her the scene had improved his sex life immeasurably.)

Ashby knew that the film's final sequence—Bob Hyde's suicide intercut with a speech Luke gives to a group of high school students—was integral to its success both as a representation of an America crippled by war and as a piece of dramatic filmmaking. Ashby felt that the most honest and powerful statements were not rehearsed and eloquent but faltering and heartfelt, so Luke's speech was completely unscripted. The day before the scene was shot, Voight called up his paraplegic vet friends and asked them what they would say in that situation, what he *should* say. He absorbed it all but still was unsure that he would be able to express it properly. Ashby just looked at him and said quietly, "You got it."[39]

As Voight sat there in his wheelchair, he looked at the kids in the audience. They weren't real high school students there to listen to a speech, just extras. "I knew they weren't interested," says Voight, "and I was determined I was going to reach those kids."[40] The resulting speech, from the moment Luke has to lower the microphone to wheelchair level to his tearful plea to think before enlisting, was instinctive and natural and deeply moving.

Salt's original idea for the film's climax involved Bob Hyde taking hostages, killing one of them, and dying in a SWAT shoot-out on the freeway believing he was back in 'Nam, but Ashby scrapped it, sure he had seen this ending on television late one night. More significantly, he refused to use it because of the responsibility he felt not to portray Vietnam vets as crazed killers.

Ashby regretted that there was not more of Bob Hyde's character throughout the film so that the audience would know him better and his suicide would be more understandable. Hyde represented the massed ranks of the American armed forces, and Ashby felt that his death "should be lyrical and a sort of heroic suicide."[41] Hellman, Voight, Fonda, and Dern all put forward suggestions about how he should end his life, but in the end Ashby decided to use his own idea of Hyde striding into the ocean. "I thought it was pretty interesting," Ashby said, "and it moved me a lot."[42] The sea held a special fascination for Ashby. He loved it but confessed that it called to him sometimes. In moments of uncharacteristic openness, Ashby would tell the story of how, during his dark days at the end of the 1960s, he had himself decided to commit suicide by swimming as far as he could out to sea. He went to the army and navy store to buy a bathing suit for the occasion, but when he couldn't find one, he thought to himself, "What am I doing?" and decided not to go through with it.[43]

Bob Hyde, on the other hand, found a fitting outfit for his send-off, turning up to take the "long swim" in full regimental dress. A skeleton crew assembled at Redondo Beach at 5:30 A.M. Ashby didn't rehearse the scene but told Haskell Wexler to let Dern undress and walk into the sea as slowly as felt right. After one take, Ashby took Dern aside and said, "I want you to come with me for five minutes." He took him to his trailer and played him the song "Once I Was" by Tim Buckley. "I want to tell you a story," he said, and told him how Buckley had auditioned to play Woody in *Bound for Glory* but had tragically died just days later. "I owe this guy big time," Ashby said, "and his song is going to be the end of this movie."[44]

They went out again, and the scene Ashby captured is as moving and as lyrical as he could have hoped. Dern played it out without knowing that it was not Bob Hyde's suicide Ashby was watching but himself walking into the water and swimming out to sea, washing away all the pain in his life that stemmed from his father's own suicide thirty-six years earlier. When Dern came out of the water, Ashby was crying. He went over to Dern, took him in his arms, and held him. Nothing was said, but nothing needed to be said.

The main shoot of *Coming Home* finished on April 23, and Ashby threw a big wrap party, inviting the numerous paraplegics who appeared in the film as special guests. Fonda made an emotional speech, after which they watched half an hour of footage featuring the paras. "They went crazy," says Voight. "It was their film. Jane and I were just extras walking through the background. Two best buddies got drunk and broke each other's noses in a fist fight in wheelchairs and the whole thing was wild."[45]

There were, however, still additional sequences of Bob Hyde's "R&R" break to be shot in Hong Kong, and on April 30, a lightweight crew, including Ashby, Fonda, Dern, Wexler, and Schroeder, arrived in the British colony, one of the most densely populated places on earth. Filming proved problematic as people kept staring directly at the camera, and Wexler had to hide in the back of a station wagon to get his shots. By the final day, Schroeder says, "Everybody on the set was sick, and it ended up being me as the 1st A.D. [assistant director] and the make-up person's assistant. We had three locations in one day; we were so proud because we got everything done and even wrapped early."[46] Finally, Ashby could relax as he and Schroeder, a keen and talented photographer, took a few days off to explore and take pictures of the vibrant, bustling city.

Afterward, they flew on to Cannes, where *Bound for Glory* was in competition. Back in the United States, UA released the film first on a test basis in New York, Los Angeles, and Denver but decided to hold its general release until after the Oscar nominations came out. The film earned six nominations, including Best Picture, but, disappointingly, Ashby was not nominated as Best Director, and Mike Haller's production design was also inexplicably overlooked. Up against two very big films, *Network* and *Rocky, Bound for Glory* was never expected to come away with much, and nominees Robert Getchell, Bob Jones (as editor), costume designer William Theiss, and Leventhal and Blumofe (for Best Picture) all left empty-handed. Nevertheless, there were deserved triumphs for Haskell Wexler's cinematography and Leonard Rosenman's score, and the film was also honored with a raft of nominations (though few victories) at the other principal nights in the awards season. It earned a disappointing $3 million, but Mike Medavoy regarded it as a very successful film. "It didn't make any money," he says, "but it was nominated for the Academy Award, and it's a landmark film. When I think about the films that I'm really proud to be a part of, that's one of them."[47]

Bound for Glory was also shortlisted for the Palme d'Or at Cannes, but the award was given to Paolo and Vittorio Taviani's *Padre Padrone.* Pierre Sauvage, the editor of the *Cannes Daily,* who interviewed Ashby during the festival, wrote to him afterward, reporting: "The jury verdict was rather controversial and unpopular. 'Tacky' was the way Bob Altman put it to Pauline Kael as we stood around nervously at the airport the following day."[48] But Ashby's disappointment was not great as his focus now was entirely on *Coming Home.*

His most immediate problem was that his editor came to him saying he didn't understand the material, that it didn't cut together. As his new cutter was clearly not a suitable replacement for Bob Jones, Ashby decided to take a risk and promote Donny Zimmerman, who had been on his editorial team since *The Landlord,* to chief editor. It would be his first film in charge, but Ashby knew that Zimmerman understood him and the way he worked as well as anyone.

Over the course of the summer, Ashby let his love of late 1960s music permeate *Coming Home;* the Rolling Stones were featured most prominently, which Ashby explained was because he'd been hanging out with Mick Jagger. He decided to have songs from 1966–1968 wall-to-wall throughout the film, as he had also planned to do in *Shampoo.*

Careful positioning of tracks heightened the impact of already powerful scenes, the music underscoring the emotion of the action, sometimes reinforcing images, sometimes acting as a counterpoint. Ashby wanted *Coming Home* to be "a new kind of musical" in which the music would remind the audience what they were doing at the time they first heard the song, allowing them to "drift in and out with the music. It can cause them to linger over a certain point, or take them somewhere else."[49] Hellman and UA were resistant to the idea owing to the cost, but this obstacle was overcome when the musicians, who were sympathetic to the film's message, gave Ashby the songs at discounted rates.

Late in the year, Ashby gathered the actors and crew together for a screening of a two-hour-and-forty-minute rough cut. Though most people were very moved by it, the abiding memory of the screening was Fonda's husband, politician Tom Hayden, coming out afterward and saying to Jon Voight as he passed him, "Nice try."[50] Hayden's cutting comment was possibly due to his anger at Fonda's sex scene with Voight (Henry Fonda demanded that the scene be cut entirely), but Ashby too saw weaknesses in the cut. He set to work tightening the film, giving the three protagonists equal prominence in the latter stages of the film. Fonda, the unenlightened woman who has her eyes opened to the nature of war through her relationship with one of its victims, was the person Ashby finally chose to close on, leaving the audience to ponder how she had grown through the course of the film.

In January 1978, a few weeks before its release, there was a highly positive special screening of *Coming Home* arranged by Hellman in Washington for veterans' groups that turned likely opponents into strong supporters. Later that month, however, the film's chance of success was dealt a huge blow when Arthur Krim and the UA top brass (including Mike Medavoy) had a falling out with Transamerica, UA's owners, and quit to form a new company, Orion. The people who had championed and were emotionally attached to *Coming Home* were replaced by new staff who viewed it as a financial liability. Rather than risk losing even more money by properly promoting it, they set out to bury it. Due for release in mid-February, *Coming Home* was to start its Los Angeles run in the third largest screen in an anonymous cinema on Wilshire Boulevard, where UA calculated it was guaranteed to be ignored.

Ashby and Hellman were distraught and faced a battle to save their film. Their relationship up to this point had been patchy at best: Hellman was a creative producer, while Ashby, who was allergic to producers, thought that *creative producer* was a contradiction in terms. Hellman often praised Ashby (and Ashby was very receptive to praise), but he also questioned his decisions when necessary (and that got Ashby's back up). They were neighbors and rode to work in the same car every morning; depending on recent dealings, either Ashby would be talkative and pleasant, or the entire journey would pass in silence. During postproduction, Ashby was reluctant to tell Hellman about screenings, and Don Zimmerman went behind Ashby's back to keep him informed. Once, a fully dressed Hellman confronted Ashby in his steam room and accused him of not telling him about screenings; an awkward Ashby, naked except for a towel, replied that he wasn't trying to conceal anything from him.

The UA crisis, however, forced them to band together. "We were working as an absolute team," says Hellman, "and that's when our friendship started."[51] Hellman was experienced in dealing with cinemas and pulled some strings to have the film moved to a much more prominent theater in Westwood. Ashby and Hellman then flew to New York and spent a week preparing for the film's opening. On February 15, the day of the first New York screening, there was a line all the way down the block, despite the film's controversial subject matter and the fact that it had been poorly publicized. In the queue was a man in a wheelchair, and Ashby and Hellman realized that they had, ironically, forgotten about disabled access; there were steps leading into the cinema and then an escalator to take people to the screen one level up. As Ashby and Hellman helped carry the man into the cinema and upstairs, no one took any notice of him. After the film, however, he was surrounded by people eager to talk to and help him.

Back in the 1950s, when Ashby was envisioning his future as a director, he had decided he wanted to make films that made a difference and changed the way people saw things. *Coming Home* was the film he'd been waiting all those years to make. Fonda, Hellman, and Ashby knew from the outset that if it were too preachy, it would fall flat on its face, so Ashby avoided polemics, favoring instead a documentary feel that brought viewers into the reality of the characters' lives. When Luke makes his impassioned speech to the high school pupils, it is much more personal than it is political. *Coming Home* was not a film about war or politics; it was a film about people whose lives are inextricably linked to war and politics.

At the start of the film, when Bob Hyde is asked what Sally thinks of the war, he says, "I don't think she really understands it all, but she accepts it." *Coming Home* was aimed at people like Sally who didn't understand but accepted, and with Fonda's character as their guide, it hoped to change their minds. The film is marked by its pauses and moments of silence, which allow viewers to absorb, just as Sally does, what they have just seen—from corridors full of paraplegics in wheelchairs to a plane returning home carrying the walking wounded, men on stretchers, and coffins draped in the Stars and Stripes. Without imposing its views on the audience, it simply presents a situation, allowing audiences to make their own judgments.

"I identify with all my characters in one way or another," Ashby said. "I never sat in a wheelchair like a Vietnam veteran, that's true. But in a sense, I transcend that reality somewhere inside me when I go to make a film like *Coming Home*. It then becomes what I would do, how I would feel if I were this particular human being in this particular situation."[52] Ashby could so easily relate to his characters because he always looked to draw out similarities with himself: he was Sally's naïveté, Luke's anger and hope, and Bob's tragic darkness. Ashby himself appears in a telling cameo in the film's climactic sequence, waving to Fonda and Penelope Milford as he drives past with Mike Haller in a Porsche Speedster that is identical to Fonda's. It was not only a return to his Hitchcockian cameos but also a mark of his affinity with the characters.

The critical reaction to *Coming Home* was decidedly mixed, which was not surprising given that—with the exception of the gung-ho John Wayne vehicle *Green Berets* (1968)—it was the first Hollywood film to tackle the subject of Vietnam. It received raves from *Variety* and the *Hollywood Reporter* as well as from *Time* and Rex Reed in the *Daily News*, who lauded the performances of Fonda, Voight, Dern, and Milford. Ashby was particularly happy to hear it favorably compared to William Wyler's *The Best Years of Our Lives* (1946), which dealt with World War II vets' return to civilian life (and happier still to learn later that Wyler himself had seen *Coming Home* and was a strong supporter). However, other prominent reviewers like Pauline Kael and the

New York Times' Vincent Canby complained that it pulled its punches politically and tried to please too many people, and Charles Champlin in the *Los Angeles Times* heaped praise on the film yet had reservations (as did others) about its persistent sound track.

However, the public reaction to the film was what really mattered to Ashby, as the more people who saw the film, the more there would be whose horizons were broadened. A cautious UA marketed the film as a romantic movie, stressing the Fonda-Voight relationship rather than the issue of the war. These ads, however, had the desired effect, and audiences flocked to see *Coming Home,* which chalked up more than $8 million and was one of UA's biggest successes of the year. For Ashby, the film was a personal triumph because of the profound impact it had on American moviegoers. "I feel as though people are starting to listen," he said, "and that's as much as I can ask for. . . . I don't think I'll ever be totally happy, but I feel satisfied right now with what I'm able to do."[53]

17

Double Feature

> The strain is beginning to show on the cast and crew. This is not what you'd call a carefree, happy set. There have been firings, and Hal Ashby has been doing a lot of yelling lately.
> —Journalist Bruce Cook on visiting the *Hamster of Happiness* shoot

> I was thoroughly at home inside of *Being There,* in significant measure because of Ashby's inarticulate empathy. The director loves his actors and his work, and that seemed just exactly right at this time with this part.
> —Melvyn Douglas

"I've always led a very simple life," Ashby reflected in early 1978. "Materially, I'm living very comfortably; I can afford the things I need. But it's not as if I've been striving for all this. It's just starting to happen now and it's all very weird to me. I just won't let it take me over. . . . I won't lose that basic value." Ashby's commitment to basic values was apparent in his filmmaking as well. In the face of the success of an emerging breed of blockbusters such as *Jaws* (1975), *Star Wars* (1977), and *Close Encounters of the Third Kind* (1977), he expressed the hope that "more films move toward personal cinema because that is where I'm at. These big-budgeted, splashy movies will always be around, they have great appeal for many. . . . But I intend to keep making personal pictures."[1]

At the time of *Coming Home*'s release, Ashby was closing in on his next project. He desperately wanted to do *The Hawkline Monster,* but he felt Richard Brautigan's screenplay was not up to scratch, so he was rewriting it himself. *American Me,* a project about low-rider gangs in East Los Angeles that Ashby's friend Lou Adler had planned to produce a few years earlier, was ready to go at Paramount. It had a strong romantic element, and though Ashby was attracted to the subject, again he felt the writing was not strong enough. By May 1978, he had passed on *American Me* (which finally appeared in 1992, directed by Edward James Olmos) and was considering *Popeye,* a live-action musical of the cartoon that was to star Dustin Hoffman and be produced by Robert Evans. Working with Hoffman was a big draw, and though a deal seemed to be in the offing—Hoffman, Evans, and Ashby went out to celebrate with vodka and caviar—Ashby withdrew after Hoffman fell out with Jules Feiffer, the satirical cartoonist hired to write the screenplay. (Robert Altman took Ashby's place and Robin Williams Hoffman's, and the resulting film was released in 1980.)

Ashby had not had an agent since Mike Medavoy moved to United Artists (UA) and instead employed his business manager, Larry Reynolds, and entertainment lawyer Jack Schwartzman to handle his affairs. Schwartzman, who was Ashby's friend as well as attorney, became a powerful Hollywood player after he joined the Coppola clan by marrying Talia Shire, Francis Ford Coppola's sister. Ever since Ashby had bought the rights to *Hawkline* in 1975, Schwartzman had insisted it was "the *special* one," identifying it as a potential goldmine if Jack Nicholson and another major male star (Dustin Hoffman and then Clint Eastwood were both considered) were to sign on.[2] MGM was very keen on the project and regularly called Ashby about it, but he was always too busy with either *Bound for Glory* or *Coming Home* and, in any case, knew the script still needed work.

In 1978, Schwartzman began negotiating a multipicture deal with UA and told Ashby that an "unprecedented" deal for *Hawkline* would be at the heart of it. However, when the talks with UA foundered, Schwartzman turned his attention to Lorimar, the television company that made *The Waltons* and *Eight Is Enough,* which had recently expanded into films. Peter Bart, previously Robert Evans's lieutenant at Paramount, had been appointed head of the film division, but Ashby didn't want to work with him after negative experiences on *Harold and Maude.* Lorimar, however, was extremely keen to attract someone of Ashby's considerable cachet, so Schwartzman opportunistically brokered an agreement where his newly formed JS Productions would act as the middleman between Ashby and Lorimar.

The reason Ashby was drawn to Lorimar, a company with no track record in Hollywood, was because it was offering him a very attractive deal. Not only would there be a fifty-fifty split of profits between Ashby and Lorimar, but he was to have full creative control over his films and a say in their distribution and marketing. Ashby stressed that the deal gave him more freedom: "I have more creative control and more budget control. I will have my own auditor and send Lorimar costs and projected costs every week from location. There's a good level of trust in that. Also, when I finish the films, I can suggest methods of distribution. I might think that one studio would be the best distributor for a particular film. And I might wind up in a better place financially."[3]

Despite the Hollywood trend toward blockbusters, Bart idealistically pledged to "make commercial movies that have innovative themes and subject matter," adding that the "key word is 'flexibility.'"[4] Proving just how willing Lorimar was to accommodate Ashby's taste, his deal included three initial projects for development: Rudy Wurlitzer's then-untitled triangular love story *Journey to India;* Bob Downey's *Victor Hiatus* (a.k.a. *Almost Together*), about a man randomly selected to save the world who is more interested in getting laid; and *Roadshow,* a modern-day Robin Hood story by novelist William Hjortsberg. In essence, these projects were Ashby's attempt to set up films with his friends and help them out financially in the process; Downey recalls that, at Ashby's request, Lorimar paid him to write the script—despite the fact that he'd already written it.

When the Lorimar deal was announced in early May 1978, the big surprise was that Ashby's first film for the company was to be *Being There,* which had suddenly been revived. It was five years since Sellers and Ashby had first talked about making the film, but the two had stayed in touch; Sellers would call Ashby and spend hours reading scripts to him, doing all the voices. Sellers had been wooing Jerzy Kosinski since the early 1970s, trying to convince the novelist to let him play the idiot savant Chance the gardener, yet, ironically, *Being There* came together for a different reason. In late 1977, Kosinski had told producer Andrew Braunsberg about plans to turn *Being There* into a film and was so impressed by his advice that he asked Braunsberg himself to produce the film. Braunsberg, who had produced several films with Roman Polanski, contacted Ashby through their mutual friend Jack Nicholson, who felt that Ashby was the ideal director. As Sellers recalled, "[Ashby and I] made a promise to each other that if we ever got a break with it, he would come to me, or I would come to him. And suddenly Hal phoned me one day in Vienna, and said, 'I hesitate to say this, but I think we've got it off the ground. It's really going to go.'"[5]

Sellers's involvement in the film, however, was still in doubt. When approached by Braunsberg to direct *Being There,* Ashby had said, "Sure, I'd be interested, but only with Peter Sellers."[6] Ryan O'Neal was Kosinski's choice, and Braunsberg too was unconvinced that Sellers—a fat, aging comic actor without significant box-office clout—was right for the part. So Sellers and Ashby arranged to have dinner in Los Angeles with the two doubters. Sellers turned up with what Braunsberg recalls was "a triple chin" but assured all present that he was going to a Bel Air clinic to have a facelift that was guaranteed to make him look the part.[7] As soon as Sellers's casting had been approved, the Lorimar deal was quickly brokered.

Kosinski, who had written a screenplay of the novel back in 1971, was hired to adapt *Being There,* and the production's start date was set for October. Ashby, however, was impatient to get on with actually making a film and in late June announced that he would shoot *The Hamster of Happiness* back-to-back with *Being There.* Frustrated with the amount of time—eighteen months, on average—it took him to make a picture from start to finish, he planned to shoot two films consecutively and then edit them simultaneously. "After being chained to one film for over a year," he explained, "you're no longer thinking straight. Your intuition is gone. You're stale. Editing two films at the same time should be fresher, healthier and less rigid. Without being too great a drain on me. I think it will enhance both films by keeping me from freezing on one set of problems."[8] He was very keen to increase his productivity and, with his fiftieth birthday just over a year away, wanted to up the pace while he still could.

Though *Hamster* seemed to come suddenly out of nowhere, Ashby had in fact read the script in 1971, when its author, Charles Eastman, had already been touting it around for two years. Eastman was one of Hollywood's most respected script doctors and the writer of *Honeybear, I Think I Love You,* which attained legendary status in Hollywood as possibly the greatest script never to be filmed. He was also briefly a director, but a two-picture deal with Warner Brothers came apart after the first film, *The All-American Boy,* spent years on the shelf before finally being released (in 1973) to a poor critical response. *The Hamster of Happiness,* the second film in the Warners deal, was canceled as a result, but Eastman had held on to the hope that he might still direct it one day. A few years later, Ashby vainly tried to convince Mike Medavoy to let Eastman make the film at UA, and by 1978 Eastman was in such dire financial straits that he was forced to sell the property to an anonymous buyer.

The buyer represented Robert Blake and film and music producer James William Guercio (director of Blake's 1973 cult hit *Electra Glide in Blue*), who then approached Ashby to direct *Hamster.* Despite his disappointment that he would not be able to direct the film, Eastman was pleased: "I felt Hal could emotionally connect to the film, liked my work, and was on my team." Eastman thought Ashby had the right sensibility. He had in fact written his "first and only fan letter" to him after seeing *The Landlord.*[9]

He was less pleased, however, about who now owned his script, as Blake (rather like David Carradine after *Kung Fu*) was not perceived as a serious actor after his stint in the television series *Baretta.* Unusually short, and lacking conventional good looks, Blake was nevertheless a capable actor and one of the more intriguing leading men of the 1970s. Moreover, Ashby had longlisted him as a casting option for Luke in *Coming Home,* Woody in *Bound for Glory,* and Johnny Pope in *Shampoo* and looked forward to using him in *Hamster,* for which his unglamorous, offbeat look was ideal. The film was about salt-of-the-earth people, a mechanic, Loyal Muke, who marries waitress and singer Dinette Dusty while on a drunken bender and then finds himself saddled with her and her three children, Human, Iota, and Sandra Dee. It was a fable-like script full of homespun wisdom, and Ashby was keen to capture the gentle comedy in a film "about people and the way they treat each other."[10]

With only a brief preproduction period, casting had to be quick. Guercio had the amusing idea of casting the leggy Jane Fonda as Dusty alongside the diminutive Blake's Loyal, but Ashby felt she was too obviously glamorous and suggested instead Melinda Dillon, his leading lady from *Bound for Glory,* who had just scored a huge hit with *Close Encounters of the Third Kind.* Blake demurred, and instead Ashby ended up casting Barbara Harris, the high-strung star of *Freaky Friday* (1976).

Guercio, who was in any case busy working with Steve McQueen on the script of *Tom Horn* (1980), realized that his and Ashby's vision for *Hamster* differed significantly and agreed he would visit the set only if Ashby were behind schedule or over budget. With Guercio, a voluntarily absent producer; Blake, a star who Guercio recalls was "in love" with his director;[11] and a budget of just under $5 million, Ashby found himself in what looked like an ideal situation. The shoot, however, would turn out to be his most challenging so far.

Mike Haller stayed behind in Los Angeles to work on ideas for *Being There*, and Ashby went off to El Paso, Texas, to shoot *Hamster* with a crew that included Haskell Wexler, Chuck Mulvehill, and Dianne Schroeder (who was both his assistant and the film's photographer). Ashby was unfortunately shooting from mid-July until the end of September, the most brutally hot time of the year, and had to tough it out in the desert during a record heat wave, the sun burning down from cloudless skies, and the temperatures up to 110°F in the shade. Ashby tried to shoot as late in the day as possible, but during daytime scenes everybody suffered from the excruciating heat. In one scene, Blake and Harris were in their car with the eponymous hamster running across the windshield; however, the heat was so intense that the hamsters kept on dying.

Ashby had been unable to involve Eastman in the film and had not had his usual sessions with the writer. He hadn't even tinkered with the script on his own. Ultimately, he says, "I felt pretty much obligated at that point to go as much with that script as I possibly could. . . . I just went with it; it was a script I liked a lot. But I wouldn't normally do that, and I'm not sure I would do it again."[12] The script was unconventional, written in a loose, free-form style with unpunctuated dialogue open to Ashby and the actors' interpretation. Ashby said that he would be "delighted" if he could come away with four or five different editing options per scene, "as boggling as that is when you come to look at the film. . . . I'm not intimidated by film, or much of anything else."[13] He was helped in the shooting process by the fact that, for the first time, he had video playback, which allowed him to watch a take straight away, rather than having to wait to see the dailies.

It quickly became apparent that the shoot was going to be a test of endurance; Haskell Wexler described it as a period defined by "confusion and division."[14] Blake, who owned the *Hamster* script and was nominally Ashby's employer, hired half the crew himself, so the company was awkwardly split into "Ashby's people" and "Blake's people." There was palpable tension throughout between the two factions, tension that worsened as Ashby's and Blake's relationship deteriorated. "Once when I was in front of the camera," says Blake, "and I was all knotted up trying to be profound and trying to show Hal how much I could feel, he said—very loud so all the crew and all the spectators could hear—'Ah, Robert! Just hit the marks and say the jokes and siddown!'" Though Blake looked back on this as Ashby "getting things in perspective" for him, at the time it stung.[15]

Blake had been a child actor in the *Our Gang* serials, and it seemed his early fame had left him with psychological scars. "He was very difficult, very moody," says Dianne Schroeder. "All I remember is he saw me once take a photograph and threatened if he saw the camera again, he'd break it."[16] Talking during the making of *Hamster* about how he approached his work, Blake said, "If you fight with me, I will fight you forever. But if you mess with me, I'll kill you."[17]

Jack and Beth Ashby visited the set and remember Hal struggling to work with Blake, who was constantly getting on his back. Blake called Eastman and told him his script was being ruined. He then phoned Guercio and said, "I don't like the way things are going. You gotta come down here." When Guercio arrived in El Paso, he found that things were, as he said, "messy" owing to the amount of drugs on set (Eastman claims there was even a cocaine budget), though there is no evidence that Ashby himself was indulging. In any case, Ashby was perfectly on schedule and within the budget. When it transpired that Blake's greatest gripe was to do with his costar, Guercio left telling him, "Any problems with Barbara, you gotta talk to Hal. He's the fuckin' director."[18]

Ashby's biggest challenge was to work around the deep hatred between his two leads. In theory, Blake and Harris made an interesting union of opposites, the gruff street brawler alongside the dainty New England princess, but in real life opposites did anything but attract. Their performances clashed horribly, Blake's shouty, over-the-top theatrics very much at odds with Harris's restraint. In an interview during filming, Ashby said that *The Hamster of Happiness* was about "two people who were at the end of their ropes and going crazy because of it," maintaining that the interplay between "Barbara and Robert works well. She's always within the character but within it she's less controlled than Robert, so you get a lot of surprise and freshness all the time. It's funny to watch the dailies. I hear myself say 'Cut!' and then laugh."[19]

Whether he was trying to put a positive spin on things or simply deluding himself, the reality was that Harris and Blake were each acting in their own film, and they were ruining Ashby's. "Both of them are nuts—certifiably over the top," says Haskell Wexler. "And they didn't try and hide their dislike of each other."[20] Blake was a loose cannon, changing tack constantly, while Harris (who was supposedly on tranquilizers) seemed to decide on one way of interpreting a scene and then stick to it no matter what. Her dislike and fear of Blake became so intense that she sometimes refused to leave her trailer. Harris was going through a period of crippling self-doubt: despite being an experienced theatrical actress, she couldn't remember her lines and had to write them on her hand or on strategically positioned bottles. It was only Ashby's admiration for her acting that made him keep faith with Harris, whose neurotic, melodramatic performances off camera tested the patience of everybody involved.

When the *Los Angeles Times* critic Charles Champlin visited the set near the end of the shoot, the two stars made no effort to hide their disdain for each other.

"We love each other," Blake told Champlin, putting his arm around Harris, "and when this is over we never want to see each other again."

Harris managed a smile.

"We got this deal that whenever she wants to be in L.A. she sends me a ticket to Baja California or any place of my choice," Blake went on, "and whenever I got to be in New York I send her and her mother tickets to Palm Beach or any place of her choice."

"It's a deal," Harris said.[21]

As shooting moved into its final month, Ashby began to feel the pressure to finish on time. It was rare for him to bring a film in on schedule, but with *Being There* due to start shooting soon after, he had very little leeway. In early September, he wrote home, saying, "All is going along pretty good—a little shaky here and there, but no real disasters."[22] Nonetheless, the final weeks were especially difficult, and Ashby uncharacteristically lost his temper a number of times; filming finally wrapped on October 3, just five days over schedule.

Although he had struggled with the cast and even been reduced to shouting at people, Ashby earned the respect of many of his collaborators on the film. Haskell Wexler talked of the continuing joys of working with his friend, Harris sang his praises unreservedly, and the veteran actor Bert Remsen (who played Voyd Dusty, Dinette's father-in-law) declared, "I'd do anything in my life to help Hal Ashby." Remsen, who called Ashby "somebody who is trying to say something special about America," explained, "He just instills in you that you have all the freedom in the world. You just feel it with him. It's a feeling of comfort. You feel completely relaxed and free."[23]

On his return to Los Angeles, Ashby learned that Peter Sellers was in the midst of making *The Prisoner of Zenda* (1979) in Vienna and, despite the fact that filming on *Being There* was scheduled to start in early November, would not be free until January. After briefly discussing the possibility of recasting the role, Ashby instead decided to push back production until Sellers was ready and spend the valuable extra months on preproduction. During the making of *Hamster,* Kosinski had produced what he considered to be close to a final draft of *Being There;* however, Ashby was unimpressed. Kosinski had rushed the screenplay, seeing it as merely a distraction from his "real work," finishing his latest novel, *Passion Play.* As a result, the screenplay (which Kosinski himself described as "competent, but . . . not inspired") lacked the quality and unique tone of the novel.[24] Ashby said that Kosinski's adaptation was "too heavy-handed" for his taste and turned it over to Bob Jones, whom he could rely on to fashion a more cinematic and nuanced screenplay.[25] Though Jones had heard rumors that Kosinski did not actually write his novels, he was shocked to find that the script he had inherited was "barely comprehensible" and began radically altering it, working more from Kosinski's original novel than from his garbled script.[26] Three weeks later, Jones had written an inspired new version. "I knew I was into the film then," said Ashby. "I'd always felt strongly about it being a film, but now I had my blueprint, my structure there. Then I sat down with Robert for three or four weeks and we worked really hard on it, eight or nine hours a day. We never worked with Jerzy on the script; [but] when we sent it to him, he loved it."[27]

The script Kosinski so approved of also included scenes that Ashby had conceived with Mike Haller inspired by Haller's scouting trip to

Washington, D.C. In *Being There,* the idiot savant Chance's simplistic statements about growth cycles and seasonal change are misinterpreted as profound economic metaphors, and he is unwittingly elevated to the position of political heavyweight. Because of the film's strong political content, Ashby had decided to move the action from New York City to the nation's capital. When in Washington, Haller had visited its black ghetto and hit on the idea that the house owned by the old man who employed Chance as a gardener and sheltered him from the outside world should be the only white holdout in the neighborhood. This idea naturally led to the interactions between Chance and the other ghetto residents when the old man's death forces him to leave his haven and go out into the world.

In his discussions with Ashby, Haller also mentioned that Caleb Deschanel, a young director of photography who had met Ashby while a film student at the University of Southern California, had just been accepted into the cinematographers' union. Ashby had kept tabs on Deschanel for over a decade and, with Haskell Wexler busy on another project, decided to hire him to shoot *Being There.* Deschanel, who was coming off shooting *More American Graffiti* (1979), read the script but struggled to see its appeal. However, after calling Ashby and hearing his descriptions of certain scenes and how he imagined the film, he suddenly became as excited as Ashby. "He told the story in such a wonderfully charming way," recalls Deschanel, "and he just had this incredible vision of it that seemed so extraordinary, so unusual, especially for an American film."[28]

Ashby and Deschanel then went on a scouting trip looking for the grand mansion that would be home to Benjamin Rand, the influential industrialist who "adopts" Chance after his limo runs him over. They went first to affluent Newport, Rhode Island, but ended up opting for the Biltmore Estate in Asheville, North Carolina, a 250-room stately home set in ten thousand acres of woodland that had been built in the late nineteenth century by George Vanderbilt. For a film about politics, wealth, and power, the awesome scale of Biltmore House and its estate perfectly embodied the trappings of success. The further fact that it had been used in only one film previously—the house's exterior appears in the 1956 Grace Kelly movie *The Swan*—made it the clear choice for the Rand Mansion.

Another integral element in the plot of *Being There* is the influence of television on Chance: for most of his cloistered life this has been his only access to the world beyond the walled garden where he works, and it has become his prime influence and guide. Ashby—who felt that television "can be the greatest tool in the world, and it can be the greatest detriment in the world"—himself tuned in only for movies, the news, and the occasional special.[29] Dianne Schroeder had a much more thorough knowledge of television culture, so he assigned her the task of finding clips to feature in the film. She ended up selecting so many clips, from drama series, game shows, and commercials, that Ashby joked that the film was "in danger of becoming a TV show, and people would be waiting for a commercial."[30] In the memorable scene in which Chance learns to kiss, however, there is a movie playing on his television set. After considering alternatives from Claude Lelouch's *Un Homme et Une Femme* (1966) and Hitchcock's *Notorious* (1946), Ashby chose the chess scene from *The Thomas Crown Affair,* not because of its personal resonance for him, but simply because it was the best passionate clinch of the three.

Production on *Being There* began in late January in Los Angeles and a week later moved to Asheville, where the majority of filming was to take place. Ashby had cast Shirley MacLaine as Eve Rand but was still pondering whom to cast as Ben Rand, whom he felt should be portrayed by someone with a real "center of strength."[31] His initial thought was Burt Lancaster, but he eventually opted for seventy-eight-year-old Melvyn Douglas, a 1930s leading man who had starred opposite Greta Garbo and Joan Crawford in his heyday and now, in his later years, exemplified fortitude tempered by a gentle humanity. For the role of the U.S. president, Ashby could not think past Jack Warden and was delighted to be working with him again, this time in happier circumstances than on *Shampoo.*

Ashby was very relaxed making *Being There,* and producer Andrew Braunsberg, who had heard stories about Ashby being difficult, was surprised by his quiet working method. Braunsberg's frequent collaborations with Roman Polanski had accustomed him to a more hands-on directorial style. "Hal," he recalled, "was invisible."[32] Ashby would say, "Let's try it again," when he wanted another take, but he held back from specific directions, which he felt were unnecessary and often counterproductive. He knew he had a reputation as a "relaxed" director but objected to the label. "I'm not laid back," he contended. "There's a tremendous energy going on all the time. What are you going to accomplish by raising your voice? Even if you're striving for some tense thing in your film, getting the crew tense isn't going to help. I went through a period in my life where I argued about everything, and I found I wasn't getting much accomplished."[33]

Fortunately, a lot was being accomplished on *Being There,* and Peter Sellers, who himself had a reputation for being difficult, was an integral part of this. Yet, just days before shooting was to begin, Sellers had had a crisis of confidence, suddenly doubting his ability to do justice to Chance the gardener. Although it was the dream role he had chased for years, he had never thought about precisely how he would play the part and now frantically searched for the two elements that would lead him to the core of the character: Chance's walk and, most important, his voice. Working alone with a tape recorder, then with his wife, Lynne Frederick, and with Ashby, Sellers perfected Chance's voice, a mid-Atlantic accent (with just a hint of Sellers's idol, Stan Laurel), clear enunciation, and a flat delivery that revealed the childlike mind behind the words.

Chance was a much more difficult character to play than his well-worn Inspector Clouseau, but once Sellers found him, he retreated inside the persona, which in fact resonated profoundly with his own sense of self. From take to take, he would tease out more and more aspects of Chance as he burrowed ever deeper into his alter ego's psyche. Sellers described the experience of working on *Being There* as "so humbling, so powerful," and would sometimes call "Cut!" in the middle of a scene because he was overwhelmed. When asked if he was all right, he would answer in a bewildered, Chance-like way, "Oh. No, no. I've just never seen anything quite like this film before."[34] Once a scene was over, more often than not he would silently withdraw to his trailer so as not to lose his connection with Chance. Sellers refused most interview requests and kept his distance from Shirley MacLaine, who complained about him going off into a corner, to which he replied, "If I hadn't I'd have broken my gardener for the day."[35] Even when he returned home to his wife, he often remained in character. Only occasionally did he return to himself, such as when he was relaxing with Jack Warden between scenes, the two raconteurs entertaining each other with acting stories until they cried with laughter.

Chance, however, never laughed and seemed to have no sense of humor, so Sellers had to be careful not to let his own laughter become part of the character. In one particular scene, he let the mask slip when he had to repeat, in his uninflected monotone, a message given to him in the ghetto: "'Now get this, honky. You go tell Rafael that I ain't taking no jive from no Western Union messenger. You tell that asshole that if he got something to tell me, to get his ass down here himself.' Then he said that I was to get my white ass out of here quick or he'd cut it." In take after take, Sellers got partway through with a straight face, then cracked up in midsentence. The lines tickled Sellers so much that in the end Ashby had to cut the dialogue.

Ashby did his best to nurture Sellers's talent and create an environment in which he could give his best. He was in awe of Sellers and let the actor's placid, unhurried rhythm set the film's pace. Ashby and Sellers worked together closely, sometimes walking off, deep in discussion, leaving the crew unsure of when exactly they would start shooting the scene. Just after Sellers's death, Ashby recalled, "I always felt while looking at his eyes how I'd never talked with anyone who was so totally vulnerable. He always let me into him through his eyes to places so deep that I wouldn't ever try to know. Places that only he, if he were aware of it at all, could know about."[36]

Ashby also had an ideal working relationship with Melvyn Douglas, whom he felt added a spiritual quality to the film owing to the fervent conviction with which he spoke his lines. Douglas called Ashby "a grown-up child" and said that his "inarticulate empathy" and "free-wheeling approach released a creativity, a kind of goofiness" in him.[37] He quickly got into the spirit of experimentation that Ashby fostered on his sets, sometimes even coming up with ideas that were too wild for Ashby to use. (One scene Douglas devised, in which Rand and Chance walk hand in hand, even unsettled the famously unshakable Sellers.)

Ashby was excited about the simplicity and clarity that Sellers and Douglas were achieving in their performances and one Sunday afternoon enthused to Rudy Wurlitzer: "Rudy, the way it's going with these characters and what's happening with them, I could have this guy walking on water at the end of the film." After a pause, he said, "I think I *will* have him walking on water at the end of the film."[38] The ending as written in the script had Eve walking up to Chance in the woods and telling him

[Left] Ashby's mother, Eileen, around 1909, the year she married Ashby's father. (Courtesy Jack and Beth Ashby.) [Right] James Thomas Ashby, Ashby's father, in the mid-1910s. (Courtesy Jack and Beth Ashby.)

Eileen and James with Ardith and "Hetz," just before James left on his mission to South Africa. (Courtesy Jack and Beth Ashby.)

Hal and Jack were nigh inseparable as kids: [left] posing, ca. 1932; [right] playing cowboys in their backyard, ca. 1933; and [below] looking grown up, ca. 1936. (Courtesy Jack and Beth Ashby.)

[Above] The Big Mug, which Ashby's father opened in the mid-1930s, was a popular watering hole in Ogden. (Courtesy Jack and Beth Ashby.)

[Right] Hal "shagging" milk, ca. 1941. (Courtesy Jack and Beth Ashby.)

Ashby's high school yearbook picture, taken in 1946, around the time he started dating his first wife, Lavon Compton. (Courtesy Jack and Beth Ashby.)

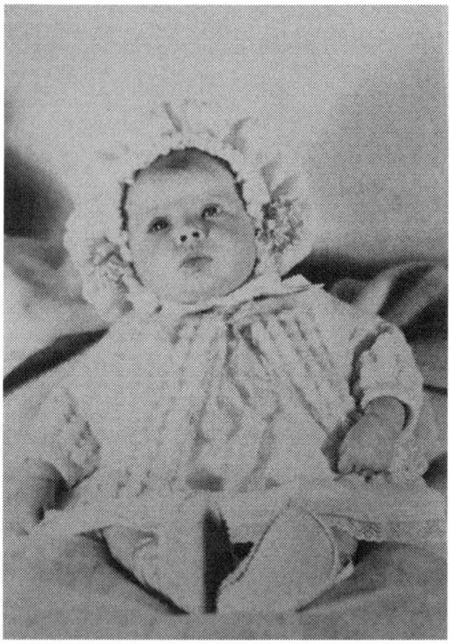

[Right] Ashby's only child, Leigh, here aged six months, not long before he left. (Courtesy Leigh MacManus.)

[Below] Ashby in Los Angeles with girlfriend Janice Austin and the bandleader Woody Herman in late 1948. (Courtesy Janice Lindquist.)

Ashby with one of his bohemian Los Angeles friends, Bill Box, ca. 1953. (Courtesy Bill Box.)

Sporting shades with effortless cool during his beatnik phase, July 1956. (Courtesy Bill Box.)

Maloy, Ashby's third wife, caught the photography bug from Ashby's friend Bill Otto. (Courtesy Leigh MacManus.)

She was never happier than when painting with her animals around her. (Courtesy Chris Cutri.)

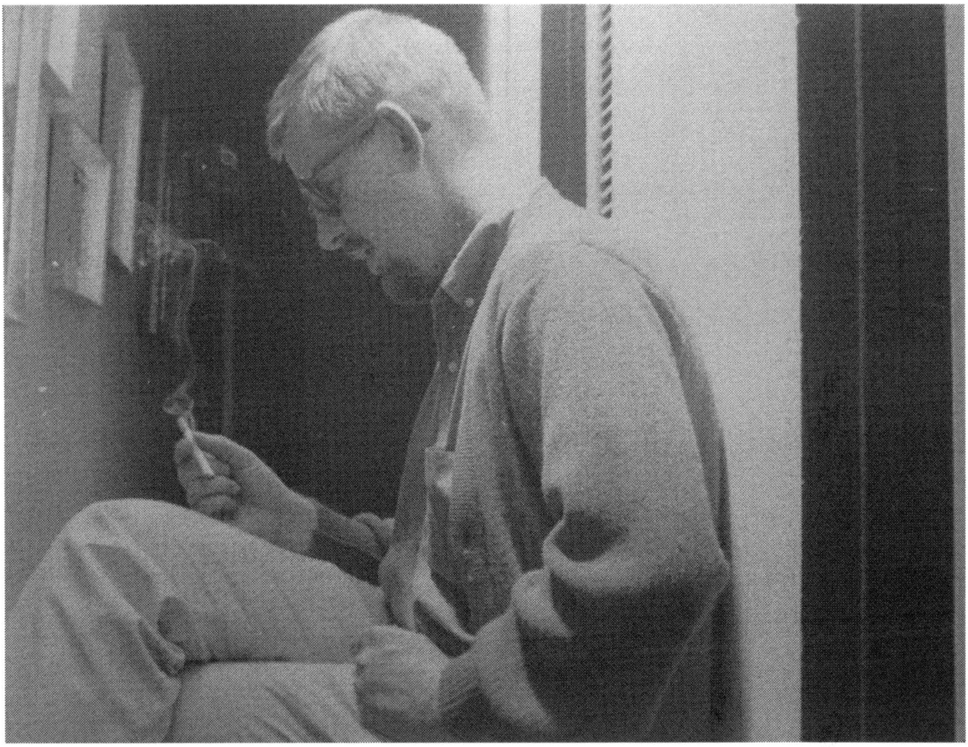

Already in the late 1950s, the highly driven Ashby knew he wanted to become a director. (Courtesy Leigh MacManus.)

Ashby almost didn't turn up to the Oscars the year he won the Best Editing award for *In the Heat of the Night,* presented to him by Dame Edith Evans. (Courtesy AMPAS.)

But afterward he seemed glad that he did. (Courtesy Jack and Beth Ashby.)

In a post-Oscar glow: probably the last time that Hetz, Ashby, Ardith, Eileen, and Jack were all together. (Courtesy Jack and Beth Ashby.)

Ashby's fourth wife, Shirley, with Teeg and Carrie, ca. 1970. (Courtesy Jack and Beth Ashby.)

Finally a director: Ashby, his mentor and friend Norman Jewison, and the actor Beau Bridges on the set of *The Landlord*. (Courtesy Photofest.)

Ashby's fifth (and last) wife, Joan Marshall, seen here in a publicity shot from 1958. (Courtesy Photofest.)

[Above] The unlikely lovers (Bud Cort and Ruth Gordon) meet for the first time in *Harold and Maude*. (Courtesy Photofest.)

[Below] Michael Haller, Ashby's production designer and great friend, shows Bud Cort how to wield a blowtorch. (Courtesy Bret Haller.)

[Right] Ashby, in befuddled guru mode, laughs with a bloodstained Bud Cort. (Courtesy Jack and Beth Ashby.)

[Left] A rare shot of Ashby, who was infamous for not returning calls, on the phone. (Courtesy Jack and Beth Ashby.)

Sporting a post-arrest trimmed beard, Ashby talks to Jack Nicholson and Otis Young during the shooting of *The Last Detail*. (Courtesy Photofest.)

[Left] Warren Beatty and Julie Christie in *Shampoo*. (Courtesy Photofest.)

[Below] Ashby had to cede much of his power to Beatty, *Shampoo*'s writer, producer, and star. (Courtesy Photofest.)

A typically cheery Ashby, ca. 1975. (Author's collection.)

[Right] The director with his Woody Guthrie, David Carradine, on the set of *Bound for Glory*. (Courtesy Jack and Beth Ashby.)

[Below] Ashby and longtime friend Haskell Wexler quickly got fed up with the problematic trains. (Courtesy AMPAS.)

Living the boxcar life, flanked by Wexler and his son Jeff, the sound mixer. (Courtesy Jeff Wexler.)

Ashby's friends say that Dianne Schroeder was the only woman who ever understood him. (Courtesy Jack and Beth Ashby.)

A workaholic who barely slept, Ashby seldom allowed himself such moments of relaxation. (Courtesy Leigh MacManus.)

[Left] After wrapping *Coming Home* in Hong Kong, a laid-back Ashby visited Cannes in 1977, where *Bound for Glory* was in competition. (Courtesy Pierre Sauvage.)

[Below] The romance between Jane Fonda's and Jon Voight's characters in *Coming Home* helped mainstream audiences connect to the film's antiwar message. (Courtesy Photofest.)

[Left] Ashby and Robert Blake had a strained relationship during the making of *Second Hand Hearts*—then called *The Hamster of Happiness*. (Author's collection.)

[Below] Jack and Beth raised Ashby's spirits when they visited the *Hamster* set. (Author's collection.)

[Left] Chance (Peter Sellers) tends his garden in *Being There*, arguably Ashby's zenith. (Courtesy Photofest.)

[Below] Ashby with Jerzy Kosinski, who definitely wrote the novel but maybe not the screenplay. (Courtesy Photofest.)

Jon Voight and Burt Young in *Lookin' to Get Out*, one of four 1980s-released films taken away from Ashby in the editing room. (Author's collection.)

Ashby elicited one of Ann-Margret's best performances in *Lookin'*. (Courtesy Larry Reynolds.)

Let's Spend the Night Together gave Ashby the chance to work with two dear friends, Pablo Ferro and Mick Jagger. (Courtesy Larry Reynolds.)

[Above] On *The Slugger's Wife,* Ashby helped the actress Rebecca De Mornay with her accent problems and rescued her when a tornado overturned her trailer. (Courtesy Photofest.)

[Right] Plagued by the interfering producer Ray Stark, Ashby was always glad to have a few quiet moments alone in the dugout. (Courtesy Photofest.)

Ashby on the set of his final film, *8 Million Ways to Die*. (Courtesy Photofest.)

that she was scared and had been looking for him, to which he responds, "I've been looking for you too, Eve." Ashby, however, felt that his idea of Chance walking on water would make a much better conclusion.

He called up Bob Downey, who had a scene in *Greaser's Palace* (1972) in which the lead character walked on water, and asked whether he could "borrow" Downey's idea.

"Why are you asking me?" Downey said with amusement. "It's in the Bible!"

"Who do I call?" Ashby deadpanned.[39]

Downey advised Ashby to use a particular type of platform, which he could borrow from an airport, that would allow him to get the shot cheaply and easily and without the need for divine intervention. However, Lorimar's representative on the set was alarmed and tried to get people close to Ashby to dissuade him from such a bizarre idea. Aware that he was in danger of losing the scene, and possibly the movie, if Lorimar got wind of what he was doing, Ashby summoned the young man to him and said, "I'm going to ask you to make a decision right now that's going to affect the rest of your life. I'm going to ask you to decide whose side you're on. . . . This is it, kid. Decide. Are you on the side of art or commerce?"[40] The "kid" chose to be loyal to Ashby.

When the scene was shot, Sellers left his umbrella by the tree for the first two takes but for the third took it with him as he walked out across the water. In a moment of inspiration, he stopped, dipped the umbrella into the water, and then started walking once again.

The new ending caused a great deal of controversy among the cast and crew, and Shirley MacLaine was one of its main detractors. Unlike Sellers and Douglas, she did not adapt quickly to working with Ashby and initially pressed him to explain Eve's actions, rather than searching for the motivation herself.

"It's almost like he was never there, really," says MacLaine. "He'd walk on the set wearing basically a janitor's outfit, and everyone thought that he was a janitor or that he came to pull the cables. That was how powerful he was in his invisibility. But then, you thought about his history, about how great he is, that's when you say, 'OK, I'm not hearing from him. He's not telling me what to do. He expects me to do it.' And that tends to stimulate creativity you didn't know you had."[41]

A particular challenge for MacLaine was preparing for the scene in the developing love story between Eve and Chance in which she misconstrues his comment "I like to watch" as a request for her to masturbate for him. A disgusted Laurence Olivier turned down the role of Ben Rand because of this scene, and the prospect of performing it was understandably daunting for MacLaine. Ashby put off filming it for as long as possible to give her time to get comfortable with the idea. When the day came, Ashby shot an incredible seventeen takes, trying to balance the needs of his actress with the knowledge that, for an edgy scene like this, he would need options in the editing room. After a while, MacLaine told Ashby she couldn't do another take. "Mmm, mmm!" Ashby laughed. "That is coffee, good to the last drop!"[42]

Lorimar had promised Ashby complete creative freedom, but it quickly became evident that "freedom" was relative. At times, Ashby had to play hardball, and he once threatened never to make another film for the studio unless he and his crew were granted the time and resources they needed. "Those guys back in the production office don't have a clue what goes on in my heart, in my head, and what I'm thinking about," Ashby said. "They don't know. They sit back there and say, 'Well, if he shoots tonight, that's going to cost $20,000.' So what!"[43]

Mostly, however, Ashby's enthusiasm for *Being There,* which he dubbed "our favorite film to be," eclipsed his concerns about Lorimar.[44] Jack and Beth Ashby found him in good spirits when they visited the set and recalled that when the actor playing the corpse of the "old man" (Chance's deceased former employer) sneezed while lying under a sheet, Ashby laughed uncontrollably for almost five minutes. The atmosphere was a world away from the tensions of *The Hamster of Happiness,* and Ashby's affection for his actors, crew, and visitors was widely remarked on. Bo Smith, who visited Asheville early on in shooting, wrote to thank Ashby, saying, "Although we found you in the midst of a hectic and intense schedule, you made us feel as comfortable and welcome as old friends. As we talked, my deep appreciation for your interest and attention was joined by an even richer realization. I came to understand that the qualities of humor, sensitivity, compassion, and extraordinary perception which so distinguish your films similarly distinguish you."[45]

These sentiments were shared by Caleb Deschanel, who relished working with someone like Ashby on only his third film. "Hal created an environment of everyone feeling welcome and creative," Deschanel says. "To this day, it's one of the best experiences I've had on a movie."[46] Ashby encouraged him to take risks, and when the cinematographer sensed that something was not quite right, Ashby always trusted his judgment. By the end of the shoot, Deschanel proclaimed, "Working with someone like Hal, you feel this incredible obligation and desire to do your best work."[47] Ashby, for his part, called Deschanel "really incredible. I can't find the words to tell you what I think of him."[48]

The warmth on set was all the more welcome given the unseasonably cold weather. In Asheville, the crew had to work wrapped in ski jackets, hats, and gloves, wading through slush and snow in freezing thirty-five-mile-an-hour winds, and the weather was no better when they traveled north in March to shoot in Washington, D.C. It was a relief to all when they returned to Los Angeles to shoot the film's final scenes.

18

Being There

> Then to be thrown into the total disorganization of release, and all those hard hours spent trying to get a campaign together, and once done, not having anybody stand behind so it would be implemented as designed. What a waste—what a disappointment, what heartache.
> —Hal Ashby

While Ashby was away in Asheville, United Artists had been enthusiastically publicizing *Coming Home* in the buildup to awards season. There had been a huge Oscar push for Jane Fonda and Jon Voight as Best Actress and Actor candidates, and Ashby himself was being touted for Best Director. When nominations were announced in February, *Coming Home* was represented in the five main categories (Best Picture, Actor, Actress, Director, and Screenplay), with Bruce Dern and Penelope Milford also up for Best Supporting Actor and Actress and Don Zimmerman in line for Best Editing on his very first film as chief editor. As the Academy Awards approached, *Coming Home* was racking up the honors at other ceremonies. Jon Voight had won Best Actor at Cannes the previous year, and he got the same accolade at the New York Film Critics' Awards, the National Board of Review awards, the Los Angeles Film Critics Awards, and the Golden Globes, with Jane Fonda also winning Best Actress at the latter two ceremonies.

In early April, Ashby was finishing *Being There* in Pasadena, where the Pasadena Historical Society was doubling as Chance's original home. While all Hollywood anxiously awaited Oscar night, Ashby calmly focused on the job at hand. During his visit to the set in Asheville, *Daily News* film critic Rex Reed had asked him about his feelings on being up for Best Director. "What a strain it is to be in competition!" Ashby had replied with a smile. "This is not why I make films, but, of course, once you're there, you want to win."[1] He was keen to see *Coming Home* do well at the Oscars, but it wasn't personal glory he wanted, as he told Haskell Wexler (who had not been nominated this time) that if he won Best Director, he would have the statuette engraved this time—but with Wexler's name instead of his own. On the day of the Oscars, Jack and Beth Ashby and their daughter, Meredith, were visiting the set of *Being There* when Hal approached Beth and Meredith and asked, "Would you guys like to take these tickets and go to the Academy Awards?"[2]

In a frenzy of delight, mother and daughter dashed off to downtown Pasadena to buy evening dresses, jewelry, and shoes for their grand night out. Surrounded by limousines and Mercedeses, they turned up in their little brown Toyota sedan and walked up the red carpet to take the two seats (just behind Gregory Peck and among a sea of other famous faces) assigned to Hal and his guest. Hal and Jack, meanwhile, were back in Malibu Colony, sitting on Hal's bed watching the show on television, drinking beer and eating potato chips.

Outside the Dorothy Chandler Pavilion, where the awards were being held, activists protested another big Oscar contender, *The Deer Hunter,* Michael Cimino's hawkish portrayal of the Vietnam War, which had particularly angered the Vietnam Veterans against the War. Despite fears expressed by other veterans that both films on the war would be overlooked in favor of Warren Beatty's decidedly uncontroversial *Heaven Can Wait, Coming Home* and *The Deer Hunter* ended up sharing the major awards. Ashby registered little emotion when Cimino was named Best Director and then *The Deer Hunter* won Best Picture, after already taking Best Editing, Sound, and Supporting Actor. But to his delight, *Coming Home* won both Best Actor and Best Actress awards, becoming only the fourth film—after *It Happened One Night* (1934), *One Flew over the Cuckoo's Nest* (1975), and *Network* (1976)—ever to do so. Fonda was handed her statuette by Shirley MacLaine and then gave part of her acceptance speech in sign language because of the heightened awareness of handicapped people that the film had given her. Voight, who had brought Lou Carello, one of his paraplegic friends from the film, to the ceremony, was sobbing by the time he acknowledged his debt to "the people in the chairs and the veterans."[3] Ashby was disappointed that *The Deer Hunter,* which he disagreed with ideologically, had done so well, but it was nonetheless impressive that on the glitziest night of the year, the spotlight had been thrown onto Vietnam.

It was testament to the impact of *Coming Home* that, as part of its Oscar coverage, the *Los Angeles Times* ran a big article on both Lou Carello and Ken Augustine, another paraplegic who featured prominently in the film. "I'm very happy," Augustine said of the film's Oscar triumphs. "I guess I'm particularly happy for Jon. But we won, too. In fact, as far as I'm concerned *Coming Home* won it all a long time ago because it gave 80 people a job and something to do."[4]

Ironically, the other category *Coming Home* won was Best Screenplay, a remarkable achievement considering that the film was essentially written as filming went along. Bob Jones and Waldo Salt happily collected their awards along with Nancy Dowd, whom a Writers Guild of America arbitration had awarded a "story by" credit because of the script she had written for Fonda back in 1973.

Haskell Wexler wrote to Ashby, "I watched the Awards on TV and thought seriously on where the movie making ability is. You are in a separate league! You have more all round film making talent and human sensitivity than Cimino would ever think of. Not to take from them, but Jon and Jane and 'the Writers' were up there mostly due to your skill. I hope you don't forget that!"[5]

A week later, Ashby had the last shot of *Being There* in the can. After Sellers's final scene, the crew clapped, whistled, and cheered for fifteen minutes while Sellers and Ashby stood by teary eyed. Ashby's admiration for Sellers had grown during filming, and he maintained that what *Being There* "proves to a whole generation is that the man's a fucking genius! Peter Sellers has every right to sit up there on his mountain in Switzerland and scream, 'I'm all right, Jack! Screw you all!'"[6]

Though Sellers's work was done, Ashby had long, hard months of editing ahead of him, during which he would also be supervising the editing of *The Hamster of Happiness.* Work on the film had already begun under the guidance of Amy Jones, a young editor on whom he had taken a chance. Ashby's offices and editing base had moved from Appian Way to Calabasas, a secluded settlement between the suburban sprawl of the San Fernando Valley and Ashby's home in Malibu, and it was now much easier for him to shuttle between home and work. Though initially he took a hands-off approach with Jones and Don Zimmerman, he was soon cutting frantically, a joint in his hand (to help him focus, he said), as he moved back and forth between *Being There* in one room and *Hamster* in the other.

"He was like a concert pianist," says Charles Clapsaddle, his personal assistant at the time. "His hands would fly, and he would be in there for hours, working like a madman. You wouldn't be in there for too long because you got a contact high off him!"[7] As Ashby had imagined, if he got stuck trying to solve a particular sequence in one film, he would simply leave it, move next door, work on the other film, and then return to the problem with a fresh perspective.

Before he started editing, however, he had to deal with the situation at Lorimar. During the shooting of *Being There*, he'd had a huge argument with Jack Schwartzman, who had tried to transfer Ashby's rights to *The Hawkline Monster* over to Lorimar, which would have meant Ashby losing control of the property. Previously, Schwartzman had expressed the opinion that Ashby's draft of the screenplay was not up to scratch, and Ashby now concluded that Schwartzman had been angling for his own screenplay of *Hawkline* (which was only fifty pages long and, in Ashby's words, "way off the mark") to be used instead.[8] Ashby, who had already spent $100,000 developing the film, suspected that Schwartzman was now trying to wrest the project away from him, using their long-established trust to con him into signing it away.

While shooting in Asheville, Ashby wrote to Lorimar boss Merv Adelson, saying he would pay the company back any funds it had spent on *Hawkline* (thus allowing him to regain control of the project), and adding, "I don't want Jack Schwartzman anywhere near me. I certainly don't want him to represent me in any way whatsoever, and I do not want him as executive producer or executive anything on any film I ever do, including *Being There*. . . . The man just let me down. I trusted him and he didn't come through. It makes me sad."[9]

Ashby's dealings with Schwartzman's company, JS Productions, abruptly ceased, but fortunately his relationship with Merv Adelson remained intact. And although Ashby had kept Andy Braunsberg at arm's length during the filming of *Being There,* by the summer of 1979 he was considering forming a business partnership with his producer, seeing an opportunity to establish his own production company and create the Utopian setup he had aimed for with the short-lived D.F. Films. Recalling the time he and Ashby spent in preproduction on *Being There*, Braunsberg says, "We had similar views on film and similar ambitions, and we started talking about a partnership."[10] Braunsberg's business sense coupled with Ashby's creative talents would be a formidable combination, and if they had their own company, then Ashby's contact with Lorimar could be reduced to an absolute minimum. Moreover, it was a chance to help talented young directors make their first films and work with established directors on projects they could not set up elsewhere.

As ever, Ashby was being inundated with offers to direct. Already in 1979, he had been approached about an adaptation of Norman Mailer's new book, *The Executioner's Song, Ladyhawke, Nine to Five,* and even *Warhead,* an unofficial James Bond spin-off. He himself was making inquiries about *Animal Factory,* another book by *Straight Time* author Edward Bunker, as well as *Creator,* a script by Jeremy Leven. He was, however, most excited about the prospect of working with Sellers and Terry Southern on Southern's audacious comic creation *Grossing Out*—about a toy designer who invents a missile, "the ultimate toy" every government in the world is desperate to get its hands on.

However, *The Hamster of Happiness,* which Southern called Ashby's "Big Bob and Fabsy-babsy epic" (a reference to Blake and Harris), became a more pressing concern as the summer wore on.[11] By the time Ashby got involved in the editing of *Hamster,* Amy Jones was already on her fourth or fifth cut. When he screened rough versions of *Being There* and *Hamster* to friends and Lorimar executives in late summer 1979, it was clear that the latter was going to be considerably more of a challenge, both editorially and in terms of finding its audience. Writing about it later, Ashby remembered, "*Hamster* suffered most. Editor, Amy Jones was far less experienced than Don [Zimmerman], and *Being There* was just a more captivating film. *Hamster* was a problem child, they [Lorimar] didn't know how to sell it."[12]

Audience reactions to *Hamster* suggested numerous flaws: people found the story confusing, thought the music was at odds with the message of the film, could not understand Barbara Harris's dialogue, and didn't know whether they were watching a comedy or a drama. The consensus was that Ashby and Amy Jones had been under too much pressure to get the film ready for a fall release and that more time was needed for editing. The release date was pushed back, and even the title was rethought, as *The Hamster of Happiness* was confusing and didn't appeal to a wide enough demographic. Market research was done on alternative titles, and after testing the public's reaction to *Bluebird of Happiness, Second Hand Hearts,* and *Neon Sunsets,* Lorimar chose *Second Hand Hearts.*

Lorimar's new release plan was to go all out to get *Being There* ready for a Christmas opening and Oscar consideration and follow with *Second Hand Hearts* in the spring of 1980. With only three months to work on the editing, Ashby knew he faced "a tough crunch" to finish *Being There* in time.[13] "This is the most delicate film I've ever worked with as an editor," said Ashby. "The balance is just incredible. It could be ruined in a second if you let it become too broad."[14] He was forced to cut a scene where Chance, who assumes the characteristics of people he meets or sees on television, imitates a homosexual man he has been talking to. The scene got big laughs, but it broke the delicate balance it was so essential to maintain.

Don Zimmerman had previously been editing the film to Ashby's specifications, but in the last six or seven weeks before the December 19 release date, Ashby took over cutting himself, with Zimmerman by his side. He was the quicker of the two, and time was of the essence. By December, Ashby was working seven days a week and barely leaving the cutting room, let alone seeing daylight. He would start work at 3 A.M., work until sunset, go home for a few hours' sleep, and be editing again by 3 A.M. the next morning.

Even during the last few days, Ashby was searching out new bits of film, takes that were better than, or just different from, the ones Zimmerman had selected, as he tried to further tighten the picture. *Being There* was to have a limited release in New York and Los Angeles cinemas, and Ashby delivered a final print to Lorimar for the East Coast opening but kept working on a few final touches. He had come up with the innovative idea of using the outtakes of Peter Sellers corpsing during his "Now get this, honky" speech over the closing credits of the film, a ploy to keep the audience in their seats until the lights came up. At 4 A.M. on the morning of the opening, Ashby made his last adjustment before delivering the print in person—complete with new closing credits sequence—to one of the two cinemas in Los Angeles that was showing *Being There.*

After visiting that cinema for a week and watching the audience reactions, Ashby decided to use that ending for every print of the film. *Being There* had an American Film Institute screening in Washington, and in the audience were Lorimar staff and Jerzy Kosinski, none of whom knew about the different end credits. They were extremely surprised to see them, but if the change upset either, it is unlikely that Ashby would have felt anything but quiet satisfaction as he had recently experienced problems with both.

Kosinski had contested Bob Jones's tentative cowriter credit and demanded that he have the sole credit. (Interestingly, it was Jones who was solely credited as "Writer" on the crew list issued during shooting.) Before the film was completed, Kosinski had distanced himself from it (telling journalists such things as, "It will be Ashby's film. I am not a filmmaker," and, "Film is not my medium. It's like tennis to me. I don't like to do it"), but with so much praise being lavished on *Being There,* he changed his tune.[15] Kosinski took his case to the Writers Guild of America, which would have dismissed his case immediately except for the fact that Kosinski apparently submitted one of Jones's drafts as his own. Accordingly, the guild found in his favor, denying Jones any credit on the film. When Ashby publicly stated that Jones's version featured "massive changes" and that what "went on in each scene was greatly different," Kosinski countered by claiming that Ashby had confided in him that he wanted to give Jones a credit to pay him back for previous unacknowledged writing work.[16] (The fact that Jones had, just months earlier, received an Oscar for Best Original Screenplay for his work on *Coming Home* makes this claim highly implausible.)

Ashby's beef with Lorimar arose over its handling of *Being There*'s publicity. After working flat out to ready the film for release, he emerged from his Calabasas offices to find that the marketing campaign he favored had been dropped and the film was being promoted on the strength of the romance between Sellers and MacLaine. "They created a lie," Ashby complained. "They were trying to make it seem as if there was this tremendous love story because people like to go to see movies about men and women. But that's not what this picture was about." His deal with Lorimar had promised significant input into marketing, and for Ashby that was "one of the key appeals" to him as a filmmaker: "It always hurts me to do battle over the marketing of my films. I have a pretty good idea of what I'm trying to say, and one of the goals of marketing is to convey some of that so people will go to see the film."[17]

Being There is seen as Ashby's masterpiece, but it is also the quintessential Hal Ashby film. Its gentleness, compassion, and optimism, as well as its intelligence and understated humor, are all manifestations of Ashby's own personality. Chance has interesting parallels with Ashby, who was almost his inverse alter ego. Though Chance is as straightforward as Ashby was complex, they had in common a softness of voice and a graceful, gentle approach to life that made both much loved and revered, as well as a desire to step back and watch silently rather than comment or get involved. For Chance, his work (in the garden) dominates his thoughts and is the only thing with which he is truly, profoundly comfortable; Ashby's relationship with film was identical.

In addition to a trademark directorial cameo (in the background of the *Washington Post* offices), *Being There* also bears Ashby's distinctive stamp through his continuing preoccupation with water and its links with death. In the iconic ending, Chance wanders into the woods during Ben Rand's funeral, tends to an ailing sapling, and then walks away over the water. The sequence has strong echoes of Bruce Dern's watery exit in *Coming Home* and is a typically ambiguous Ashby ending, one that leaves us doubtful that Chance will ever return.

Despite the fact that *Being There* came out at Christmas time, when numerous other films were opening, its critical reception was nothing short of rapturous. Vincent Canby, Andrew Sarris, and Rex Reed immediately put it on their lists of the year's top films, and it got raves from seemingly every critic who saw it. Sellers drew the greatest praise, with most reviews calling his performance either his greatest ever or his best work in years, but the supporting cast of Shirley MacLaine, Jack Warden, and particularly Melvyn Douglas was also highly lauded. Unfortunately, the focus was so much on Sellers that the efforts of those behind the camera were almost totally ignored, with little recognition for the remarkable work of Mike Haller and Caleb Deschanel. Even Ashby, whose directorial powers were arguably at their zenith, was left in the shade by Sellers, though reviews usually gave him a brief laudatory mention.

Considering its critical reception, *Being There* did not make as big an impression on awards voters as might have been expected. Peter Sellers won Best Actor (Musical/Comedy) at the Golden Globes but lost out to Dustin Hoffman for Robert Benton's *Kramer vs. Kramer* at the Oscars, and Melvyn Douglas picked up Best Supporting Actor prizes at the Oscars *and* the Golden Globes as well as from both the New York and the Los Angeles Film Critics awards. Ashby received just one Best Director nomination, at the Golden Globes, but did not win.

In the midst of awards season, *The Last Detail* producer Gerry Ayres wrote to Ashby praising *Being There* and saying, "I continue to marvel that you achieve what no one else is in this town. You are getting the companies to make films that their every instinct tells them not to, and you're making them with a high level of art and they are working at the box office."[18]

Being There was indeed doing very well commercially, quieting the naysayers who had called it a "one-joke film." It took $10 million in North American rentals and was Lorimar's biggest-ever hit both domestically and internationally, yet everyone thought it could have done better, and Lorimar blamed Ashby for the film's lack of success. The studio felt that letting him use the print advertising campaign of his choice (featuring Chance in silhouette) had negatively affected box office. Conversely, Ashby lay the blame on Lorimar and pointed to the fact that Merv Adelson had vetoed East Coast radio ads, saying, "Nobody listens to the radio in New York," and that Lorimar had marketed the film only tentatively on its nationwide release.[19] His marketing guru, Mike Kaplan, concurred, deeming Lorimar's promotional push for the rerelease in September 1980 (to cash in on election fever) "half-hearted."[20] Disagreements over the promotion of *Being There* marked the beginning of tensions between Ashby and Lorimar that were to continue, in one form or another, for the best part of a decade.

Writing to Adelson just before the fall rerelease, Ashby complained about the ad execs who had not bothered to watch *Being There* with a paying audience, and had thus classed it as "a special little film," rather than going to "watch those audiences rock with laughter, and know they had a gold mine. People do love to laugh—lots of them pay lots of money to do just that, and BEING THERE gives them all they want, and it doesn't leave them with holes waiting for the next joke. I went to the theatre a number of times, and saw it with many different, but paying, audiences, and I swear to you the way they responded was something to see. Merv, they honest to God lost us millions of dollars with their stupid ass 'little—special' bullshit. . . . It makes me real aware of how many million will see the film and what it has to give to them."[21]

Being There had been released as "A Northstar International Picture," "Northstar" being the name chosen by Ashby and Andy Braunsberg for their newly formed production company. Northstar, housed in the famous Selznick building, had a three-year nonexclusive contract with Lorimar that allowed Ashby to make films elsewhere should he wish to do so. The formation of the company was announced in late January; Lorimar promised $50 million in backing for the company and a salary of $750,000 per year for Ashby. Five films were planned for 1980, and the first of these was already in production: Bob Rafelson's *The Postman Always Rings Twice,* starring Jack Nicholson, who was finally getting to make the film he and Ashby had planned as *Three Cornered Circle* eight years earlier.

Ashby wanted to make Northstar a haven where filmmakers could create daring, original, and *successful* films. Crucial to this was the fact that Ashby and Braunsberg—two creative people with a firsthand understanding of filmmaking—were running the show, not the studios. Ashby revealed a lot about the roots of his problems with authority when he explained the setup at Northstar by saying, "I'm not a kid anymore who has to go up to daddy and say, 'Daddy, I was thinking about riding the bike 100 miles an hour down to the corner.' 'Well, I don't know if you ought to do that son, I don't know if it'll sell.'"[22]

Though at the time Braunsberg stressed how close Northstar's relationship with Lorimar was, he now says that there was no script approval from Lorimar, as studio representatives never read anything, but "if there was glory or profit, it was OK."[23] The projects that Ashby and Braunsberg were hoping to make certainly suggested that there would be an abundance of both. Their formidable list of films mooted for production included *Lie Down in Darkness,* from the novel by William Styron, to be directed by Jack Nicholson; *Barfly,* Barbet Schroeder's 1987 film of Charles Bukowski's screenplay; *The Dreamers,* Orson Welles's ultimately unfinished cinematic interpretation of short stories by Isak Dinesen; another Welles film, based on Jim Harrison's novel *Revenge,* that was to star Nicholson; *Vicksburg,* an American Civil War film from

Robert Altman; and *Black Sands,* to be directed by Brazilian director Bruno Baretto from Oscar-winning writer Bo Goldman's script.

Ashby also saw an opportunity to give talented, up-and-coming directors a first shot, just as Jewison had done with him. "I've always wanted to have a company," he said, "because I want to help young filmmakers. It's stupid not to do it. And morally, you've got to do it. The studios don't have a clue, when it comes to new filmmakers. When they have little flurries, and they try new filmmakers, nine times out of ten what they do is listen to the guy that talks the fastest."[24] Ashby was hoping to get Jonathan Demme, a director he had befriended in the early 1970s, to direct Jeremy Leven's *Creator* and give the University of Southern California film grad Jamie Foley (whom he had met at a party while pursuing actress Colleen Camp) a chance to bring his own script, *Cowboys of the American Night,* to the big screen. Also on Ashby's wish list of films to make at Northstar were, inevitably, *The Hawkline Monster* and *Henderson the Rain King* as well as *Grossing Out.*

Grossing Out's future, however, had been put in doubt after Sellers saw Ashby's outtake ending, which he felt undermined the impact of *Being There.* In a rushed and emotional telex sent to Ashby in March 1980, he said, "I must reiterate once again, that the out-takes you have placed over the credits do a grave injustice to the picture for the sake of a few cheap laughs. It breaks the spell, do you understand? Do you understand, it breaks the spell! I'm telling you how it breaks the spell and as I said in my previous telegram there's not much point in the film going to Europe as I saw it last night."[25] Sellers believed that the outtakes had hurt his chance of winning the Best Actor Oscar, so, in an attempt to repair their friendship, Ashby changed the European prints to have the regular credits that Sellers favored. Ashby was apparently forgiven as by midsummer there were reports that Sellers would make *Grossing Out* for an enormous $3 million plus a percentage cut of profits. However, on July 24, 1980, Sellers died in London after suffering a massive heart attack. Southern, who was always keen to work with Ashby, tried to keep the project alive after Sellers's death. "There is going to be a *gigantic audience* for the kind of film we are talking about," he told Ashby. "And there is bound to be a veritable deluge of such films within the next couple of years. Why not have the *first* and the *best???*"[26] To Ashby, however, doing the film without Sellers was inconceivable.

19

Lookin' to Get Out

> Directors who have the reputation of always coming in on schedule are in steady demand even if they've had a long line of box-office failures and their work is consistently mediocre, and . . . directors who are perfectionists are shunned as if they were lepers—unless, like Hal Ashby, they've had some recent hits.
> —Pauline Kael

> But you must understand if somebody says *me,* then they are automatically saying *the film.* For we are one and the same.
> —Hal Ashby

Once again, it was time for Ashby to line up his next film. Given the range of projects on the table, *Lookin' to Get Out* was a typically idiosyncratic choice. In the mid-1970s, the singer Chip Taylor had introduced his brother, Jon Voight, to his manager, Al Schwartz, who was writing a screenplay with dialogue that Taylor thought particularly impressive. Schwartz, who had quit high school after ninth grade and learned life's lessons hustling on the New York City streets, had produced thirty-odd pages about the misadventures of two gamblers in New York City. Voight was so taken with the material that he started helping Schwartz with the script and trying to get the film made. Voight approached Burt Reynolds, Bruce Dern, and Peter Falk and actually convinced James Caan and Alan Arkin to play the leads, until Arkin pulled out. Voight resisted acting in the film himself, but he says, "I finally came to the point where I was looking at a lot of scripts and I admitted at last that the script I had in my hand was the best thing I had."[1]

Once Voight decided to play Alex Kovac, the compulsive gambler heavily based on Schwartz, he quickly brought character actor Burt

Young and Ann-Margret on board to play Alex's best friend, Jerry, and old flame, Patti, respectively. The film was a shambolic comedy, virgin territory for Voight, and the actor felt that Ashby, whom he colorfully described as "an extremely gifted humorist, witty and bright, part W. C. Fields and part some kind of mystic," was just the person to guide him through it.[2] With a package in place, Voight approached Ashby with the script. "I said, 'Read it this time,'" Voight remembers, "because I'd showed it to him about six months earlier, and I'm never sure if Hal actually reads anything. He got hurt, he got insulted, but he came back and said, 'I think we can do it.' . . . With his help, I knew I could solve any problems with the film, because he cares as much as I do."[3]

Ashby asked Jerry Hellman whether he would produce the film, but Hellman turned him down and advised him against directing it. There was a feeling among a number of Ashby's close friends that he was doing it for the wrong reasons—as a favor to Voight and because it was ready to go with a cast and a script, rather than because he was genuinely passionate about it. Nonetheless, when Voight's friend Robert Schaffel, the man who had started *Crawdaddy* magazine in the 1960s, came on board as producer, things began to get rolling.

Lorimar approved *Lookin' to Get Out* as the third film in Ashby's three-picture deal, and a start date of February 1980 was announced. However, complications repeatedly pushed production back. After three months spending almost every hour of every day rushing *Being There* to completion, Ashby was exhausted. "I've never worked as hard as I did editing *Being There*," he wrote. "It damn near did me in."[4]

Though the Northstar deal was announced in late January 1980, because the contract negotiations were still ongoing, the company had yet to see any money from Lorimar. Back in September, during the first Northstar talks, Merv Adelson had told Ashby and Braunsberg that they wouldn't get any development money until the deal was done but had assured them, as Ashby recalled, that "everything we would want, or need, wasn't any farther than a phone call away."[5] However, Ashby was having to put tens of thousands of dollars of his own money into the company to keep operations going while his phone calls to Adelson asking for funds were brushed away with the promise that money would be forthcoming—once the deal was signed.

Ashby was still trying to save *Second Hand Hearts*. He had laid off some of the editorial staff but had kept faith with Amy Jones, convinced that the problem was Barbara Harris's inflexible performance. However, as he looked more closely at what footage Jones had and hadn't used, he concluded, "My inexperienced editor had been wrong about the film going together."[6] Realizing that Jones's editing approach was probably fundamentally flawed, he started looking at every scene, essentially going back to square one. As the start time for *Lookin'* was put back again and again, he spent most of March and April in the editing room working on *Second Hand Hearts*. The projected spring release date was scrapped as Ashby tried to ensure his "problem child" was in the best possible shape when he let it out into the world. He still believed he could make the film good and further felt that if he could influence its distribution and marketing, it would find its audience.

When he wasn't in the editing room trying to coax *Hearts* back to health, he was prepping *Lookin' to Get Out*. Schwartz and Voight were busy polishing their rough diamond of a script, and Ashby was overseeing the rewrites as well as doing some work on the script himself. During preproduction, Ashby admitted, "I'm not quite sure where we're going with it. In the end, I think it's a film about learning to let go."[7] Though Alex Kovac was Schwartz's alter ego, one reason Ashby was drawn to the project was that he felt a connection with the character himself. For him, letting go meant facing issues from his past, and he drew on his own experiences in his contributions to the script. In one of Ashby's scenes, Jerry's parents discuss the reasons for Alex's problems in life:

> FELDMAN'S LIVING ROOM—Jerry sits alone on the couch listening to Mother and Father in the Pantry
>
> MOTHER (V.O. [voice-over]) It's never been easy for him, Harold. Remember when he lost his father?
>
> FATHER (V.O.) His father was never around anyway."[8]

Ashby had never directly addressed the impact of his father's death in his films, and this brief exchange was the closest he would ever come to doing so. In just a few words, it reveals the huge significance he placed on the event and the effect that it had on the person he became. The scene was ultimately cut, but Ashby's own life was similarly imposed onto Alex Kovac's in another equally revealing aspect of the script. One of the important plot developments revolves around Alex's discovery that Patti was pregnant with his child when he left her five years earlier and that he has been unaware that he is a father. In the original script, the child was a boy called Josh; however (probably under Ashby's influence), the character became a girl, Tosha.

This story line resonated deeply with the situation surrounding Ashby's first marriage and his (lack of a) relationship with his daughter, Leigh. Though he had told Eileen that he wanted to meet Leigh "when everything is right," years had passed, and he had never arranged to do so. Leigh herself had made a number of attempts to contact Ashby, but he never returned her calls or answered her letters. In 1980, he was a fifty-year-old man who had never had any contact with his thirty-two-year-old daughter except for the first few months of her life, and he seemed pathologically incapable of remedying the situation. He could tell himself she was best off without him, but his decision not to allow her into his life had been made only to protect himself from his guilt. In the same way that the ending of *Coming Home* drew on Ashby's preoccupation with swimming to his death, so the scene in *Lookin'* where Alex meets Tosha allowed Ashby to play out a meeting with Leigh and vicariously experience that moment. Ashby's fear of commitment is palpable in the encounter: Alex is introduced to Tosha as a friend of her mother's, and after their brief but touching conversation, he is able to walk away.

Just days before production was due to start on *Lookin' to Get Out,* a major crisis arose when Lorimar declared that the Northstar contract being negotiated was "not what they were talking about."[9] In light of these problems, Merv Adelson suggested pushing back production until May so that Ashby would not be shooting while preoccupied by unresolved issues. While attempts were made to clarify what the contract would include, Ashby, along with Haller, Voight, Schaffel, Haskell Wexler, and production designer Bob Boyle jetted off to scout locations. In New York, Ashby researched the gambling scene and later met up with Melvyn Douglas, with whom he talked late into the night, despite Douglas's failing health; in Vegas, everyone stayed at the legendary MGM Grand Hotel, which was to be the setting for most of the film's action.

Back in Los Angeles, with a week to go before filming began, Ashby discovered that he was in financial trouble: because of the contract delays, no money had been forthcoming from Lorimar, and Ashby had been keeping Northstar afloat with his own money. In what he would later describe as a "not enough time to think" mistake, he wrote an impassioned, handwritten letter to Merv Adelson in an attempt to temporarily resolve his company's—and his own—financial difficulties.[10] Ashby and Adelson had an oral agreement that the director was to receive $1 million to direct *Lookin';* however, Ashby's letter asked for $1.25 million so that he could pay his staff until the contract negotiations were concluded, which would not be until after *Lookin' to Get Out* wrapped. "I need the money," Ashby wrote. "I have heavy obligations, which have become even heavier, and I'm sure the less stress I have regards being broke and owing money, especially while shooting, the better off I and the film will be and that is not a threat, it's just common sense."[11]

The personal and heartfelt nature of Ashby's note had the required effect, and, as a gesture of good faith, Adelson agreed to pay him the extra money. It was a relief to Ashby, who looked back on the period from September 1979 to May 1980—the editing of *Being There,* the problems surrounding its release and marketing, the recutting of *Second Hand Hearts,* and the Northstar contract crisis and financial difficulties—and called it "as horrendous a time as I've ever gone through."[12] With one problem at least temporarily solved, Ashby spent his last few "free" days before leaving for Las Vegas finishing his cut of *Second Hand Hearts.* He had lengthened some sequences, shortened others, and replaced some footage altogether, and at last he began to feel like the film was coming together. In the last available hours, he laid out sound effects and music and left detailed notes on how the editing was to be completed. He left the editing room at midnight on Saturday night, returned home for four hours' sleep, and then climbed into his red Mercedes and set out on the five-hour drive from Malibu to Las Vegas.

Ashby was on edge because of recent tensions, so much so that when he arrived in Vegas and found that there was a problem with his hotel room, he got into his car and drove home again. Panic ensued, but it was still a few days before shooting began, and Jon Voight volunteered to bring Ashby back. He went to Malibu Colony and joked with Ashby about the situation, putting him at ease. "Let's go back, fight the fights, and get this thing done," he said.[13]

"*Lookin' to Get Out* was the start of things going wrong," says Jeff

Wexler. "It was done as a favor to Jon Voight. We started the film with a few characters, a loose idea, and basically no script."[14] The film was to have been shot in fourteen weeks at a cost of $12 million, but its troubled production period doubled to twenty-eight weeks, and it came in about $4 million over budget. It was decidedly strange that the film had such a high budget to start with, as it was essentially an intimate, low-key piece about friendship whose style and focus on character rather than plot were reminiscent of John Cassavetes. But because Las Vegas and New York City were expensive locations and elaborate sets had to be built on the lot, it had a massively inflated budget.

Since making *Coming Home,* which had won a Best Screenplay Oscar despite not having a shooting script, Ashby had grown confident of his ability to elevate a less than perfect screenplay. "One of the reasons he made *Lookin' to Get Out* with a lousy script," Haskell Wexler explains, "was he was very arrogant about what he could fix in the editing. Rather than try and rewrite it, he would say, 'We'll shoot this, and I'll cut to the reaction of this guy, it'll be fine.'"[15] However, Al Schwartz was on set every day, and the script *was* constantly being rewritten (at one stage it ballooned to a massive 196 pages) until the end of September.

Despite worries about the logistics of shooting in Las Vegas, the company's time there was highly successful. Ashby and Voight were both put up in lavish suites at the MGM Grand, their main location, and the hotel staff did everything to ensure filming went as smoothly as possible. The company was allowed to shoot in the hotel and its casino during the day, the paging system was switched off while they were rolling, and, to Ashby and the crew's great relief, the gamblers were so engrossed that they didn't stare at the camera.

Voight and Ashby were happy to be working together once again, and Ashby had brought together lots of other familiar faces—Bob Boyle, Pablo Ferro, Dianne Schroeder, and Haskell and Jeff Wexler. It was, however, the first film since *Shampoo* on which Chuck Mulvehill was absent, as he was producing another Northstar movie, *The Postman Always Rings Twice* (1981). He had turned down Ashby's invitation to run Northstar ("I just saw a fuckin' mess," Mulvehill says) and felt it was time for him to work independently of Ashby, the man he had idolized—and whose dirty work he had done—for so long. Though Mulvehill and Ashby's relationship had been mutually beneficial, it had become uncomfortably close. "I was under his mesmerizing spell," says Mulvehill. "There was a whole lot of convoluted psychological webs."[16]

Arguably, Mike Haller had taken Mulvehill's place as Ashby's closest friend, and at the time of *Lookin' to Get Out,* Ashby was trying to get him his first film as a director, on an unpromising cop movie, *Flasher.* Twentieth Century–Fox offered Haller a contract to direct it (if Ashby and Braunsberg were the producers), but the terms were so unfavorable that Haller ultimately passed, and the project was shelved. At the time, however, Haller was still hoping to get started on *Flasher,* so Bob Boyle was brought in as the production designer on *Lookin',* and Haller took on an uncredited role as a creative assistant to Ashby on the film. (In the credits of *Lookin' to Get Out,* Ashby extends special thanks to Haller for "Being Here.")

"Mike Haller had a lot to do with taking Hal's ideas and developing them," Voight explained. "He's like a Jeffersonian personality. Mike's real quiet, has a toothpick in his mouth, and he's looking at things like a painter, like a visual artist. And he'll come up with these ideas: he'll just pick at whatever you do. No matter what you do, he'll have six other different ways, and he'll pick the most outlandish, and he'll write a little something like that. Sometimes he comes up with wonderful, wonderful ideas. He just pokes around, and that's what Hal would want him to do."[17]

One of Haller's ideas came from his discovery of a huge room in the MGM Grand with doors all the way down two sides. It was worked into the film by having Voight and Burt Young find themselves there while they are being pursued by bookies they owe money to. In a surreal, inspired chase sequence, Voight and Young try door after door, all locked, as they try to get out of the cavernous room while engaged in a petty argument about Young's ex-wife. It was a quintessential Ashby moment, simultaneously surreal and emotionally incisive, and the kind of scene that no other filmmaker would think to put in a film.

Two weeks into filming, Ashby and company had a moment of genuine drama when their filming of Siegfried and Roy's famous stage spectacle went horribly wrong. Ashby was shooting a routine involving the two entertainers and one of their trained tigers when the tiger got agitated. Pablo Ferro recalls that the animal was startled when Haskell Wexler put up a new light, but Voight reveals there was more to it than that. "I was fooling around with Burt, who was making funny faces and going 'Ooooh!' at the tiger," Voight confesses, "and then the light glinted off his glasses, and the tiger got spooked."[18] At first it refused to come out of its cage; then it suddenly rushed into a section of the audience of extras, dragging Roy with it. Ashby's assistant director, Chuck Myers, calmly told everybody to let the trainers handle the tiger, and further drama was avoided. Three people with minor injuries were sent to the hospital, the other extras were quickly asked to sign disclaimer forms, and filming resumed two hours later.

Just the day before, an exasperated Ashby had fired his four editors back in Los Angeles because of his dissatisfaction with their work. They had failed to spot that one of the shots he had sent back to them in Los Angeles was slightly out of focus, and he had concluded that they weren't watching the footage properly. "We were all working on the film, very young and inexperienced, and he was in Las Vegas," remembers one of the editors, Eva Gardos. "It was a high-tension situation, and we were far too inexperienced."[19] Ashby wanted to give young editors their first break at Northstar, but his novice crew was a huge frustration to him. Ashby had also noticed that the dailies were sent late and out of sync. One night, out of pure frustration, he sat down in his hotel room after a full day's filming and set about syncing up the dailies. The last straw was when he received a print of *Second Hand Hearts,* which had allegedly been completed according to his instructions but was far from what he had envisioned. He found himself spending every available moment undoing the mistakes of his "totally inept editorial crew" who, to add insult to injury, were reinstated because they had been terminated without proper cause.[20]

It was mid-June when filming wrapped in Las Vegas. The last scenes there were between Jon Voight and his five-year-old daughter, Angelina Jolie (playing Alex's daughter, Tosha), who was making her first screen appearance. The day after, Ashby drove back home with his assistant, Charles Clapsaddle, and dropped him at his home on the Calabasas Canyon Road. Just minutes later, overworked and exhausted, Ashby fell asleep at the wheel. The car drifted sideways, and he woke up to find it smashed up and leaking oil; it was pure luck that he emerged unscathed.

Back in Los Angeles, Ashby was filming at a number of different soundstages at Laird International Studios, where a hotel room—the Dr. Zhivago Suite, complete with suede walls, brass plumbing fixtures, and a working jacuzzi—and the Metro Club casino had been re-created at great cost by Boyle and art director Jim Schoppe. Only a few weeks after shooting at Laird had begun, the Screen Actors Guild (SAG) announced a strike over payments for Pay-TV and video cassettes, and on July 21 actors staged a walkout, halting all production. An appeal was made to the guild to sign an interim agreement allowing the actors in *Lookin' to Get Out* to continue work, but it became clear that any such pact would be slow in materializing.

During the interim period, Ashby wrote a long letter to Merv Adelson complaining about the financial difficulties he and Braunsberg were suffering owing to Lorimar's failure to sign the Northstar deal promptly. Furthermore, the company was charging them a 10 percent overhead (amounting to almost $2 million) for premises it was not using. Pondering his strained relationship with Lorimar as a whole, Ashby concluded, "I don't think there's any way to turn it around, now, because the real problem has to do with the different levels of faith we all have in regards to me, and my films."

He felt strongly that Lorimar's handling of *Being There* had resulted in the film underperforming and told Adelson he was fearful this would happen with *Second Hand Hearts* and *Lookin' to Get Out*. "It just doesn't add up right if you walk around feeling real anxious about decisions made regarding directions you're taking," Ashby wrote, "and I sense real strong how uneasy you've always felt about the films you've given me the money to make. You've told me, a few times, how you never would have gone for *Being There* if it hadn't been me bringing it to you, and the same goes for *Second Hand Hearts* (the lower cost/risk helped here, too). Then we come to *Lookin to Get Out*, and I know, from things said, you really don't feel good about it either. It worries you more than it should. 'It was too much money in the first place, and now Hal's over schedule.' 'Let's do some research on the title, we don't like the title.' 'We don't really understand the script, etc.;' all kinds of things to keep you feelin' good about the film."[21]

Robert Blake, who came by the editing rooms sometimes, was getting irritated that, two years after he had shot the film, it had not yet been released, and during an appearance on Johnny Carson's *The To-*

night Show he told Ashby to hurry up. Lorimar had actually submitted the film to the Motion Picture Association of America (MPAA) for a rating—a major step toward releasing it—but Ashby was disappointed to find that because of three instances of the word *fuck* (none of them in a sexual context), the film had received an R rating, massively limiting its potential audience. Convinced it deserved a PG rating, he applied for an appeal; however, when the MPAA contacted Lorimar about the standard payment of $100 for the appeal screening, the legal department said the studio would not be bothering with an appeal.

Fortunately, Ashby found out about this, and his subsequent appeal was successful. However, he was exasperated that Lorimar could take such thoughtless, irresponsible actions, especially without consulting him. Though Ashby had always done his best to maintain a good relationship with Merv Adelson, his feelings toward Lorimar were now unreservedly negative. Lee Grant remembers meeting Ashby around this period at Warren Beatty's house and noting him anxiously talking to Beatty about his situation and the problems on *Lookin' to Get Out*. "He didn't have time for anything else; he was monomaniacal about it," says Grant. "He was desperate. He was single-minded, so concerned, so worried, and all he wanted to do was get some help from Warren. The feeling I got from him was 'Save me.'"[22]

During the SAG strike, Ann-Margret's husband, producer Roger Smith, came to Ashby to propose that he direct her next film, *Dreams* (a.k.a. *A Question of Direction*), a vehicle based on her battle with alcoholism and its impact on her career and marriage. Ashby, though interested, was cautious about committing, not only because he was already overloaded with projects he was developing for himself or others, but also because of his working relationship with Ann-Margret. Like Shirley MacLaine, she wasn't used to the freedom Ashby extended to his actors and the expectation that they should experiment, push themselves, and ad-lib lines. (The situation probably wasn't helped by the fact that she started drinking again during production.) "Ann was sometimes very uncomfortable because she didn't know what was being asked of her," Jon Voight recalled, "and sometimes I would use that as an actor. I would want her to be uncomfortable in a scene because I knew that would be the scene."[23]

On August 20, SAG signed an interim agreement allowing production to resume (while the strike went on until October 23), and Voight again threw himself into the role of Alex Kovac. At the start of filming, he had enthused about what the other actors should expect from working with Ashby, telling Ann-Margret and Burt Young, "You're going to be on the set and you'll never have expected you're going to be able to really go. And he'll let you go as far as you want."[24]

Young wasn't disappointed by the experience and described the safe feeling he got from Ashby as like working under an umbrella. Because the film had a loose, improvisational feel to it (despite being tightly scripted), Ashby pushed his actors to avoid obvious interpretations of a line or scene and viewed their so-called mistakes as simply another way that the action could go. "If I was way off in a scene," Voight says, "he would simply see what happened to the character in that kind of stress or confusion. And that stress or confusion would sometimes lead to very valuable and beautiful moments."[25]

This unconventional approach inevitably led to Ashby shooting even more film than usual. Voight said that Ashby's dealings with Bob Schaffel were better than previous interactions with his producers, and Schaffel supported Ashby, saying, "His first consideration is to get the best on film artistically which he always does, and he achieves this with a thorough knowledge and genuine concern for budgetary requirements."[26] However, Ashby did not, in fact, seem to have any concern for the budget, and without an experienced producer to reign him in, shooting on the soundstages at Laird dragged on for two months longer than scheduled, in addition to the month's hiatus caused by the SAG strike. At one point, a young Lorimar exec came to tell Ashby to cut the budget. He responded by tearing out a few pages of the script and snapping, "There, I've cut $100,000. That's the only way I can save money, and if you start cutting, then we're in trouble."[27]

Ashby nurtured his actors, but as the pressure to finish the film mounted, he showed less patience with the crew. "There were a lot of bad vibes coming from that picture," says Haskell Wexler. "Hal went crazy. We had this casino set, and we spent ten, twelve days with multiple cameras, shooting inserts—dice, cards. Hal wanted the second camera guy to pan to one card, and the guy missed. Hal got furious, fired him right there. I just felt Hal had lost it. Something flipped."[28]

"I saw him when he was erratic—he was not in the best shape on that film," says Voight. "He would be difficult. He would have temper fits and then march off and then be unreachable."[29] There were rumors going around the set that Ashby was using cocaine again, but Voight himself never saw Ashby using any drug other than marijuana. "He was erratic and irrational," Haskell Wexler adds, "but that was because he wasn't happy with the film and took substances to alleviate his unhappiness."[30]

Ashby himself later said he thought "*Lookin'* was jinxed or something," and though this may seem somewhat superstitious in light of his own culpability in the protracted production period, this assessment is not entirely unfounded.[31] On top of a string of tussles with Lorimar, the Northstar deal (or lack of), his car crash, the ineptitude of his editorial staff, and the actors' strike, in late October there were a string of bizarre thefts from the soundstages where he was shooting in which a $5,000 antique bronze buffalo and (bafflingly) some plants were stolen. (It should also be noted that the infamous fire that hit the MGM Grand in 1980, killing 84 and injuring 679, happened on November 21, the very day that *Lookin' to Get Out* finally wrapped. What's more, Bob Boyle tells the story that when Ashby first arrived at the hotel, he pointedly remarked to Boyle, "This is funny. There are no exits.")[32]

After cramming the final two weeks' worth of filming into just five days in New York, Ashby wrapped on *Lookin'* and once again turned his attention to *Second Hand Hearts,* which was now to be released by Paramount. Ashby had previously sent a letter to his lawyers laying out what influence he felt he should have in his films' releases, specifically, approval of the marketing strategy and distributor and the right to exclude Lorimar from the distribution process. He wrote that he would rather abandon his films than "deal with the heartache and indignities" of continuing to work for Lorimar. "As much as I truly love 'Lookin' to Get Out,' 'Hamster,' and 'Being There,'" he continued, "no matter how much of my life, and blood, and heart is in each and all of them, I would rather walk away from them now, than go through all that pain."[33]

However, it was not in Ashby to jump ship; his films were too important to him, and relinquishing all control was worse than having less control than he wanted. While a new, more competent chief editor worked on a rough cut of *Lookin',* Ashby tried to get *Hearts* back on track by bringing in his old friend Bill Sawyer, who had cut *The Landlord* and *Harold and Maude,* to oversee the ongoing recut. In late August, *Hearts* had premiered at the Montreal Film Festival, where there were walkouts and it received a decidedly lukewarm review from *Variety.* It had also been test screened yet again by two separate market research companies, both of which reported that the feedback was almost universally negative, as evidenced by their transcripts of viewers' scathing remarks. Though Mike Kaplan told him he felt that he could successfully market the film only if changes were made, Ashby remained upbeat about *Hearts,* maintaining that he was "very, very pleased with the picture."[34] Nevertheless, he allowed Sawyer to hire a young editor to make changes based on audience responses, on the understanding that the original sequences would be reinstated if Ashby wasn't happy with the alterations.

While editors worked on both his films, Ashby turned his focus to his probable next project, an adaptation of Truman Capote's novella *Handcarved Coffins,* a supposedly factual small-town crime story akin to Capote's seminal *In Cold Blood.* Lester Persky, a producer on both *The Last Detail* and *Shampoo,* had fallen in love with the book when it was published in its entirety (a mere thirty thousand words) in Andy Warhol's *Interview* magazine in December 1979 and immediately snapped up the film rights for $350,000, then the most expensive dollar-per-word sale ever. After initially pursuing Roman Polanski to direct, Persky turned to Ashby, and a deal with United Artists was soon in the works for him to start shooting in March. However, Judith Rascoe's script failed to live up to expectations, and the project was put on hold while it was rewritten.

When Ashby sat down to look at both his films around January 1981, he had a shock. As he had anticipated, *Lookin' to Get Out* needed a lot of work, but he was horrified when he saw *Second Hand Hearts,* which he had expected to be all but ready to release. The editor whom Sawyer had brought in to make alterations had unwittingly butchered the film and in some parts even erased the master dub tracks Ashby had spent days making.

"It was a mess," Ashby recalled. "I basically have a very positive philosophy on life, because I don't feel I have anything to lose. Most things are going to turn out OK. But when I saw (the re-edited version) of *Second,* for the first time in my life I thought someone was ruining my picture."[35] At a time when he had hoped to be in preproduction on *Handcarved Coffins* and putting the finishing touches to *Lookin'* and *Hearts*—thus ending the painful Lorimar chapter of his life—he found himself sucked back into personally salvaging both films. Almost three years after work on *Second Hand Hearts* had begun, Ashby was the only person who knew exactly what had been undone, so he had no choice but to sit down and painstakingly re-create what had been lost. It took him five weeks working twenty hours a day to get it back to where it had been the previous May, and Ashby would look back with bitterness on this time that had been taken from him.

By now, stories were circulating that drugs had taken over Ashby's life and that he was incapable of finishing a film. (Ashby later told a friend that someone high up at Lorimar had called every Hollywood studio boss and told them not to hire him because he was a drug addict.)[36] As Ashby already had a reputation as a dopehead and *Second Hand Hearts* had been stuck in postproduction for years, it didn't matter that there was no proof of these allegations; the stories began to take on a life of their own. Ashby was even more frustrated than Lorimar by the delays to *Hearts,* but while it was financial concerns and contractual obligations that the studio was fretting over, for him it was his creative reputation and his career that were at stake. "Nobody was more unhappy than I about the delays," he insisted. "I'm not crazy—I would have liked nothing better than to look at *Second Hand Hearts* and think it was great. But I didn't, so I ended up putting a load on myself. And instead of getting help in the form of support from Lorimar, I got BS encouragement that you don't even waste your time listening to because you know it's not sincere."[37]

By late January 1981, however, Lorimar's encouragement had been exhausted, and the studio's lawyers insisted Ashby deliver the picture immediately so that Paramount could release it in the spring as planned. It was indicative of the lack of communication between the parties that Ashby had, in fact, already shown *Hearts* to Paramount and was working on changes suggested by both Lorimar and Paramount boss Frank Mancuso. Lorimar had not confirmed how it wanted the credits to read, so while Ashby waited for word from them, he and Mike Haller wrote an introductory poem that would serve as a prologue, which he and

Mancuso hoped would set the tone for the film. The prologue, however, was arguably just an attempt to explain a confusing film, and even Ashby, the film's staunchest defender, was finally realizing that he would never be happy with it.

"He would edit whole sequences of *Second Hand Hearts,* take them out the next day, and then put them back in," Charles Clapsaddle remembers. "He didn't really know what to do with it. It just didn't seem right for him. But he gave it the care and attention it needed; he took so much care over everything. It took him a long time to realize that he had to just let go."[38]

By the time Ashby handed over the "finished" version of *Second Hand Hearts* to Paramount, he had "emotionally cut loose from the film."[39] Judith Crist, the esteemed critic who had vehemently attacked *The Landlord* but loved Ashby's subsequent work, championed the film, getting it screened at the Dallas Film Festival, where it struck something of a chord with down-to-earth Texans, and also showing it at one of her film weekends in Tarrytown, New York. The Tarrytown reception, however, was disappointing, and it was becoming clear that metropolitan audiences could not relate to the film.

When *Second Hand Hearts* opened in more rural Austin, Texas, to mixed reviews and disastrous box office, it began to look like the film simply had no viable audience. Lorimar, in any case, had already decided it was going to be a failure and was having Paramount release it in only a handful of major cities for one week each to qualify for network television money. In a word, it was buried: no trailers or posters were used for the openings in New York, Los Angeles, Washington, Detroit, San Francisco, or Boston, press materials were not sent to journalists, and Mike Kaplan's marketing plan was mostly ignored by Paramount. Kaplan had strongly advised that as a weaker, more "niche" film, *Second Hand Hearts* be kept back until after *Lookin' to Get Out* had been released, but Lorimar didn't want to change its release schedule. When Kaplan went to Frank Mancuso with the idea of showing an old *Our Gang* short starring an infant Robert Blake before each screening of *Hearts* and showing the film in a double bill with *Harold and Maude* (another Ashby "odd couple" romance) to help it at the box office, he was flatly turned down. The reason, according to Kaplan, was that *Hearts* was a "small" film and "Mancuso didn't give a shit about it."[40]

Paramount did, however, allow Ashby to use the print marketing campaign that he had devised, which featured a crude line drawing of Blake and Harris and the confusing tagline "A Recession Romance." Ashby had strongly objected to Paramount's marketing strategy, which promoted the film on Ashby's name and past success, as he felt that the use of his previous credits "tells the public that the film cannot stand on its own and that Paramount does not have confidence in it, as it must resort to a tired and uninspired device which has never worked."[41] That said, Ashby's own campaign was not strictly based on the film's true merits, as his ads quoted as many vaguely positive extracts from reviews as possible. In one instance, the *New York Post*'s Archer Winsten seemed to be raving about the film, saying it was "played to the hilt by Barbara Harris. . . . I don't think there has been anything like it." But the review *actually* ended as follows: "I don't think there has been anything like it and hope there never will again."[42]

At the first Los Angeles press screening, the reaction from critics was awful. One said that because Ashby had made the universally adored *Being There*, after *Hearts* there was "still hope for him," and others asked incredulously whether Ashby had *really* directed it.[43] A sentiment shared by many was that it might have been best not to release the film at all. When the reviews emerged, they were predominantly very poor, though most did their best to judge the film on its merits. Though Ashby had thought Barbara Harris's performance was the film's greatest weakness, Harris was actually the one person who was almost universally praised. Despite widespread disbelief that Ashby had directed a film this poor, the criticism was doled out gently, and the *Motion Picture Product Digest* reviewer summed up the thoughts of many when he said that Ashby was "entitled to a lapse now and then."[44] Writer Charles Eastman (whose reputation was already shaky) took the biggest hammering. Dinette and Loyal's homespun wisdom was widely attacked, and the *New York Times*' Vincent Canby said that Eastman treated his "characters as if they were waste baskets to be filled with prose that any self-respecting writer would hide from his best friend."[45] (Eastman, for his part, hated Blake's and Harris's acting and, when asked whether there was any element of the film he liked, replied, "No.")[46]

There were good reviews, however, such as Crist's and those in the *LA Weekly* and *LA Reader*. A glowing appraisal of the film, headlined

"A brilliant ode to Americana," by Bruce McCabe in the *Boston Globe*, made the Boston box office takings the biggest by far. Nonetheless, at the end of the year, the film was featured in *Rolling Stone*'s top box office bombs of 1981: having cost $7 million, it had staggeringly grossed less than $10,000. (Nielsen figures now list it as having taken only $19,450, though a year after its release it had earned back almost $2 million from worldwide receipts and television and video money.)

Second Hand Hearts is a puzzling film, above all because it seems almost inconceivable that Ashby made it. Though there are a remarkable number of aspects of Loyal that Ashby could relate to (his restlessness and inability to commit, a family inherited by marriage, the voyage to California's promised land, having been an encyclopedia salesman, and having fallen in love in Ogden), he is flippant, loud, and unthinking and thus a fundamentally atypical Ashby hero. Tonally, the film is completely antithetical to Ashby's other work, with a manic chaos that pervades almost every moment. Confusion is rife owing to the rapid-fire, oddly expressed dialogue (spoken in accents so strong that Ashby at one point even considered having subtitles) and bizarre, befuddling plot situations. Everything is overplayed, and the few moments of quiet or restraint are a blessing for viewers.

After an incredible run in the 1970s, Ashby had to accept that his films would not always turn out how he imagined them. Or as Loyal Muke says, "You can't win 'em all, you've got to lose some of 'em. You've got to take the bitter with the better, that's my philosophy."

20

Like a Rolling Stone

> I'm supposed to be a director, and a director is supposed to have a body of work. All I have is a body of frustration!
> —Hal Ashby

> The studios were basically frightened of him because he was their antithesis. As sweet as he was, he was a tough guy. You could not move him if he felt the enemy was in the room. And the enemy was anyone who was going to make him compromise what he felt was the truth of what he was doing. . . . When he was protecting the truth, he was a warrior. He was beautiful, sweet, lovely, but also ferocious—a ferocious angel.
> —Dustin Hoffman

As soon as Ashby had handed *Second Hand Hearts* over to Paramount, he began supervising the editing of *Lookin' to Get Out.* On hiring a new chief editor to oversee the cutting, he had noted that, unlike his predecessor, the replacement "did know how the basic mechanics worked, so things got done, and my life seemed more pleasant, for awhile, in that area." Now, however, he began to notice a new problem: "In a few short weeks I was able to see how bad my new editor was, not the mess of before, just not much reason behind any of the juxtapositions used in placing one piece of film after another."[1]

Finally, Ashby ran out of patience and took over the editing himself. He had all the footage transferred to videotape (at considerable cost) so he could use an innovative new editing technique and brought in the ever-reliable Bob Jones to share the workload with him. Having determined that the current cut was inherently flawed, Ashby insisted that he and Jones start over from scratch. With 130 hours of footage to wade through, the two friends faced a huge challenge. From spring through summer, they worked almost twenty-four hours a day, Jones doing day shifts and Ashby doing nights, trying to get it ready for the October release that Lorimar and Paramount were planning.

Ashby had recently gotten into the Police and decided to make their music an integral part of *Lookin' to Get Out,* selecting twenty-four tracks from their first three albums to put in the film. He cut scenes to the songs, using the beat to dictate the rhythm of the editing, but was still just thinking about the film a sequence at a time. He had not yet screened a rough cut for anybody and indeed seemed actively resistant to the idea of doing so, though he did show significant portions of what he had done to the increasingly vexed Lorimar suits.

Ashby had never really seemed to need much sleep (which he apparently did for only an hour or so at a time, with his eyes half open), so he often edited at night. His editing staff, who'd all heard the rumors about his hedonistic tendencies that had been going around Hollywood, drew their own conclusions when he turned up at 4 A.M., sometimes barefoot and with a towel wrapped around him. "When he showed up, you never knew what Hal had had, whether he had eaten mushrooms, whether he was on acid or coke," says Janice Hampton, one of his editors on *Lookin'*. "We would hear his Mercedes, and we would say, 'Here comes Captain Wacky to the bridge.'"[2] Ashby would then silently settle down with a joint, often encouraging the other editors to join him, and work with fiendish concentration for hours on end. Hampton recalls that a stoned Ashby would play sadistic mind games with her, trying to baffle her with his editing expertise, but still she maintains, "Everything I've learned of value I learned from Hal."[3]

While there was certainly a degree of truth in the rumors of Ashby's drug use, they were unreasonably inflated, in part because of people's preconceptions about Ashby as a hippie, and possibly also because of Lorimar's alleged attempt to blacken his name. Another editor who worked with him during this period, Eva Gardos, did not see him as being in any way an exceptional case. "He smoked a lot of marijuana freely, and sometimes came in with a bag of mushrooms and said 'These are really good,' but I never saw him take coke," she recalls. "Drugs were rampant at the time—he was no different from anybody else."[4]

While Ashby was working nights editing *Lookin' to Get Out,* he was spending his daylight hours developing future projects. Around the time *Handcarved Coffins* was put on ice, Ashby had been approached by his friend Mick Jagger about directing an adaptation of *Kalki,* a novel by Truman Capote's great literary rival, Gore Vidal. The book, which Jagger had bought the rights to when it was published in 1978, is a jet black comedy about an American GI who starts his own religion and then predicts the coming of the apocalypse. It seemed an ideal project for Ashby. "It was because of *Being There* and because I admired him as a director that I thought he was perfect for *Kalki,*" says Prince Rupert Loewenstein, the Rolling Stones' business manager, who helped set up the film. "He was an educated, sensible, sensitive man. He was all those things with humor, which is rare. He had a sense of the ironic, a sense of the ridiculous, and a sense of proportion. All three are essential ingredients in a great director. I can't think of any other director who had that specific talent and humor."[5]

Jagger had not only bought the rights to *Kalki* but also convinced Vidal to write the screenplay and was putting up a significant chunk of his own money. However, Ashby and Jagger still needed to find a studio to provide the rest of the budget. In early 1981, it was reported that *Kalki* would start shooting in the latter part of the year, but this plan had to be revised as too many elements of the film were a turnoff to the major studios. The shoot would be long and expensive regardless—not least because bribes would be required to get permission to shoot in the proposed locations in India and Nepal—and this left less money with which to attract big-name stars. Jagger initially wanted a good comic actress—Goldie Hawn, Diane Keaton, or Jane Fonda—to play the role of the lesbian Teddy, but none was willing to take the risk, and in the end the only well-known actor who committed himself to *Kalki* was Alec Guinness. The film was generally something of a hot potato as it scathingly satirized religion, the CIA, and America as a whole, and although Paramount and Twentieth Century–Fox expressed interest, both ultimately passed.

Around the same time, Ashby was contacted by Dustin Hoffman.

There had been some discussion earlier in the year that they would work together on an adaptation of *Laughing War,* Martyn Burke's novel about a comedian sent to entertain U.S. troops in Vietnam; however, Hoffman had now found another film he wanted Ashby to direct. *Tootsie,* which Hoffman had announced back in 1979, was a cross-dressing comedy in which a struggling actor (Hoffman) passes himself off as a woman in an attempt to get the female lead in a soap opera. When Dick Richards, the man originally slated to direct, chose to do *Man, Woman and Child* (1983) instead, Hoffman (who had a deal for the film at Columbia giving him creative control plus a huge $4.5 million fee) saw his chance to bring Ashby on board. Since Hoffman became involved with the project in 1979, it had gone through numerous changes symptomatic of the actor's insecurity about his transformation from serious actor to comedic transvestite.

Ashby's *Tootsie* contract was far from ideal as his engagement was subject to a formal commitment from Hoffman, who also had final cut. It was understood that Ashby and Hoffman would work out creative aspects between them, including final cut, but had it not been for Ashby's friendship with Hoffman and the implicit trust between them, he would have been unwilling even to consider such a contract. The prospect of collaborating with Hoffman, however, seemed to override any doubts Ashby may have had, and it quickly became clear that *Tootsie* was going to be a lot of fun.

Hoffman seemed to love cross-dressing and would turn up at Ashby's editing complex in full drag. In mid-May, Ashby had Haskell Wexler shoot a screen test of Hoffman dressed as his female persona, Dorothy Michaels, at Ashby's house in Malibu Colony. Hoffman, made up beyond recognition and wearing the large glasses, was clearly having a ball as he vamped it up in various outfits, including a nurse's uniform. Hoffman sang to his eight-week-old son Jake as "Dorothy" and bounced him on his lap. Ashby then let him teeter around on his high heels and improvise scenes where he flirted with an elderly female neighbor (whose bottom he pinched) and responded to men hitting on him. Even Ashby got involved in the hilarity, lifting up Hoffman's dress; the actor responded by perching on his director's lap. Hoffman was quite brilliant; all present were in hysterics, and Hoffman himself often burst out laughing midsentence.

The plan was to shoot *Tootsie* in the fall when *Lookin' to Get Out* would be nearly completed and Ashby's obligation to Lorimar would be all but fulfilled. Lorimar's patience with Ashby had by that time long been exhausted; as *Lookin'* was the final film in the three-picture deal, there was no further attempt to be diplomatic. At the start of the year, Lorimar had ceased paying Northstar staff, and Ashby and Braunsberg's company was in the process of closure. By the summer, it was little more than a name and some nearly deserted offices (Lorimar representatives had entered the premises after hours and snatched the furniture), and the two founders were left to look back on an idea ultimately too ambitious to succeed. With the exception of *The Postman Always Rings Twice,* there had not been a single Northstar film that Ashby had not directed himself; all the other projects had stalled in development.

Creator, Barfly, and *Revenge* did, in fact, all get made four or more years down the line (Ivan Passer's *Creator* was released in 1985, Barbet Schroeder's *Barfly* in 1987, and Tony Scott's *Revenge* in 1990), but it was projects like Orson Welles's *The Dreamers* and James Foley's *Cowboys of the American Night* that were truly symbolic of Northstar's fortunes. Braunsberg had fostered a friendship with Orson Welles and was tremendously excited about being the architect of his return to Hollywood, but when he went to Warner Brothers with the idea, he was told Welles was a liability and unceremoniously shown the door.

Cowboys of the American Night was at the other end of the spectrum, a script by a first-time writer-director, but it proved equally difficult to get funded. In a moment of financial desperation, Braunsberg had sold an eighteen-month option for *Cowboys* to Playboy Productions without Ashby's knowledge, to fund much needed rewrites on other Northstar projects and pay some of the staff. Braunsberg's actions drove a wedge between him and Ashby and, in many ways, signaled the end for Northstar. The reason Braunsberg hadn't told Ashby was because he was locked in the editing room cutting *Lookin'* and Braunsberg had long since grown used to working around Hal's unavailability.

"Hal never appeared, of course," recalls Braunsberg, "because he always stayed in his house." Looking back, Braunsberg says Northstar was "a lovely idea" that worked on paper but not in practice. "We started that company with a lot of idealism," he continues, "but our feet were not firmly on the ground. Hal was too much of a poet, and I wasn't enough of a businessman. It seemed like two different companies pulling in two different directions."[6]

As Northstar was falling apart, Braunsberg wrote to Ashby in an attempt to heal the rift, stressing their shared beliefs, and underlining that he too felt betrayed by Lorimar and the Northstar films' distributors. "The major companies seem to have more ego than the film makers," Braunsberg wrote. "Why is it that one sounds so naïve when all we are asking for is a *joint* agreement. The answer of course is money, which is nearly always used as a weapon. The main thrust of my future work will be to find solutions to these problems."[7]

Sadly, Braunsberg's heartfelt letter did not soften Ashby's feelings, and further attempts at reconciliation were equally unsuccessful. Bob Downey recalls visiting Ashby once at the Colony when Braunsberg appeared outside and began knocking on the window. When Downey asked what was going on, Ashby said, "Ignore him, Bob." Eventually, when Braunsberg did not go away, Ashby went over to the window and said, "Andy, there are three people in the world I can talk to, and you're not one of them."[8] Braunsberg seemed heartbroken.

Any inclination he had left to reestablish a working relationship was quickly eroded by Ashby's inflexibility. "Both of us were right, and both of us were wrong," says Braunsberg. "It was very sad because he was an *exceptional* person. We knew each other, even though we didn't know each other. It could have worked out. We had an amazing synergy. We had an incredible opportunity that we blew."[9]

During the summer, the October release for *Lookin' to Get Out* was scrapped by mutual agreement after both Ashby and Lorimar acknowledged that the film was still a problematic "work in progress." Braunsberg says that Ashby was attempting to make the film work, that he was looking for "a miracle he couldn't figure out. It had a debilitating effect on Hal. He became like Howard Hughes, and he was chain-smoking grass, which I think induced paranoia. He looked like a fright, and became unavailable."[10] Surrounded by the miles of film he had shot, Ashby created version after version of the same scenes, unsure of what worked best. He was philosophical about the possibility of *Lookin'* being a failure and once, during his struggles with Lorimar, said, "Hey, I can always go back and live on the beach."[11]

At the same time, Ashby was enthusiastically looking forward to making *Tootsie*. The start date, however, had been pushed back to November at the request of a jittery Dustin Hoffman, who wasn't happy with either of the drafts the film's latest screenwriter, Larry Gelbart, had produced. Yet Hoffman's dissatisfaction had more to do with his continuing personal fears. Jeff Wexler, who had been brought on board the film by Ashby along with his father, Haskell, Mike Haller, and a number of other Ashby regulars, says, "Dustin was very insecure, unsure he could actually pull off the movie."[12]

Jack Ashby recalls that when he was staying with Hal in Malibu around this time, Hoffman's wife brought a tearful Dustin to Ashby's house. "Dustin was just crying and sobbing and saying 'I don't wanna go to New York to do the first scene,'" Jack recounts. "And Hal just says, 'Well OK, Dusty,' and treated him just like a little kid. He says, 'That's just fine. If you don't wanna do that we'll work out some other way to do it.' Hoffman kept saying, 'I don't wanna do that, I don't wanna do it,' and Hal kept just talking to him and patting him. Pretty soon he calmed down, and his wife says, 'Thanks for talking to him. He was driving me crazy!'"[13]

Hoffman's jitters were, in turn, making Ashby uneasy as he was well into preproduction on *Tootsie* and Hoffman had yet to make a firm commitment to the film—meaning that Ashby was working without pay and essentially without a contract. Columbia couldn't even give him an estimated budget for the film but demanded his exclusive services, which he could not offer since he was still working on the editing of *Lookin'* and had no idea when production on *Tootsie* would actually begin.

Events took a drastic turn for the worse when, on September 30, Lorimar announced it would sue Ashby and Columbia if he began work on *Tootsie* before he had delivered *Lookin' to Get Out*. Two days later, Columbia said it could not offer employment to Ashby while the threat of legal action was hanging over the studio, and, despite Ashby's lawyers' assertions that Lorimar had no lawful grounds to sue, three days later Ashby's job on *Tootsie* was terminated. Lorimar's lawyers had maintained that Ashby's services were not available until he had finished what Lorimar deemed an acceptable version of *Lookin'*, despite the fact that, as Jack Schwartzman had explained to Ashby in 1979, the deal brokered with Lorimar stipulated that his "commitment to Lorimar was and is non-exclusive. You agreed to give them first look at your projects during the course of the agreement. Any project they did not want to develop could be set up elsewhere. You could accept pictures from other companies."[14]

Ashby's lawyers made desperate attempts to get Columbia to reconsider, and for a few days it looked as if Ashby might be reinstated. Frank Price, Columbia Pictures' chairman and president, told the *Hollywood Reporter,* "Hoffman wants Ashby, and we do, too, but we can't interfere with contractual relationships. There's nothing definitive at this point. To our knowledge, Hal's occupied with another picture. The situation is a little loose. He could return to the project but preproduction time is important."[15]

Columbia wanted the exclusive services of *Tootsie*'s director for the ninety days of preproduction, and Ashby's ties to *Lookin'*—whether legally binding or not—were too much of a risk for the studio to stick with him. Lorimar had prized Ashby from an exciting and lucrative project by playing a game of high-stakes legal bluff with Columbia and left him high and dry.

"It was retribution for the problems on *Lookin' to Get Out,*" says Kenneth Kleinberg, one of Ashby's lawyers who tried to get Ashby $1.5 million compensation for the loss of earnings incurred by Lorimar's actions.[16] However, though Ashby's contract promised to pay him $1.5 million for *Tootsie,* it was valid only once Columbia had received a "formal" commitment from Hoffman, which the actor had not yet given. As a result, Ashby never saw a single cent for his work on *Tootsie,* which ultimately was directed by Sydney Pollack and released in 1982.

On October 9, in the midst of his despondency over what had happened with *Tootsie,* Ashby went to see the Rolling Stones at the Los Angeles Coliseum. They were on the lengthy American leg of their *Tattoo You* world tour, the first all-stadium tour in rock-and-roll history. It was during the show, as the band watched the sun setting, that Jagger had the idea of commissioning a film of the tour. Ashby had very particular ideas about how a music film should be made, so when Jagger asked him after the show which directors he could recommend, he said, "Why don't I do it?"[17]

As it was far from certain that *Kalki* would ever get made, Jagger jumped at the opportunity to work with Ashby, who was relieved to have a replacement for *Tootsie* fall into his lap. Within just a few days, Jagger had convinced the band members to put up $2.5 million of their own money (of which Ashby would receive a modest $150,000), and a shooting schedule was drawn up. To prepare for the movie, Ashby attended and taped a few more Stones shows (the fact that they played the same twenty-five songs in the same order every night helped) to formulate ideas on how to approach the venture and brought in old friend Pablo Ferro as his codirector.

Jagger wanted a departure from the way that previous films, particularly the Maysles brothers' *Gimme Shelter* (1970), had shown the band: instead of interviews and vérité behind-the-scenes footage, he favored a straightforward document of the tour. The Stones had a huge, colorful stage setup that Ashby was excited about capturing on celluloid, and he wanted to make a concert film that would focus on the energy and excitement of the Stones' music. "My initial, basic idea," Ashby said, "was to make a real good hour-and-a-half-long rock and roll album, and capture some real good images to go with it."[18]

Though Lorimar had forbidden Ashby to do *Tootsie,* insisting that nothing should keep him from finishing *Lookin' to Get Out,* Merv Adelson inexplicably allowed him to direct the Stones film. Admittedly, Ashby would be shooting for only a handful of days, but there were also lengthy pre- and postproduction periods to be factored in. After the ruthlessness of Lorimar's actions over *Tootsie,* Adelson's decision seems bizarre, though it may have simply been a demonstration to Ashby that the company was in charge. Ashby summed it up by saying, "Lorimar had blown my *Tootsie* deal, but Merv said okay to the Stones Film—it was getting nuttier all the time."[19]

Shortly after getting the green light for the Stones movie, Ashby completed a cut of *Lookin' to Get Out* (seemingly close to three hours in length) that he was happy with. Unfortunately, however, he had discovered that using songs by the Police, a British band, was in conflict with Northstar and Lorimar's agreement with the American Federation of Musicians to use only music recorded in the United States in their films. Only a significant payment would have allowed Ashby to have the sound track of his choice, so the Police songs had to be scrapped. *Lookin'* had already cost close to a staggering $18 million, and as Ashby said, by the time he showed his version of the film to Lorimar, "everyone was pissed and down on the film."[20]

A few years earlier, Ashby's editors had cut *Being There* with Erik Satie's music as a temporary track, and then John Mandel wrote a symphonic sound track that uncannily recalled Satie's style—so much so that the French arm of the film composer's association (unsuccessfully) sued him. Ashby now decided to have Mandel write a sound track in the style of the Police, expecting that it would be done in time for the film's new release date of February 1982.

Less than a month after the idea for the Stones movie had been conceived, production began on the as-yet-untitled concert film. The first two Stones shows Ashby shot were on November 5 and 6 at the Brendan Byrne Arena, Meadowlands, New Jersey. Ashby had brought in Ron Schwary, producer of the most recent winner of the Best Picture Oscar, *Ordinary People* (1980), and reunited with Caleb Deschanel, one of two directors of photography on the film, along with Gerald Feil. Ashby and Ferro sat in front of a bank of video monitors, giving instructions to the fourteen camera operators covering every possible angle of the spectacle. "Hal was directing half the cameras and I had the others," says Ferro. "We'd be yelling into the operators' headsets, 'Camera One, stay with Mick, stay with Mick,' and 'Camera Three, looks good on Keith Richards, don't lose him,' and all the while everything they were shooting was being recorded on videotape. It was exhausting, and it got pretty crazy."[21]

The great efforts the Stones had made to dazzle the masses visually as well as musically translated well to Ashby and Ferro's wide-screen cinematic vision. At every show, twenty-five thousand balloons were released in the crowd, and the carnival atmosphere was capped by a huge fireworks display set to Jimi Hendrix's explosive rendition of *The Star Spangled Banner.*

Jagger had an active role in the film, readily contributing ideas for both the film and the pay-per-view show in Hampton Roads, Virginia, at the end of the tour, which Ashby was also to direct. The other band members, however, were not so keen on the idea of yet another film, which to them was one more obligation on an already busy tour. "There was definitely a greater bond between Mick and Hal than there was with the rest of the band," says Prince Rupert Loewenstein. "Mick was a man who was the incarnation of the band for Hal and also much more interested in the filming side than all the rest."[22]

Jagger was a natural entertainer, and even his backstage activities had a charm and flamboyance, something that was not true of some of his bandmates. Richards was particularly uncooperative. While Ferro and Caleb Deschanel were shooting backstage, he grumpily told them to stop filming him in the greenroom. Even worse, Richards turned up drunk for one of the Meadowlands gigs, and although the visuals that night were fine, it sounded so bad that filming had to be abandoned.

The Stones were infamous for their drinking and drug taking, and it was inevitable that Ashby—some fifteen years their senior—would join in their hedonism. There is a degree of uncertainty surrounding the events that took place before the show at the Sun Devil Stadium in Tempe, Arizona, the final filmed concert; however, on the night of the show Ashby had to direct while lying on a gurney with an IV in his arm. The consensus opinion was that Ashby had overdosed, and Jeff Wexler says fifty-two-year-old Ashby was "partying way beyond his capabilities with the Stones."[23] However, Pablo Ferro and Caleb Deschanel, the two people on the film who were closest to Ashby both professionally and personally, both say Ashby was genuinely ill, suffering from a severe bout of the flu.

"I heard that he couldn't attend for medical reasons," remembers Prince Rupert Loewenstein, "so I rang him and said, 'You've *got* to turn up.' I believe what I was told was a minor heart attack, but, from ninth-hand gossip, I assumed it was something else. I would not call into question his dedication to the project; I just think that it was the unfortunate effect of dope or drink. I think he was a highly dedicated artist."[24] To his credit, Ashby soldiered on, despite not being completely functional. Ironically, the Sun Devil show turned out to be the best of the three, and footage from that concert makes up more than half the completed film. Twenty cameras were employed, one of them in a helicopter that captured a stunning aerial shot as it rose above the mountains to reveal the stadium below and then swooped down over the stage as the Stones opened their set with the pounding "Under My Thumb."

"There was this really beautiful backdrop of desert and mountains, and we had 70,000 people," said Mick Jagger, recalling the concert during the film's editing. "We filmed it so that you see me singing in front of lots of bright colors, like a painting really, but a helicopter pulls the camera back and you see I'm actually performing in front of a gigantic guitar. I just saw a rough cut of the scene, and to tell you the truth I hadn't thought it would look as spectacular as it does."[25]

The Tempe show was full of memorable Jagger moments. During "Let Me Go," he climbed down into the audience and sang as he walked through crowds of fans. He danced with scores of chorus girls (including his girlfriend, Jerry Hall) for "Honky Tonk Women." And he rose into the air in a hydraulic cherry picker as he belted out "Jumpin' Jack Flash."

Garrett Brown, the cinematographic magician behind the groundbreaking Steadicam shot in *Bound for Glory,* filmed the band behind the scenes that night and followed them as they walked onto the stage, capturing an ideal opening sequence for the film. (Keith Richards got so annoyed with Brown walking after him he nearly started a fight with him.) Over the three nights in New Jersey and Arizona, Ashby and Ferro amassed more than sixty hours of footage, but at the end of it all, Ashby was probably just glad to be alive. "It's one of the most difficult things I've ever done," he said. "And the most fun."[26]

After the stress of the Sun Devil concert, the pay-per-view HBO show at Hampton Roads five days later was a less demanding affair, but only just. It was a massive operation, a two-and-a-half-hour program broadcasting to sixteen U.S. cities, composed of thirty minutes of backstage buildup, a brief support spot from George Thorogood and the Destroyers, and then the Stones' *Tattoo You* tour extravaganza in full. Ashby had no previous experience of the pressures of live television, especially on such a huge scale, but used what he'd learned in the past weeks to get him through—and justify the $100,000 fee he was earning for a single night's work. The broadcast's inspired opening sequence gave the names and frequencies of all the radio stations simulcasting the show (so, as Jagger was originally scripted to tell viewers, they could hear the sound "through proper speakers and avoid that awful little box on your TV"), which were painted onto a naked girl, the camera informatively moving up and down her body.[27] The backstage material ranged from run-of-the-mill footage (Keith Richards jamming, Jagger warming up for the show, Bill Wyman playing table tennis) to surreal staged moments such as when the cameraman wandered into the bathroom and found sheep, chickens, and ducks, naked women and men in the shower, and a woman standing at the urinal while snakes slithered on the bathroom pipes.

As it was the first ever pay-per-view concert, everyone involved was nervous. But when Jagger told the hordes at home he hoped they were having a good time drinking beer and smoking joints, suddenly it was just another night on tour with the Stones.

21

Getting Out

> The world is ripped up. Real good people stand around and try to figure out *why* they're ripped up.
>
> —Hal Ashby

In January 1982, Merv Adelson sent Ashby a letter with a document detailing the money spent on *Lookin' to Get Out*. "Just so that you are aware of the ridiculous costs of this film as it now stands," Adelson wrote. "This kind of thing is part of what is wrong with our business today. These costs do not include interest or overhead. When is it going to stop[?]"[1] The film had been budgeted at $12 million but was more than $5 million over budget and estimated to cost a further $1 million before completion. To ensure that it was finished as quickly as possible, Lorimar had Ashby sign an agreement stating that if he did not deliver *Lookin'* within one week of receiving the sound track from John Mandel, "Lorimar shall forthwith thereafter have complete control of the Picture, and materials and elements, and to be required to affectuate its control."[2] This would have been a fail-safe move, if not for the fact that the music didn't materialize for months.

During that time, Ashby wrote to his lawyer, Kenneth Kleinberg, in a cathartic attempt to explain why he was "so bloody angry" about the ongoing Lorimar situation. Reflecting on the deal he had made four years earlier, he asserted that the partnership he signed on for had never been honored: "I sincerely can't see myself accepting a deal where I was told I was considered an employee. Partners, what a joke. Along with all the other broken promises, I was anything but a partner. From the time I was away in Texas shooting the first film 'Hearts,' and Lorimar made the deal with U.A. to distribute, to the negotiation with Paramount, when they were scrambling for money, and refused to tell, even to this day, what kind of deal they were trying to make, or did make, on some film on which I was a so-called partner. I wonder what they thought I'd feel when I was told the ultimate fate of my film is none of my business. A great way to run a partnership, huh? . . . I do understand it is, and was, my responsibility to take a walk, once I discovered, or was aware of the deception, dishonesty, or whatever you want to call it, but it seems I let continued hope, and promises guide me instead of my own good common sense. For this, I have truly learned one of the bigger lessons."

In addressing Lorimar's snide comments about how long it was going to take to edit *Lookin' to Get Out,* he said that because of "an editorial crew on both 'Hearts' and 'Lookin''" that had "continually" let him down he didn't start editing the film until the previous April: "And at that time it was like starting on a virgin film, as I was so unhappy with the so-called edit of the film."

Nevertheless, he did acknowledge that recently, with just a few small tasks remaining, he had found himself unable to work on *Lookin':* "It has to do with my Creative, ha ha, person. You see, it seems I'm only so good at working night and day, for almost 4 years, while trying to create, ha ha, 3 films for Lorimar, and all the while receiving no more support than a few broken promises, served up with a good dose of out and out lying. Most certainly, Lorimar has never even come close to saying thanks for a job well done. Well, as a result of this kind of treatment, my creative, ha ha, self sometimes starts to feel real sick inside, and even goes so far as to get very depressed at times. Of course, a lot of this has to do with the silly notion that this life, as we know it, is not a dress rehearsal. It is, in fact, the real thing. But what the hell, why should 4 unappreciated years, matter[?]"[3]

Anticipating that Mandel's music would be in his hands soon, he said he expected *Lookin'* should be ready (even if it were not entirely finished) for Lorimar's planned screening at the Cannes Film Festival in early May. However, Mandel's music did not turn up in time, adding to the notoriety of the film, which hyperbolic newspaper articles had stated "reportedly cost about $27 million."[4]

By this time, editing on the Stones movie was already at an advanced stage. Ashby and his crew were stationed at the postproduction complex he had set up in an old courthouse in Malibu. It was a somewhat surreal place to work (Ashby's business manager, Larry Reynolds, had an office in the building with bars on the door), but progress was relatively quick by recent standards. Ashby's four young editors, Lisa Day, Michael Tronick, Lori Hollingshead, and Sonya Sones, were working on the film song by song, and as they completed each number, he would look at what they had done and give them notes. Ashby had not initially assigned anyone the role of chief editor, but after turning up at 4 A.M. one morning to find Day familiarizing herself with the video editing system he was using on *Lookin'*, he casually offered her the job. She had feared she was going to be sacked but instead found herself promoted.

Ashby took it upon himself to be a friend and mentor to Day. "What I learned most from him was looking at film," she recalls. "He just loved it: the smell of it, the touch of it, the look of it. He was like a kid. I can't think of a better person to work for." Day says that very occasionally Ashby would turn up under the influence but that this was the exception rather than the rule. "He wasn't there to party," she says.[5]

There was pressure from Prince Rupert Loewenstein to finish the film as soon as possible so as to cash in on residual excitement about the tour, and the strain sometimes showed. Sonya Sones remembers that very early on in postproduction, an exasperated Ashby yelled at her. "It was probably the first time he sat down to work with me," she says, "and I was flustered because it was the great Hal Ashby. He was trying to communicate what he wanted done, and I wasn't understanding. I just remember being flustered and then being stunned because he was screaming at me. After that I was happy to edit [alone] and have somebody else work with him."[6]

There had been initial interest in the Stones film from Don Simpson, Barry Diller, and Michael Eisner at Paramount, who identified it as a potential gold mine if properly marketed and distributed. Ashby had given it Mike Kaplan's suggested title, *Time Is on Our Side* (from the Stones' song "Time Is on My Side"), and Jagger was touting it as a hit movie just waiting to happen: "If *The Last Waltz* grossed $5 million, and it wasn't a very good movie, we could gross at least that."[7] Kaplan himself compared it to the seminal *Woodstock* (1970) and predicted that *Time Is on Our Side* should make $20 million in rentals, adding that that was a "perhaps conservative figure."[8]

After finishing the European leg of the Stones' tour, Jagger joined Ashby in Los Angeles to help finesse the film's sound track. Sound rerecording mixer and longtime Ashby collaborator Robert "Buzz" Knudson remembers that Ashby and Jagger "would come in so fresh in the morning and by 11 or 12 o'clock they'd go out a couple of times together and come back, and after that they were just . . . rocking and rolling! They were great guys, though. They were really nice. Hal was one of my favorite people, as a matter of fact."[9]

A rough cut of *Time Is on Our Side* was screened to international distributors at Cannes and snapped up by the German distributor Tobis, which was to release the film in all the German-speaking countries in Europe as soon as possible. The finished seventy-millimeter print, however, was still a few months off, in part because its director was exhausted. Writing to Jagger to apologize for his noncommunication, Ashby explained, "It seems every time I come up for air and see where I'm at, it isn't the right time to call, or I'm just too bloody tired to make sense or or or. . . ."[10]

Ashby was in the process of finishing off the final version of *Lookin' to Get Out* and gave a copy of the print to Merv Adelson in early June. Though Ashby still had to do a final check and add end titles, Adelson did not return it as agreed. When Paramount execs saw the film, they declared it unreleasable and demanded it be reedited and shortened. Though Ashby's contract unambiguously gave him final cut, Lorimar stated that it had control of the film. Ashby responded by writing to Richard Zimbert, the senior vice president of Paramount, saying that he would sue if he didn't approve of the version Paramount proposed to release. However, Ashby ultimately had neither the stomach nor the will to follow through with the threat.

"There was too much studio politics," says Mike Kaplan, "and he gave up."[11] Just as he had done with *Second Hand Hearts,* Ashby emotionally switched off and let Paramount go ahead with its plans. Jon Voight, who loved the film as it was, worked with Bob Jones to cut fifteen to twenty minutes out of Ashby's version and create something more commercial. The fact that Jones, Ashby's favorite editor, had turned against him by helping Lorimar, "the enemy," butcher his film drove a wedge between them. Once the changes had been made, Jones contacted Ashby, hoping he might watch the new version and maybe even give his blessing. "I called him," remembers Jones, "said, 'Hal, we're screening this, I want you to see it,' and I couldn't get any response. 'Hal it's being released,' no response."[12]

Ashby had, in fact, given Voight permission to supervise the editing, but had he seen the final cut, he never would have approved. (Looking back on the changes he made to the film, even Voight admits, "I didn't do anything right.")[13] Ashby could not follow through on his initial decision to completely abandon *Lookin'* and ruefully admitted a few months later that the editing was his responsibility: "I can't negate that by saying, 'Hey, if they [audiences] don't like it, it's your [Voight and Jones's] fault, not mine.' That's bull. I'm the one who said, 'OK, do what you want' instead of 'No, I'm sorry. The version I have here is my cut, it's my film and I don't care what any of you think.' From now on, that's what I'm going to say."[14]

Paramount had accepted what seemed an undeserved R rating and planned only a limited release, and it appeared that the studio had decided to treat *Lookin' to Get Out* in much the same way as *Second Hand Hearts,* letting it slip by with the least possible embarrassment and money spent. Ashby disapproved of both the trailer and Paramount's choice of poster, which he told Paramount staff was "misrepresentative" and "will further alienate the audience."[15]

When *Lookin' to Get Out* was released on October 8, the critical reception almost killed it stone dead. Reviews expressed a continuing respect for Ashby and Voight but were unrestrained in their harsh opinions about the film itself. "False" and "ill-conceived" was how *Variety* saw the film, adding, "Voight and Young are an entertaining team but presented in an untenable vehicle."[16] Across the board, there was criticism of the improvisational feel of the film, and reviewers almost universally disliked the two main characters. The *Hollywood Reporter* called Voight's Alex Kovac "unsympathetic" and said that both Young's and Voight's screen personas were "too alien for empathy, and unconvincing."[17] In the *Los Angeles Times,* Sheila Benson opened her review by saying, "It is hard to understand the vision that attracted a director of Hal Ashby's sensibilities and overall track record . . . to the strident charmlessness of *Lookin' to Get Out.*"

There were also a handful of good reviews, notably from Gene Siskel and Judith Crist, plus others in the *New York Post, Newsweek, US Magazine,* and the *LA Weekly,* but it was possibly Benson's senior colleague at the *Los Angeles Times,* Charles Champlin, who best encapsulated the problematic film and its reception when he discussed it in his "Critic at Large" column.

"The film has been greeted in many reviews as a felony rather than a misdemeanor," Champlin wrote, "because (the backhanded compliment that can leave bruises) the critics on past evidence hoped for more from the assembled talents. What took place—in the making and, therefore, the perceiving of the film—is that a fairly serious film about the compulsive gambler acquired so many farcical and slapstick moments that it looked like a funny caper picture that wasn't funny enough, rather than a hard-edged and cynical film whose cutting edge was dulled. . . . I found *Lookin' to Get Out* more interesting than I expected it to be ("interesting" being one of those critical words that sound evasive even when they're not). Voight . . . struck me as taking a big risk for a star actor of creating a character who was essentially unlikable if possibly pitiable."[18]

The main reason that *Lookin' to Get Out* failed to appeal was arguably because it was out of line with the popular cinema of the 1980s. In the 1970s, the emergence of New Hollywood directors pushed the marginalized and underrepresented to the forefront of American cinema, and antiheroes, subversives, and losers were the protagonists of many highly successful films. But this had changed as increasingly aspirational Americans replaced former peanut farmer Jimmy Carter with failed Hollywood leading man Ronald Reagan. (Ashby was staunchly anti-Reagan and said that he "thought it was a joke" when he "heard Ronald Reagan was running for governor" of California. "I'm so naïve that I didn't think people were really going to get down to it."[19] According to producer Robert Shaffel, when Reagan wanted to visit the set while *Lookin' to Get Out* was shooting, Ashby threatened to shut down production for the day if Lorimar staff let him set foot on the lot.)[20] Alex Kovac is a loser with a smile who offers no excuse for himself, and there was no place for such an unrestrained and unsympathetic "hero" in Hollywood cinema of the 1980s. "Audiences want to identify with somebody in the picture," *Lookin' to Get Out*'s production designer, Bob Boyle, reflected, "and it was kind of hard to identify with these two losers."[21]

The film was awkward, unsettling, and staunchly individual, the opposite of what the successful films of the era were like as mainstream Hollywood movies became slicker and less complex. The reaction to *Lookin'* and Ashby was indicative of a general trend as the New Hollywood directors who had thrived making personal, challenging, and distinctive films under the permissive regimes of the studio heads of the

1970s almost all found themselves yesterday's men, outdated and marginalized. Coppola, Mazursky, Friedkin, Bogdanovich, Rafelson, and particularly Altman hit a slump during the "me" decade of the 1980s from which most would never recover.

However, not only was the film out of sync with the times, but the released version of *Lookin' to Get Out* suffered from its reediting after Ashby was forced to give it up. (Its failure should be set apart from that of *Second Hand Hearts,* a film gone so wrong that it never realistically had a chance of success.) The greatest flaw with the version of *Lookin'* the world saw was that it was an attempt to make an unconventional film seem more conventional. Nevertheless, there are still signs of quality marking it as a Hal Ashby film, particularly the performances of the leads: Voight plays totally against type and brings Alex Kovac vibrantly to life; Burt Young is wonderfully understated as Jerry, adding just enough compassion to the character to make him strangely charming; and Ann-Margret, though perhaps underused, is unusually good under Ashby's direction.

Considering its R rating and limited release, *Lookin'* had a respectable opening weekend, taking just over $500,000. However, owing to Paramount's lack of patience, it lasted barely more than a week or two in cinemas and grossed a little under $1 million, a staggering loss considering its $18 million price tag.

It was to be the last Lorimar film released for some years. Lorimar Films, a venture Merv Adelson had championed against the wishes of his partner, Lee Rich, had floundered horribly because of the inexperience, naïveté, and mistrust that extended throughout the company. Ashby's inability to thrive under Adelson and Rich was the rule rather than the exception, as other highly talented and individual directors like James Toback and Sam Fuller had equally miserable experiences. "There were a lot of petty, stupid things that in a better atmosphere would have been solved," says Kenneth Kleinberg. "I think they were unwilling to accept that they had made mistakes and that they hadn't handled a lot of things correctly; they wanted to pretend they were as important a studio as any major studio."[22]

Having ignored Bob Jones's invitation to watch his and Voight's amended version of *Lookin' to Get Out,* Ashby also declined to see the film on its release, though much of his bitterness seemed to have dissipated. "I directed it, it's a Hal Ashby film," he conceded. "I made the decision to allow what (Jon Voight) did to the cut. I choose not to see it, not because I disagree with the cut, but because I don't want to second-guess him."[23] However, in November 1982, UCLA organized a retrospective of Ashby's work from *Harold and Maude* onward, and presented him with a unique opportunity to show his own version of *Lookin' to Get Out.* According to Bob Schaffel and Voight, there are scenes and sequences in this version that they had never seen before, meaning that Ashby must have continued editing the film after he gave it to Lorimar, despite the fact that this unofficial version would never be seen by more than a handful of people.

Comparing the two versions of *Lookin' to Get Out,* one is struck by the scenes that are only in Ashby's version. The opening sequence—in which Alex collects his white Rolls Royce and has an unrestrained conversation with the Asian parking attendant, painting a hilarious, wildly imaginative, but extremely politically incorrect picture of what America would be like if the Chinese took control of it—shows that he is a chancer and an unashamed bullshitter, while the released version's opening scene sets him up as a more conventional leading man. Indeed, the scenes that are in Ashby's cut alone are arguably some of the most inspired, the perfect example being the chase sequence where Alex and Jerry are pursued through the MGM Grand by Harry and Joey, the heavies to whom they owe money. An abbreviated version exists in the released film, but in Ashby's it becomes a highly unusual chase owing to the off-kilter interludes: we see Alex and Jerry in the showgirls' dressing room donning oversized wigs, and then, as described previously, they get stuck in the room with numerous doors and begin bickering about Jerry's ex-wife. Another significant omission is the scene near the end where, after seeing his daughter for the first and last time, Alex is shown in a long shot sitting sad and alone, listening to Jerry having sex with the hotel hooker in the next room. It is a daring, emotionally powerful moment that perfectly expresses the poignancy of the situation, which Ashby typically captures with silence.

Overall, the pacing and feel of Ashby's cut are strikingly different from the released version. While Jones and Voight tried to generate a quicker pace to make it like a straightforward comedy, instead creating an awkward, stuttering progression, Ashby's cut is consistent throughout. From the first scene, nothing is rushed, and the film meanders and ambles with a sureness and ease toward its conclusion.

On the night Ashby showed his version of *Lookin'* at UCLA, he also premiered the Stones film, now titled *Let's Spend the Night Together.* It had been released a few months earlier in East and West Germany, Switzerland, and Austria under the title *Rocks Off!* and had been a considerable success. Ashby, however, had decided to reedit the film for its domestic release, which he was able to do because, despite considerable interest, the film had failed so far to find a U.S. distributor.

Ashby and Mike Kaplan had formulated an ambitious plan for a "road show" release, inspired by an editing session on the big screen at the Todd-AO studio. "Everybody just started dancing," says Kaplan, recalling how the idea came about.[24] Ashby wanted to re-create the scenario for audiences by showing the film on a big screen with an even bigger sound system and space for people to dance. This could be achieved by showing the film not in cinemas but in clubs. The film would travel to the big cities, taking an advanced audio setup with it, just like a rock-and-roll band.

"I want to do a road show kind of thing," Ashby explained, "because the film has got a lot of energy in it. Every time I screen it people come up to me afterwards and say, 'My God!,' so I want to take a 70mm, six-channel stereo print and put it up where people can have some fun. I want to screen it where people can get up and dance."[25]

There were precedents for Ashby's idea, as the Venice Film Festival had screened a seventy-millimeter print of the movie in St. Mark's Square, and 300,000 Stones fans had crammed into a stadium in São Paolo for a special screening to mark its Brazilian release. Before filming had started, Jagger met with Douglas Trumbull, the special effects wizard and director of *Silent Running* (1971), who had suggested that the film be shown on his own invention, Showscan, a system similar to IMAX. That plan had been shelved because there were no Showscan cinemas, and the road-show idea foundered too, owing to a combination of impracticality and expense. Though the film was making good money internationally, the Stones' management had already invested considerable funds in pursuing a U.S. distributor and saw the road-show scheme as too much of a financial risk.

Much later than Loewenstein had hoped, *Let's Spend the Night*

Together found an American distributor, Embassy Pictures, which released it on February 11, 1983. Though a seventy-millimeter print with six-track sound was put out and played at drive-ins as well as normal cinemas, Ashby's dream of audiences dancing to the film in clubs was never realized. The critical reception was very positive, though reviews tended to qualify their praise by acknowledging the film's rather limited ambitions. *Variety* dubbed it "a solid, technically sophisticated concert pic," and the *Hollywood Reporter* noted, "[What] Ashby did is mount a straightforward attempt to capture them [the Stones] in performance. He succeeds admirably."[26] Though Janet Maslin similarly noted the film's modest brief as "just a concert," she nevertheless described it as "probably the handsomest rock-and-roll movie ever made" and "the classiest of concert movies. . . . The scale is enormous, almost as though this were a western."[27]

The credits list Ashby as the sole director, only because Pablo Ferro forgot that his Directors Guild of America membership had lapsed ten years earlier. "Pablo is actually the co-director of the film," Ashby stressed. "Only guild requirements prevented him from having that title. He's been an integral part of this project from the beginning and has been involved in all of the film's creative work."[28] To make up for Ferro being credited only as "Creative Associate" on the film, Ashby surprised him by giving him the original storyboards for *The Russians Are Coming, the Russians Are Coming* and the "multiples" contact sheets from *The Thomas Crown Affair,* reminding him of their earliest collaborations and how their friendship had endured over the years.

One of Ferro's many contributions was the montage of black-and-white newsreel footage—soldiers brutally beating prisoners, a decapitated head on a spike, a man on fire, the pope being carried aloft through the streets, and a naked dying man lying in the dirt—that runs as the Stones play "Time Is on My Side," a variation on Jagger's idea of using stock footage and cutting erotica in with concert footage.

During the same song, pictures of the Stones as they progressed from infancy to adulthood and clips of them playing throughout their career were also interspersed, but what was surprising was the scarcity of moments like this in the film, when it was truly cinematic and not "just a concert." There was the helicopter shot, small amounts of backstage footage, a time-lapse sequence showing the band's elaborate stage set being assembled from scratch, and smaller montages showing Jagger's bows, whirls, jumps, kisses, etc., or Richards's dynamic guitar playing, but for a ninety-minute film featuring twenty-four songs, it was precious little. The film was essentially a more elaborate, up close version of what audiences experienced at the concerts, showcasing the band rather than Ashby's directorial skills.

Jagger, however, seemed very happy. He called the film "a much bigger, more accurate, interesting view of the concert than we'd had before in any film."[29] He also said, "I'm quite pleased that the band managed to achieve a film like this in the middle of all the insanity of a big tour. I think the Stones really *deserved* it."[30] The rest of the band was unimpressed, and Keith Richards even publicly criticized the film, saying that he didn't "think it's *Gone With the Wind*" and that the interest shown "doesn't justify pretending it's a real movie, it isn't."[31] Loewenstein contends, "Keith, Charlie [Watts], and Bill Wyman were never keen on the film angle. They said 'We tour, we perform, and we don't want to have to do anything else.' But because of [Ashby's] name and reputation I said, 'You can't turn down such a talented director.' They imagined the film would turn out as it did, whereas Mick and I thought the opposite. They just said 'I told you so.'" Loewenstein's regret was that the film lacked "creative thought, wit, intelligence—all the things that you had before with Hal Ashby."[32]

Despite the fact that Ashby had seemingly delivered exactly what Jagger asked for, Loewenstein and many others came away feeling that they expected more from "A Hal Ashby Film." But if *Let's Spend the Night Together* falls short of the mark, it is in large part because Jagger's idea of a "document" of the *Tattoo You* tour was too simplistic to be satisfying.

22

Old Man

I've been first and last
Look at how the time goes past
But I'm all alone at last
—Neil Young, "Old Man"

In *Let's Spend the Night Together,* as Mick Jagger sings the lines "When you're old, when you're old / Nobody will know" from "She's So Cold," there is a cut to Ashby sitting on a sofa backstage, bare chested and wearing shades, waving at the camera. And he does look old, the effects of the stress, trauma, and hard work of the past few years all too visible on his face. This cameo appearance was a dig at himself but also an acknowledgment that he was no longer a young man of boundless energy, that he didn't get up so quickly anymore when he was knocked down.

"You know, some people think you're dying," Jack Nicholson had told him sometime in 1982.

"Dying?" Ashby responded with an incredulous laugh.

"Yes!" said Nicholson.

Ashby related this story to Dale Pollock, arts editor of the *Los Angeles Times,* quipping, "I never got swamped by so much damn work in my life, but I didn't know it killed me."[1]

Ashby had spoken to Pollock just after the release of *Lookin'* in an attempt to give the film a push, breaking his silence after a number of years of not giving interviews. Mike Kaplan, who set up the interview, wrote to Ashby saying that Pollock, a friend of Kaplan's, was "a fan (saw *Being There* four times) and can be trusted. I discussed the *Lookin' to Get Out* situation with him—off the record, and he feels it can be finessed without hurting the movie."[2]

Over the course of two interview sessions, Ashby and Pollock had in-depth discussions about Ashby's life and, in particular, the events of recent years. When asked about the rumors of his heavy drug use, Ashby ascribed them to the fact that he had admitted to smoking marijuana, saying, "I hear all this stuff, but I personally don't get alarmed. As I go on with my life, I can't recall the last thing I heard about myself that was true."[3]

He called his time at Lorimar "as heavy a period in my life as I ever want to have." "I've run into more frustration than I could ever imagine," he continued, enigmatically adding, "It's made me think about things I don't usually think about." Having his house and editing rooms in Malibu, an hour from Los Angeles, had inevitably earned him a reputation as an "inaccessible" recluse, but Ashby had no regrets about his isolation from Hollywood. "I see people there start to fall into the wrong things," he said. "They start living their lives on simple levels where they didn't know the difference between right and wrong."[4]

While Pollock's article gave such intriguing insights into Ashby's views, it was ultimately sensationalist. Titled "Whatever Happened to Hal Ashby?" it focused on the failure of *Second Hand Hearts* and *Lookin' to Get Out* and even included a sidebar of numerous quotes from (mostly negative) reviews of the latter. Ashby was, however, given a forum to detail how Lorimar had systematically mishandled his films. (Lee Rich responded to these accusations by saying, "They're all ridiculous. Why even dignify them by answering them? They deserve no answer.") Nevertheless, the portrait Pollock painted of Ashby was one of a director in decline. The article opened by saying, "For the last three years, Hal Ashby seems to have disappeared. . . . There have been ugly rumors that Ashby was in ill health, burned out by drugs, incapable of completing a movie."[5] This negative image was compounded by a huge, unflattering photo of Ashby, looking spaced out.

An incensed Mike Kaplan wrote to the *Times*, criticizing Pollock's article, and giving the backstory behind the druggy-looking photo of Ashby: "During the first interview session, which lasted over two hours, nearly 50 photographs must have been taken by The Times photographer. Ashby wears glasses all the time, alternating the tints depending on the light. After the first hour or so of the session, he removed his glasses to readjust his eyes and pause for a moment. It was then that what appears as the cover shot was taken, providing the reader with a decidedly distorted look at Ashby, but one which when joined with the exploitative headline, fulfills the editorial intent."[6]

Pollock cannot particularly be blamed for tailoring his piece to fit the existing perception of Ashby. By this stage, Hollywood had already made up its mind that the widely expressed explanation for Ashby's career decline—namely, that he was burned out on drugs—was true. Ashby had long been an unashamed pot smoker and in 1977 had (naively) admitted to using cocaine to none other than the *New York Times,* so there was a degree of logic in the assumptions of those who ascribed the failure of his films in the early 1980s to problems with drugs. Yet many of the people making these claims conceded that they had never seen Ashby taking drugs and, moreover, that he had always been lucid, charming, and businesslike in his dealings with them.

The truth was that during this period Ashby did indeed use other drugs than marijuana and would sometimes take cocaine, usually with friends, or quaaludes with his girlfriend, editor Cathy Peacock. Chuck Mulvehill, who was close with Ashby for much of his professional career, says Ashby used drugs, "but I never thought of him as an addict." According to Mulvehill, because of Ashby's hippie image, "people just assumed he was a drug addict," and drugs became a scapegoat.[7] However, while Ashby's drug use may have made him difficult to be around at times and exacerbated the darker sides of his personality, it did not significantly change the way he directed. And Ashby himself certainly did not think so. When asked later about the decline in the quality of his films in the 1980s, he said, "Not quality. Success. Difference."[8]

While Ashby publicly insisted that the idea of a decline in his work was a fallacy, he was nevertheless well aware that he was no longer working in a Hollywood that supported artists like himself. Yet there is no question that, drugs aside, Ashby himself had contributed to the problems of his Lorimar films. His idealistic insistence on giving young editors a break led him to consistently engage inexperienced crews unqualified to competently edit the large amounts of footage he shot, and more damaging still was his uncommunicative and alienating attitude toward his employers.

After cutting all ties with Lorimar, Ashby found himself being sued by his former employers, who claimed he was liable for the huge costs incurred on *Lookin' to Get Out*. Faced with the possibility of having to pay the approximately $2.3 million that Lorimar was demanding, Ashby filed for bankruptcy, a calculated move to prevent the studio from getting a penny out of him in the foreseeable future.

The situation was further complicated by Ashby bringing a counterclaim against Lorimar in 1984 on multiple counts, a move he had considered making three years earlier. Lorimar's treatment of Ashby radically and detrimentally changed the course of his career, and although Ashby stopped doing business with the studio in 1982, it was a tragic irony that his court battles with Adelson's company dragged on until 1987, past the time when he directed his last film.

Ashby's recent lack of success made him cautious about taking on a new film, but he nevertheless attached himself to a number of projects and continued to seek out new ones. (He also got an agent for the first time in almost a decade, Jeff Berg at ICM, who was presumably brought in by Ashby to act as a buffer between him and the moneymen.) *Handcarved Coffins* still had not been made, but it appeared to have slipped away from Ashby, as a number of other directors (Roman Polanski, Jonathan Demme, Sidney Lumet) were being linked with it, while *Kalki* was put into turnaround in early 1983. In the latter stages of 1982, Ashby was leaning toward doing *Hawkline Monster* with Jack Nicholson, but the idea was put on ice when it briefly looked like Ashby's former *Coming Home* colleague Bruce Gilbert would hire him to direct *Jack the Bear* (which was finally released in 1993, directed by Marshall Herskovitz). Ashby continued to flirt with musical projects, including Willie Nelson's idea of turning his as-yet-unreleased album *Tougher Than Leather* into a film: the legendary country singer invited Ashby to his ranch near Austin, Texas, and even flew him there on his private jet, but the film never got past the drawing-board stage.

Mike Medavoy at Orion Pictures was keen to reestablish a partnership with Ashby after their success together at United Artists and suggested two possible projects. The first was *Modern Bride,* a romantic comedy starring Diane Keaton, who had twice previously tried to get Ashby to collaborate with her. Unfortunately, it collapsed—owing to problems over the budget and differences with Keaton—just as contracts were about to be signed. *Bake and Shake,* the second proposed film, was a basketball comedy written for Ashby by longtime friend Rudy Wurlitzer, with their mutual friend Nicholson touted as a possible star. A zippy, picaresque comedy about down-on-his-luck black pimp Shake Indigo and his old friend Bake MacLain, a white basketball coach, it didn't ultimately strike the right note with either Orion or Universal, which both passed on it.

In late 1982, Dustin Hoffman announced that he wanted to make a sequel to *Kramer vs. Kramer,* and he and Ashby began working on it. In the follow-up film, which was referred to as *Kramer II* or simply *K-II,* Ted Kramer and his son move in with a divorcée who has a child with Down syndrome. Along with producer Gail Mutrux, Ashby learned everything he could about Down syndrome, reading articles and studies on the subject, and meeting families who had children with the condition.

At the same time, Ashby, Hoffman, and Mutrux were researching Hiroshima with an eye to developing a related film. Ashby's interest in the subject had been reignited after reading John Hersey's 1946 extended *New Yorker* article "Hiroshima" in book form. The dropping of the atomic bomb had been a preoccupation for Ashby, as it was—like the day of the 1968 presidential election, around which *Shampoo* was based—a time at which America took a huge and irreversible step in the wrong direction. In 1963, he had written to his mother, saying, "I wonder if Man will ever stop hating Man? We always want to lash out and hurt somebody else. It makes me sick at heart whenever I think about it. I saw a show last night with some of the crew from the plane that dropped the Atom Bomb on Hiroshima. As you know, none of them knew exactly what it was they were dropping. It has had tremendous after-effects on many of them. . . . [The pilot] was so moved that he wrote, 'My God, what have we done?' I did see this man on a show some years ago and as he told about it he started to cry. Right on TV, in front of millions of people, he broke down and cried. I wanted to tell him we were all responsible, not just him. Well, I'm upset now. . . ."[9]

While Ashby and Ian Bernard had been inexperienced unknowns when they attempted to examine the repercussions of Hiroshima in *The Sound of Silence,* Ashby was now a veteran director whose handling of the fallout from Vietnam in *Coming Home* amply qualified him to tackle America's collective guilt about Hiroshima. In the spring of 1983, Ashby went to Japan (just as his alter ego, David Cassidy, had done in

The Sound of Silence) to see and absorb the atmosphere of the places he had only read about or seen in pictures. It was not an enjoyable trip; he got very ill in Tokyo as the city's smog irritated his lungs, still sensitive after the damage done by the dust storm on *Bound for Glory*. Though his interest in the subject continued, the Hiroshima film was yet another project that never came to fruition.

Just before his trip to Japan, Ashby had gone to Iowa with actress Jessica Lange and writer William Witliff to meet with local farmworkers in Des Moines. Impressed by Ashby's work, and *Bound for Glory* in particular, Lange had interested him in a project with the working title *Modern Day Farm Drama* (later called *Country*), a contemporary film about farmers' extreme financial difficulties, in the vein of *The Grapes of Wrath*. He was signed on to supervise Witliff writing the screenplay and to direct the movie in the fall of 1983, capturing the corn harvest on film as it happened. The Ladd Company, headed by former Fox boss Alan Ladd Jr., had taken on the film but was obliged to drop the project after financial problems with *The Right Stuff* (1983) and other films. Lange and Witliff shopped the project around every studio in town, but none saw the appeal of a dour picture about failing farmers. They were close to giving up when Touchstone, Disney's new offshoot that made live-action films for a more mature demographic, agreed to fund *Country* if the budget could be reduced from $11 to $8 million. The very next day, Ashby inexplicably withdrew from the project. As it had been sold as a package that included Ashby as director, this almost scuppered the Touchstone deal.

Looking at Ashby's activities in 1983, one is struck by the fact that, despite the rumors of a drug addiction that made him unemployable, many of Hollywood's major players were clamoring to work with him. And yet despite the huge number of projects he was involved in, he did not direct a single one of them. It is very revealing that exactly when *Country* had received a definite green light and was only weeks away from starting, he said he had no desire to direct it. Ashby was in the habit of attaching himself to projects, but when it came down to it, it seems he had neither the appetite nor the energy to take on a major production in the wake of his experiences with Lorimar.

In Ashby's old pad on Appian Way, one of the most striking things he had added to the decor was a montage painting of the Rolling Stones and Neil Young, his two favorite recording acts at the time. Young, like Jagger, was also a friend. *Let's Spend the Night Together* had sprung from Ashby's kinship with Jagger, and, after dropping out of *Country,* Ashby reconnected with Young to film one of his concerts, thirteen years after their aborted collaboration on *The Landlord.*

Young and Ashby's career trajectories had been remarkably similar. Both started out in the late 1960s to great success and peaked in the 1970s—when Ashby was making his landmark films and Young recording classic albums such as *Harvest* and *After the Gold Rush*—and both had major career slumps in the 1980s. Finding his folk-rock stylings no longer of interest to the public, Young visibly floundered, trying to acclimate to the change in musical taste. In 1983, he released two records, *Trans,* in which he experimented with electronic music, and *Everybody's Rocking,* which was recorded with the 1950s throwbacks the Shocking Pinks.

The concert Ashby was asked to film—at the Harrah Arena in Dayton, Ohio, on September 18, 1983—was part of Young's 1983 *Solo Trans* tour. The show was staged in three parts: first he played his much-loved songs from the 1960s and 1970s, then he moved on to the electro-pop of *Trans*, and finally, after a costume change, reappeared with the Shocking Pinks. Ashby's production was framed by contributions from faux television anchorman Dan Clear (played by Newell Alexander), whose enthusiastic backstage reportage was seen by the audience on a big screen at the back of the stage. It was yet another aspect of the show that was self-consciously modish and an unfortunate misjudgment on a par with Young's decision to do a vocoder reworking of "Mr. Soul," a song he had first recorded with Buffalo Springfield in 1968.

Ashby, with a crew of thirty-five people, turned up in Dayton the day before the show and employed a much less elaborate and expensive approach than he had with the Stones, opting for just seven cameras. The film crew and the road crew gelled quickly but faced a serious setback when Young discovered that the stage had been made five feet high, far too elevated for the cameramen to get the shots needed. Overnight, the roadies took down and then reassembled the stage so as to be ready in time. "I'm going to have T-shirts made with 'Mr. Popularity' on the chest," Young joked, "and below that, 'Pull It Down And Put It Up Again Lower.'"[10]

Ashby was unfazed by the drama, having dealt with much greater crises in the past. The morning after the panic, Ashby took Young through the plans for the show, letting him climb up onto the camera crane to see exactly how certain shots would look. That night, the show went well, and the audience loved Young. He began with his classic songs "Heart of Gold," "Old Man," and "Ohio"; after that, his adoring fans were putty in his hands despite the fact that he was clearly struggling with his musical identity.

It must have been poignant for Ashby to reflect on the difference between the film director and the singer: while Young could go from city to city, feeling the appreciation of fans everywhere by playing old songs, Ashby had no such luxury. As a director, he was an unseen figure, almost totally unacknowledged by the public, whose fate lay in the hands of his employers.

23

The Slugger's Wife

> I guess the idea of losing is enough to turn most people, especially men, into full out idiots. In sports it's better. You don't like to lose, but it's okay if you do. You're trained for it in sports. Crowds will boo, hiss, put you down for losing, but they'll keep coming back for the wins. It doesn't work the same way in life—when you lose, you're a loser. You can't keep getting up like they do in football. Actually, you can, it just doesn't seem like it.
>
> —Hal Ashby

Producer Ray Stark was a fan of Hal Ashby's, having twice gone to the trouble of writing him to say how much he admired his work. He had told Ashby he'd done "a damn good job" on *The Last Detail*.[1] Later, he mentioned in a letter that Peter Sellers had told him about *Being There* while they were shooting *Murder By Death* (1976), adding: "[Sellers was] very lucky . . . that [he] didn't make the film [*Being There*] with me. I never could have contributed to the making of a film from a book which I wasn't quite knowledgeable enough to know how to dramatize." Ashby, he said, was "a remarkable talent with a remarkable range and I hope someday we'll have the privilege of working together."[2]

Though a latecomer to filmmaking, Stark had established himself in the mid-1960s as one of the most powerful producers in Hollywood, starting with initial hits *Night of the Iguana* (1964) and *Funny Girl* (1968) and then consolidating with a string of films with Neil Simon, arguably the most respected comic dramatist of the period. Stark's dominance as a producer was fueled by a desire to control everything: his telephone conversations began "Are you alone? . . . Are you sure? . . . And what we say will go no further? . . . *Swearzy?*"[3] Though the bedrock of his success was his close and highly lucrative relationship with Simon, the pair had fallen out after making *Seems Like Old Times* (1980), a film based on Simon's marital problems with his wife, actress Marsha Mason. In 1982, Stark and Simon were reconciled, by which time Stark had produced the infamous flop *Annie* (1982) and Simon was on a run of uncharacteristically mediocre films, including *I Ought to Be in Pictures* (1982) and *Max Dugan Returns* (1983), that were ever more thinly veiled ponderings on his own life and relationships.

In 1983, Simon and his muse, Mason, announced their divorce; however, Simon received a welcome boost when Stark proposed they recommence their partnership on Simon's latest script, *The Slugger's Wife,* a soppy romance about a baseball player's strained relationship with a pop singer. Stark had a reverence for anything Simon wrote, while Simon respected Stark's absolute authority as a producer (because it was used to grant Simon immense authorial control), and the two were excited about working together again, convinced that this latest collaboration would be the hit they both needed—despite the fact that, in retrospect, the confidence in Simon's screenplay seemed like a case of the emperor's new clothes.

Initial whispers in Hollywood suggested that Stark had pulled off a coup by getting Warren Beatty (who had not acted since directing himself in 1981's *Reds*) to play the male lead in *The Slugger's Wife*. Though he saw potential in the script, a cautious Beatty prudently decided not to take the role of home-run hitter Darryl Palmer. He wasn't willing to be just an actor for hire and wanted a creative role on the film if he were to be involved at all. "The problem with *The Slugger's Wife* was Doc Simon," he recalls. "Doc Simon always had complete control—Neil and I didn't agree, so I just didn't do the movie."[4]

Stark had hired Martin Ritt, the veteran director of *Hud* (1963) and *Norma Rae* (1979), to direct, but health problems forced Ritt to pull out; instead, he acted in the film as Burly DeVito, the wily manager of Darryl's team. (Ritt was ultimately relieved not to have directed the film for Stark, who he declared "has no taste.")[5] In mid-November 1983, Ashby was announced by Stark as Ritt's replacement, with Michael O'Keefe unveiled at the same time as the film's star. Though *Caddyshack* (1980) star O'Keefe had won a Best Supporting Actor Oscar nomination for his debut role in *The Great Santini* (1979), it was clear to all that Stark's director and actor were not his first choice.

Ashby's decision to sign on was somewhat puzzling as the project was badly mismatched with his directorial style and themes, and one suspects that he must have been aware of the general poor quality of the script. However, the control-obsessed Stark's decision to ask Ashby—who now had a reputation as being a loose cannon—to direct *The Slugger's Wife* is positively baffling, particularly in light of subsequent events. Caleb Deschanel, Ashby's director of photography on the film, offers the opinion: "Stark hired him because he was down-and-out, and they thought they could push him around. I was too embarrassed to ask Hal why the fuck he did it!"[6] It is likely that Ashby assumed that working with Simon and Stark would give his career the kick-start it needed, gambling on a problematic script by a great writer because of the cachet he believed the project would give him.

Both Ashby and O'Keefe certainly seemed grateful to be integral players in such a high-profile film. O'Keefe embarked on a rigorous baseball training program so that he would look like a real slugger, and Ashby did his own preparations. His focus, however, was watching stylish comedies from Hollywood's Golden Age, including Ernst Lubitsch's *Ninotchka* (1939), *The Shop Around the Corner* (1940), and *Trouble in Paradise* (1932), and Frank Capra films like *Mr. Smith Goes to Washington* (1939), *Meet John Doe* (1941), and *It's a Wonderful Life* (1946). As he had done before shooting *Bound for Glory,* he also watched Preston Sturges's films, which he found witty, earthy, and deeply human, the epitome of great comedy.

Ashby and Neil Simon were an unusual pairing of director and writer, an odd couple to rival Simon's own; Rebecca De Mornay, who played O'Keefe's love interest, Debby Huston, called Ashby and Simon "the most unlikely combination I could think of."[7] De Mornay, like Ashby and O'Keefe, was a surprising choice, given that Stark's preliminary wish list for Debby included just about every A-list actress, up-and-coming starlet, and comedienne in Hollywood—except De Mornay. And yet when the front-runner for the role, Darryl Hannah, passed after tentatively agreeing to be in the film (incurring the wrath of Stark, who sent her a bilious memo and a bouquet of dead flowers), De Mornay was offered it instead. Riding high after her eye-catching performance as a sexy prostitute opposite Tom Cruise in *Risky Business* (1983), De Mornay was delighted to now be working with Ashby: as a teenager she had been enchanted by *Harold and Maude*, which had made her wonder what kind of director made strange films like that.

As early as six weeks before production began, Stark was already showing what kind of a producer he was going to be. He wrote to Ashby complaining about Caleb Deschanel, who wanted four or five thousand extras for baseball stadium scenes, rather than the fifteen hundred Stark proposed. "I believe there must be a clarification," an agitated Stark stressed, quickly adding, "Of course you will have as many extras as you want. . . . Everyone works differently, Hal, and I certainly respect the way you want to work and we will all do everything to facilitate this."[8]

This passive-aggressive tone cannot have reassured Ashby that Stark would indeed do whatever he (and his trusted collaborators) felt was necessary for the film, yet neither did it prepare him for just how intrusive Stark would turn out to be. Despite Ashby having a number of his regular crew (Deschanel, Jeff Wexler, his old assistant Lucile Jones, costume designer Ann Roth) on board, it soon became clear that *The Slugger's Wife* was not *his* film but a film he was making for Neil Simon, Ray Stark, and Columbia. Long before production began, he was given the dates by which his cut and the final answer print of the film were to be ready, and he was expected to have product placement for certain companies and baseball teams.

The Slugger's Wife had originally been set in Houston but was moved to Atlanta, supposedly because the Houston Astros' ground was not a hitter's park but the Atlanta Braves' Fulton County Stadium was. The fact that Atlanta was the home of Coca-Cola, which owned Columbia, may also have been a factor.

After a week of rehearsals, the planned twelve-week shoot began in Atlanta on March 14, 1984, and Ashby was immediately made to feel accepted. On his arrival, he found a card from Ray Stark: "Dear Hal, It's going to be a ball—and a ballgame! Love, Ray."[9] Simon similarly showed a reassuring positivity and warmth toward Ashby by sending him a 1920 first edition of Zane Grey's *The Redhead Outfield and Other Baseball Stories*, inscribed, "To Hal, Thought this might make a good sequel. Looking forward to the 'Slugger.' Warmest wishes, Neil Simon."[10]

De Mornay was excited about her role, which, after the switch from Texas to Georgia, had been changed from a country-and-western singer to a pop singer from Atlanta. Unfortunately, however, despite two months of vocal lessons, there were problems right from the start. Two weeks in, Ashby lost confidence in De Mornay's ability to pull off a Southern drawl and was forced to scrap all her dialogue he had shot so far and reshoot with her speaking normally. In Michael O'Keefe's opinion, "Rebecca De Mornay was in over her head with the singing and acting aspects of the role."[11] This view was reflected by Jeff Wexler, who called her "clueless, just impossible."[12]

Ashby coaxed De Mornay through the film as best he could, and the actress today recalls how his "liberal, non-judgmental vibe created an environment where you felt free to do or say anything."[13] Ashby was particularly protective of her after, on top of her accent problems, she was dealt another blow—this one literal. Tornadoes hit the set on three separate occasions during the shoot, and the winds were so extreme during the first storm that De Mornay's trailer, where she was working with her drama coach, was picked up by a violent gust and landed with its door facing upward, trapping her inside.

"I remember hearing someone hacking his way through the door screaming, 'Baby!'" says De Mornay. "It was Hal, his long hair wringing wet in the rain, and wearing this jean vest, with his arms coming through. No one else tried to help, but here was the director on top of the trailer, trying to pull me to safety. That completely symbolized the beauty and soul of Hal."[14] De Mornay's drama coach sustained torn ligaments in his arm, but De Mornay came through with only a bruise over her right eye that was covered up with makeup and disappeared in a few weeks.

Ashby worked hard to get the best possible performance from De Mornay, but it wasn't easy, and Stark was very disappointed by his leading lady. "When she was burdened with an accent, her creative concept of hair styles and a confusion on her makeup, her work on the film became a terrible problem for you and, therefore, for us," he wrote to Ashby, a month into production. "However, it was solved expeditiously and pleasantly with the proper results, because of our working together."[15] Stark often stressed the virtues of "working together," although this basically meant that he, or production manager Jerry Baerwitz ("a weaselly, slimy guy," according to Caleb Deschanel), should be consulted about every decision, because he didn't trust Ashby to make any on his own.[16]

Stark began the same letter by telling Ashby, "Both Neil and myself could not be more pleased with the film that has been shot and with the good relationship amongst us. I have complete confidence in you, Hal. In spite of the fact that the basic communication is really between you and Caleb, I am most pleasantly surprised at what appears in the rushes." While he expressed his concern here about Ashby's lack of communication (a criticism, as ever with Stark, expressed in a seemingly positive way), he went on to stress, "As with all the films I do with Neil, my primary concern is that Neil's original script is faithfully executed. By no means should this frustrate the director's creative work, but it should be the result of a communication between you and Neil, which so far has been terrific."[17]

Despite his praise of Ashby's work so far, Stark's inability to control his director, and also Caleb Deschanel, increasingly frustrated him. Deschanel says that Stark and Baerwitz "were trying to sabotage [Ashby's] movie" as all they wanted was "a filmed play," which Deschanel and Ashby had no interest in delivering. When conflicts arose between Stark and Deschanel, Ashby always sided with his cinematographer because he trusted his artistic instincts over those of a producer. "In the midst of all that, Hal was always really cool," Deschanel says, "always on the side of the creative people who were trying to make the film better."[18]

Stark was critical of Deschanel for supposedly undermining the film's comic elements with his somber lighting, but it was clear to everyone else that the lack of laughs was the fault of the writer. Simon, downbeat after his divorce, had produced a script that wasn't particularly funny in any of its numerous versions. "I was on the set every day rewriting as we went along, changing scenes, changing dialogue, adding material," said Simon. "I have no loyalty to a funny line. If the scene works better without it, out it goes."[19] And out they seemingly went, as his declining mood changed the film from a (nominally) romantic comedy to a decidedly bittersweet romance with only occasional glimpses of Simon's comic gifts.

While Simon was constantly changing the script, even grabbing actors just before a take to alter a line, Ashby's contract apparently stipulated that *he* was unable to change even the smallest aspect of the script. For Ashby, who thrived on working out dialogue with actors, this was a serious creative handicap, especially given the material he was working with. Michael O'Keefe recalls that Simon's script "was not in the best shape but I was too inexperienced to really notice that."[20] Ashby had realized this too and tried to shoot scenes so as to give himself options in the editing room.

Stark, who was also aware of problems with the ever-changing screenplay, dealt with them by, as O'Keefe remembers, "trying to go around Hal's back like scheduling B camera shoots to pick up scenes that Hal had no idea about to be inserted later on. It was pretty childish stuff from both of them. The production manager, Jerry [Baerwitz], and Ray started making things difficult for Hal when they both realized that the film wasn't working. . . . They didn't handle it well and the final outcome reflects that."[21]

Ashby was helpless, inhibited by a writer whose every whim he had to follow and a producer more powerful and intrusive than he had ever encountered before. "Hal had no mechanism to protect himself from producers," says Jeff Wexler. "He couldn't promote himself; he wasn't a showman. He just wanted to get the right people together and make the movie."[22] However, Ashby didn't have the right people, and it was clear now that this was far from the right movie. When Rudy Wurlitzer visited him in Atlanta, he recalls that Ashby "was really suffering. He paid too big a price—it was not his film, and he used up too much energy."[23]

One of the reasons Ashby was using up so much energy was because he was battling to get the film made the way he wanted it in the day and then staying up half the night. A significant amount of the film was shot at the Limelight nightclub in Atlanta. In the film, it is where the baseball players congregate and Debby works as a singer, and the venue also became the cast and crew's after-hours hangout. Jeff Wexler recalls that there was a lot of drinking going on at night and that there was so much cocaine around that even Wexler (who usually steered clear) occasionally indulged. The police officer in charge of security on the film told Guy D'Alema, a Limelight liaison on *Slugger,* that Ashby was discovered on several occasions at 3 or 4 A.M. "in a somewhat intoxicated state sitting outside the club's side entrance. They would take him back to his hotel and see to it that they got him up to bed."[24]

Dianne Schroeder had expressed concern to Ashby when she heard that Lucile Jones, who she said had in the past cajoled Ashby into snorting cocaine with her, was working on the film. "I hope that she doesn't influence you in any negative ways," she had written. "*I* don't mean to be negative, but I *care* about you, and never trusted her. So for what it's worth. . . ."[25] Since *Bound for Glory,* Ashby had tried to stay away from cocaine, particularly when in production, but in this case he wasn't helping himself with the company he kept: in addition to having Jones around, during his time in Atlanta he was living with an extra from the Limelight, the focal point of the film's nighttime hedonism.

Ashby's difficulty committing to one project at this time had a parallel in his inability to commit to even one woman. During the course of *The Slugger's Wife,* he received correspondence from five different women declaring their love to him—not including his girlfriend back in Los Angeles, Karen Stephens. His reluctance to be tied down, combined with his charming and lovable nature, often led these women to become obsessive, and Ashby's disinclination to reply to their letters only fueled their fixations. Friends such as Beau Bridges have referred to Ashby as a magical, wizardly figure, his white beard contributing to the aptness of the image, and some of Ashby's conquests felt he had put them under his spell. One of them, known only as "The fuckin fairy" or "Princess Carleigh," called him Merlin and drew postmarks saying "Oz" or "Fairyland" on her letters. For years she wrote him emotionally intense letters in an attempt to get him to reciprocate her obsessive love.

"Darling H—I tried to call your hotel in Atlanta but they don't seem to have you registered or something," she wrote in April 1984. "I was worried about u becuz i heard you were fucking someone + dislocated your shoulder or something maybe your penis—who knows? Well as usual i feel like i'm writing to the wizard of OZ cuz i never hear from you only heresay [*sic*] like the dislocated prick! . . . No one can figure out my sex life cuz i don't have one except for you the Easter bunny who i see once a year + then you give me time to take off my clothes + then get dressed again. Honestly Hal stop dragging my heart around. I've more than payed for anything I've put you through."[26]

"Hal was getting high back in those days," O'Keefe contends, "and it didn't do much for him except give him a break at the end of the day. He was not communicating well and had I read the signs earlier in our work together I could have saved all of us a lot of trouble by asking questions earlier. Like 'How come Hal can't really articulate a vision of the film when we speak?'" The actor says that he did not object in theory to Ashby using drugs "as long as it doesn't interfere with personal or professional relationships" but adds, "Unfortunately, I think it probably did interfere."[27] While there is likely some truth in O'Keefe's rather broad statement, the problems with *The Slugger's Wife* went a great deal deeper.

At the end of May, all the dialogue had been shot, and Simon left Atlanta to return to his home in New York. On his departure, he expressed major concerns about what he had turned *The Slugger's Wife* into. In a letter to Stark, he declared himself "pretty positive" but admitted, "It's always so hard to tell how you feel about a film until you see it put together. . . . We've done so much cutting, rewriting and changing of tone, that I hope we haven't lost any consistency or forgotten to tell the story, which is what we set out to do in the first place. My feeling, as I left, was that it was getting to be a musical and as we both know, it's neither a story about singing or baseball. It's a love story and if we don't have that, we don't have 'nothing.'" He also had grave reservations about Rebecca De Mornay and the lack of emotion in her performance: "God knows 'emotion' is a very broad term and I'm not looking for Lillian Gish in *Way Down East* but as we know, Rebecca has had her problems in that department, although by and large, Hal has done a great job with her when he goes after what we want."

Simon ended the above letter by admitting, "I have another eighty page rewrite on the script but I haven't the heart to send it in."[28] Even after Ashby had shot everything to Simon's specifications, the writer knew it still wasn't right. Nevertheless, two days later, after Stark showed a large portion of the footage to the studio, he wired Ashby: "The reaction of the three Columbia executives to the film this morning made me very proud for all of us."[29]

All that remained now was to shoot the crowd scenes in Fulton County Park, scenes that were all-important in making the baseball sequences exciting and realistic. For months, Stark and his team had plotted how to attract the largest possible number of people to the stadium on the first two weekends in June, given that they'd just be sitting around and cheering on cue as there would be no game actually being played. Stark publicized the filming of the crowd scenes on a local radio station, announcing that there would be prizes for the first people into the ground and free Coke and hot dogs for all. He confidently predicted that there would be twenty-five to thirty thousand but was hoping for fifty thousand. On the hot morning of Saturday, June 2—the first shooting day for these scenes—a mere fifteen hundred turned up. Ashby and Caleb Deschanel had to tell Stark that this was not even enough to fill the relatively small area behind home plate. Stark later complained to Ashby that the picture had been budgeted at $19 million but cost $20 million, yet he spent a significant amount of money desperately trying to bribe the city to come to a nonexistent baseball game. A Pontiac Firebird, a Domino's Pizza Indy-racing-style go-cart, a motorcycle, and numerous other tempting gifts were all offered up as prizes the following day, with $500 given away promptly every half hour, to provide further incentive not just to come but to stay.

With filming almost over, tensions between Stark and Ashby were now obvious to all. When Ashby offered a bet of $100 that the crowd of twenty-five thousand that Stark predicted would not materialize, the producer immediately accepted. Ashby won. The turnstiles registered that seven thousand spectators came into the ground, but there was a maximum of only four thousand at any one time.

On the morning of the following Saturday, Ashby's much-needed sleep was disturbed by an incessantly ringing phone that he declined to answer. When he came on the set, he found a memo from Stark complaining that the film was over schedule and over budget (which it was marginally) and further pressuring Ashby to finish as soon as he could, "even if we have to work through the night."[30]

While waiting for the crowds to turn up later that day, Ashby dictated an incensed reply:

> I've been working very hard and not sleeping so well, and much to your disappointment I fell asleep this morning and slept through, for the most part, except for the phone ringing which kept waking me up, but I decided not to answer and try to go back to sleep. Thank God, for if I'd answered and all you had to say was what is in the memo, then I would have been so angry I'd never have gotten back to sleep.
>
> As to your constant reference to communication, please, give me a break! When have *you*, or your *production team* ever

> asked a question that wasn't answered. . . . I don't think Jerry [Baerwitz] will have to ask me three or four times a day if I'm doing my work. I believe I gave him full answers to every question when I started into the stadium today. Before I received this memo, which sent me back to my camper with enough anger to almost shut me down permanently for the day. However, I'm sure I'll rise above it and again go out and at least give 80% to the film, and maybe even 100%, once I get involved and can forget how angry I am that people can actually stand around and see how hard we're all working and still not see it.

Though Stark was pushing Ashby to finish up production, he had slowed down the shooting of an airplane scene by engaging only fifty extras, despite there being three hundred seats on the plane set. "I know you don't care how it looks to have fifty people on a plane that holds over 300, but I do. I think it would look stupid," Ashby complained. "But what the hell, that's my problem, right[?]"[31]

To everyone's relief, the film wrapped a few days later. "We just knew it wasn't going to be a good movie," Jeff Wexler admits.[32]

After driving cross-country back home to California, it wasn't long before Ashby got into yet another argument with Stark, this time over his desire to edit in Malibu rather than in Los Angeles. Ashby was in the end allowed to edit the film at his home, on the express condition that he be available to communicate with Stark and his associates as and when they required. By this time, Neil Simon's regular supervising editor, Margaret Booth, a legendary figure in Hollywood whose career began in the 1920s, had put together her cut of the film. Stark and Columbia were determined that the film should have a December release, so Ashby was required to have a director's cut within a few days. It was, however, a few weeks before he was ready to show it to Stark and Simon. He had made some radical changes, most significantly, scrapping the script's flashback framework, which he felt was necessary to overcome the film's narrative problems.

"The big problem came," Ashby said, "when I found out some days later the cut was to [*sic*] radical for good ole Neil and he wouldn't look past reel 2."[33] Ashby was stung by Simon's reaction and refused to answer his phone when a furious Stark called repeatedly to reprimand him for his audacity in straying from Simon's script. Finally, Ashby agreed to attend a screening on July 31, after which he and Stark were to discuss the editing of *Slugger.* Ashby did not, however, turn up.

Ashby was reluctant to participate in the editing process when he was being treated like Stark's employee and Simon had such sway, but he wasn't ready to give the film up. Columbia's Robert L. Robinson informed him that if he persisted in his behavior, the film would be edited without him. Trying to force Ashby's hand, Robinson told him a few days later that reshoots and additional filming had been scheduled and that if he wished to be involved, he would have to respond by the end of the day. Ashby did not respond but instead contacted the Directors Guild of America (DGA) in an attempt to protect his right to edit *The Slugger's Wife* as laid out in the DGA regulations.

Ashby's decision to involve the DGA changed the whole complexion of the conflict. Columbia countered by writing to Ashby, "Your unprofessional conduct during the past several months has been and continues to be shocking to us, is violative of your contractual obligations and has jeopardized the timely completion and release [of *The Slugger's Wife*]."[34] Through the deliberate choice of words and phrases and claims of "unprofessional conduct," Columbia demonstrated that it was poised and willing to sack Ashby.

Not wanting an unnecessary battle, Ashby recalled, "I stepped out of the picture so they could continue on to meet the Xmas date. All I asked was to view the film, when they felt it was ready, to see if I wanted my name on it. They said I could look at it right away. So I looked, thought it was dreadful, and asked to have my name taken off."[35] Ashby was not alone in his opinion. In an attempt to rescue *Slugger,* Columbia Pictures' president, Guy McElwaine, begged Ashby to come back onto the film and got Stark to agree that this was the best course of action. A plan was concocted to say that Ashby needed oral surgery and use this excuse to explain why the Christmas release had been scrapped and the film would now come out at Easter. A settlement agreement was prepared by Stark's lawyers in an attempt to clear up the dispute between him and Ashby, but the proposed terms on which Ashby was to be brought back were far from favorable. He was obliged to deliver the finished film by a date in early 1985 and waive all creative rights, including the right to use a pseudonym (such as the traditional Alan Smithee credit) if he were unhappy with how the movie ended up. Stark had final cut rather than Ashby, and though he could initially cut the film to his own wishes, after that Stark could tell him how to change it if he did not approve of Ashby's editorial choices.

Once again, Ashby wanted to cut the film in Malibu, but after the previous problems, Stark was understandably unwilling to yield on this point. In a desperate move, Ashby met with Stark (who attended with no less than nine of his attorneys) and asked to be allowed to leave the film, even offering up 5 percent of his fee ($75,000). McElwaine once again stepped in, insisting that Ashby was to be paid in full, and then asking him to take a look at the film and offer any suggestions.

A plea to salvage the film appealed to Ashby's rescuing impulse, and in October he sat down to try to bring the best out of *The Slugger's Wife*. Two months later he had completely recut the film and managed to solve a major problem by balancing the events leading up to Darryl and Debby's marriage with the other half of the story, the breakdown of their marriage. Ashby showed the first half of the film to Columbia and Stark, and Ashby remembered receiving their "support which they gave wholeheartedly. They were thrilled and amazed at how much I'd done in so short a time."

With only the final baseball game to cut, Ashby screened the rest of the film: "And that's when Ray started with that b.s. that he was just going to have Maggie [Booth] make some changes to show me, and I told him it didn't work that way."[36]

Ashby withdrew from the film a second time, though this failed to end the conflict. On December 20, *Variety* reported, "Ashby and Stark have been trying to resolve differences over the final cut, and they've been trying almost as hard to keep the squabble from becoming a public confrontation. [Neil] Simon . . . said he has been told by Stark that the problems between him and Ashby have been ironed out and that both are 'delighted' with the present version. However, Ashby did not subscribe to that view when informed of it, and acknowledged that he is not 'tickled pink.' He begged off further comment in the hope that remaining conflicts may be resolved quietly behind the scenes."[37]

Stark and Columbia punished Ashby's departure from the film by moving his "Directed by" credit from the opening credits to the closing credits. Despite the fact that Ashby had wanted the right to remove his name from the film if he wished, their actions angered him on principle. His reaction was to once again approach the DGA, which agreed that his directorial rights had been infringed upon but awarded him a minimal $2,500 in damages.

In February 1985, Ashby was interviewed by Catherine Wyler for *Directed by William Wyler* (1986), a documentary about her father. In a telling moment, he recalled pointing out to Wyler that his 1939 film *Wuthering Heights* was playing at a cinema across the street. "I just poked Willy and I said, 'Hey look, how 'bout that?'" Ashby related. "I'm sure his mind was well into the other picture [*The Children's Hour* (1961), which was then being edited], but he said, 'Oh, yeah. You know I shot a much better ending than is on the picture.' I was astounded. I said, 'What do you mean?' He proceeded to tell me . . . that Goldwyn didn't like the ending that Willy had on the picture, and that he had had another ending shot. I mean, my God, that's absolutely amazing. . . . I remember at first it just startled me, and it made me see how strong a person Goldwyn was, and it also showed me the incredible thing about how you get *over* something, how at a later time you can not have the . . . Because it didn't bother Willy, he just said it, matter of fact. It was like, 'Oh sure, that went on,' and so forth."[38]

For Ashby, whose battles over *Slugger* were still raw, painful memories, Wyler's calm, impassive response to his experience with *Wuthering Heights* was an example of a detachment he was incapable of feeling. Wyler cared deeply about his films but had taught himself to let go when he had to; Ashby, however, saw every skirmish on every film as intensely personal and could not let go of the hurt.

It is unclear what changes were made to *The Slugger's Wife* after Ashby's departure in December 1984, though Stark's intention of having Margaret Booth (who had a reputation as a biddable editor willing to tailor a film to the studio's needs) alter Ashby's work suggests that it most likely underwent a significant transformation. Michael O'Keefe says, "Margaret and Ray didn't use the best takes, ignored Hal's selected takes and notes from shooting, and used the last take, instead of the best take. At that point the word 'disaster' would best describe what came of it."[39]

By early March, Columbia was selling *Slugger's Wife* T-shirts and the sound track featuring Rebecca De Mornay singing the film's theme song, "Oh, Jimmy," in anticipation of its release later that month. Reviewers, who had excitedly anticipated the film on the basis of its roster, brutally attacked *Slugger* after actually seeing it. In the *New York Times*, Janet Maslin called it "resoundingly unfunny" and said that Ashby had made "a mess of *The Slugger's Wife*" with direction that was "humorless and unsteady."[40] Rex Reed, a huge fan of *Being There,* now declared, "[Ashby has] no aptitude for comedy, and from the looks of things, he hasn't got much aptitude for anything. What happened to the once-stylish, deeply committed director of films like *Coming Home* and *Harold and Maude?*"[41]

Merrill Shindler of *Los Angeles Magazine* expressed the opinions of many by admitting: "Though the credits say that the film was written by Neil Simon and directed by Hal Ashby, it's hard to believe either of them was genuinely connected with it." The review went on to deem *Slugger* "a bad Hal Ashby film from a very bad Neil Simon script."[42] *Newsweek*'s David Ansen simply declared that it would have been "better [if] someone had stolen the whole script and hidden it."[43]

There was widespread criticism of not only the leads' acting but also the attempt to appeal to a young audience, and *Variety* dismissed *Slugger* as "yet another example of a soundtrack album accompanied by a film."[44] Caleb Deschanel, the target of much of Stark's wrath during production, actually emerged from the film with much distinction, and Martin Ritt's turn as weary Braves manager Burly De Vito also drew well-deserved praise. There was a terrible irony that the best performance came from Ritt, a director who had only ever acted once before.

Ashby's legal agreement with Stark contained a disparagement clause that essentially prevented Ashby from bad-mouthing the film—Simon, however, was free to say whatever he wanted. Though he did publicity for the film, just two weeks after its release he declared his true feelings about it. "I saw the first screening and said, 'What happened to the movie?'" he admitted. "You don't like to air dirty laundry and complain publicly about a picture and say, 'Well, that's not really my movie.' . . . And I've had pictures that have bombed out and I say, 'Well, I didn't do that well.' But I don't say that about *The Slugger's Wife* because what's left of what I'd done is very little. They've decided—other people, I don't know who—that we've got to market this for the kids, which is not what I wrote about. I have 50 pages of script that never appear in the film. There would have been very little music in the film. They decided to make an MTV out of it. It's what happens when somebody aims a picture at a certain market and one of the reasons I get nervous about films."[45]

The Slugger's Wife is perceived by Simon as such a low point in his career that it is his only film or play that does not get a single mention in either of his two volumes of memoirs. Stark, conversely, seemed compelled to bring up the film regularly, to demonstrate that he was aware what a terrible picture it was and that he regretted his role in its production. He said he blamed himself most for hiring Ashby.

Ashby himself made no public declaration about *The Slugger's Wife* but when asked a year or so later what he thought of it said, "I didn't like *Slugger's Wife*. That is . . . the picture I liked the least."[46] *Hollywood Reporter* critic Duane Byrge wrote that one had "to assume that Hal Ashby may have chosen to direct this one from the third-base dugout,"[47] and in fact just how much of it was Ashby's film remains unclear. During filming, Ashby was hounded and impeded by Stark and compelled to cede control at times to Simon, and even during his stint of editing the picture he claimed it was being cut behind his back by Stark or others. Ashby departed the film three months before it was deemed finished, so presumably Stark and Simon were the primary forces behind the film's final cut. It seems genuinely confusing then—given that Stark had told Ashby that his "primary concern is that Neil's original script is faithfully executed" and then was incensed when Ashby's initial cut of the film did not conform to Simon's screenplay—that Simon was so publicly critical of the film and blamed others for its major faults.

What is truly unique about *The Slugger's Wife,* when compared with any of Ashby's previous films, is how bland and devoid of his directorial presence it is. Whereas in all his other efforts his personality was discernible to one degree or another, here it seems to have been entirely suppressed. The only signs that it is a Hal Ashby film are his cameo (he plays a customer in a café who sits opposite O'Keefe just before the actor smashes up the place in anger) and the dominant presence of popular music, although the latter is so faddish and mediocre that it no doubt had more to do with Stark and Columbia's attempt to make the film hip than Ashby's own taste.

The critical mauling *The Slugger's Wife* received had a massive impact on its box-office performance. Though a high-profile, megabudget movie made by highly respected individuals, it was a huge flop, taking only $1.8 million in receipts, less than 10 percent of what it had cost. Fortunately—or maybe not so fortunately—by the time it came out, Ashby was already deeply involved in his next directorial project.

24

8 Million Ways to Die

> Hal had pissed off Merv Adelson, pissed off Ray Stark, and Mark Damon and John Hyde were already pissed off when he met them. Let's just say, the planets were aligned.
> —Chuck Mulvehill

> If you think a director can direct a movie with those kinds of knives and blades hovering about, then you've got another thing coming.
> —Hal Ashby

Around Christmas 1985, Ashby was sent a copy of Oliver Stone's script for *8 Million Ways to Die*. It was an adaptation of two crime novels by Lawrence Block, *8 Million Ways to Die* and *A Stab in the Dark*, both featuring New York detective and recovering alcoholic Matt Scudder. Stone and former Creative Artists Agency "superagent" Steve Roth had bought the books a few years earlier intending to make the film at Embassy Pictures with Stone as director but were unable to get funding. By the end of 1985, Roth had produced two other films and managed to interest PSO (Producers Sales Organization) in *8 Million Ways to Die*. PSO, a former sales company founded by the leading man-turned-producer Mark Damon, had just moved into production and also had *Short Circuit* (1986), *9½ Weeks* (1986), *Flight of the Navigator* (1986), and *Clan of the Cave Bear* (1986) in the works.

Although the gritty violence of Stone's script was antithetical to Ashby's usual style, he connected with the antihero Scudder sufficiently to tell Roth that he would be pleased to direct the film. Early in the new year, Roth took him to meet Mark Damon, and he was introduced to the PSO boss as the only man for the job. After the meeting, it appeared that PSO would hire Ashby, but it also came out that Damon had actually been interviewing him. Ashby was deeply insulted. "I haven't done that for a long time," he said. "I have pictures that people can look at to see what kind of work I do."[1] Ashby's hurt pride no doubt came also from the suspicion that PSO half expected him to be a washed-up junkie.

However, despite Roth's continuing reassurances that he wanted Ashby on the film, no deal materialized. A subsequent discussion at Damon's house in late January clarified that PSO had opted not to go with Ashby after all, although Damon acknowledged that he was "a highly talented, highly unique filmmaker" who had "had a profound effect on international cinema." He added, "I would be proud to work with you . . . one day."[2] PSO's interest in Ashby had flagged because the studio wanted to get Walter Hill and Nick Nolte, the director-star team responsible for the massively successful *48 Hours* (1982): Hill's hard-edged direction was ideal for Stone's script, and Nolte, a notorious drinker and Hollywood wild man, seemed a natural for alcoholic ex-cop Scudder.

Hill, however, rejected PSO's offer. So, just two weeks after being snubbed, Ashby was hired to direct *8 Million Ways to Die* after all. In a curious chain of command, Mark Damon and his business partner John Hyde's company PSO was employing Steve Roth, through his company SFR Films, to produce the film, which in turn was engaging Ashby, through his company Carbon State. Relations between Ashby and Damon were off to a bad start, so it was decided Ashby would liaise predominantly with Roth.

Ashby met with Oliver Stone to discuss the script, but he would take it in a very different direction than the writer imagined. He began to have second thoughts about the New York setting, partly for budgetary reasons, but also because there had been so many New York crime films before that he felt he had nothing new to add to the genre. Ashby and Roth decided to shoot in Los Angeles, which would eradicate travel costs and, as Roth explained, "also lets us use a much broader vista, something along the lines of *Point Blank*."[3] John Boorman's classic 1967 film, more a psychological tale of revenge than a crime film, was the kind of movie Ashby was aiming for, and he had very definite ideas about how to handle the material. He wanted to avoid the clichéd hard-boiled cop formula of Stone's script and focus on Scudder's battle with alcoholism as much as his attempts to catch his nemesis, the Columbian drug lord Angel, who

Scudder believes murdered a prostitute called Sunny. To research the world of the film, Ashby read "The Social World of the Female Prostitute in Los Angeles," a Ph.D. thesis, and went to Alcoholics Anonymous (AA) meetings. Noting the habits alcoholics developed to stop themselves from thinking about liquor, he laughed, "*God Almighty,* have you seen so many people eating, and smoking, and drinking something?"[4]

Although it had been years since Ashby himself had been a drinker, he could easily relate to people with substance-abuse problems and found himself strongly attracted to the ideas of AA. After *The Slugger's Wife,* where there were once again rumors of drugs interfering with his work, it seems that he made a concerted effort to clean up his act. According to Chuck Mulvehill, he would periodically purge himself—ceasing all drug use and sometimes even fasting—and he appears to have felt the need to do this again. Looking at the parallels between the film and Ashby's life, it seems no coincidence that at the start of *8 Million Ways to Die,* the hero is a maverick with long, shaggy hair and a beard who has decadent tendencies that have all but destroyed his career, but who ultimately ends the film clean, sober, and happy.

As Stone was busy in Mexico shooting *Salvador* (1986) and thus unable to rework the screenplay before production began, Ashby started to write his own script for the film. He worked from both Stone's script and Lawrence Block's novel *8 Million Ways to Die* as well as his own research. The fifty pages of script that Ashby wrote had neither the fiercely evocative color of Stone's screenplay nor particularly exciting dialogue, yet they were the starting point for a much more complex and psychologically interesting film and were consciously designed as a blueprint that the actors and possibly other writers could move forward with later.

Ashby gave these first fifty pages to Steve Roth (who said he liked them) but abruptly stopped work on his screenplay when he discovered that, without his knowledge, PSO had hired Canadian author R. Lance Hill to rewrite Stone's script. Ashby, who had confidence in his own screenplay, felt hurt and told Roth, "I don't think I have ever had that one happen to me before."[5] He was further upset on learning that Hill was to report to Damon, cutting Ashby out of the rewriting process completely.

Ashby accordingly focused his energies on casting. For the part of Matt Scudder, it was a choice between Al Pacino and Jeff Bridges. However, as Pacino's desire to make the film about alcoholism clashed with Roth's vision of "an adventure movie in which alcoholism is just one of the demons which the hero must vanquish," Bridges got the nod.[6] Ironically, in Bridges's preparation for the film, he became fascinated by the hero's addictive personality. "I was interested in exploring the obsessive side of his character," Bridges says. "I went to AA meetings and found it to be an incredible organization, with an interesting perspective on how to live your life whether you're an alcoholic or not. I wanted to put some of that out. I wanted to explore the spiritual aspects of what an alcoholic goes through."[7]

Meanwhile, Ashby's main challenge was to cast the two main female parts, Scudder's love interest, Sarah, and the murdered woman, Sunny. Both characters were prostitutes, which made it difficult to interest big-name stars in the roles. Cher, who had been a huge fan of *Coming Home,* was touted as a likely Sarah, but it was Jamie Lee Curtis who was finally chosen to play opposite Bridges. However, when Curtis wasn't happy with her fee, she jumped ship and was replaced by Rosanna Arquette, who had made a big impression alongside Madonna in the just-released *Desperately Seeking Susan* (1985). (Incidentally, Ashby had been offered that film a few years earlier.)

For the role of Angel, Ashby hired an exciting unknown actor, the Cuban-born Andy Garcia: Garcia was so keen to be in the film, he had begged to audition not only for Angel but also for Chance the pimp so as to have two shots at being cast. He recalls with amusement when Ashby told him he wanted him as Angel and then said he looked forward to seeing him the next day for his second audition. With all the other major parts cast, Ashby continued to struggle to find the right actress for Sunny. Only after filming had started did he finally pick fresh-faced twenty-two-year-old Alexandra Paul to play the doomed prostitute.

In late May, coproducer "Doc" Erickson quit the film after a fight with Steve Roth, and Ashby called Chuck Mulvehill asking, "What are you doing?" Since parting company with Ashby around 1980, Mulvehill had worked with Bob Rafelson, Jonathan Demme, Ivan Passer, and Karel Reisz and established himself as a well-regarded producer and production manager. Mulvehill remembers that his wife advised him to be cautious about working with Ashby again, knowing how emotionally convoluted their relationship had been in the past, but Mulvehill felt comfortable with the idea. As it turned out, their dealings on *8 Million Ways to Die* were much more pragmatic. As Mulvehill says, "The rose-colored spectacles were off, but it was the best relationship we'd ever had."[8]

Just after Mulvehill joined the film, Lance Hill's script arrived, but his rapid rewrite was a disappointment not only to Ashby but also to PSO, Roth, and the cast. Stone's grit and vibrant realism were gone, and instead Hill had tried to put an intellectual stamp on the film, with prostitute Sarah quoting the obscure German poet Heinrich Heine, whom she had supposedly read in a journalism course. Ashby felt major changes were still necessary, not least because Hill's draft, which included a huge climactic battle at an airport (which Ashby called the "*Rambo* ending"), would push the budget up to $16 million. On a personal level, Ashby was also deeply frustrated that Hill was sending new pages to PSO rather than him.

While Ashby was trying to reestablish his authority on the film and get PSO to let him work directly with Hill, PSO told him that Robert Towne was available. Because of their friendship and the success of their previous collaborations on *The Last Detail* and *Shampoo,* Ashby convinced Towne to be the film's script doctor for only $250,000, a quarter of his usual fee. PSO had told Hill that it was very pleased with his work but wanted him to come to Los Angeles to make a few changes; however, that plan was quickly abandoned when Towne was hired. PSO told Hill that a close friend of Ashby's was making some "minor cuts" in order to reduce the budget, work that would, he was assured, take a few days at most.

Hill was extremely hurt and wrote to Ashby, "Hal, I went to the wall and supported both of you all the way, assuming the same united stance you had proposed to me. I supported your position ultimately by telling PSO I would walk unless you and I could work together the way we must. Instead of ultimately supporting me, you let me take the fall. Make no mistake about it. Even by Hollywood standards, this is as unprincipled and unconscionable an act as there is. No movie and no circumstance is worth that kind of compromise."[9]

Despite his usual loyalty to creative people, Ashby felt that the quality of the film was more important than persisting with the wrong writer simply to save his feelings. Moreover, he couldn't turn down the opportunity to work with Towne: "I knew Bob would lift us right out of the good film category and put us into another level immediately. There is nobody like him!"[10] However, Ashby soon discovered PSO was refusing to pay Towne's full salary and was insisting that Ashby and Roth cover $150,000 of it. Ashby agreed but found it decidedly strange that PSO "didn't even care enough about the picture to pay a full fee for a writer that I thought to be the best for the picture, . . . a writer that they first suggested."[11] "It didn't sit well with me though," he said later, "that I had to become an investor in the film in order to protect us and give us the best possible shot of having something to really be proud of. For all of us."[12]

Contrary to what Damon had told Hill, Towne was in fact changing the script substantially and doing so with a whole entourage of collaborators, including an ex-cop he had befriended. One of Towne's first decisions was to change the title to *Easy Does It* (a popular AA slogan), which signaled his allegiance to Ashby's original intent to move the film away from its thriller elements and into more profound psychological territory.

Towne was highly critical of Hill's efforts, saying, "If this script had anymore clarity, it might have risen to the dignity of an exploitation film." Ashby agreed and confided to Towne that Jeff Bridges had told him, "Hal, we gotta figure out how to make this not just another movie for exploitation of sex and violence."[13] Both Bridges and Arquette had agreed to do the film almost entirely because they wanted to work with Ashby, and he was determined not to let their faith in him prove unfounded.

By mid-July, Towne had written approximately one-third of the new screenplay, but Chuck Mulvehill's estimated budget based on those pages was nearly $14 million, $2.5 million more than PSO wanted to spend. Mulvehill told Ashby that with smaller locations and a shorter production time *8 Million Ways to Die* (or was it *Easy Does It?*) could be delivered on budget, though this would naturally increase the pressure on Ashby.

PSO also decided to push production back by a week, without consulting Ashby. Furious, Ashby told Mulvehill, "Any change of the start date made only by the production entity is tantamount to a shut down of the production as it would mean they had decided, for whatever reasons, to tell the director he no longer is the skipper of the ship."

Responding to a memo from Mulvehill, he addressed issues of control on the picture and also frankly addressed his negative reputation in Hollywood. "From the looks of it," Ashby wrote to Mulvehill, "if you continue to maintain the control you [PSO] have so far, this movie stands about as good a chance of going in the toilet as anything I've ever seen. Now that I'm on the subject, what's with all the inference that I'm somehow out of control, and I must be controlled in order to stop these horrendous costs, and bring them into line. That's just plain bullshit and you know it! If I'm out of control, it's because the production entity has continually refused to let me have control. You can't direct a film when every decision you make is either counter-manded or questioned as if you were out to do harm to the financiers instead of trying to make a good film. Doesn't that approach sound dumb to you. Paying me all that money just so I can put you, them, me, and the film in jeopardy."

"Does anyone really believe I will break or be bent into some other shape than I really am," he continued. "Please! Give me a break! I am what I am and I make the movies I make, and I'm not going to become someone else. If anything I have more resolve, and more strength than ever before. I should have, I know more than I ever knew before. I get smarter and stronger all the time.

"As you know Chuck, I've had a lot of crud thrown my way the last couple of years. My, my the things that have been said about me. You are also one of the only people who really know I've never been addicted to anything but work. So most of everything said about me is totally false. In fact the only thing anyone could honestly say about me in a negative sense is that I'm very difficult to deal with. Especially when the dealing entails my rather strong point of view and how it relates to the film I happen to be making. . . . I guess if they were really fearful because of all they've heard, and this made them believe I was some burnt out being just pretending to be me, then they would be suspect of every move I make. But, my god, if that's what's going on please try to make them understand it would really be the wisest thing to replace me as quietly as possible."

"What is the need to control the so called wayward director—to make him more tame, more timid," he asked. "Those things can break a spirit, and in turn rob that spirit of those bold dreams that are sometimes needed when something special is done. This is something I feel about all of my films; that they were and are something special. All of them except the last and the lessons I learned from that experience are something else again. I know it's so heavy on my soul that I will carry the mistake with me for the rest of my life. Any stigma acquired by my failure would pale in the shadow of the fact I overrode my heart and mind. Something I've never done before, and believe me, will never do again. But it lays very heavy in me."[14]

As the start date neared, the budget caused ructions between Ashby and PSO: Ashby was willing to shoot the film for a realistic figure of $13.5 million, but Damon and Hyde would not budge from their $11.5 million estimate. Though PSO's directors acknowledged it was impossible to estimate accurately given that the script wasn't even half finished, they said they could not continue with Ashby as director and told him that he was fired. Attorneys were immediately brought in on both sides, and just six days before shooting was due to begin, crisis talks were held in which PSO proposed a new budget of $12.8 million (including a 10 percent contingency). Roth and Ashby had an option to collectively post a further $550,000 from their salaries (on top of the $150,000 they had already posted to pay for Towne's services). If they did this, PSO would add another $600,000 contingency to the budget, bringing it to just over $14 million; if they did not, Roth and Ashby would not be reinstated.

Once again putting the film before himself, Ashby swallowed his pride and agreed to PSO's conditions. He came back on the film supposedly with a clean slate but was immediately angered by his employers' actions when they informed him of imminent screen tests for a number of actresses. Ashby was told he had to attend these because the screen tests were in the week when shooting had originally been scheduled to start, meaning he was being paid for that period. "So, before I had taken step one under our new reunion, I was, once again, treated like a hired hand," an exasperated Ashby wrote to John Hyde. "It didn't even matter that I'd been fired off the picture. Well John, even if I am a hired hand, I'm not a hired hand. I kid you not!"

In the memo to Hyde, Ashby expressed severe doubts about his continued involvement in *8 Million Ways to Die,* asking, "Will I be able to make my film? What are the compromises being asked? Are they too great for me to realize the dream?" Ashby was aware that his reputation had changed radically since the 1970s but felt that he was no different now than in those years of heady success. "The implication always seems to be that I'm out to be devious and do some vile, harmful thing to the film," he told Hyde. "And I can't think of anything further from the truth or fact. I'm a tireless worker, and my concern, and cares, for any film I do, are so deeply rooted that it makes the idea of my being irresponsible in any way, ludicrous."

Ashby made it clear that he could not make the film if PSO's level of influence and interference continued and maintained that not even Ray Stark had been as difficult to work with. "On the intimidation level: No more 'I better show up because I've been paid for the week,'" he wrote. "No more of that stuff, because I don't like it and I don't function at all well with it around. Again, the next time someone from PSO feels the need to threaten me, I will feel inclined to consider the threat as a fact that I've been fired again."[15]

Though written in frustration rather than anger, Ashby's memo enraged PSO, and his involvement in the film was once again thrown into question. After Damon's initial anger had passed, he actually took on board Ashby's concerns and proposed that PSO leave Ashby alone during production, on the condition that there be a PSO representative on set to keep an eye on him. Ashby suggested Mulvehill, but Damon was understandably concerned about conflicting loyalties and instead chose a writer and former stuntman, Don Edmonds. Ashby was happy to have Edmonds around—despite his allegiance to PSO—because he was an alcoholic and could be used as a "technical adviser" on the film.

Principal photography began on July 29, but only because Ashby's, Jeff Bridges's, and Rosanna Arquette's "pay or play" contracts required PSO to pay them more if filming did not start by the end of the month. The situation was highly reminiscent of *Coming Home:* there were still only thirty-three pages of script, Ashby "wasn't sure what we were going into,"[16] he was essentially shooting from a beat sheet (a rough description of scenes and action) rather than a real script, the actors were improvising many of their lines, and there was no ending to replace the elaborately violent one deemed too expensive to shoot.

Towne was sending pages to the set once he was happy with them, but Ashby needed to find a way to move ahead without a complete script. His solution was to shoot all the major scenes that he had first and then move on to the smaller connecting scenes, thus allowing the actors to follow the arc of the story. Despite the challenging circumstances, there was a good atmosphere on set simply because Ashby was relaxed and having fun, and that began to transfer itself to everyone around him. A phrase Ashby was very fond of at the time was "God Almighty!" which he would say with his big laugh when he was particularly happy, such as when one of the actors nailed a take.

Ashby quickly established an easy relationship with his new director of photography, Stephen H. Burum, whom Caleb Deschanel had used on his directorial debut, *The Escape Artist* (1982), and especially recommended to Ashby. Burum, who was aware of Ashby's tarnished reputation as a director, remembers Ashby as a model professional: "When I worked with him, he was completely clean—nothing. I worked with a lot of people who were on drugs, and it's very easy to tell when someone's a druggie or an alcoholic. He was always on time, he was always coherent, he didn't have mood swings, his eyes weren't dilated. And he was right there. He paid attention to what he was doing, and he was very smart about what he did. And the actors just *loved* him! They would do anything for him."[17]

The cast was particularly fond of Ashby because he devoted himself fully to their needs, listened to their suggestions, and made them feel that the film was a shared vision they were all working toward. "For my money, Hal Ashby was a master filmmaker, making some of the best movies of the 70's," says Jeff Bridges. "He was also a favorite of mine to work with. He created an environment of fun and excitement. Hal had huge creative *cojones*. A script for him was simply an outline. He approached the work with a Zen attitude—'not knowing' played an important role in the making of his movies. I was asked, as many other actors he worked with were, to work through improvisation to discover the realities of scenes."[18]

Bridges's style of acting was based on studious preparation, involving visits to AA meetings and long conversations with the film's two police consultants, as he tried to get to the core of Matt Scudder. But while he was excellent at building up an in-depth backstory for his character, Bridges was not so confident with the improvisational aspects of the film, so Ashby would sometimes get Rosanna Arquette to cut him off halfway through a line to bring a greater spontaneity to his performance. Arquette, like all the other actors, felt hugely supported by Ashby and called him "a great actor's director; he's always there with you. The guy's an artist, a true, true artist. Hal lets you do your thing with a very strong guiding hand."[19]

The whole cast's fierce loyalty to Ashby was also due to the calm, gentle way he let them know that he always had their backs. One morning, Arquette appeared with tears streaming down her face, her makeup ruined, and said to Ashby, "Hal, you don't want me to take off my clothes, do you?"

"No!" he exclaimed. "Who said that?"

"Steve Roth came to my trailer and said I had to take off my clothes in this picture."[20]

Ashby took Arquette off the set to calm her down, but it was a full five hours later before she was ready again. "I guess they hired me because they wanted me to show my tits," she says. "PSO was flipped out because I didn't do any nudity. Hal and I decided, 'Why do we have to show a hooker fuck?'"[21]

Alexandra Paul, who was playing the other prostitute, had a nude scene in the film and says, "Despite being a little nervous, I remember being very comfortable with Hal and not having any problem with his being in the room when I had to have no clothes on. We had a real-life prostitute that was my consultant, and I interviewed her about my role. She was on set, and they gave her a small part, and Hal was very business-like, whereas there were other people on the set who were *not* so businesslike. (I saw one of the crew go upstairs with her!) I remember being impressed with that and feeling more comfortable with him."

Paul admits that when Ashby discussed certain scenes with her "he would talk a mile a minute with a little high-pitched 'Ha-ha' interspersed [and] I would sit there and nod and not really know what he was saying because I was young and stupid."[22] However, when it really mattered, Ashby knew exactly what to say. When Paul was worried about people seeing a scar she had when she did her nude scene, Ashby said maybe the reason Sunny had become a hooker was because she was ashamed of the scar. "Ah," said Paul, satisfied by this suggestion.[23]

Just six weeks after starting work on *Easy Does It,* which Ashby viewed as an original screenplay rather than an adaptation, Towne delivered the remaining sections of the script. Towne was famously slow and careful, so it was almost inevitable that the script he had rushed off was not up to scratch. PSO demanded rewrites, but Towne was not available, so Ashby took it on himself to make the necessary changes and actively involved his principal cast members in the process.

Unfortunately, this meant it would be impossible for Ashby to complete the film in sixty days as Damon had requested. Doc Erickson had originally proposed a $13 million budget and a seventy-odd-day shoot, and Damon's request to spend less money in less time became a vain hope when Ashby, Bridges, and Arquette began spending significant portions of shooting days scripting the scenes they were about to film. "We were busting our butts, writing and shooting at the same time," says Bridges. "I've never worked so hard on a picture in my life! We were locked in our dressing rooms writing our asses off." Addressing a possible misperception of their actions, he added, "It's not like we were in there doing coke or anything. This was the cleanest, hardest-working set I've ever been on. I never saw anyone do anything."[24]

Throughout the course of the film, all the writers who had been involved at various stages expressed dissatisfaction at some aspect of how the film was being made. On the very first day of filming, Ashby shot the opening scene, in which, during a police drugs bust, Towne had written that a rocking chair should be grabbed and used as a weapon by one of the characters. However, Ashby discovered that none of the rocking chairs provided were suitable, as they were either too large to lift or too small to be threatening, and he changed the chair to a baseball bat. Towne, who had failed to tell Ashby that the rocking chair had a deeper, symbolic relevance within the script, was upset that his work had been altered.

According to a (questionable) account by Steve Roth, "Robert went ballistic. Psychotic. He thought he was the greatest thing since sliced bread. He was this raging egomaniac with a whole group of sycophants around him. He was envious of Hal being a big director, and he thought he did him this big favor in rewriting the movie. It was the ugliest fight I ever saw in my life. Hal was down on his luck at that point. . . . Towne was vicious. Said he was over-the-hill and gone. A cripple. 'I'm not gonna be fucked by this guy one more fucking time.' What was sad was these guys genuinely liked each other. They took an entire relationship and threw it away. I don't think they ever spoke again."[25]

Ashby, however, remembered Towne's reaction differently: "He said that he felt that a baseball bat was too lethal. I said, 'I'm sorry, Bob. I didn't have any choice.' . . . We certainly saw a lot of each other after that and he claimed he wasn't angry. I certainly didn't feel he was angry with me after that."[26]

Though Lance Hill did not come down to Los Angeles, both Oliver Stone and Lawrence Block did visit the set. Stone, who was unaware that while he'd been shooting *Salvador* his screenplay had been reworked by no less than three different writers, was very upset at what the film had become and felt that Ashby was solely to blame. "He gave it to Robert Towne behind my back," says Stone. "Robert later called me and was very nice about it, but it wasn't his fault. Hal wanted it totally changed. He was on a completely different wavelength than I was. I remember going over to their set in Malibu and seeing this L.A. crew driving up in Porsches, eating shrimp barbecue. It was just rich and decadent. They were way over budget. Hal and Jeff Bridges would sit in the trailers for hours and talk about the script. And Hal and the producers were fighting like dogs and cats. They were going to take the movie away from him. That's part of the reason I work in overdrive when I direct. I have this nightmare image of that set."[27]

Block, who happened to be in Los Angeles for a wedding, stopped by the set with his wife, met Ashby and the actors, and left again two hours later. He was understandably disgruntled about the change of setting and, though he was impressed by the acting from both Bridges and Andy Garcia, later called the film "dopey."[28] Elsewhere he went further, saying, "It was lousy. I can say that now, because the director is no longer in the building."[29]

While Ashby was oblivious to Stone and Block's visits, PSO staff were constantly interfering and made sure Ashby acknowledged their presence on set. Ashby's lawyers later stated: "Principal photography regularly was interrupted by visits to the set by PSOP [PSO Productions] officers and employees. During these visits, which often occurred in the middle of the night, the cast and crew would stand by while PSOP employees yelled at Mr. Ashby regarding the budget or the number of shooting days, demanded changes in the script, such as how to shoot the ending, or threatened Mr. Ashby with termination."[30]

Steve Burum recalls that on six or seven occasions, PSO employees appeared on set and took Ashby away to his trailer to have an "important private chat" with him.[31] "I had heard that the film was in terrible shape, but the only bad thing was them coming to the set and hovering with their bad vibes," says Rosanna Arquette. "They come on with doom and blackness and time and money and pressure."[32] PSO execs were regularly telling Ashby to speed up shooting, what he should and shouldn't shoot—which, in turn, slowed shooting down—all because of their inability to trust him. Although Ashby was not contractually obliged to do so, PSO forced him to sign a budget agreement and then withheld two weeks' pay because it had taken him two weeks to agree to sign it.

Another point of contention was what would replace the costly "*Rambo* ending." Ashby conceived an ultrarealistic shoot-out between Angel and Scudder in an empty warehouse, a location Ashby had chosen because it offered no place to hide. Designed to be disarmingly uncontrolled, the scene was sufficiently unconventional to prompt Mark Damon to suggest that Angel and Scudder instead have a fistfight on a balcony. Damon ultimately softened and let Ashby shoot his ending, on the understanding that he would film Damon's ending if PSO felt it necessary. Ashby had his actors improvise the scene, allowing it to play out naturalistically, but got only two takes in the can because Garcia lost his voice from all the shouting. The scene has since acquired a degree of infamy because its chaotic realism is so unexpected in a thriller, and it is apparently one of Quentin Tarantino's favorite action scenes. "I did not like the scene at the end where they're all screaming at each other, fighting," admits Alexandra Paul. "Now, I think it's great, but then I couldn't stand it because it looked to me like the chaos that was our set. My friend Eric Stolz says how much he loves that scene because it's so real, and it is so real because everybody's just yelling F-words."[33]

After giving his input on the warehouse scene, Damon said he would not be coming on set anymore, which was a relief to Ashby. However, a month later Chuck Mulvehill told Ashby that Damon was planning an impromptu set visit; Ashby threatened to walk if he showed up. "I liked Mr. Damon. I just didn't want to be hassled any more," Ashby said. "There were a lot of them. . . . Just enough hassles to make me not want to have any more. I felt they were imposing upon what I was doing in making the film."[34] It was all the more frustrating for Ashby because PSO was actually very pleased with the dailies—Mark Damon said he thought Jeff Bridges's performance was as good as Jon Voight's in *Coming Home*.

Ashby felt he did not have creative control over the film and maintained, "You can't make a movie unless you do. You can't direct it."[35] Creative control had become a major issue between Ashby and PSO, culminating in PSO execs demanding that Ashby run any script changes by them before scenes could be shot. Ashby had not been granted final cut (though PSO allowed him "full and meaningful consultation"); however, Steve Roth (who shared creative control with PSO) had ceded his creative rights to Ashby.[36] The upshot of all this was, quite simply, confusion: both sides felt they lacked the necessary power, but PSO execs knew that they could fire Ashby if they wanted to, while Ashby was obviously in no position to replace PSO.

Ashby was concerned about being sacked again and was concerned that PSO had failed to alter the mid-April delivery date when the film had to be ready for TriStar to release, despite principal photography starting late and the delays caused by script problems. There were further delays because of PSO's decision to make Villa Casablanca in Malibu one of the film's locations (apparently because it was owned by a friend of a senior PSO employee). The house, positioned high on a hill and with its own funicular, was visually compelling but unfortunately positioned, as the gunfight being staged there disturbed the affluent neighbors on either side. After complaints, the crew was restricted to shooting only about three hours a day, so what should have taken three or four days ended up taking twelve.

It was now impossible for Ashby to complete a sixty-day shoot, so he signed an agreement saying he would finish the film in seventy days or less, though this was to prove equally impractical. Ashby was constantly under pressure, a direct result of there still not being a full screenplay. PSO's completion bond company wanted to see the script before footage was shot, but the reality was that Ashby could show only scraps and only once they had been written, which was usually moments before scenes were to be shot. He was under massive pressure, writing and directing on set, and frustrated that he had no downtime to work alone on the script. He called Bob Jones, whom he had fallen out with over the editing of *Lookin' to Get Out,* in the hope that he could come and work on the script based on Ashby's notes, but Jones was busy.

Ashby's one saving grace was that, though he was significantly behind schedule, he was *not* over budget. When the film finally wrapped on November 26, after eighty-six shooting days, he had miraculously spent only about $11 million. (According to Andy Garcia, however, filming ended not because it was finished but because PSO pulled the plug, and there were still scenes that needed to be shot.)

The day after production ended, Ashby received a letter from his first assistant director, Andy Stone, whose words revealed the impact Ashby had had on the people he had worked with on the film. "From the moment I arrived for my interview with you," Stone wrote, "to this last day, you've treated me with more courtesy, warmth, understanding and friendship than any other director for whom I have worked. You allowed me to do my job with total support and without censure or constraint. This breeds loyalty and support in return—not only me, but the entire crew would march into battle with you anytime. . . . Give 'em hell."[37]

Though filming was over, the pressure was still very much on. PSO refused to raise the postproduction budget to help Ashby meet the delivery date, and he was expected to have his first cut ready in only a month. After repeated bad experiences with young editors on recent films, Ashby hired Bob Lawrence, a friend since they were both junior editors on *The Pride and the Passion,* to edit *8 Million Ways to Die.* Ashby had wanted Lawrence to cut *The Landlord,* but he had been busy on another film, and now, sixteen years later, they were finally working together again.

When production ended, Ashby took a well-deserved break and handed the film over to Lawrence, who promised him an assemblage by Christmas. Ashby then turned his attention to *The Hawkline Monster.* The novel's author, Richard Brautigan, had committed suicide in October 1984, and Brautigan's estate had extended Ashby's option by eighteen months to give him a chance to make the film. Mike Haller had always been lined up as the film's producer, but now Ashby seemed to be setting him up to direct it as he announced that Haller would take over from him if his schedule prevented him from taking on the film. (It appeared Ashby was hoping to re-create the situation in which Norman

Jewison had elevated him to director, by setting up *The Landlord* for himself and then passing it on to Ashby.) Pacific Films, a New Zealand production company, said it wanted to make *Hawkline,* then Jeff Bridges became interested in the lead and was trying to get his brother Beau involved also, and it briefly looked as if the film was really going to happen. But then the film's executive producer, Henry Honeckman, developed colon cancer, the New Zealand film industry hit a financial slump, and only half of the $8 million budget could be raised, and hopes of *The Hawkline Monster* being made vanished.

As Lawrence began to piece together an assemblage of *8 Million Ways to Die,* he wrote a sympathetic note to Ashby, saying:

> Dear Hal,
> I know how you felt after the end of shooting
> And I know who you felt like shooting
> But Amor Vincit Omnia,—at the end you shall triumph[38]

Ashby's triumph looked unlikely, however, as PSO blamed him for the film going over schedule and was incensed that he was not working with Lawrence on the assemblage. Ashby, who had never worked on an assemblage with an editor before, refused to take PSO's phone calls to discuss the issue. PSO then wrote to Ashby, accusing him (in rhetoric Ashby knew indicated an imminent firing) of being "irresponsible" and "unprofessional." Stung, Ashby responded to the allegations in a letter to his lawyer, Michael Sherman:

> The only time I've been irresponsible and non-professional on this film was during that week prior to shooting. I went against all of my instincts, and professional experience, and allowed myself to be coerced by people who didn't have a qualm in the world when it came to renegotiating my contract after I'd already been working for almost six (6) months on the film.
>
> At the time, I told myself it was the responsible thing to do. For me, the film, Jeff, Rosanna, PSO, and all the others who'd been working or waiting around for months. Well, it's turned out to be the worst move of my life, so far.
>
> I thought I would never cap the one of believing I was good

> enough to make something out of the last movie. The big difference on this one is not having to contend with Mr. Simon and cohort Mr. Stark. But the big mistake was in feeling I should defer to Neil because of who he is! What he represents! It was stupid of me, and I call that irresponsible.
>
> On this one: There were always plenty of signs, but most of them had to do with how tough it was for PSO to put up with all of those normal decisions being made by me, or the production company, without getting the consent of PSO first. You know, things like casting, not Jeff and Rosanna, but all the other roles. What Cameraman I wanted, what composer. All those things that are obviously best selected by the person actually making the film.

It was very upsetting to Ashby that although he had completed shooting the film within the 10 percent contingency, he was "being maligned and treated [like] a no account, no talent, evil minded rat that has nothing in mind but the destruction of PSO." "I wonder sometimes if the actions and words from PSO aren't just some great need, urge, secret desire, to see if I will bend," he continued. "It seems to me, it would really be some kind of fool's game to put up all that money on the chance you could bend or change somebody whose [*sic*] come down the road as far as I have. I know there are better candidates out there for bending than me." Ashby was definitely not going to bend on helping with the assemblage, and he pointedly stated that he "gave up work as an assistant editor quite some years ago."[39]

Berg, aware of Ashby's position, reminded an increasingly anxious and irritated Mark Damon that Ashby had no (contractual) obligation to speak to him until he had completed his first cut of the film. Allegedly, Berg added that if PSO execs really wanted to speak to Ashby, they should do so at a Directors Guild of America "hotline" meeting. PSO took this as an invitation to fire Ashby.

25

The Last Movie

> The film was not going to be linear in the way it was going to be cut. We tried to explain to PSO how they were going wrong with the editing, but they wouldn't listen.
> —Andy Garcia on *8 Million Ways to Die*

> Hal shouldn't see the film; it would kill him. It's a horrible, horrible thing.
> —Rosanna Arquette

On December 16, 1985, just twenty days after Ashby finished shooting *8 Million Ways to Die,* a five-ton truck arrived at the cutting rooms where Bob Lawrence was working. Producers Sales Organization (PSO) representatives confiscated the footage and refused Ashby and Lawrence access to the film. "PSO's attitude was 'Fuck him, he's going to take the film to Malibu and cut it as some unreleasable art film,'" says Chuck Mulvehill.[1]

The following day, Ashby received a letter from PSO saying his uncommunicative behavior was being interpreted as an indication that he had resigned from the film—but that if he had not, he would be fired. There has never been a clear explanation given for why Ashby was fired. Mark Damon said later, "I think I'm a total professional, and what was done was done with the best interests of everybody. Our firing Hal wasn't because we disagreed with or distrusted Hal's creative vision of the film. It was a business decision."[2]

After all the tussles and Machiavellian machinations so far, Ashby didn't regard his firing as by any means final—it simply seemed like more of the same from PSO. His contract gave him complete control over postproduction, PSO had influence only after he'd completed three cuts of the film, and anyway SFR, not PSO, was Ashby's employer, so PSO was in no position to sack him. Two days after his "firing," Ashby wrote a patient letter to Mark Damon in which he pledged to do "everything possible" to have the film ready for the April release date: "Now, Mark, I would really appreciate it, if you and the rest of your people over at PSO would please, at long last, give me a break, and quit telling me how to do my job. I really do know more about making movies than anybody and everybody at PSO, and I'm getting a little sick and tired of being called irresponsible just because I went ahead and made a film from no script. Please don't say you ever handed me a *script* that you thought should be shot. There were three (3) scripts that nobody—*nobody* wanted shot. So, what's so irresponsible on my part[?]"[3]

Meanwhile, Ashby's lawyers told PSO that it didn't legally have the right to fire Ashby; PSO's response was to force Steve Roth to fire him. The cast and crew were dismayed and distraught when they heard. "PSO thought they could edit the film better than Hal Ashby," says Rosanna Arquette. "What kind of mind thinks that way? Who do they think they are? Confiscating that film was the lowest thing anyone could do." Jeff Bridges said that Ashby's firing made him feel "ripped around. In the first place, I did the picture to work with Hal. To have it pulled away at the stage where all his expertise lies—which is in the *editing*—made no sense to me whatsoever."[4]

Work recommenced on the film in the new year, when Lawrence was given the few remaining days he needed to complete his assemblage. He only returned in the hope that he could convince PSO to bring Ashby back. Instead, however, the company brought in a new editor, Stuart Pappé, and encouraged Lawrence to work alongside him. Lawrence, however, remained loyal to Ashby and quit the film in protest.

Now it was clear that his firing was permanent, Ashby went to the Los Angeles Superior Court, backed by the Directors Guild of America (DGA), claiming that both his contract and the DGA's code had been violated when he was fired. He sued PSO for the money he had posted, $10 million for damage done to his reputation and loss of possible future business opportunities, and $50 million in punitive damages. The judge remanded the case to the DGA, deeming that it had jurisdiction over the dispute: Ashby produced documents to back up his case, but PSO claimed it needed time to produce the paperwork. PSO's stalling appears simply to have been intended to prevent Ashby from being reinstated on the film. But not even Ashby was hoping for that outcome, saying he probably would have "end[ed] up having to hand the film over unfinished. It would have been too frustrating. And there would have been nothing to stop them releasing *their* version in the meantime."[5]

On January 21, 1986, Ashby began a three-day testimony at a deposition hearing in the case of Ashby vs. PSO, during which PSO's lawyers tried to prove that he was irresponsible and a drug addict. Ashby explained why he was suing PSO, saying, "I got into directing after being an editor. I have always been known as a very, very good editor. I was an Academy award–winning editor. I believe . . . when the picture was pulled away from me, I wasn't doing anything wrong, and I believe that that damages me. People don't know what goes on. All they know is that I am not editing the picture. It is a very, very small community and . . . that is why I believe I was damaged."[6]

At the end of the three days, none of the dirt thrown at Ashby had stuck. He had answered the easy questions; the leading, argumentative, or difficult questions had been thrown out by his counsel; and his interrogation had turned up nothing new. The DGA arbitration panel gave Ashby and his company, Carbon State, damages of $550,000, which covered personal reputation, personal distress, and loss of business reputation. Ashby accepted the outcome, but his attitude surprised people.

"They gave him some money, and he just said, 'Ah, fuck it,' and left," says Chuck Mulvehill. "He would never have done that in the '70s—it would have been a fight to the death."[7] Now, however, Ashby had little fight left and didn't want to put himself through any more unnecessary punishment. When Mulvehill asked him why he wasn't trying to get the film back, Ashby said, "What's the point in fighting it? I'm just going to sweat blood to do my version, and then they'll just recut it their way."[8]

He was sad but ultimately philosophical about how things had ended up with PSO. "It's just a case of them not wanting me," he reflected. "Maybe they thought I wouldn't get it finished on time. I'm not quite clear. . . . I don't even know what the arguments were. The wire that I got said I was totally irresponsible and non-professional. I think they have to say that to fire you, but it's a little hard when you've been working so hard."[9] He confided to Mike Kaplan that he had shot a lot less footage than usual on *8 Million Ways to Die* so that there weren't many editing options and "they couldn't fuck it up."[10] However, PSO got round this by doing reshoots. "That's when I got the feeling stuff was going wrong with the film," says Alexandra Paul.[11]

Ashby took consolation from the fact that despite any further damage his reputation may have sustained, he was still being considered to direct major film projects. In mid-February, Dustin Hoffman called to ask whether he would be interested in working with him on a film version of Elmore Leonard's novel *La Brava,* about an ex–secret service agent who becomes involved in blackmail. The project already had a long and checkered history: the list of people who had tried and failed to get the film made included actor Roy Scheider and directors Ted Kotcheff, Volker Schlöndorff, and Martin Scorsese. The film's producer, Walter Mirisch, set up a deal with Cannon Films—a company run by Israeli cousins Menahem Golan and Yoram Globus—which was best known for low-budget exploitation films but was looking to move upmarket. Cannon was willing to pay the big money Hoffman wanted for the film, so a deal was brokered in late January 1986. Francis Ford Coppola dropped out of talks to direct at the same time as Ashby became available, and it initially seemed a perfect fit.

La Brava was due to start filming in Miami in August, but Hoffman was unhappy with the script and had been working on his own version of it with regular writing partner, Murray Schisgal. Ashby, confident after the work he had done on *8 Million Ways to Die,* had also started a draft of his own. He was excited about the film's possibilities, particularly the love story: Hoffman's protagonist falls for a fifty-something film star, who Ashby hoped would be played by one of the leading ladies of Hollywood's Golden Age, such as Debbie Reynolds, June Allyson, or Kathryn Grayson.

Hoffman, however, was insecure about having a love interest so much older than he was, and until he had approved the script the deal hung in the balance. He had wanted to be a codirector with Ashby, which the DGA would not allow, but was happy for Ashby to be the sole director so long as he retained script approval and primary creative control. In early March, Ashby was publicly unveiled as the film's director; however, two weeks later, Hoffman quit the project.

Hoffman claimed that Walter Mirisch had set up the Cannon deal "without telling anybody. I didn't back out—I flew out. I was frightened of Cannon. They could do anything, and would."[12] Cannon had already run two adverts using Hoffman's name without his approval, but when it ran double-page ads in both *Variety* and the *Hollywood Reporter* with a huge picture of a smiling Hoffman next to the caption "Welcome to the Cannon Family," it was the last straw. Al Pacino was briefly interested in the project, but on April 22 Ashby, who had taken on the film only to finally work with Hoffman, also pulled out.

Three days later, *8 Million Ways to Die* was released. The film was now radically altered from Ashby's original conception as the new editor, Stuart Pappé, had had no contact with Ashby and acted under instruction from PSO. Ashby had ensured his name did not feature too prominently and, in order to reflect his diminished role in the film, had asked PSO not to put "A Hal Ashby Film" on any of the posters or promotional materials. Though Ashby was acknowledged by the Writers Guild of America as one of the contributors to the script (along with Oliver Stone, Lance Hill, Robert Towne, and Don Edmonds), the screen credit had been given to Stone and "David Lee Henry," Hill's screenwriting nom de plume.

Ashby was certain that *8 Million Ways to Die* was far from the film he had set out to make as a "committee of editors . . . can't possibly think the same way [as I do]. They offered me the opportunity to see the film to see if I wanted 'A HAL ASHBY FILM' on it—it was in my contract—but I couldn't look at it. I said it's obviously not 'A HAL ASHBY FILM' unless *I* make it. I ended up with a payment, but what does that do? It doesn't give you your film."[13]

On its release, the film received predominantly negative reviews, and many critics clearly wanted to like it more than they did. The *Variety* and *Hollywood Reporter* reviewers, who knew of Ashby's firing, both reflected on the film as a wasted opportunity to tackle alcoholism in a more meaningful way. *Variety* said, "What could have been a better film delving into complexities . . . instead ends up an oddly paced work that is sometimes a thriller and sometimes a love story, succeeding at neither." The reviewer guessed that the film's "unevenness" was due to the fact that Ashby "wasn't privvy to what happened in the editing room."[14] Though the *Hollywood Reporter* said the film was "an entertaining and hard-edged cinematic yarn," it stated it was still "only another hard-noir, coke ring tale. Handled harder, more honestly, the film could have really been something."[15]

The *Reporter* review did, however, praise both Bridges and Arquette, though performances of the whole cast were dubbed "loud and aimless" by Walter Goodman in the *New York Times.* Goodman contended that Ashby seemed "to have been made desperate by the desultory and disjointed nature of the material. He has the characters constantly shoving and yelling insults at one another, fills the many interludes with headache-making music and winds things up with as clumsy a burst of bang-bang as you've ever seen."[16] A Pauline Kael review in the *New Yorker* blamed Ashby for every one of the film's shortcomings. Though Kael backhandedly complimented *8 Million Ways to Die* by calling it "more enjoyable than the other pictures Ashby has made in the last half-dozen years," she said that viewers could not "always distinguish between what's intentional and what's unintentional. . . . You don't know what's going on, or if the director does either."[17]

Almost everyone involved was deeply upset about the released version of the film, and an article in the *LA Weekly* entitled "How to Kill a Movie," by a friend of Ashby's, Michael Dare, gave the principals a forum to voice their grievances. Rosanna Arquette, derided for her acting, revealed that the inconsistency of her performance was due to poor editorial choices. "We'd purposely do takes where we'd overact, then calm down and do a take right after that was perfect," she explained. "[In the film] I go from a tough chick to suddenly I'm nice. It wasn't like that at all, and *I'm* getting attacked because they left all these scenes out. I was really proud of what I did in this movie. It was a completely different character from my others. But they made me look like a jerk, like I decided to play it that way, and I didn't. It was the most painful experience in the world to know that Hal didn't get to decide what takes to use."[18]

Speaking more than ten years later, Arquette showed her feelings were just as strong. "Hal was such a great guy," she told director Mike Figgis. "I felt like they killed him, I really did. Because he was so hurt, so angry. If you could have seen what Hal would have done, his cut and his music, it would have been a great movie. So that was kind of tragic. I was very bitter and angry in those days."[19]

Arquette said that she suspected PSO had hired Ashby only in order to lure big names like herself and Jeff Bridges to the film and admitted that she had done it only to work with Ashby. She did, however, describe it as "one of my greatest experiences," a sentiment that Jeff Bridges echoed. "I had one of the most creative times working on this picture I've ever had," Bridges told Dare. "Hal gave us space to create, and it wasn't just jerking off—we came up with good stuff. Unfortunately, they cut against the way Hal shot and conceived the film. He's one of the best directors I've ever worked with. He's an artist, though his process may look strange to people who aren't artists. They shouldn't have hired Hal in the first place if they wanted some other kind of film. We were going out of our way *not* to make a shoot-'em-up drug movie."[20]

Bridges maintained, "In the final film, they goosed up all the stuff we were trying to avoid. It was a case of fixing something that wasn't broken."[21] His sentiments are understandable, given the way Ashby's footage was used: often the last, rather than the best, take was used, so the film lacks a consistency of tone, and the performances oscillate wildly. Steve Burum maintains that Pappé and his editors "were cutting against the material and didn't understand Hal's intentions. There are a lot of things in that picture that are out of sequence, wrong-intentioned, all that."[22]

At the end of each shooting day, Ashby had asked his actors to improvise surreal sequences he saw as Scudder's alcoholic dreams and hallucinations, such as Bridges and Garcia on a pedestal and Garcia and Randy Brooks pouring champagne over Alexandra Paul while she was crying. They were abstract and needed to be handled carefully, but Andy Garcia recalls that after shooting a number of these scenes, Ashby excitedly told him, "I've found my movie."[23] None of these drunken montage sequences (which Burum remembers as quite brilliant) were used, but footage of Sunny's death from one of them was incorporated into the film as if it were a normal scene: it looked extremely out of place, as it was intentionally overdramatized and had been shot in a completely different style and palette.

There were more major deviations from Ashby's vision as well. Voice-overs, which Ashby never used, featured heavily, and Jeff Bridges was made to rerecord two hundred lines of dialogue for postdubbing, meaning that, as Dare's article noted, "more than half of the audio version of [Bridges's] performance was directed by editor Stuart Pappé."[24] Additionally, PSO asked composer James Newton Howard to make his score sound like the music on the hit television show *Miami Vice,* then bizarrely used pieces of music meant for one sequence in others.

Defending himself against the suggestion that PSO had botched the film, Damon claimed, "Ashby doesn't shoot a lot of footage, and he very much edits in camera. Therefore, any editor coming on cannot, in my estimation, go very far afield from Ashby's intentions."[25] Years after Ashby's death, he went further, blaming Ashby completely for the film's shortcomings, saying, "Ashby at that time, his mind was blown. He'd had too much coke. . . . It's a flawed picture with moments of brilliance. It was from a script by Oliver Stone and rewritten by Robert Towne, two of the best writers we had. Ashby threw the script out and had the writers improvise every day. It was mind boggling."[26]

Though much of the material in *8 Million Ways to Die* is of a relatively high standard—good acting and high production values are to be found throughout—the film's major problem is that Ashby did not edit it. As Jeff Bridges says, "'the puddings' that had come out of Hal's 'oven'" before had shown how important his skills as an editor were, especially with his own directorial work, and PSO firing Ashby to ensure the film was ready for its delivery date was lunacy.[27] While one can understand the studio's concern as a fledgling company that did not want to get a bad reputation, it failed to see the bigger picture and understand that had Ashby been allowed to cut the film, it would have been significantly better and therefore likely much more critically and financially successful. As it was, what Stuart Pappé cooked in *his* oven was a "pudding" in the most derogatory sense, one that took a pitiful $1.3 million at the box office.

There are still some bona fide Ashby moments in among the misguided editorial choices that blight *8 Million Ways to Die*. The scene where Scudder and Angel confront each other while eating snow cones and the warehouse face-off both have a compelling spontaneity, although one is left wondering how much better they might have been had Ashby's tight editing shaped them. The use of a beautiful Gaudí house, which Angel has just bought and rhapsodizes about, is also vintage Ashby, as is the moment in the opening scene where Scudder walks past a gravestone marked "Adelson," a sneaky dig at the Lorimar boss. And, like in so many Ashby films, the ending involves water: Scudder walks along the beach with his arm around Sarah, looking out at the Pacific Ocean as the camera dwells on the couple in long shot. Though Ashby's best-known movies all eschew (straightforward) happy endings, this rosy final image hinted at a new positivity in Ashby's perspective on life.

26

Starting Over

> His childhood was no sweet treat. But he had a lot of joy in him, despite what had happened. I think he'd experienced so much as a kid, anything he was experiencing in Hollywood was just small potatoes. So he'd always be laughing, and he had that perspective about what was important.
> —Sean Penn

> Steve, Thanks for the letter. Hope you are having a good year. My hobby is making movies.
> —Hal Ashby (autograph inscription, 1987)

Since the start of the 1980s, Ashby had had four films taken away from him in the editing room and then flop at the box office, had turbulent business relationships with Ray Stark and the Producers Sales Organization (PSO) and a nightmare partnership with Lorimar that descended into a prolonged legal battle, and seen his utopian production company Northstar flounder and fail and his reputation in Hollywood change from that of a charmed maverick to an aging hippie burned out on drugs. Weary after this litany of negative experiences, the fifty-six-year-old Ashby now took time out to rethink his lifestyle and the way that he wanted to work. He broke his life down to its essentials, focused on what was important. He knew that he could not continue as before, so, as Bob Jones says, he "turned his life around."[1] He stopped smoking dope, took greater care in his appearance, and took long walks along the beach at Malibu, almost immediately looking healthier for it.

After the *La Brava* deal fell through, Ashby briefly developed the modern-day Western *Road Show* (a.k.a. *Spangler*) before a rights issue put it into turnaround. As he now wasn't committed to any project, Ashby decided to have a change of location and perspective and go to

New York, where he stayed for a month or so. He had an apartment on the sixtieth floor of a high-rise on the Upper East Side two blocks from Central Park, a place he would periodically escape to over the next couple of years.

When Rudy Wurlitzer visited Ashby's apartment, he was struck by the fact that it had hardly any furniture, a manifestation of his spartan lifestyle. Ashby was a great admirer of Wurlitzer's wife's work as a photographer and wanted one of her pictures on his wall but asked whether he could rent one. "I'm not buying at the moment," he explained. Wurlitzer noticed a fundamental change in Ashby's attitude to life, saying, "It was a very haunting moment when I realized he was facing something profound, and doing it in his own way, in the context of his own privacy."[2]

When he went to and from New York City, Ashby would drive cross-country in his red 1984 Chevrolet Corvette, often taking detours to visit friends on the way. Novelist Jim Harrison, a friend who regularly tried to provide Ashby with possible scripts they could collaborate on, recalls, "One summer morning in 1987 . . . Ashby stopped by the cabin. I could hear his Corvette thumping its bottom along my rumpled two-track for minutes before he drove into the clearing. He had called the tavern the night before saying that he was driving from New York to L.A. and would be in the area. This seemed to be a little odd because the cabin was about a thousand miles out of the way from a direct line between New York and Los Angeles." Harrison writes, "We spent several hours pleasantly talking and he said he understood why I loved the cabin."[3]

Wurlitzer says he thinks Ashby "was communing with himself by being on the road,"[4] but he was also communing with America. Though he was often frustrated and upset by the state of his country, he embodied a quintessentially American rebelliousness and desire to better himself. "I hope every one of my movies tells something about America," he said in 1976. "They're all made in America, by Americans, for Americans. I feel very strongly about this country."[5] Talking about his love of America four years later, he said, "I didn't [previously] realize how fortunate I was as an individual that I was born in this country. . . . You don't get, I don't think, those kind of opportunities in most other places in the world. And certainly not in countries where there are hardships because there are too many people and not enough money. This is the Land of Plenty, even though we're a little tight now."[6]

Back in Los Angeles, Ashby made a conscious decision to shift his focus from directing and editing to writing and directing: he closed down his editing rooms in Malibu, sold the equipment to old apprentices or donated it to the UCLA Film Department, and took on a new creative partner. Rick Padilla had originally worked with Ashby as a consultant on *8 Million Ways to Die,* helping him with high-tech tools for directing, but now started helping him develop scripts. Padilla says Ashby was doing some of his best work in years, having finally found the confidence to become a full-fledged screenwriter rather than just a director. Padilla had a background in acting and writing as well as business, and his take on film was very close to Ashby's own. He was an ideal collaborator for Ashby and fondly remembers how they brought out the best in each other.

"Even brilliant as he was, he was jumping plateaus, and he was growing," says Padilla. "He was always wanting to ask and probe and put his ego to one side. I've never seen someone work so hard, and it was magic *every day.* He was *so* focused. When you were working with him, you found yourself working in that way too. He had extreme clarity and was so humorous and so pleasant to be around. I would have stayed in that job forever because it just didn't get any better than that."[7]

Always reclusive, Ashby now distanced himself from the Hollywood system and worked only on carefully chosen projects, at the pace he wanted. He never forced ideas when they did not come freely. He and Padilla would take breaks and sit out on the sun deck, watching the dolphins playing only one hundred meters away in the ocean, waiting for inspiration. Rudy Wurlitzer describes collaborating with Ashby by saying, "It was like you were dreaming a project together, and it was a journey. But the studios took away the dream process."[8] Ashby loved the dreaming and so took all the time he wanted creating films on paper, knowing that as soon as a studio became involved the perfection of what he had in his head would start to unravel.

Adding to Ashby's sense of a fresh start was the fact that his legal battle with Lorimar had finally come to an end, with him receiving a settlement from his former employers. Though Ashby himself had footed the bill for the years of legal fees, he didn't keep the money he was given but instead donated it to a camp for children suffering from cancer and a charity that helped battered women.

Peter Bart, the former Lorimar Films president and Bob Evans's underling at the time of *Harold and Maude,* dined out with Ashby around the same time and recalls him being "both bitter and bemused by the ups and downs of his career."

"Trying to deal with movies on an orderly basis is like trying to be rational about your love life," Ashby told him with a wry smile. "Reality keeps getting in the way. You start a project under the worst possible circumstances and the stars are fighting and you don't have the money to finish, and you end up with a smash. And then you get to do it the right way, and you end up in a mess. What the hell do you make of it?"

"Not much," said Bart.

"I mean, in the end, you look at the ledger and hope you have something to show for all of it. I've managed to do all the things directors were supposed to do. I made some good pictures and I made some bad. I managed to make a lot of money and then lose all of it. I mean, that's the gig, right?"[9]

Bart was struck by the fact that Ashby "didn't have anything to pitch, didn't ask my help on anything" and writes, "I never understood the scenario for that meeting."[10] The reason Ashby did not try to set up a film with Bart was not, as Bart had suspected, because he was washed up or devoid of ideas but because he had become extremely careful about whom he chose to work with. Though he readily admitted that he could be difficult to deal with, he was honest and straightforward with everybody and expected the same in return. However, he had been shocked at the underhanded, cutthroat way Lorimar, Ray Stark, and PSO had done business and could no longer work with people who viewed him as another employee whom they could mistreat. Ashby decided from then on he would collaborate only with producers he knew and trusted. "On my last films, the producers turned out to be liars, and I'm never going to do that again," he told Padilla. "Whatever we're going to work on, it's going to be with producers that I know, and who I know their word means everything."[11]

When Ray Stark came to Ashby with the idea of directing *Revenge,* the Jim Harrison novel Orson Welles had been slated to direct at Northstar, he turned him down without hesitation. (Ashby's decision was made easier because he had heard that Stark had previously engaged John Huston on the project but had inexplicably sacked him because his script did not include any camera setups.) Similarly, Ashby spent only a brief time working for producer Elliott Kastner on a screen version of Noel Behn's quirky comic novel about the FBI, *Seven Silent Men*. Kastner had given him free rein to pick his leading man and approved Ashby's choice, Timothy Hutton, but then backtracked when Al Pacino expressed an interest in the role. Ashby had already shaken hands with Hutton and would not be moved, so Kastner tried to get Padilla to change Ashby's mind for him. When this failed, Kastner asked Ashby to go to New York to speak to Pacino, but when Ashby told him all he would tell Pacino was that the part was already taken, it was agreed that it would be best if Ashby did not remain on the film. Ironically, just weeks after he had left the project, it came out that Kastner had not actually bought the rights to the book, and Noel Behn contacted Ashby saying he still wanted him to make the film. Ashby brought in Jerry Hellman as his new producer and settled down to write the screenplay himself.

In his newly relaxed frame of mind, it was much easier for Ashby to be philosophical about life's hardships. When Robert Blake visited him at the Colony and was downcast about the difficulties in his own career, Ashby told him to appreciate how lucky he was. "You know, Bobby," he told Blake, "when we pass on, we can count our films. They will count their money."[12]

Ashby had always tried to help aspiring directors climb up the Hollywood ladder, as Norman Jewison had done with him, and now once again acted as a mentor. Ashby had met John Teton in the late 1970s through their mutual friend Ken Kesey and in 1986 was asked to be a creative consultant on *Lightning,* a modern-day romantic drama about mining that Teton had cowritten with novelist Gurney Norman. Ashby was impressed by the script and did not hesitate to attach his name to the project, as he knew it would be a major help to Teton in trying to get funding.

"Hal was supportive and gracious working with me on *Lightning,*" says Teton. "His confidence that I could do a first-rate job directing the movie was a big morale-booster for me." Ashby also tried to get Teton an agent, put him in touch with Jerry Hellman, agreed to a more prominent role as executive producer (for which he deferred his salary), and encouraged Teton to send his script out and get actors to commit to the film. "All of the first seven well-known creative talents approached to attach themselves to *Lightning* agreed to do so," Teton recalls, "including 3 others who, like Hal, were past Academy Award nominees—this despite the project coming to them from a newcomer intending to direct based hundreds of miles from LA without an agent. I was in for a rude awakening when, despite the bright showers of praise generated from the creative talent and occasional promising meetings, the many overtures to studios and prospective investors in those years turned up dry."[13]

Ashby was also a mentor to Padilla, whom he thought had great promise as a director, and tried to pass as much expertise as he could on to him. Padilla cherished his working relationship with Ashby and was very appreciative of the education he was receiving. "You shouldn't be paying me, *I* should be the one paying to work with you," he would say to Ashby. Padilla says Ashby had two criteria for the projects they were working on: "Firstly, do something that no one else had done before. And secondly, create something that has entertainment as a base but has something to say."[14]

One of these projects was *The Ditto List,* based on the 1985 book of the same name by Stephen Greenleaf that Dustin Hoffman had told Ashby about when it was still in galleys. The novel was about D. T. Jones, a self-employed divorce lawyer (the titular "ditto list" is his secretary's term for the divorce court calendar) who dedicates his life to helping the women he represents. The story particularly appealed to Ashby because of the complexities of the protagonist, who is himself divorced and has self-destructive tendencies. Jones was a perfect Ashbyesque hero whom Hoffman seemed well suited to play, and the actor now asked Ashby to adapt Greenleaf's book for his company, Punch Productions. In just eight frenzied days, Ashby wrote a script that, far from being rushed and substandard, was described by Lynn Stalmaster, Ashby's casting director since the 1960s, as the best he had read in twenty years.

Joe Kanter, the chairman of the Bank of Florida and president of the Kanter Company, which had produced the Jack Nicholson–Meryl Streep film *Ironweed* (1987), knew Ashby and, according to John Mandel, was "enthralled" and "bowled over by him."[15] There was some discussion of a film loosely based on Kanter's life, but Kanter and Ashby were more excited by the prospect of bringing *Wonderland Avenue,* an as-yet-unpublished memoir by Danny Sugerman, to the screen. Sugerman had grown up as a fan of the Doors and by the age of thirteen was handling their fan mail, but his association with the band, and particularly with its iconic frontman, Jim Morrison, had led him to becoming a heroin addict on the brink of madness. Written with verve and humor, Sugerman's account of the Los Angeles rock-and-roll scene in the 1960s and 1970s was a compelling read and particularly interesting to Ashby, as he had lived among its principal players.

To support himself while developing these projects, Ashby also took a couple of short-term, high-paying directing jobs. In the fall of 1987, he was hired to direct the pilot episode of *Beverly Hills Buntz,* a spin-off from the hugely successful cop show *Hill Street Blues.* In the final episode of *Blues,* gruff, no-nonsense cop Norman Buntz (Dennis Franz) punched out the police chief and turned in his gun and badge; in the new series, the show's creators, Jeffrey Lewis and David Milch, dispensed with gritty realism as they transported Buntz to the affluent streets of Beverly Hills, where he becomes a private detective. Partnering Buntz with a colorful sidekick, Sid "the Snitch" Thurston (Peter Jurasik), who goes west with him, the show's main focus was not private investigator plots but comedy derived from Buntz's inability to adapt to Los Angeles life and Thurston's underhanded ways of making a buck.

Ashby was engaged not to shoot but to reshoot the pilot. According to an article by Jeff Jarvis in *People Weekly,* the producers had decided the look of the original version was too dark, and NBC executives felt it "needed a clearer beginning and a neater ending." It was also three and a half minutes too long, so the pilot was ditched, two roles were recast, and Ashby was brought in to fix things. The version that aired was deemed by Jarvis to be "the production-line model without the subtlety, fine shadings, grace and unpredictability of the original," a surprising statement given that these are exactly the qualities one would expect Ashby to bring to the proceedings.[16] The episode contains moments of sharp dialogue and moderately funny broad comedy, but though Ashby elicited spirited performances from Franz and Jurasik (who had been playing the characters on *Blues* for years), his fingerprints are barely discernible on the episode. The flashy television editing (in which Ashby was not involved) further accentuates the difference between this and his other work.

Variety's review said the *Beverly Hills Buntz* pilot was "not a smash, but does look like it will work as a regular series."[17] The *Hol-*

lywood Reporter's Richard Hack had high praise for Franz and Jurasik, saying, "The pair make classic comedy." Hack continued by praising a show "filled with gentle comedy and physical excesses, directed with refreshing aplomb by Hal Ashby. To watch Buntz describe a fellow cop-turned-private-eye as 'a mixture of goat puke and fruit' is to watch magic."[18] Premiering on November 5, 1987, *Beverly Hills Buntz* was one of NBC's "designated hitters," an experimental ploy the channel used for its Thursday night prime slot—between *Cheers* and *L.A. Law*—to try out four different shows on a four-week rotation. Predictably, the system was a failure and proved the undoing of *Buntz,* as viewers who enjoyed the show had to wait a full month between episodes while the rest simply forgot it existed.

In 1987 Ashby pledged to help casting director Don Phillips make a film based on the life of Scottish missionary and explorer David Livingstone, whose adventures in nineteenth-century Africa promised to be compelling viewing. Though there had previously been a film, *Stanley and Livingstone* (1939), starring Spencer Tracy and Cedric Hardwicke and Phillips had little more than a treatment, the project appealed to Ashby because Sean Penn was tentatively attached to play Livingstone. Penn had announced himself as one of the most rawly talented and exciting actors of his generation with performances opposite Timothy Hutton in John Schlesinger's *The Falcon and the Snowman* (1985) and in *At Close Range* (1986), directed by his best friend, former Ashby acolyte James Foley, but had been thrust into the public eye for different reasons after marrying pop superstar Madonna. Penn struggled with fame and served a month's jail sentence after two incidents of assault (against a paparazzi he caught in his hotel room and an extra who was taking photos of him) but also used his high profile to befriend his heroes, including legendary writer Charles Bukowski, Dennis Hopper, and a number of Ashby's own friends, Warren Beatty, Jack Nicholson, and Harry Dean Stanton. Penn listed *The Last Detail* as one of his favorite films and sought out Ashby, who happened to be his neighbor in Malibu. The two quickly became close.

"I first met Hal in the Colony with Tim Hutton," Penn remembers. "Later I got to know him much better—he started coming to my house in Malibu. We spent a lot of time together in the period that was my first marriage. When she [Madonna] was out of town, that house was Hal and I, playing pool."[19] Ashby gave Penn comfort and company during 1987 and 1988, a troubled period when Penn's marriage was on the rocks. It is a sign of how close their relationship became that Ashby, who rarely opened up about his past, talked to Penn about his early years in Ogden and his father's death.

During more upbeat periods, Penn would visit Ashby, sometimes with Don Phillips or Adam Nelson, one of his actor friends. Penn later told how Ashby helped Nelson when Nelson's career was flagging and, in Penn's words, he was "in a desperate moment; somewhere between suicide and just running away from Los Angeles."[20] Nelson had recently done a short film called *Hotel November* that Penn liked very much, so he invited Ashby over to watch it in an attempt to raise Nelson's spirits. Ashby was so impressed that he began talking about developing a film for both Nelson and Penn.

"We went down to his house," Nelson recalls, "and what a sweet guy. Those are the kind of people that Sean gravitates to: very talented, maybe on the fringe a little bit sometimes, people who the business forgets about." Nelson, who lived in Culver City, used to regularly pass by Ashby Avenue and would think about Hal whenever he saw the street sign. One day, Nelson mentioned the sign to Penn and said, "Hey, man, it'd be cool if we could hand it to Hal as a present."[21] And thus was born the grandly titled "Operation Blue Board."

To put the plan into action, Penn says, "Adam and I went over to a hardware store and got metal-clippers. Adam was the lookout, and I climbed the pole and snipped the sign. We wrote on the back of it. 'You Are Now In Possession Of Stolen Property.' And then, quite late at night, we called Hal and said we had a present for him. We put it in the trunk of the car, an early 80s or '79 model Caprice, and met Hal at the Malibu shopping center about two in the morning. The local police saw our two cars pull in together and wondered what the hell was going on. All we needed was them to ask us to open the trunk . . . but they recognized Hal as a long-term resident of the area and they took off. And we gave the sign to him right there."[22] Penn's actions were all the more daring and meaningful because he was on parole at the time.

In early 1988, Ashby accepted work directing another television pilot, this time for CBS, and in this instance he seems to have been genuinely attracted to the project. The job would take him to England to direct the first episode of *Jake's Journey*, a series loosely based on Mark Twain's novel *A Connecticut Yankee in King Arthur's Court* and developed by ex–Monty Python member Graham Chapman and his partner, David Sherlock. Chapman admitted that when he was first approached, he "wasn't particularly keen on writing any TV at that particular moment." But, he said, the prospect of shooting in England—and the money on offer—made him think, "Wait a minute. For twenty-three minutes of material, which won't get made *anyway* . . . why not?"[23] His pilot script introduces Jake Sibley—an American teenager from Dayton, Ohio, struggling to adapt to his new life after his father's business takes the whole family to London—who learns to tackle life head-on with the help of his mentor, the time-traveling knight Sir George. In the enjoyably silly plot, Jake suddenly finds himself back in Arthurian times, as Sir George's knave, and has to go to Castle Greed to woo the Princess Yeugh on behalf of Prince Kevin the Rich. There were obvious parallels with the Arthurian antics of *Monty Python and the Holy Grail* (1975) as Chapman's script featured crones, a witch, a troll, an eccentric innkeeper, and a wonderfully ridiculous king and queen—not to mention two lobsters on a cycling holiday!

The show was less a situation comedy than a fantasy comedy, or "fantacom," as Chapman called it, and was written with such warmth and humor that it's no surprise that Ashby signed on to direct. The sixteen-year-old Chris Young, who had appeared in the *Max Headroom* television series, played Jake and was surrounded by a raft of talented British comedy actors, including Rik Mayall, Griff Rhys Jones, Alexei Sayle, Liz Smith, and Celia Imrie. True to form, Chapman himself played the queen (who only ever says "Good evening"), while another behemoth of British comedy, Peter Cook, was perfectly cast as the stuffy king. Ashby went to London in February to audition actors with casting director Joyce Gallie, who describes him as "just divine, really lovely to work with."[24] After their casting sessions, the only major part that remained uncast was that of Sir George. At the last minute, Chapman decided to play the part himself, explaining, "I secretly cherished the notion of playing that role, but didn't want to because of several other considerations. . . . I quite enjoyed it, despite the fact it meant going back into armour, albeit even worse, because it was a full set of armour, and rusting."[25]

The pilot was shot in the second half of March at Shepperton Studios, just outside London, with a substantial $1.2 million budget. The actors knew Ashby only through his films and were surprised when he was not, as they had expected, a director in the brash, loud Hollywood mold. "The thing I remember about him was that he was *terribly* softly spoken," says Celia Imrie. "I thought how interesting for a man of obvious fame and power that you don't have to be screaming and shouting all over the place, which is of course what you're given to believe of American directors. My overall feeling was that I thought, 'If this is American directors, then what a thrill!' He was *absolutely* sweet and particularly kind and gentle with [Chris Young]. They had a very good relationship, and I thought how lucky he was to have such a man as his mentor."[26]

Young indeed relished his time on *Jake's Journey* and fondly recalls the experience of working with Ashby. "He was one of the very first people to acknowledge me on a professional level, even though I was a kid," Young says. "He made me part of the process and said he wanted me every night at dailies. I thought he was the coolest guy. He was reserved and in good spirits; he was smiling, cheery, and respectful. My image of him is standing around with a smile on his face. You had the sense that he was happy to be doing what he was doing, and he was the kindest, gentlest man he could be."[27]

Young and Ashby were both put up in London's Athenaeum Hotel, and during their stay there, the young actor played a practical joke on his director: Young got hold of some police tape so that one day Ashby came back to find his room had been locked off as a crime scene.

There was a general sense of fun on the set, and Young describes Ashby and Graham Chapman as "a good pairing. [I remember] Hal sitting back, amused by Graham's absurdity."[28] As a result, they produced good work. Though the brief modern-day sequences are clichéd and weak in comparison (the episode concludes with Jake conquering his fear and asking out the girl he likes and then punching the air in freeze frame), the rest of the pilot is marked by originality, humor, and vitality. The dialogue is excellent, the scenes between Cook and Chapman a true delight, and the burgeoning partnership between Chapman and Young, whom Chapman described as "very good indeed," promised much for the future.[29] Unfortunately, CBS was put off by the wacky, surreal elements in the show, which it felt would alienate audiences, and decided not to commission more episodes. A few months later, a strike by the Writers Guild of America (of which Chapman was not a member) had CBS scrambling for shows, and five more episodes of *Jake's Journey* were written, although none were ever produced. In 1989, the Disney Channel picked up the pilot (which it showed occasionally) and hoped to commission more episodes, but by this time Chapman was terminally ill.

During Ashby's time in London, he received a call from Lester Persky, who five or six years earlier had given up trying to get Ashby to clear his schedule to direct *Handcarved Coffins*. Despite past problems with the screenplay, Persky had decided to have another go at bringing Capote's novella to the screen and found Ashby was both available and eager to be a part of the film. "Lester, I'll be coming back on Sunday," Ashby told Persky. "Is Wednesday too late for a meeting?"

His enthusiasm for directing reignited by *Beverly Hills Buntz* and *Jake's Journey,* Ashby threw himself into preparing *Handcarved Coffins* for production. "His command of the medium, his understanding, was unabated," said Persky. "He was brilliant. He put together a script that I think really licked the problems we'd had in the past, and we were set to go ahead."[30]

In July, Ashby and Persky went to New Mexico to scout locations for the film. They were looking for a small, secluded Western town that would be a fitting atmospheric backdrop for Capote's (probably fabricated) tale of bizarre serial murders. Though the producer went back to Los Angeles after five days in the sweltering heat, Ashby stayed on alone. Soon after, Jack Nicholson signed on to play the lead, detective Jake Pepper, and filming was scheduled for summer 1989, after Nicholson had finished shooting *Batman* (1989) in England.

Ashby's willingness to get back into directing a major film was due in no small part to the fact that Lester Persky was a producer he knew and trusted after working with him on *The Last Detail* and *Shampoo.* One of the few other producers whom he had stayed in contact with over the years was Jerry Hellman, with whom he had fostered a friendship during their battles to save *Coming Home* from the new regime at United Artists. The following year, Ashby gave Hellman a small part in *Being There,* and subsequently the two neighbors occasionally went round to each other's houses to complain about their respective woes. They were now collaborating again, on the planned *Seven Silent Men,* and in late 1987 Hellman proposed that they make a film of Thomas Berger's novel *Vital Parts.* Ashby had, in fact, been pitched that same idea back in 1971, when Berger's ex-agent Joel Steinberger had unsuccessfully tried to get the film made with Walter Matthau.

Ashby and Padilla wrote a draft of *Vital Parts* and then passed it on to Bob Jones for rewriting. The screenplay for *Handcarved Coffins* was ready to go, and in the gap before Ashby was to start shooting he met regularly with Hellman to discuss *Vital Parts.* Danny DeVito had agreed to play Carl Reinhart, the antihero in midlife crisis, and Gene Hackman the enigmatic figure from his past, Bob Sweet. Ashby was also trying to finally get *Hawkline* off the ground. He had Padilla put together a step outline and lined up Nicholson and Harry Dean Stanton to play the two cowboys.

The plan was to shoot *Coffins* in the summer, *Vital Parts* the following winter or spring, and then do *Hawkline.* Ashby was very excited about the prospect of directing again—these were projects he had long been passionate about, and for the first time since 1980 he would be working with producers who would support rather than undermine his talents. "He was vital and active: he had a couple of other projects in development that I knew of, there was a constant parade of young filmmakers to his house, he was always there for council and guidance and encouragement," Hellman recalls. "During all that time he was working at such a high level of creative energy and intelligence and craft."[31]

One day, when Ashby was due at Hellman's house to discuss *Vital Parts,* he called and asked whether the meeting could be moved to his house. When Hellman arrived, Ashby had one leg propped up. He rolled up his sweatpants to show Hellman the leg, which was black and blue. "I don't know what it is," Ashby said, pointing at what appeared to be a badly discolored bruise. "It's traveling around. One day it's in my arm, the next it's in my leg, and then my back."[32]

Rather than see a doctor, Ashby tried to ignore the problem, but soon after, he visited Warren Beatty and showed the bruise to him. Beatty frowned and said, "I don't like the way that looks. It looks to me like phlebitis."

"What the hell is phlebitis?" said Ashby.

"You know, what Nixon had," Beatty replied. "Let me send you a doctor."[33]

Ashby, however, still stalled. "Hal's approach to medicine was opposite to mine—he didn't have an approach," Beatty remembers. "Hal didn't want to go to a doctor when he first had these bumps on his legs—he didn't even *have* a doctor then."[34] Ashby finally went to a doctor at UCLA who said it was a rash and that phlebitis never affected both legs, but Beatty was not satisfied and wanted a second opinion. When Beatty's father had been ill with cancer, he had been treated at Johns Hopkins Hospital in Baltimore (Ashby had gone with Beatty to see him), so Beatty called up the doctors at Johns Hopkins to ask for expert advice on Ashby's symptoms. He was told that they were consistent with migratory phlebitis, a condition in which a blood clot moves around the body through the bloodstream, a symptom of excessive blood clotting or cancer.

Beatty called Ashby and insisted he immediately see a doctor, so Ashby took a break from working with Padilla to go for an appointment at Cedars Sinai Hospital in Los Angeles. He returned a few hours later, shaken and angry, with tears in his eyes.

"Motherfucking doctors!" he said.

"What is it!?" asked Padilla.

"I'm a dead man," said Ashby. "They tell me I've got cancer of the pancreas and say I've only got months to live."[35]

27

Do Not Go Gentle

> Grave men, near death, who see with blinding sight
> Blind eyes could blaze like meteors and be gay,
> Rage, rage against the dying of the light.
>
> And you, my father, there on the sad height,
> Curse, bless, me now with your fierce tears, I pray.
> Do not go gentle into that good night.
> Rage, rage against the dying of the light.
> —Dylan Thomas, "Do Not Go Gentle into That Good Night" (1951)

> He found out that he had cancer. He knew he was going to die but he never complained. He had a smile for everyone. At the start he didn't want to take any drugs. But then he had to.
> —From Hal Ashby's script for *Handcarved Coffins* (1988)

After hearing Ashby's prognosis, Beatty took him to Johns Hopkins for more tests, CAT scans, and pancreatic scans, which revealed that there were malignant tumors in his pancreas and the cancer had almost entirely consumed his liver. His doctors recommended an aggressive treatment beginning with surgery, but Ashby refused. "I think you should have the surgery," Beatty told him.[1] Ashby could not be convinced, however, and returned home. Agreeing to surgery would have been admitting he might die, so as he had often done in his life, he chose denial instead.

Back home, Ashby kept working and even tried to take over *She's De Lovely,* a script by his friend John Cassavetes that Sean Penn wanted to do. Penn had initially been set to make it, but when Cassavetes became terminally ill, he had to pass the project on. Not long after, it became clear that Ashby too was in no shape to consider taking on the film. (It was later filmed, after significant changes, as the 1997 *She's So Lovely,* with Penn directed by Cassavetes's son, Nick.) Soon after his return, Ashby's blood clots made him suffer a stroke that caused hemisphere damage. "After that," says Padilla, "he wasn't the same. He didn't know what was going on; he was mentally different. He was like a five-year-old: if you'd asked him for a check for $10,000, he probably would have written you one."[2]

The ailing Ashby was being looked after by Lynn Griffis, a striking southern blonde known to everyone as Grif who had gotten to know him after writing him a fan letter, hoping he might cast her in one of his films. Though in his last years Ashby had enjoyed the company of many women without committing to, let alone living with, any of them, after his stroke Griffis appointed herself Ashby's live-in nurse and girlfriend and set out to heal him. Ashby was desperate to get better and hopeful that he could be cured, and Griffis persuaded him to try New Age methods and alternative medicines. Though Ashby had been given three months to live, Griffis admits now that she was convinced they were going to beat the cancer through alternative therapies and that Ashby would then make a film letting the world know how he had miraculously cheated death. Ashby had money, so she brought healers from all over the world who laid hands on him, tried to draw out the tumors, "zapped" him. Nothing worked, however, and he became visibly more ill.

As word got out, a stream of friends came to visit him at the Colony. "I set up a schedule with all the calls that started to come in from his friends who had heard about Hal's illness," Griffis says. "We set up every afternoon for people to come by and sit on the bed and be with Hal. . . . We always had no more people than could sit on the bed at one time. . . . It actually was the bed from *Being There,* so it was a big bed and could hold a lot of friends at one time."[3] Many of those who visited Ashby pleaded with him to go back to Johns Hopkins, but Warren Beatty recalls, "It was about five or six weeks—I felt they were crucial weeks—before me and Jack [Nicholson] and Haskell finally talked him into going back and having the surgery."[4]

Ashby made the decision suddenly one afternoon when Dustin Hoffman was visiting him. "Dustin happened to be there and he planned right then and there to fly with us, and the three of us left and went to a private plane and went straight to Johns Hopkins," Griffis recalls. "I cannot say enough about Dustin for the way he just 'picked up' and changed his life for that time and chose to be with Hal."[5]

Between them, Hoffman and Beatty managed to get the Warner Brothers jet to fly Ashby to Baltimore. "We drove in a limo to the airport," Hoffman remembers. "Every few miles, he would throw up, black rivers of it."[6] He was operated on at Johns Hopkins, where his spleen and parts of his liver and pancreas were taken out in an attempt to remove the tumors. However, the cancer had already spread too much for the surgery to have the positive effect doctors had hoped for, and Ashby regretted having been talked into it. He was in severe pain that even morphine could not dent and felt angry and humiliated by what the doctors had done to his body. Weak and now suffering from failing eyesight, he was desperate to escape from the hospital, where everything around him reminded him that he was a dying man. Still, he welcomed visits from his friends, and Quincy Jones, John Mandel, and Jon Voight chartered a plane to come out to see him. "He was still Hal, even when he was sick," remembers Dustin Hoffman, who stayed by Ashby for four days in the hospital.[7] On one occasion, he weakly tried to climb out of bed and said to Hoffman, "Come on, let's go. They've got some great crabcakes round here!"[8]

Though he had retained some of his sense of humor, Ashby acknowledged now that he was facing his own mortality. He was not getting any better at Johns Hopkins, so a week after his surgery he walked out of the hospital and checked himself and Griffis into a hotel and found the next flight back to Los Angeles. If he were going to die, he wanted to do it at home, by the ocean, with his friends around him.

The next day, they returned to Malibu, and Griffis set about making sure he had everything he needed. At first, he came downstairs in the morning and spent his days on the couch in the kitchen, looking out at the sea. His nephew, Guy, Jack's son, happened to be working nearby in Malibu and would come by sometimes and carry him up to the roof so he could have a bird's-eye view of his beloved ocean. As time went on, he got weaker and was able to move about much less, and in the final month of his life he rarely left his bedroom. He had a huge television and top-of-the-range hi-fi system set up there and would lie in bed watching movies and listening to music, often in the company of Al Schwartz. The writer of *Lookin' to Get Out* had not seen him since 1980, but when he found out Ashby was ill, he called up the house immediately and asked whether he could come visit. The two spent the whole day together, and as the sun was setting Ashby said, "Can you come back?"

"Sure," said Schwartz. "When?"

"How about tomorrow?"

After that, Schwartz came to see Ashby every day, spending up to twenty hours at a stretch looking after him alongside Griffis and a nurse who had quit his job at Johns Hopkins to work for Ashby. He was increasingly frail and needed help getting in and out of bed, going to the bathroom, and getting up and down the stairs, but much of the time Schwartz just sat with him, rubbing Ashby's body to alleviate some of the incredible pain he was suffering. "It made me feel good to take care of him, but it was a horrible thing to see someone dying," says Schwartz. "He never took any painkillers because he wanted to know how he felt. He couldn't stay in one spot for long, he was in so much pain. We were constantly moving him, rolling him, rubbing him."[9]

Having his aching body rubbed was one of the few things that gave Ashby any comfort, and many of his friends participated in this ritual. "In life, Hal was a recluse," says Don Phillips. "But in death, he wanted everybody around him. And, any given night, you might see Jon Voight, Jack Nicholson, Warren Beatty, Shirley MacLaine, Jane Fonda, Sean [Penn]. . . . Nobody in Hollywood would believe this, but they loved him and they were there to comfort him. Everybody would take a body part, his arms, his legs, six or seven or eight people rubbing him, caressing the skin, just to ease his terrible pain. And he loved having everybody around. That's not the way he was in life."[10]

Like Schwartz, Pablo Ferro came to see him every day, while other friends visited whenever they could: Bob Jones came several times a week, and Quincy Jones, whom Ashby had visited daily after Jones's brain surgery in 1974, was another regular visitor, often with Norman Jewison. Ashby was now almost blind, so Sean Penn would bring a book to read to him. When John Teton turned up to see Ashby, he found him in too much pain to be able to speak and recalls, "The way he apologized when he told me he couldn't talk now struck at the heart. Even in what was obviously a death's-door crisis, he took care to make sure I did not feel brushed-off."[11]

When Bob Downey went to see him, Ashby had lost most of his sight but still recognized his old friend. "I'd know that voice anywhere," he told Downey. "Look, I'm really sick now, but I'm going to get better."[12] Despite his rapid and painful decline, he remained outwardly positive. "When something like this happens, you fight it," he told Lester Persky. "And then afterwards, I guess you have to be philosophical about it."[13]

Despite his condition, Ashby continued to think about work and had recently talked with Ian Bernard about a screenplay Bernard had written that Ashby promised to try to set up for him with Persky or Jerry Hellman. Hellman himself later said, "Hal's spirit was intact, and in lucid moments right up, literally, until he died, Hal was talking with passion about Hal Ashby films that he hoped to make. And I'm sorry that he won't get to make them. We're all a lot poorer for it."[14]

Hellman recalls that Ashby's eccentric humor was undimmed by his illness, citing an incident when he was sitting by his bedside and Ashby suddenly began to sing "Let Me Call You Sweetheart." When Bob Downey brought Bruce Dern to see him, the actor was shocked by just how ill Ashby looked but was heartened that "the first thing he'd say [was], 'Dernsie, tell me something funny.' He was trying to hold on to that joy he always had."[15]

Ashby's friends also did their best to keep him in good spirits. One time, Jon Voight tried to cheer him up by saying, "Let's call Haller and make him laugh." "Oh, Jon, I can't," Ashby replied weakly. Still, he raised himself up and called Mike Haller. "He would be in such pain, and cranky," says Voight, "but he would get on the phone and leave these messages, and I so wish I had these messages because they would make you laugh. Here's a guy that's facing death, and he's making you laugh about it."[16]

Ashby, however, was also prone to sporadic angry outbursts, venting the emotions that he had bottled up not just during his illness but throughout his life. He was still deeply troubled by the events of his Ogden years but had never been able to resolve his feelings about them because of his reluctance and, ultimately, his inability to tackle them head-on and deal with the pain. Just before he was diagnosed, Ashby was helping Padilla through a tough divorce and showed great sympathy toward him and his three-and-a-half-year-old son, of whom Ashby was extremely fond. "I was having a *really* hard time because of my son and the effect that it was having on him," Padilla says, "and one day Hal showed up, and he had . . . this poetry from the *New York Times*. If I remember correctly, it was some young Russian girl who was ten or twelve years old and had written this incredible poetry. And he read it to me, and he *wept;* he was crying. It was basically about the fact that when you are cruel and say cruel words as an adult to a child, that it was like arrows that pierce your heart. He was weeping, and I was crying too because of how I was feeling about my kid, and we both sat there, and we wept. I really felt that he was talking about himself."[17]

Jon Voight, who knew about the shadow that Ashby's father's death had cast over his life, did his best to help Ashby forgive him before he himself died. "I tried to bring up his dad so he wouldn't have to go through all of this," Voight recalls. "I said, 'Think of all he went through, the pain he was in.' I tried to be a little bit of a healer. But he couldn't do it; he couldn't go to that point."[18]

Norman Jewison, whose mother had died of pancreatic cancer, tried to comfort Ashby but says that his emotion on facing death was "total anger."

"Fuck, man, why is it happening to me?" he asked Jewison.

"Hey, man," his old mentor said. "It's a common end we all share."

"You don't share my fucking death!" Ashby replied angrily.[19]

Knowing that his fight with cancer was a losing battle, Ashby would vent his anger on those around him and lash out at people. When Chuck Mulvehill came to see him, hoping to resolve their conflicted friendship, he found that Ashby's turbulent emotional state made this impossible. When Ashby found out that Mulvehill's wife, Shari, was there, he started to cry. He had introduced Shari to Mulvehill back at the time of *Harold and Maude* and was the best man at their wedding, which was held at Ashby's house up on Appian Way, but he had not seen her in years. Mulvehill remembers an attempt to break the tension of the moment: "Somebody made a joke, and we all laughed, and then Hal turned on everybody, I mean, it was vicious. . . . Everybody was on eggshells."[20]

When he wasn't so angry, Ashby faced his death with surprising clarity. He discussed his will—in which Griffis and his brother Jack were the two principal beneficiaries—and spoke to his sister, Ardith, for one last time on the phone. "He couldn't talk to me very long because he was very sick," she reflected sadly afterward.[21] Even though Jack and

Beth had moved there almost twenty years earlier, Hal had never visited them at their home in Fresno, California, but he now planned to spend Thanksgiving with them, knowing it would be his last. Sadly, however, with his frail condition and all the tubes that he was hooked up to, it proved impossible. Instead, he spent Thanksgiving at home: Jon Voight brought the turkey, and Voight, Al Schwartz, and Ashby ate perched on Hal's bed.

As the end neared, he also made sure that his friends would be looked after. One of the reasons he had been so keen to get *The Hawkline Monster* made was because it was Michael Haller who first brought it to him; Ashby felt guilty that he had never managed to make the film and that he had not been able to help Haller become a director as he felt he would have excelled in the role. "When Hal was dying and Michael came to see him, they held each other's hands," says Al Schwartz. "And these were not emotional guys. Hal said, 'I never gave you what you deserved on these films, and I should have brought you further.' It brought a tear to my eye."[22]

Haller's cinematic sensibilities were strikingly similar to Ashby's, and he was part of the filmmaking family Ashby hoped would keep the spirit of his work alive after he was gone. In his last days, Ashby told Don Phillips, "Next movie you make, the first person you hire is Michael, because he is the artist who has the keys to the black box."[23] Phillips was as good as his word and hired Haller for *The Indian Runner* (1991), Sean Penn's directorial debut, which led to Penn establishing a close professional and personal relationship with Haller. Ashby also looked to his "brother" Quincy Jones, with whom he had wanted to direct a miniseries based on *The Manchild in the Promised Land* (1964), Claude Brown's seminal novel about growing up in Harlem in the 1940s and 1950s. He constantly encouraged him right until the end to become a director and even left him his viewfinder and director's chair.

Just over a week before he died, Ashby called up Jeff Berg and made him promise he would get work for Rick Padilla after he died as he was going to be a great director. Ashby once confided to his nurse that Padilla was the only person to share his view of cinema and he wanted to pass on the baton to him after he was gone. "Never sell out," Ashby begged Padilla.[24]

One day in mid-December, as winds whistled round the house, rattling the shutters, Ashby turned to Jeff Berg, who was sitting by his bedside, and quietly said, "Well, they're here."

"Who's here?" asked Berg, confused.

"Them. Can't you hear them?" said Ashby. "The people who are taking me away."[25]

A few days before Christmas, Bud Cort came to see Ashby and brought a priest with him, in the hope that he might help Ashby find peace. "Hal," the priest said, "you have to let go." Ashby nodded quietly in agreement. "After that, he went downhill," says Al Schwartz.[26]

Ashby now slipped in and out of consciousness, struggled to breathe properly, and was bloated and jaundiced because his liver had ceased to function. In a moment of delirium, he told Bob Jones, "They're calling me across the river—don't let them take me."[27]

"I've never seen anyone more afraid of facing death," recalled Jerry Hellman. "Most of the time he was frightened and didn't want to sleep. He would lie down and then sit bolt upright."[28] Ashby knew that the next time he fell asleep might well be the last and, despite his exhaustion, would sleep only for five minutes at a time. On Christmas Eve, Ashby's ex-wife Joan Marshall relieved Griffis from her vigil so that she could get some well-earned rest. As she sat by his side, he drifted off and at last slept peacefully.

When Bob Downey came to the house on Boxing Day, he asked the nurse who was watching over the now comatose Ashby, "Does he have a chance?"

"Look at him," she said, "he's turning yellow. He won't be here tomorrow."[29]

Burt Young, Jon Voight's costar in *Lookin' to Get Out,* had visited Ashby and was distressed to see him so sick and so afraid of dying. But on the morning of December 27, he dreamed he was doing another film with Ashby, who was now healthy and with a trimmed beard. When he awoke, Young discovered that Ashby had passed on.

For years, Ashby had dreamed of making films outside the studio system, finding a way to act independently of the studios, and had even talked about buying a piece of land away from everything and setting up a film commune. In 1980, he had told an interviewer about his desire to set up a foundation to help young directors make their first film: "Instead of trying to raise a family, I would rather, as I go along, get more into young people and be helpful to them in whatever way I can. What I want to do is set up a foundation. I want to do something with my money that helps people. . . . [The foundation] would take young people and hire them to write screenplays, then try and follow through to the end result of becoming a film. And if there's a profit, it goes right back in, so the foundation perpetuates itself. I want to set it up where the people will run it themselves. . . . I want to see the money being used that way. I think it's of real value to do that; it's a chance to use what you've got."[30]

Though he had never set up the foundation, in the days after Ashby's death people were asked to make a donation to the Hal Ashby Film Scholarship Fund rather than sending flowers. There was no funeral, but Bud Cort, Pablo Ferro, Mike Haller, and Jeff Wexler organized a memorial service at the Directors Guild building three days after Ashby's death in order to, as Cort put it, "raise the industry's consciousness of his gifts to film."[31] Ferro cut together clips from Ashby's films, and proceedings began with a montage of Ashby's cameos. Though he was gone, he was up there on the screen, a director who had always avoided the limelight now the center of attention. Jeff Bridges was the master of ceremonies and moved through Ashby's career in chronological order, introducing clips from *The Landlord* through to *8 Million Ways to Die*. After each clip, an actor from the film shared memories of Ashby. At the base of the lectern was the "Ashby" street sign Sean Penn had stolen; behind it was a huge picture of Ashby smiling, his grin extending almost from one side of the stage to the other.

In his final days, Ashby had told Griffis, "I want you to think of me as being alive. Don't refer to me in the past when I'm gone."[32] And it was as if he were still there, as one after another the speakers who came onstage turned to the picture of Ashby behind them, larger than life, and started talking to him. Speaking first, Beau Bridges affectionately noted that Ashby "never liked big social events. I think if he was here, then he probably would have stayed home. But if he was here, he'd be sitting in the back row there with some friend, giggling over some pompous remark that someone had made, which he'd share with them later on. And then when the lights came on after the show, and you'd look for him back there, he'd be gone. He always left early."[33]

Following him, Bud Cort had everyone laughing after he announced matter-of-factly, "I was Hal's favorite." The whole event was a celebration, sad and reverential, but nevertheless joyful, as a string of actors, producers, colleagues, and friends spoke of their love for Ashby and the impact he'd had on their lives. His sense of humor and love of life were much commented on, and a number of jokes were made about his legendary reluctance to pick up the phone. A message sent by Tom Skerritt ended: "I will miss you, and I will understand why you don't return my calls."[34]

Lynn Stalmaster, Ashby's casting director, who spoke after the starrier names had said their piece, aptly described the memorial as "a living monument of friends."[35] Those who could not be there, such as Quincy Jones and Jack Nicholson, sent written tributes, and messages were also read out from John Cassavetes, Michael Cimino, and Martin Scorsese. People were crying throughout, but perhaps the most poignant and moving moment came when Ronny Cox and Melinda Dillon did a duet of Ashby's favorite song from *Bound for Glory,* "Hobo's Lullabye." As they sang, Cox and Dillon struggled to hold back the tears; by the end of the song, everyone was crying.

There was one person present who felt the emotions of the occasion with a unique poignancy, and that was Leigh, Ashby's daughter. Over the years, her various attempts to contact her father had been unsuccessful, despite the efforts of people close to him to get him to acknowledge her, and she was at the memorial service only because Jack and Beth had brought her as a guest. She had never known the man whose memory was being honored that day, and when she introduced herself to fellow mourners afterward, they were shocked to learn that Ashby had a daughter.

A few months later, a group of friends, including Jeff Wexler, Jeff Bridges, and Jerry Hellman, took Hal Ashby's ashes out on a boat off Malibu to scatter them on the ocean as he had requested. It was a calm day, but as they scattered the ashes, suddenly a wind came and blew Ashby's remains back toward them, covering the friends who had gathered to say their final farewell.

Filmography

The Naked Hills (1956)

La Salle Productions/Allied Artists Pictures
Director: Josef Shaftel
Producer: Josef Shaftel
Writers: Helen S. Bilkie (story); Josef Shaftel (screenplay)
Cinematographer: Frederick Gately
Art Director: Rudi Feld
Editors: Gene Fowler Jr.; Hal Ashby (assistant editor, uncredited)
Cast: David Wayne (Tracy Powell), Keenan Wynn (Sam Wilkins), James Barton (Jimmo McCann), Marcia Henderson (Julie), Jim Backus (Willis Haver), Denver Pyle (Bert Killian/Narrator)
Running Time: 72 minutes
Release Date: June 17, 1956

The Pride and the Passion (1957)

Stanley Kramer Productions/United Artists
Director: Stanley Kramer
Producer: Stanley Kramer
Writers: C. S. Forester (novel: *The Gun*); Edna Anhalt and Edward Anhalt (screen story and screenplay); Earl Felton (uncredited)
Cinematographer: Franz Planer
Production Designer: Rudolph Sternad
Editors: Ellsworth Hoagland, Frederic Knudtson; Hal Ashby (assistant editor, uncredited)
Cast: Cary Grant (Anthony), Frank Sinatra (Miguel), Sophia Loren (Juana), Theodore Bikel (General Jouvet), John Wengraf (Sermaine)
Running Time: 132 minutes
Release Date: July 10, 1957

The Big Country (1958)

United Artists
Director: William Wyler
Producers: Gregory Peck, William Wyler; Robert Wyler (associate producer)

Writers: Donald Hamilton (novel); Jessamyn West, Robert Wyler (adaptation); James R. Webb, Sy Bartlett, Robert Wilder (screenplay)
Cinematographer: Franz Planer
Art Director: Frank Hotaling
Editors: Robert Belcher, John Faure, Robert Swink; Hal Ashby (assistant editor)
Music: Jerome Moross
Cast: Gregory Peck (James McKay), Jean Simmons (Julie Maragon), Carroll Baker (Patricia Terrill), Charlton Heston (Steve Leech), Burl Ives (Rufus Hannassey), Charles Bickford (Major Henry Terrill), Alfonso Bedoya (Ramón Guiteras), Chuck Connors (Buck Hannassey)
Running Time: 165 minutes
Release Date: October 1, 1958

The Diary of Anne Frank (1959)

George Stevens Productions/Twentieth Century–Fox
Director: George Stevens
Producers: George Stevens; George Stevens Jr. (associate producer)
Writers: Frances Goodrich, Albert Hackett (screenplay adapted from their own play); Anne Frank (book: *Anne Frank: The Diary of a Young Girl*)
Cinematographer: William C. Mellor
Art Directors: George W. Davis, Lyle R. Wheeler
Editors: David Bretherton, William Mace, Robert Swink; Hal Ashby (assistant editor)
Music: Alfred Newman
Cast: Millie Perkins (Anne Frank), Joseph Schildkraut (Otto Frank), Shelley Winters (Mrs. Petronella Van Daan), Richard Beymer (Peter Van Daan), Gusti Huber (Mrs. Edith Frank), Lou Jacobi (Mr. Hans Van Daan)
Running Time: 180 minutes
Release Date: March 18, 1959

The Young Doctors (1961)

Millar/Turman Productions/United Artists
Director: Phil Karlson
Producers: Stuart Millar, Lawrence Turman
Writers: Arthur Hailey (novel); Joseph Hayes (screenplay)
Cinematographer: Arthur J. Ornitz
Production Designer: Richard Sylbert
Editor: Robert Swink; Hal Ashby (assistant editor)
Music: Elmer Bernstein
Cast: Fredric March (Dr. Joseph Pearson), Ben Gazzara (Dr. David Coleman), Dick Clark (Dr. Alexander), Ina Balin (Cathy Hunt), Eddie Albert (Dr. Charles Dornberger)

Running Time: 100 minutes
Release Date: August 23, 1961

The Children's Hour (1961)

The Mirisch Corporation/United Artists
Director: William Wyler
Producers: William Wyler; Robert Wyler (associate producer)
Writers: Lillian Hellman (adapting from her own play), John Michael Hayes (screenplay)
Cinematographer: Franz Planer
Art Director: Fernando Carrere
Editors: Robert Swink; Hal Ashby (assistant editor)
Music: Alex North
Cast: Audrey Hepburn (Karen Wright), Shirley MacLaine (Martha Dobie), James Garner (Dr. Joe Cardin), Miriam Hopkins (Mrs. Lily Mortar), Fay Bainter (Mrs. Amelia Tilford)
Running Time: 107 minutes
Release Date: December 19, 1961

Captain Sindbad (1963)

King Brothers Productions/MGM
Director: Byron Haskin
Producers: Frank King, Herman King
Writers: Ian McLellan Hunter, Guy Endore
Cinematographers: Günther Senftleben, Eugen Schüfftan (uncredited)
Art Directors: Isabella Schlichting, Werner Schlichting
Editors: Robert Swink; Hal Ashby (assistant editor)
Music: Michel Michelet
Cast: Guy Williams (Captain Sindbad), Heidi Brühl (Princess Jana), Pedro Armendáriz (El Kerim), Abraham Sofaer (Galgo), Bernie Hamilton (Quinius)
Running Time: 85 minutes
Release Date: June 19, 1963

The Best Man (1964)

Millar/Turman Productions/United Artists
Director: Franklin J. Schaffner
Producers: Stuart Millar, Lawrence Turman
Writer: Gore Vidal (from his own play)
Cinematographer: Haskell Wexler
Production Designer: Lyle R. Wheeler
Editors: Robert Swink; Hal Ashby (editorial consultant)
Music: Mort Lindsey

Cast: Henry Fonda (William Russell), Cliff Robertson (Joe Cantwell), Edie Adams (Mabel Cantwell), Margaret Leighton (Alice Russell), Shelley Berman (Sheldon Bascomb), Lee Tracy (President Art Hockstader), Ann Sothern (Sue Ellen Gamadge)
Running Time: 102 minutes
Release Date: April 5, 1964

The Greatest Story Ever Told (1965)

George Stevens Productions/United Artists
Directors: George Stevens; David Lean, Jean Negulesco (uncredited)
Producers: George Stevens; George Stevens Jr., Antonio Vellani (associate producers); Frank I. Davis (executive producer)
Writers: Fulton Oursler (book); Henry Denker (source writings); James Lee Barrett (screenplay); George Stevens (screenplay); Carl Sandburg (uncredited)
Cinematographers: Loyal Griggs, William C. Mellor
Art Directors: William J. Creber, Richard Day, David S. Hall
Editors: Harold F. Kress, Argyle Nelson Jr., J. Frank O'Neill; Hal Ashby (assistant editor)
Music: Alfred Newman; Hugo Friedhofer, Fred Steiner (uncredited)
Cast: Max von Sydow (Jesus), Dorothy McGuire (the Virgin Mary), Robert Loggia (Joseph), Charlton Heston (John the Baptist), Robert Blake (Simon the Zealot)
Running Time: 225 minutes
Release Date: February 15, 1965

The Loved One (1965)

MGM/Filmways Pictures
Director: Tony Richardson
Producers: John Calley, Haskell Wexler; Neil Hartley (associate producer)
Writers: Evelyn Waugh (novel); Terry Southern, Christopher Isherwood (screenplay)
Cinematographer: Haskell Wexler
Production Designer: Rouben Ter-Arutunian
Editors: Hal Ashby, Brian Smedley-Aston, Antony Gibbs
Music: John Addison
Cast: Robert Morse (Dennis Barlow), Jonathan Winters (Henry Glenworthy/the Reverend Wilbur Glenworthy), Anjanette Comer (Aimee Thanatogenous), Dana Andrews (General Buck Brinkman), Milton Berle (Mr. Kenton), James Coburn (Immigration Officer), John Gielgud (Sir Francis Hinsley), Tab Hunter (Whispering Glades Tour Guide), Margaret Leighton (Mrs. Helen Kenton), Liberace (Mr. Starker), Roddy McDowall (D. J. Jr.), Robert Morley (Sir Ambrose Ambercrombie)
Running Time: 122 minutes
Release Date: October 11, 1965

The Cincinnati Kid (1965)

MGM/Filmways Pictures
Director: Norman Jewison
Producers: Martin Ransohoff; John Calley (associate producer)
Writers: Richard Jessup (novel); Ring Lardner Jr., Terry Southern (screenplay); Charles Eastman (uncredited)
Cinematographer: Philip H. Lathrop
Art Directors: Edward C. Carfagno, George W. Davis
Editor: Hal Ashby
Music: Lalo Schifrin
Cast: Steve McQueen (the Cincinnati Kid), Edward G. Robinson (Lancey Howard), Ann-Margret (Melba), Karl Malden (Shooter), Tuesday Weld (Christian), Joan Blondell (Lady Fingers), Rip Torn (Slade)
Running Time: 102 minutes
Release Date: October 15, 1965

The Russians Are Coming, the Russians Are Coming (1966)

The Mirisch Corporation/United Artists
Director: Norman Jewison
Producer: Norman Jewison
Writers: Nathaniel Benchley (novel: *The Off-Islanders*); William Rose (screenplay)
Cinematographer: Joseph F. Biroc
Art Director: Robert F. Boyle
Editors: Hal Ashby, J. Terry Williams
Music: Johnny Mandel
Cast: Carl Reiner (Walt Whittaker), Eva Marie Saint (Elspeth Whittaker), Alan Arkin (Lieutenant Rozanov), Brian Keith (Police Chief Link Mattocks), Jonathan Winters (Norman Jones), Paul Ford (Fendall Hawkins), Theodore Bikel (the Russian Captain), Tessie O'Shea (Alice Foss), John Phillip Law (Alexei Kolchin)
Running Time: 126 minutes
Release Date: May 25, 1966

In the Heat of the Night (1967)

The Mirisch Corporation/United Artists
Director: Norman Jewison
Producers: Walter Mirisch; Hal Ashby (assistant to producer)
Writers: John Ball (novel); Stirling Silliphant (screenplay)
Cinematographer: Haskell Wexler
Art Director: Paul Groesse
Editor: Hal Ashby
Music: Quincy Jones

Cast: Sidney Poitier (Detective Virgil Tibbs), Rod Steiger (Police Chief Bill Gillespie), Warren Oates (Officer Sam Wood), Lee Grant (Mrs. Leslie Colbert), Larry Gates (Eric Endicott), James Patterson (Purdy)
Running Time: 109 minutes
Release Date: August 2, 1967

The Thomas Crown Affair (1968)

Simkoe/The Mirisch Corporation/United Artists
Director: Norman Jewison
Producers: Norman Jewison; Hal Ashby (associate producer)
Writer: Alan Trustman
Cinematographer: Haskell Wexler
Art Director: Robert F. Boyle
Editors: Hal Ashby, Byron "Buzz" Brandt, Ralph E. Winters
Music: Michel Legrand
Cast: Steve McQueen (Thomas Crown), Faye Dunaway (Vicki Anderson), Paul Burke (Eddy Malone), Jack Weston (Erwin), Biff McGuire (Sandy), Addison Powell (Abe), Astrid Heeren (Gwen), Gordon Pinsent (Jamie), Yaphet Kotto (Carl)
Running Time: 102 minutes
Release Date: June 19, 1968

Gaily, Gaily (1969)

The Mirisch Corporation/United Artists
Director: Norman Jewison
Producers: Norman Jewison; Hal Ashby (associate producer)
Writers: Ben Hecht (novel); Abram S. Ginnes (screenplay)
Cinematographer: Richard H. Kline
Production Designer: Robert F. Boyle
Editors: Ralph E. Winters, Byron W. Brandt; Hal Ashby (editorial consultant, uncredited)
Music: Henry Mancini
Cast: Beau Bridges (Ben Harvey), Melina Mercouri (Lil), Brian Keith (Sullivan), George Kennedy (Johanson), Hume Cronyn (Grogan), Margot Kidder (Adeline), Roy Poole (Dunne), Wilfrid Hyde-White (the Governor), Melodie Johnson (Lilah), Hal Ashby (cameo)
Running Time: 107 minutes
Release Date: December 16, 1969

The Landlord (1970)

Cartier Productions/The Mirisch Corporation/MGM
Director: Hal Ashby
Producers: Norman Jewison; Patrick J. Palmer (associate producer)

Writers: Kristin Hunter (novel); Bill Gunn (screenplay)
Cinematographer: Gordon Willis
Production Designer: Robert F. Boyle
Editors: William A. Sawyer, Edward Warschilka
Music: Al Kooper
Cast: Beau Bridges (Elgar Winthrop Julius Enders), Lee Grant (Joyce Enders), Diana Sands (Francine "Fanny" Marie Johnson), Pearl Bailey (Marge), Walter Brooke (William Enders Sr.), Louis Gossett Jr. (Copee Johnson), Marki Bey (Lanie), Hal Ashby (cameo), Douglas Grant (Walter Gee Copee)
Running Time: 112 minutes
Release Date: May 20, 1970

Harold and Maude (1971)

Paramount Pictures
Director: Hal Ashby
Producers: Charles B. Mulvehill, Colin Higgins; Mildred Lewis (executive producer)
Writer: Colin Higgins
Cinematographer: John Alonzo
Production Designer: Michael Haller
Editors: William A. Sawyer, Edward Warschilka
Music: Cat Stevens
Cast: Ruth Gordon (Maude), Bud Cort (Harold Parker Chasen), Vivian Pickles (Mrs. Chasen), Cyril Cusack (Glaucus), Charles Tyner (Brigadier General Victor Ball), Eric Christmas (Priest), G. Wood (Psychiatrist), Hal Ashby (cameo)
Running Time: 91 minutes
Release Date: December 20, 1971

The Last Detail (1973)

Acrobat Productions/Bright-Persky Associates/Columbia Pictures
Director: Hal Ashby
Producers: Lester Persky, Gerald Ayres; Charles B. Mulvehill (associate producer)
Writers: Daryl Ponicsan (novel); Robert Towne (screenplay)
Cinematographer: Michael Chapman
Production Designer: Michael Haller
Editor: Robert C. Jones
Music: Johnny Mandel
Cast: Jack Nicholson (Seaman's Mate First Class Billy "Bad Ass" Buddusky), Otis Young (Gunner's Mate First Class "Mule" Mulhall), Randy Quaid (Seaman Larry Meadows), Clifton James (Master at Arms), Carol Kane (Young Whore), Michael Moriarty (Marine Duty Officer), Hal Ashby (cameo)

Running Time: 103 minutes
Release Date: December 12, 1973

Shampoo (1975)

Rubeeker Films/Columbia Pictures
Director: Hal Ashby
Producers: Warren Beatty, Lester Persky; Charles H. Maguire (associate producer)
Writers: Robert Towne, Warren Beatty
Cinematographer: Laszlo Kovacs
Production Designer: Richard Sylbert
Editor: Robert C. Jones
Music: Paul Simon
Cast: Warren Beatty (George Roundy), Julie Christie (Jackie Shawn), Goldie Hawn (Jill), Lee Grant (Felicia Karpf), Jack Warden (Lester Karpf), Tony Bill (Johnny Pope), Hal Ashby (cameo, deleted), Carrie Fisher (Lorna Karpf)
Running Time: 109 minutes
Release Date: March 13, 1975

Bound for Glory (1976)

United Artists
Director: Hal Ashby
Producers: Robert F. Blumofe, Harold Leventhal, Jeffrey M. Sneller; Charles B. Mulvehill (associate producer)
Writers: Woody Guthrie (book); Robert Getchell (screenplay)
Cinematographer: Haskell Wexler
Production Designer: Michael Haller
Editors: Robert C. Jones, Pembroke J. Herring
Music: Leonard Rosenman
Cast: David Carradine (Woody Guthrie), Ronny Cox (Ozark Bule), Melinda Dillon (Mary/Memphis Sue), Gail Strickland (Pauline), John Lehne (Locke), Ji-Tu Cumbuka (Slim Snedeger), Randy Quaid (Luther Johnson)
Running Time: 147 minutes
Release Date: December 5, 1976

The Stronger (1976)

American Film Institute
Director: Lee Grant
Producers: Hal Ashby, Joseph Feury; Antonio Vellani (executive producer)
Writers: August Strindberg (play); Lee Grant (adaptation)
Cinematographer: Andrew Davis
Cast: Edward Ashley, Katharine Bard, Anthony Costello, Dolores Dorn, Dinah Manoff, Hanns Manship, Susan Strasberg
Running Time: 30 minutes (approx.)

Coming Home (1978)

Jerome Hellman Productions/Jayne Productions Inc./United Artists
Director: Hal Ashby
Producers: Jerome Hellman; Bruce Gilbert (associate producer)
Writers: Nancy Dowd (story); Waldo Salt, Robert C. Jones; Rudy Wurlitzer (uncredited)
Cinematographer: Haskell Wexler
Production Designer: Michael Haller
Editor: Don Zimmerman
Cast: Jane Fonda (Sally Hyde), Jon Voight (Luke Martin), Bruce Dern (Captain Bob Hyde), Penelope Milford (Vi Munson), Robert Carradine (Bill Munson), Robert Ginty (Sergeant Dink Mobley), Hal Ashby (cameo)
Running Time: 127 minutes
Release Date: February 15, 1978

Being There (1979)

Lorimar/Northstar International/United Artists
Director: Hal Ashby
Producers: Andrew Braunsberg; Charles B. Mulvehill (associate producer); Jack Schwartzman (executive producer)
Writers: Jerzy Kosinski (adapted from his own novel); Robert C. Jones (uncredited)
Cinematographer: Caleb Deschanel
Production Designer: Michael Haller
Editor: Don Zimmerman
Music: Johnny Mandel
Cast: Peter Sellers (Chance), Shirley MacLaine (Eve Rand), Melvyn Douglas (Benjamin Rand), Jack Warden (President "Bobby"), Richard Dysart (Dr. Robert Allenby), Richard Basehart (Vladimir Skrapinov), Ruth Attaway (Louise), Hal Ashby (cameo)
Running Time: 130 minutes
Release Date: December 19, 1979

Second Hand Hearts (1981)

Lorimar/Paramount Pictures
Director: Hal Ashby
Producers: James William Guercio; Charles B. Mulvehill (associate producer)
Writer: Charles Eastman
Cinematographer: Haskell Wexler
Production Designer: Michael Haller
Editor: Amy Jones
Music: Willis Alan Ramsey
Cast: Robert Blake (Loyal Muke), Barbara Harris (Dinette Dusty), Sondra Blake

(Ermy), Bert Remsen (Voyd Dusty), Shirley Stoler (Maxy), Collin Boone (Human Dusty), Amber Rose Gold (Iota)
Running Time: 102 minutes
Release Date: May 8, 1981

Lookin' to Get Out (1982)

Lorimar/Northstar International/Paramount Pictures
Director: Hal Ashby
Producers: Robert Schaffel, Andrew Braunsberg, Edward Teets
Writers: Al Schwartz, Jon Voight
Cinematographer: Haskell Wexler
Production Designer: Robert F. Boyle
Editor: Robert C. Jones
Music: Johnny Mandel, Miles Goodman
Cast: Jon Voight (Alex Kovac), Burt Young (Jerry Feldman), Ann-Margret (Patti Warner), Bert Remsen (Smitty Carpenter), Jude Farese (Harry), Allen Keller (Joey), Richard Bradford (Bernie Gold), Stacey Pickren (Rusty), Samantha Harper (Lillian), Hal Ashby (cameo)
Running Time: 105 minutes
Release Date: October 8, 1982

Let's Spend the Night Together (1983)

Northstar International/Raindrop/Weintraub Entertainment Group/Embassy Pictures Corporation
Directors: Hal Ashby, Pablo Ferro (credited as "creative associate")
Producers: Ronald L. Schwary; Kenneth J. Ryan (associate producer)
Cinematographers: Gerald Feil, Caleb Deschanel
Editor: Lisa Day
Cast: Mick Jagger, Keith Richards, Charlie Watts, Bill Wyman, Ron Wood, Hal Ashby (cameo)
Running Time: 95 minutes
Release Date: February 11, 1983

Solo Trans (1983)

Director: Hal Ashby
Producers: L. A. Johnson, Neil Young; Elliot Rabinowitz (executive producer); Jeanne Field (line producer)
Writers: Newell Alexander, L. A. Johnson, Neil Young
Cinematographer: Bobby Byrne
Cast: Neil Young (as himself), Newell Alexander (Dan Clear), Inez Drummond (Baby), Craig Hayes (Vito Toledo), Rosemarie Lovell (Crystal Clear), Connie Simmons (Connie Sue), Pegi Young (Honey)
Running Time: 60 minutes

The Slugger's Wife (1985)

Rastar Films/Columbia Pictures
Director: Hal Ashby
Producers: Ray Stark; Margaret Booth (executive producer)
Writer: Neil Simon
Cinematographer: Caleb Deschanel
Production Designer: J. Michael Riva
Editors: Don Brochu, George C. Villaseñor; Margaret Booth (supervising editor)
Music: Patrick Williams, Quincy Jones
Cast: Michael O'Keefe (Darryl Palmer), Rebecca De Mornay (Debby [Huston] Palmer), Martin Ritt (Burly DeVito), Randy Quaid (Moose Granger), Cleavant Derricks (Manny Alvarado), Lisa Langlois (Aline Cooper), Loudon Wainwright III (Gary), Hal Ashby (cameo)
Running Time: 105 minutes
Release Date: March 29, 1985

8 Million Ways to Die (1986)

PSO/TriStar Pictures
Director: Hal Ashby
Producers: Steve Roth; Charles B. Mulvehill (coproducer); Mark Damon (executive producer)
Writers: Oliver Stone, Lance Hill (as David Lee Henry); Robert Towne, Hal Ashby, Don Edmonds (uncredited)
Cinematographer: Stephen H. Burum
Production Designer: Michael Haller
Editors: Robert Lawrence, Stuart Pappé
Music: James Newton Howard
Cast: Jeff Bridges (Matt Scudder), Rosanna Arquette (Sarah), Alexandra Paul (Sunny), Randy Brooks (Willie "Chance" Walker), Andy Garcia (Angel Moldonado)
Running Time: 115 minutes
Release Date: April 25, 1986

Beverly Hills Buntz (Television Pilot) (1987)

MTM Enterprises/NBC
Director: Hal Ashby
Producers: David Milch, Jeffrey Lewis (executive producer); John Romano (coproducer); Jessie Ward (associate producer); Michael Vittes (supervising producer)
Writers: Jeffrey Lewis, David Milch
Cinematographer: Robert Seaman
Editors: Jonathan Pontell, Alec Smight

Cast: Dennis Franz (Norman Buntz), Peter Jurasik (Sid "The Snitch" Thurston), Dana Wheeler-Nicholson (Rebecca Giswold), Guy Boyd (Lieutenant Pugh), Joe Pantoliano (Montaigne)
Running Time: 30 minutes
Air Date: November 5, 1987

Jake's Journey (Television Pilot) (1988)

HTV/Witzend Productions
Director: Hal Ashby
Producers: Allan McKeown, Mike Merson
Writers: Mark Twain (novel: *A Connecticut Yankee at King Arthur's Court*); Graham Chapman, David Sherlock
Editor: John Farrell
Cast: Graham Chapman (Sir George/Queen), Peter Cook (King Arthur), Rik Mayall (Troll), Chris Young (Jake)
Running Time: 30 minutes

Notes

Unless otherwise noted, all letters and other primary source documents are held at the Margaret Herrick Library, Los Angeles.

Prologue

1. American Film Institute (AFI) Seminar with Hal Ashby, March 12, 1975, interview by Rochelle Reed.

2. Hal Ashby, "Breaking Out of the Cutting Room," *Action* 5, no. 5 (September/October 1970): 10.

1. Enter Hal

Epigraph: Ashby, "Breaking Out of the Cutting Room," 7.

1. "Salt Lake News," *Ogden Standard,* March 19, 1901.

2. "Diary of Important Days," October 9, 1916. Courtesy Jack Ashby.

3. Ibid., September 8, 1917.

4. Ibid., April 19, 1919.

5. Diane Jacobs, "*Coming Home*—It's Hal Ashby at His Best," *Minneapolis Star,* May 12, 1978, C2.

6. Letter from Eileen Ashby to Hal Ashby, August 22, 1960.

7. Letter from Ardith Ashby, ca. September 2, 1932. Courtesy Mary Myers.

8. Jack and Beth Ashby, interview with the author, Fresno, CA, October 29, 2004.

9. Ibid.

10. Letter from Hal Ashby to Eileen Ashby, September 17, 1962. Courtesy Jack Ashby.

11. Jack Ashby, telephone interview with the author, November 19, 2003.

12. E-mail from Jack and Beth Ashby to the author, July 2, 2008.

13. Ibid.

14. Jack and Beth Ashby, telephone interview with the author, February 6, 2004.

15. Aljean Harmetz, "Gambling on a Film about the Great Depression," *New York Times,* December 5, 1976, 2-13.

16. Peter Biskind, *Easy Riders, Raging Bulls* (London: Bloomsbury, 1998), 170.

17. “Dairy Official Succumbs from Gunshot Wound,” *Ogden Standard Examiner,* March 23, 1942, 12.

18. Jack and Beth Ashby, interview with the author, Fresno, CA, October 28, 2004.

19. Harmetz, “Gambling on a Film,” 2-13.

20. Letter from Hal Ashby to Richard Avedon, March 25, 1974.

21. Ashby, “Breaking Out of the Cutting Room,” 7.

2. The Artist as a Young Man

Epigraph: Letter from Hal Ashby to Eileen Ashby, October 4, 1963. Courtesy Jack Ashby.

1. Bob Ballantyne, email to the author, February 13, 2006.

2. Bob Busico, telephone interview with the author, February 23, 2006.

3. Nancy Frizzelle, “Hip Rip,” *Women's Wear Daily,* February 3, 1972.

4. Jack and Beth Ashby, interview with the author, Fresno, CA, October 29, 2004.

5. Puget Sound Naval Academy Web page, http://www.interisland.net/cwlindenberg/psna.htm.

6. Jack Swanson, telephone interview with the author, August 5, 2004.

7. Gus Cooper, telephone interview with the author, July 29, 2004.

8. Jack Swanson, telephone interview with the author, August 5, 2004.

9. Ibid.

10. Ibid.

11. Ibid.

12. Gus Cooper, telephone interview with the author, July 29, 2004.

13. Jack Swanson, telephone interview with the author, August 5, 2004.

14. Bob Ballantyne, telephone interview with the author, February 27, 2006.

15. Jack and Beth Ashby, interview with the author, Fresno, CA, October 28, 2004.

16. Ibid.

17. Letter from Hal and Lavon Ashby to Eileen Ashby, ca. March 1, 1947. Courtesy Jack Ashby.

18. Jack and Beth Ashby, interview with the author, Fresno, CA, October 28, 2004.

19. Jack and Beth Ashby, telephone interview with the author, December 18, 2003.

20. Jack Ashby, telephone interview with the author, November 19, 2003.

21. “Biography of Hal Ashby,” *Harold and Maude* Paramount production notes, 1971.

3. Los Angeles

Epigraph: John Fante, *Ask the Dust* (1939; repr., Santa Rosa, CA: Black Sparrow, 1980), 13.

1. William Avery, "Hal Ashby: Getting the Right Drift," *Soho Weekly News,* February 23, 1978, 18–19.

2. Janice Lindquist, telephone interview with the author, July 1, 2008.

3. Ibid.

4. Ibid.

5. Haskell Wexler, interview with the author, Santa Monica, CA, December 5, 2006.

6. Max Grow, telephone interview with the author, January 14, 2006.

7. Jacobs, "Hal Ashby at His Best," C2.

8. Harmetz, "Gambling on a Film," 2-13.

9. Ralph Appelbaum, "Positive Thinking: Hal Ashby in an Interview with Ralph Appelbaum," *Films and Filming,* July 1978, 13.

10. Sylviane Gold, "Hal Ashby's Climb to Glory," *New York Post,* December 2, 1976, 26.

11. Jacobs, "Hal Ashby at His Best," C2.

12. Letter from Hal Ashby to Eileen Ashby, October 22, 1948. Courtesy Jack Ashby.

13. Letter from Janice Grow to the author, December 30, 2005.

14. Harmetz, "Gambling on a Film," 2-13.

15. Jack and Beth Ashby, email to the author, July 2, 2008.

16. Dale Pollock, "Whatever Happened to Hal Ashby?" *Los Angeles Times,* October 17, 1982, Calendar section, 23.

17. Janice Lindquist, telephone interview with the author, July 1, 2008.

18. Ashby, "Breaking Out of the Cutting Room," 7.

19. David Sterritt, "'That Special Okie Southwest Flavor, That Humor,'" *Christian Science Monitor,* February 4, 1977, 31.

20. AFI Seminar with Hal Ashby, interview by Sam Grossman, January 11, 1972.

21. Jacobs, "Hal Ashby at His Best," C2.

22. Gold, "Hal Ashby's Climb to Glory," 26.

23. Tay Garnett, "Hal Ashby," in *Directing: Learn from the Masters* (Filmmakers, no. 48), ed. Anthony Slide (London: Scarecrow, 1996), 1.

24. Robert Ballantyne, email to the author, February 13, 2006.

25. Richard Fernandez, "Cinema Chat with Hal Ashby," *Audience* 10, no. 2 (1978): 25.

26. Gerald Early, ed., *The Sammy Davis Jnr. Reader* (New York: Farrar Straus Giroux, 2001), 551.

27. Gloria Box, telephone interview with the author, February 11, 2004.

28. Sammy Davis Jr., with Jane Boyar and Burt Boyar, *Sammy: An Autobiography* (New York: Farrar Straus Giroux, 2000), 123.

29. Maloy Barreto, telephone interview with the author, September 10, 2004.

30. Bill Box, telephone interview with the author, March 19, 2006.

31. Betty Gumm, interview with the author, Los Angeles, November 30, 2006.

32. Ian Bernard, telephone interview with the author, April 28, 2004.
33. Ibid.
34. John Mandel, telephone interview with the author, March 18, 2006.
35. Bill Box, interview with the author, Los Osos, CA, November 28, 2006.
36. Ian Bernard, telephone interview with the author, April 28, 2004.
37. J. D. Salinger, *The Catcher in the Rye* (London: Penguin, 1958), 5.
38. Ian Bernard, telephone interview with the author, April 28, 2004.
39. Gloria Box, telephone interview with the author, February 11, 2004.
40. Bill Box, telephone interview with the author, February 11, 2004.
41. Ian Bernard, telephone interview with the author, April 28, 2004.
42. Bill Box, email to the author, February 11, 2004.
43. Bill Box, telephone interview with the author, February 11, 2004.
44. Ibid.
45. Bill Box, email to the author, February 11, 2004.
46. John Mandel, telephone interview with the author, March 18, 2006.
47. Ian Bernard, telephone interview with the author, April 28, 2004.
48. John Ridley, *A Conversation with the Mann* (New York: Warner Books, 2002), 244.
49. Ian Bernard, telephone interview with the author, April 28, 2004.
50. Ian Bernard, email to the author, April 30, 2004.
51. Maloy Barreto, telephone interview with the author, February 22, 2006.

4. Doors Open . . .

Epigraphs: Antoine de Saint-Exupéry and Irene Testot-Ferry, *The Little Prince* (1943; repr., Ware: Wordsworth Editions, 1995), 82; letter from Hal Ashby to Robert Swink, April 29, 1968.

1. Bill Box, telephone interview with the author, February 11, 2004.
2. AFI Seminar with Hal Ashby, interview by Sam Grossman, January 11, 1972.
3. Ashby, "Breaking Out of the Cutting Room," 7–8.
4. Maloy Barreto, telephone interview with the author, February 22, 2006.
5. Ibid.
6. Ibid.
7. Ibid.
8. Ibid.
9. Ibid.
10. Ibid.
11. Sterritt, "'That Special Okie Southwest Flavor,'" 31.
12. Ashby, "Breaking Out of the Cutting Room," 8.
13. Hal Ashby, interview by Catherine Wyler February 12, 1985, outtake held by the Academy Film Archive, Los Angeles.
14. Ashby, "Breaking Out of the Cutting Room," 8.
15. Hal Ashby, interview by Catherine Wyler, February 12, 1985.

16. Ibid.
17. Ibid.
18. Ibid.
19. Ian Bernard, telephone interview with the author, April 28, 2004.
20. Ibid.
21. Tom Blackwell, telephone interview with the author, March 28, 2006.
22. Ian Bernard, telephone interview with the author, April 28, 2004.
23. Tom Blackwell, telephone interview with the author, March 28, 2006.
24. Ibid.
25. Letter from Maloy Barreto to Hal Ashby, ca. 1980.
26. Maloy Barreto, telephone interview with the author, September 10, 2004.
27. Hal Ashby, interview by Catherine Wyler, February 12, 1985.
28. Ian Bernard and Wm. Hal Ashby, *The Sound of Silence*.
29. Appelbaum, "Positive Thinking," 16.
30. Memo from Leona Epstein to Society of Motion Picture Film Editors, October 27, 1958.
31. Ashby, "Breaking Out of the Cutting Room," 8.
32. Maloy Barreto, telephone interview with the author, February 22, 2006.
33. Ibid.
34. Ian Bernard, telephone interview with the author, April 28, 2004.
35. Maloy Barreto, telephone interview with the author, September 10, 2004.
36. Maloy Barreto, telephone interview with the author, February 22, 2006.
37. Maloy Barreto, telephone interview with the author, September 10, 2004.
38. Ibid.
39. AFI Seminar with Hal Ashby, interview by James Powers, January 30, 1980.
40. Hal Ashby, interview by Catherine Wyler, February 12, 1985.
41. Maloy Barreto, telephone interview with the author, April 6, 2006.
42. Maloy Barreto, telephone interview with the author, February 22, 2006.
43. Maloy Barreto, telephone interview with the author, April 6, 2006.
44. Complaint for Divorce (No. 100932), December 29, 1961.
45. Maloy Barreto, telephone interview with the author, April 6, 2006.
46. Maloy Barreto, telephone interview with the author, September 10, 2004.
47. Letter from Maloy Barreto to Hal Ashby, ca. 1980.
48. Maloy Barreto, telephone interview with the author, September 10, 2004.

5. The Family Man

Epigraphs: Carl Sandburg, *Remembrance Rock* (New York: Harcourt, Brace and Company, 1948), 7; letter from Hal Ashby to Eileen Ashby, September 17, 1962. Courtesy Jack Ashby.

1. Jack and Beth Ashby, interview with the author, Fresno, CA, October 28, 2004.
2. Letter from Hal Ashby to Eileen Ashby, September 17, 1962. Courtesy Jack Ashby.

3. Ibid.

4. Ibid.

5. Letter from "Carrie Ashby" (typed by Shirley Ashby) to Eileen Ashby, November 12, 1962. Courtesy Jack Ashby.

6. Letter from Hal Ashby to Eileen Ashby, August 6, 1962. Courtesy Jack Ashby.

7. Letter from Hal Ashby to Eileen Ashby, March 22, 1963. Courtesy Jack Ashby.

8. Letter from Hal Ashby to Eileen Ashby, October 4, 1963. Courtesy Jack Ashby.

9. Letter from Hal Ashby to Eileen Ashby, January 2, 1963. Courtesy Jack Ashby.

10. Letter from Hal Ashby to Eileen Ashby, August 7, 1963. Courtesy Jack Ashby.

11. Letter from Hal Ashby to Eileen Ashby, June 20, 1963. Courtesy Jack Ashby.

12. Letter from Hal Ashby to Eileen Ashby, September 15, 1963. Courtesy Jack Ashby.

13. Letter from Hal Ashby to Eileen Ashby, August 7, 1963. Courtesy Jack Ashby.

14. Letter from Hal Ashby to Eileen Ashby, September 15, 1963. Courtesy Jack Ashby.

15. Letter from Hal Ashby to Eileen Ashby, September 17, 1962. Courtesy Jack Ashby.

16. Letter from Hal Ashby to Eileen Ashby, June 20, 1963. Courtesy Jack Ashby.

17. Letter from Hal Ashby to Eileen Ashby, October 4, 1963. Courtesy Jack Ashby.

18. Letter from Hal Ashby to Eileen Ashby, February 18, 1964. Courtesy Jack Ashby.

19. Ibid.

20. "Harold Kress," in *Selected Takes: Film Editors on Editing*, by Vincent LoBrutto (New York: Praeger, 1991), 10–11.

21. Ashby, "Breaking Out of the Cutting Room," 8.

22. AFI Seminar with Hal Ashby, interview by Rochelle Reed, March 12, 1975.

6. Norman

Epigraph: Norman Jewison, *This Terrible Business Has Been Good to Me: An Autobiography* (New York: St. Martin's, 2004), 112.

1. Letter from Budd Cherry to Hal Ashby, December 31, 1968.

2. Charles Champlin, "'Loved One' Already Exciting," *Los Angeles Times*, August 2, 1965.

3. Tony Richardson, *Long Distance Runner: A Memoir* (London: Faber & Faber, 1993), 166.

4. Ashby, "Breaking Out of the Cutting Room," 8.

5. Stephen Rebello, "A Mild and Wild Maverick," *Vlife*, December/January 2005, 96.

6. Jewison, *This Terrible Business*, 98.

7. Norman Jewison, telephone interview with the author, April 25, 2006.

8. Ibid.

9. Ibid.

10. Ian Bernard, email to the author, March 31, 2006.

11. Norman Jewison, telephone interview with the author, April 25, 2006.

12. Jewison, *This Terrible Business*, 98.

13. Ibid., 102.

14. David Weddle, *Sam Peckinpah: "If They Move . . . Kill 'Em!": The Life and Times of Sam Peckinpah* (New York: Grove, 1994), 258.

15. Jewison, *This Terrible Business*, 109.

16. James Powers, "Dialogue on Film: Hal Ashby," *American Film*, May 1980, 59.

17. AFI Seminar with Hal Ashby, interview by James Powers, January 30, 1980.

18. Robert J. Emery, "Norman Jewison," in *The Directors—Take One* (New York: TV Books, 1999), 198; Jewison, *This Terrible Business*, 114.

19. Ashby, "Breaking Out of the Cutting Room," 8.

20. Whit., "*The Cincinnati Kid*," *Daily Variety*, October 14, 1965.

21. James Powers, "'Cincinnati Kid' Superb Picture with Fine Cast," *Hollywood Reporter*, October 14, 1965, 3.

22. James Powers, "'The Loved One' a Satire with an Offbeat Message," *Hollywood Reporter*, October 12, 1965, 3; Whit., review of *The Loved One*, *Daily Variety*, October 12, 1965.

7. Motion Picture Pioneers of America

Epigraph: Haskell Wexler, commentary, on *In the Heat of the Night* DVD, dir. Norman Jewison (MGM, 2001).

1. "Confrontations: Norman Jewison Interviewed by Gordon Gow," *Films and Filming*, January 1971, 22.

2. Larry Salvato and Dennis Schaefer, "Hal Ashby Interview," *Millimeter*, October 1976, 37.

3. Norman Jewison, telephone interview with the author, April 25, 2006.

4. Ashby, "Breaking Out of the Cutting Room," 8.

5. "Oral History with Robert F. Boyle," interview by George Turner, with an additional interview by Barbara Hall, August 21, 26, 1992, © AMPAS 1998, p. 222, 223.

6. AFI Seminar with Hal Ashby, interview by James Powers, October 20, 1976.

7. Pablo Ferro, interview with the author, Winnetka, CA, October 20, 2004.

8. Murf., review of *The Russians Are Coming, the Russians Are Coming, Daily Variety,* May 24, 1966.

9. James Powers, "'Russians Coming' Brilliant Comedy Headed for Top Returns at Box Office," *Hollywood Reporter,* May 26, 1966, 3.

10. Rebello, "A Mild and Wild Maverick," 96.

11. Army Archerd, "Just for Variety," *Daily Variety,* August 4, 1965.

12. Wayne Warga, "Civil Rights and a Producer's Dilemma," *Los Angeles Times,* April 14, 1968, Calendar section, 1.

13. Lee Grant, telephone interview with the author, July 22, 2006.

14. Memo from Hal Ashby to Norman Jewison et al., September 21, 1966.

15. Memos from Hal Ashby to Norman Jewison et al., September 26–October 13, 1966.

16. Memo from Hal Ashby to Norman Jewison et al., September 27, 1966.

17. Memo from Hal Ashby to Norman Jewison et al., October 12, 1966.

18. Memo from Hal Ashby to Norman Jewison et al., October 1, 1966.

19. Memo from Hal Ashby to Norman Jewison et al., October 4, 1966.

20. Draft of undated letter from Hal Ashby to Norman Jewison, late October 1966.

21. Norman Jewison, commentary, on *In the Heat of the Night* DVD.

22. Powers, "Dialogue on Film: Hal Ashby," 59.

23. Norman Jewison, telephone interview with the author, April 25, 2006.

24. Harmetz, "Gambling on a Film," 2-13.

25. Rebello, "A Mild and Wild Maverick," 96.

26. Jewison, *This Terrible Business,* 150–51.

8. 1968

1. Radie Harris, "Broadway Ballyhoo," *Hollywood Reporter,* June 9, 1967.

2. Letter from Hal Ashby to Shirley Ashby, October 13, 1967.

3. Norman Jewison, telephone interview with the author, April 25, 2006.

4. AFI Seminar with Hal Ashby, interview by James Powers, October 20, 1976.

5. Jewison, *This Terrible Business,* 164.

6. AFI Seminar with Hal Ashby, interview by James Powers, October 20, 1976.

7. Biskind, *Easy Riders, Raging Bulls,* 172.

8. James Lipscomb, "Improvise!—Films Are Made with Whimsy," *Life,* November 10, 1967, 89.

9. Murf., review of *In the Heat of the Night, Variety,* June 21, 1967.

10. John Mahoney, "'In the Heat of the Night' One of the Year's B.O. Winners," *Hollywood Reporter,* June 21, 1967, 3.

11. Haskell Wexler, commentary, on *In the Heat of the Night* DVD.

12. Memo from Hal Ashby to Norman Jewison et al., October 10, 1966.

13. AFI Seminar with Hal Ashby, interview by James Powers, October 20, 1976.

14. Letter from Hal Ashby to Shirley Ashby, October 13, 1967.

15. Norman Jewison, commentary, on *The Thomas Crown Affair* DVD, dir. Norman Jewison (MGM, 2002).

16. AFI Seminar with Hal Ashby, interview by James Powers, October 20, 1976.

17. Powers, "Dialogue on Film: Hal Ashby," 59.

18. Letter from Hal Ashby to Shirley Ashby, January 3, 1968.

19. Court Memorandum, in the Matter of the Adoption of Baby Boy Lawrence (No. WE A.D. 1937), May 15, 1968.

20. Letter from Hal Ashby to Shirley Ashby, September 15, 1970.

21. Jewison, *This Terrible Business*, 151–52.

22. Quincy Jones, *Q: The Autobiography of Quincy Jones* (London: Hodder & Stoughton, 2001), 216.

23. Letter from Quincy Jones, read at Hal Ashby memorial service, December 30, 1988.

24. Mason Wiley and Damien Bona, *Inside Oscar* (New York: Ballantine, 1996), 411.

25. Jewison, *This Terrible Business*, 153.

26. Memo from Hal Ashby to Norman Jewison et al., October 13, 1966.

27. Richard Cuskelly, "A Rip Van Winkle Beard and a Calm Demeanor," *Los Angeles Herald Examiner*, April 2, 1972.

28. Will Jones, "Film Guru Ashby Enjoys View from the Mountain," *Minneapolis Tribune*, February 1976.

29. "Film Editor from Ogden Wins Oscar," *Ogden Standard Examiner*, April 12, 1968.

9. Where It's At

Epigraph: Ben Hecht, *Gaily, Gaily* (1963), quoted at the beginning of *Gaily, Gaily* (Norman Jewison, 1969).

1. Note from Marilyn and Alan Bergman to Hal Ashby, April 11, 1968; telegram from Buzz Brandt to Hal Ashby, April 15, 1968.

2. Telefax from Steve McQueen to Hal Ashby, April 11, 1968.

3. Letter from Hal Ashby to William Wyler, April 25, 1968.

4. Letter from Hal Ashby to Bob Swink, April 29, 1968.

5. Ashby, "Breaking Out of the Cutting Room," 9.

6. Bridget Byrne, "Dream Weaver Hal Ashby," *Los Angeles Herald Examiner*, April 18, 1976.

7. Jones, "Film Guru Ashby."

8. Harmetz, "Gambling on a Film," 2-13.

9. Letter from Hal Ashby to Eileen Ashby, June 5, 1968.

10. Jewison, *This Terrible Business*, 172.

11. Norman Jewison, telephone interview with the author, April 25, 2006.

12. Christopher Sandford, *McQueen: The Biography* (London: HarperCollins, 2001), 202; Murf., review of *The Thomas Crown Affair*, *Daily Variety*, June 19, 1968.

13. John Mahoney, "Mirisch's 'Crown' Flashy," *Hollywood Reporter,* June 19, 1968, 3; review of *The Thomas Crown Affair, Los Angeles Times,* June 28, 1968.

14. Letter from Laurence Babb to Hal Ashby, July 19, 1968.

15. AFI Seminar with Hal Ashby, interview by James Powers, October 20, 1976.

16. Beau Bridges, telephone interview with the author, November 4, 2004.

17. Ibid.

18. Letter from Margot Kidder to Hal Ashby, May 27, 1970.

19. Kenneth Bowser, dir., *Easy Riders, Raging Bulls: How the Sex, Drugs and Rock 'n' Roll Generation Saved Hollywood* (Shout! Factory, 2004).

20. Letter from Margot Kidder to Hal Ashby, April 1, 1970.

21. "Norman Jewison Directs *And Justice for All,*" *Millimeter,* October 1979.

22. "Oral History with Ralph E. Winters," interview by Jennifer Petersen, May 24, 2000, AMPAS, Los Angeles, 2003, p. 289.

23. Ashby, "Breaking Out of the Cutting Room," 9.

24. Powers, "Dialogue on Film: Hal Ashby," 57.

25. Ashby, "Breaking Out of the Cutting Room," 9.

26. Ibid., 9–10.

27. Beau Bridges, telephone interview with the author, November 4, 2004.

10. The Director

Epigraph: Jessica Hundley, "The Ultimate Hollywood Outlaw," *Premiere,* October 2006, 89.

1. Telegram from Jan Schrader to Hal Ashby, May 29, 1969.

2. Ashby, "Breaking Out of the Cutting Room," 10.

3. Powers, "Dialogue on Film: Hal Ashby," 57.

4. Beau Bridges, telephone interview with the author, November 4, 2004.

5. Howard Gensler, "Absentee Landlord," *Premiere (U.S.),* August 1992, 96.

6. Frances Taylor, "'The Landlord' a Tenant in LI Home," *Long Island Press,* August 3, 1969.

7. Letter from Pearl Bailey to Hal Ashby, December 10, 1969.

8. Beau Bridges, telephone interview with the author, November 4, 2004.

9. "Oral History with Robert F. Boyle," 224.

10. Ashby, "Breaking Out of the Cutting Room," 10.

11. Beau Bridges, telephone interview with the author, November 4, 2004.

12. "Shooting at the Virshups: A Scene within a Scene," *Great Neck Record,* July 31, 1969, 8.

13. Norman Jewison, telephone interview with the author, April 25, 2006.

14. Ibid.

15. Ashby, "Breaking Out of the Cutting Room," 10.

16. Lee Grant, telephone interview with the author, July 22, 2006.

17. Salvato and Schaefer, "Hal Ashby Interview," 38.
18. Frizzelle, "Hip Rip."
19. Norman Jewison, telephone interview with the author, April 25, 2006.
20. Program for Hal Ashby's wedding to Joan Marshall, August 21, 1969.
21. Norman Jewison, telephone interview with the author, April 25, 2006.
22. Lee Grant, telephone interview with the author, July 22, 2006.
23. Norman Jewison, telephone interview with the author, April 25, 2006.
24. Ibid.
25. Letter from Sheri Marshall Ashby to Hal Ashby, October 8, 1969.
26. Memo from Hal Ashby to Marvin Mirisch, ca. November 7, 1969.
27. Letter from Hal Ashby to Diana Sands, December 17, 1969.
28. AFI Seminar with Hal Ashby, interview by Sam Grossman, January 11, 1972.
29. Letter from Hal Ashby to Norman Jewison, January 8, 1970.
30. Al Kooper, *Backstage Passes and Backstabbing Bastards* (New York: Billboard Books, 1998), 152.
31. Letter from Margot Kidder to Hal Ashby, April 1, 1970.
32. Norman Jewison, telephone interview with the author, April 25, 2006.
33. Letter from Hal Ashby to Joe Baltake, May 25, 1971.
34. Sue Cameron, "Lee Grant Thinks, Talks Strong on Career Progress," *Hollywood Reporter,* April 29, 1971.
35. Letter from Hal Ashby to Sue Mengers, June 2, 1970.
36. Letter from Hal Ashby to Julie Newmar, July 29, 1970.
37. Letter from Maloy Baretto to Hal Ashby, ca. 1980.

11. *Harold and Maude*

Epigraph: AFI Seminar with Hal Ashby, interview by James Powers, January 30, 1980.

1. Frizzelle, "Hip Rip."
2. Robert Evans, *The Kid Stays in the Picture* (London: HarperCollins, 1995), 169.
3. AFI Seminar with Hal Ashby, interview by Sam Grossman, January 11, 1972.
4. Salvato and Schaefer, "Hal Ashby Interview," 42.
5. Chuck Mulvehill, telephone interview with the author, April 12, 2006.
6. Robert Downey Sr., interview with the author, New York, January 3, 2006.
7. Steve Toy, "Director Hal Ashby's Office Is a House with Psychedelic Walls," *Daily Variety,* December 24, 1971, 14.
8. Ruth Gordon, *My Side* (New York: Harper & Row, 1976), 391.
9. Letter from Norman Jewison to Hal Ashby, ca. early November 1970.
10. Gordon, *My Side,* 392.
11. Letter from Hal Ashby, December 3, 1970.

12. Memo from Hal Ashby to Sheila Woodland et al., November 19, 1970.

13. AFI Seminar with Hal Ashby, interview by Sam Grossman, January 11, 1972.

14. Letter from Hal Ashby to Robert Evans, December 1, 1970.

15. Gordon, *My Side*, 395.

16. Powers, "Dialogue on Film: Hal Ashby," 56.

17. Alex Simon, "Life in the Court of Bud," *Venice*, May 2005, 78.

18. Ibid., 78.

19. Hal Ashby memorial service, December 30, 1988.

20. AFI Seminar with Hal Ashby, interview by Sam Grossman, January 11, 1972.

21. Jeff Wexler, interview with the author, Venice, CA, November 6, 2004.

22. Gordon, *My Side*, 391.

23. Telegram from Peter Bart to Hal Ashby, February 18, 1971.

24. Letter from Hal Ashby to Cyril Cusack, April 12, 1972.

25. AFI Seminar with Hal Ashby, interview by Sam Grossman, January 11, 1972.

26. Simon, "Life in the Court of Bud," 78.

27. Ruth Gordon, interview by Leticia Kent, *New York Times*, April 4, 1971.

28. Robert Downey Sr., interview with the author, New York, January 3, 2006.

29. Letter from Hal Ashby to Norman Jewison, March 29, 1971.

30. Ibid.

31. Telegram from Peter Bart to Hal Ashby, July 29, 1971.

32. Michael Shedlin, "*Harold and Maude*," *Film Quarterly*, Fall 1972.

33. Peter Bart and Peter Guber, *Shoot Out: Surviving Fame and (Mis)Fortune in Hollywood* (London: Faber & Faber, 2002), 185.

34. Biskind, *Easy Riders, Raging Bulls*, 173.

35. Charles Champlin, "*Harold and Maude*," *Los Angeles Times*, December 19, 1971; Judith Crist, "*Harold and Maude*," *New York*, December 20, 1971; Pauline Kael, "*Harold and Maude*," in *5001 Nights at the Movies* (New York: Holt, Rinehart & Wilson, 1982), 242.

36. Bowser, dir., *Easy Riders, Raging Bulls*.

37. Review of *Harold and Maude*, *Playboy*, April 1972.

38. Bowser, dir., *Easy Riders, Raging Bulls*.

39. AFI Seminar with Hal Ashby, interview by Sam Grossman, January 11, 1972.

40. Cuskelly, "A Rip Van Winkle Beard."

12. Nicholson

Epigraph: Harmetz, "Gambling on a Film," 2-13.

1. Biskind, *Easy Riders, Raging Bulls*, 174.

2. Robert David Crane and Christopher Fryer, "Hal Ashby," in *Jack Nicholson, Face to Face* (New York: M. Evans, 1975), 110.

3. Chuck Barris, telephone interview with the author, January 6, 2006.

4. Marilyn Beck, "Director Charges Studio Was Afraid of 'Maude,'" *Philadelphia Evening Bulletin,* January 25, 1972, B33.

5. Chuck Mulvehill, telephone interview with the author, April 12, 2006.

6. Email from Deanna Benatovich to the author, May 7, 2005.

7. Ibid.

8. Cuskelly, "A Rip Van Winkle Beard."

9. D.F. Films reader's report on *The Last Detail,* ca. September 1971.

10. Crane and Fryer, "Hal Ashby," 113.

11. "Biography: HAL ASHBY," *The Last Detail* Columbia production notes, January 15, 1974.

12. Bridget Byrne, "Fighting for 'The Last Detail,'" *Los Angeles Herald Examiner,* February 10, 1974.

13. Lawrence H. Suid, *Guts and Glory: The Making of the American Military Image in Film* (Lexington: University Press of Kentucky, 2002), 297.

14. Norman Jewison, telephone interview with the author, April 25, 2006.

15. Email from Deanna Benatovich to the author, April 19, 2005.

16. Email from Deanna Benatovich to the author, May 7, 2005.

17. "Directors of the 9th Era," *Esquire,* February 1975, 69.

13. *The Last Detail*

Epigraph: Ted Demme and Richard LaGravenese, dirs., *A Decade under the Influence* (IFC Films, 2003).

1. Hundley, "The Ultimate Hollywood Outlaw," 89.

2. Hal Ashby memorial service, December 30, 1988.

3. AFI Seminar with Hal Ashby, interview by James Powers, October 20, 1976.

4. Joe Baltake, "Ashby Likes His Characters, Warts and All," *Philadelphia Daily News,* February 8, 1980, 25.

5. Letter from Gerry Ayres to Hal Ashby, ca. mid-November 1972.

6. AFI Seminar with Hal Ashby, interview by James Powers, October 20, 1976.

7. Salvato and Schaefer, "Hal Ashby Interview," 37.

8. T. Starr, "High on the Future," *Ticketron Entertainment,* June/July 1973, 9.

9. Kathleen Miller, "Kathleen Miller—Notes," *Stay Hungry* United Artists production notes.

10. AFI Seminar with Hal Ashby, interview by Rochelle Reed, March 12, 1975.

11. Janet Maslin, "Finishing Up the Last Details," *Boston Phoenix,* February 6, 1973, 2-3.

12. Powers, "Dialogue on Film: Hal Ashby," 57.

13. AFI Seminar with Hal Ashby, interview by James Powers, October 20, 1976.

14. Robert C. Jones, telephone interview with the author, April 14, 2006.

15. AFI Seminar with Hal Ashby, interview by James Powers, October 20, 1976.

16. Letter from Ken Kesey to Hal Ashby, ca. May 1973.

17. Letter from Ken Kesey to Hal Ashby, June 18, 1973.

18. AFI Seminar with Hal Ashby, interview by James Powers, October 20, 1976.

19. Al Schwartz, interview with the author, Los Angeles, January 26, 2007.

20. Mary A. Fischer, "Peter Sellers' Chance of a Lifetime," *Rolling Stone*, April 19, 1979, 63.

21. Biskind, *Easy Riders, Raging Bulls*, 180.

22. Fischer, "Peter Sellers' Chance of a Lifetime," 64.

23. Teletype message from Gerry Ayres to David Begelman, August 23, 1973.

24. Salvato and Schaefer, "Hal Ashby Interview," 65–66.

25. Ibid.

26. Jack and Beth Ashby, telephone interview with the author, December 18, 2003.

27. Letter from Eileen Ashby to Hal Ashby, November 23, 1969.

28. Letter from Eileen Ashby to Hal Ashby, March 17, 1970.

29. Andrew Sarris, "Salty Way to Naval Prison," *Village Voice*, February 7, 1974.

14. *Shampoo*

Epigraphs: Directed by Hal Ashby, documentary (TV Ontario, 2005); Lee Grant, telephone interview with the author, July 22, 2006.

1. Biskind, *Easy Riders, Raging Bulls*, 193.

2. Letter from Hal Ashby to Sheila Woodland, November 26, 1973.

3. Salvato and Schaefer, "Hal Ashby Interview," 44.

4. Suzanne Finstad, *Warren Beatty: A Private Man* (London: Aurum, 2005), 414; Ellis Amburn, *The Sexiest Man Alive: Warren Beatty, the Biography* (London: Virgin Books, 2003), 177.

5. Finstad, *Warren Beatty*, 414.

6. Warren Beatty, telephone interview with the author, January 18, 2007.

7. Miller, "Kathleen Miller—Notes."

8. "Robert Towne," in *Filmmakers on Filmmaking*, ed. Joseph McBride, 2 vols. (Los Angeles: J. P. Tarcher, 1983), 2:76.

9. Ken Gross, "Lee Grant," *People Weekly*, October 23, 1989.

10. Lee Grant, telephone interview with the author, July 22, 2006.

11. Christopher Wilson, *Absolutely . . . Goldie: The Biography* (London: HarperCollins, 1999), 105–6.

12. AFI Seminar with Hal Ashby, interview by Rochelle Reed, March 12, 1975.

13. Warren Beatty, telephone interview with the author, January 18, 2007.

14. Email from Peter Sorel to the author, February 7, 2004.

15. "Warren Beatty on Discretion, Valor and Better Parts," *Films Illustrated*, May 1975, 333.

16. AFI Seminar with Hal Ashby, interview by Rochelle Reed, March 12, 1975.

17. Warren Beatty, telephone interview with the author, January 18, 2007.

18. Finstad, *Warren Beatty*, 417.

19. Biskind, *Easy Riders, Raging Bulls*, 193–94.

20. Ibid., 193.

21. Jeff Wexler, interview with the author, Venice, CA, November 6, 2004.

22. AFI Seminar with Hal Ashby, interview by Rochelle Reed, March 12, 1975.

23. Jacobs, "Hal Ashby at His Best," C2.

24. James Spada, *Shirley and Warren* (New York: Collier, 1985), 168.

25. Email from Deanna Benatovich to the author, May 14, 2005.

26. Letter from Tom Blackwell to Hal Ashby, June 1, 1974.

27. Wiley and Bona, *Inside Oscar*, 493.

28. Warren Beatty, telephone interview with the author, January 18, 2007.

29. Letter from Ellen Burstyn to Hal Ashby, February 28, 1980.

30. Michael Butler, telephone interview with the author, January 7, 2004.

31. Ibid.

32. Michael Butler, "*Hair:* Getting the Film Together," October 2, 2000, http://www.orlok.com/orlok/michael/film.html.

33. AFI Seminar with Hal Ashby, interview by Rochelle Reed, March 12, 1975.

34. Warren Beatty, telephone interview with the author, January 18, 2007.

35. Rudy Wurlitzer, telephone interview with the author, April 17, 2006.

36. Chris Nashawaty, "The Warren Report," *Entertainment Weekly*, March 1, 2000.

37. Hal Ashby's Daily Journal, February 6, 1975.

38. Salvato and Schaefer, "Hal Ashby Interview," 64.

39. "Dialogue on Film: Robert Towne," *American Film*, December 1975, 44.

40. AFI Seminar with Hal Ashby, interview by Rochelle Reed, March 12, 1975.

15. Glory Bound

1. David Carradine, interview with the author, Los Angeles, October 14, 2004.

2. AFI Seminar with Hal Ashby, interview by Rochelle Reed, March 12, 1975.

3. Warren Beatty, telephone interview with the author, January 18, 2007.

4. Julia Phillips, *You'll Never Eat Lunch in This Town Again* (London: Heinemann, 1991), 196.

5. Erica Jong, *Fear of Fifty: A Midlife Memoir* (New York: Tarcher, 2006); Phillips, *You'll Never Eat Lunch in This Town Again*, 205.

6. Richard Thompson, "In the American Grain (an Interview)," *Sight and Sound*, Summer 1976, 143.

7. Harmetz, "Gambling on a Film," 2-13.

8. Joseph McBride, "Song for Woody," *Film Comment*, November–December 1976, 27.

9. Biskind, *Easy Riders, Raging Bulls*, 195.

10. Mireille "Mimi" Machu, telephone interview with the author, October 18, 2006.

11. Pierre Sauvage, "Hal Ashby: On *Bound for Glory*," *Cannes Film Daily*, May 18, 1977, 48.

12. Robert Downey Sr., interview with the author, New York, January 3, 2006.

13. Bernard Weinraub, "Carradine Plays Woody 'Like Me,'" *New York Times*, December 4, 1976.

14. David Carradine, *Endless Highway* (Boston: Journey Editions, 1995), 417.

15. David Carradine, interview with the author, Los Angeles, October 14, 2004.

16. Fernandez, "Cinema Chat with Hal Ashby," 25.

17. Thompson, "In the American Grain (an Interview)," 143.

18. Appelbaum, "Positive Thinking," 15.

19. AFI Seminar with Hal Ashby, interview by James Powers, October 20, 1976.

20. Demme and LaGravenese, dirs., *A Decade under the Influence*.

21. Email from Michael Dare to the author, February 21, 2004.

22. AFI Seminar with Hal Ashby, interview by James Powers, October 20, 1976.

23. Jon Carroll, "Hey Hey, Woody Guthrie, We'll Make You a Star," *Village Voice*, October 13, 1975, 132.

24. Frances Taylor, "Director's Vision Vital to Success," *Long Island Press*, November 21, 1976.

25. Edward Kaufman, "Haller—Visually Creating Time and Space," *Los Angeles Herald Examiner*, March 8, 1977, B6.

26. Robert Downey Sr., telephone interview with the author, December 30, 2005.

27. David Carradine, interview with the author, Los Angeles, October 14, 2004.

28. Joseph McBride, "*Bound for Glory*, about a Month over Sked, Called 'Murderous' by Blumofe," *Daily Variety*, December 29, 1975.

29. Rebello, "A Mild and Wild Maverick," 97.

30. Biskind, *Easy Riders, Raging Bulls*, 196.

31. Aljean Harmetz, "Cocaine and Hollywood," *New York Times*, July 9, 1978.

32. Robert Downey Sr., interview with the author, New York, January 3, 2006.

33. Carradine, *Endless Highway*, 418.

34. David Carradine, interview with the author, Los Angeles, October 14, 2004.

35. Ibid.

36. Harmetz, "Gambling on a Film," 2-13.

37. David Barry, "The Making of a Maverick," *Women's Wear Daily,* May 21, 1976, 12.

38. Ibid.

39. Letter from Pete Seeger to Guthrie Thomas, December 20, 1975.

40. Memo from Mike Medavoy to Hal Ashby, February 2, 1976.

41. Dustin Hoffman, interview with the author, New York, February 15, 2007.

42. Haskell Wexler, interview with the author, Santa Monica, December 5, 2006.

43. Mireille "Mimi" Machu, telephone interview with the author, October 18, 2006.

44. Chuck Mulvehill, telephone interview with the author, April 12, 2006.

45. Dianne Schroeder Hanks, telephone interview with the author, April 20, 2006.

46. Dianne Schroeder Hanks, telephone interview with the author, January 22, 2007.

47. Ibid.

48. Lee Grant, "Film Clips," *Los Angeles Times,* July 12, 1976.

49. David Carradine, interview with the author, Los Angeles, October 14, 2004.

50. Baltake, "Ashby Likes His Characters," 25.

51. McBride, "Song for Woody," 26.

52. AFI Seminar with Hal Ashby, interview by James Powers, October 20, 1976.

53. "Our Critic Eyes the Future and Blinks," *Village Voice,* September 13, 1976, 107.

54. Sterritt, "'That Special Okie Southwest Flavor,'" 31.

55. McBride, "Song for Woody," 26.

16. *Coming Home*

Epigraph: Tim Buckley, "Once I Was," *Goodbye and Hello,* Elektra Records, 1967; Damien Love, "Bruce Dern," *Uncut,* January 2004, 98.

1. Jerome Hellman, telephone interview with the author, August 2, 2006.

2. Note from Jerome Hellman to Hal Ashby, December 13, 1973.

3. Appelbaum, "Positive Thinking," 13.

4. Powers, "Dialogue on Film: Hal Ashby," 55.

5. Janet Maslin, "For Jon Voight, a Coming Home," *New York Times,* February 13, 1978, C15.

6. Appelbaum, "Positive Thinking," 11.

7. Ibid.

8. Jacobs, "Hal Ashby at His Best," C2.

9. Note from Haskell Wexler to Hal Ashby, ca. August 1976.

10. "Dialogue on Film: Jerome Hellman," *American Film,* June 1978, 36.

11. Jerome Hellman, telephone interview with the author, August 2, 2006.

12. Memo from Jane Fonda to Hal Ashby, Jerome Hellman, Bruce Gilbert, Waldo Salt, et al., November 24, 1976.

13. Jane Fonda, *My Life So Far* (London: Random House, 2005), 361.

14. Appelbaum, "Positive Thinking," 12.

15. "Dialogue on Film: Jerome Hellman," 36.

16. Appelbaum, "Positive Thinking," 12.

17. Kirk Honeycutt, "The Five-Year Struggle to Make 'Coming Home,'" *New York Times,* February 19, 1978, 2-13.

18. Powers, "Dialogue on Film: Hal Ashby," 55.

19. Rudy Wurlitzer, telephone interview with the author, April 17, 2006.

20. Powers, "Dialogue on Film: Hal Ashby," 55.

21. Ibid., 56.

22. Gregg Kilday, "Jon Voight," *Moviegoer,* July 1982, 14.

23. "Coming Back Home" documentary, on *Coming Home* DVD (MGM, 2002).

24. Demme and LaGravenese, dirs., *A Decade under the Influence.*

25. "Coming Back Home" documentary.

26. Jon Voight, telephone interview with the author, October 20, 2006.

27. Ibid.

28. Letter to Chuck Mulvehill from John D. Chase, January 13, 1977.

29. Avery, "Hal Ashby: Getting the Right Drift," 19.

30. Appelbaum, "Positive Thinking," 13.

31. Maslin, "For Jon Voight, a Coming Home," C15.

32. Appelbaum, "Positive Thinking," 13.

33. Maslin, "For Jon Voight, a Coming Home," C15.

34. Benjamin Bergery, *Reflections: Twenty-One Cinematographers at Work* (Hollywood, CA: ASC Holding Corp., June 2002), 135.

35. Robert Carradine, interview with the author, Edinburgh, August 27, 2004.

36. Powers, "Dialogue on Film: Hal Ashby," 55–56.

37. "Guardian/NFT Interview: Jane Fonda," *Guardian,* June 3, 2005.

38. Fonda, *My Life So Far,* 372.

39. Demme and LaGravenese, dirs., *A Decade under the Influence.*

40. "Coming Back Home" documentary.

41. Tony Crawley, "The Loneliness of the Long-Distance (Silent) Runner," *Films Illustrated,* October 1978, 53.

42. Appelbaum, "Positive Thinking," 14.

43. Carrie Ashby, interview with the author, Laguna Beach, CA, December 3, 2006. See also Biskind, *Easy Riders, Raging Bulls,* 354.

44. "Coming Back Home" documentary.

45. Rex Reed, "Jon Voight," in *Travolta to Keaton* (New York: William Morrow, 1979), 214.

46. Dianne Schroeder, telephone interview with the author, April 20, 2006.

47. Mike Medavoy, interview with the author, Culver City, CA, September 21, 2004.

48. Letter from Pierre Sauvage to Hal Ashby, June 13, 1977.

49. Jeff Freedman, "Ashby Ponders 'American,' 'Hawkline' as Next Project," *Hollywood Reporter*, February 23, 1978.

50. Jerome Hellman, telephone interview with the author, August 2, 2006.

51. Ibid.

52. Jacobs, "Hal Ashby at His Best," C2.

53. Fernandez, "Cinema Chat with Hal Ashby," 27.

17. Double Feature

Epigraphs: Bruce Cook, "Stalking the *Hamster of Happiness*," *American Film*, December 1978–January 1979, 27; Melvyn Douglas and Tom Arthur, *See You at the Movies: The Autobiography of Melvyn Douglas* (London: University Press of America, 1986), 228.

1. Fernandez, "Cinema Chat with Hal Ashby," 27.

2. Letter from Hal Ashby to Merv Adelson, February 27, 1979.

3. Aljean Harmetz, "Hal Ashby Tries 'Doubling Up' as a Film Director," *New York Times*, June 25, 1978.

4. Ibid.

5. Roger Lewis, *The Life and Death of Peter Sellers* (London: Arrow, 1995), 605.

6. Todd McCarthy, "Hal Ashby's Prod'n Experiment Doubles His Feature Film Output," *Daily Variety*, November 26, 1979, 2.

7. Andrew Braunsberg, telephone interview with the author, April 4, 2006.

8. Harmetz, "Hal Ashby Tries 'Doubling Up.'"

9. Charles Eastman, interview with the author, Venice, CA, November 6, 2004.

10. *Second Hand Hearts* Northstar press notes.

11. James William Guercio, telephone interview with the author, July 15, 2006.

12. Jordan R. Young and Mike Bruns, "Hal Ashby: Satisfaction in Being There," *Millimeter*, May 1980, 94.

13. Charles Champlin, "Robert Blake Shifts Gears for 'Hamster,'" *Los Angeles Times*, October 8, 1978, Calendar section, 34.

14. Haskell Wexler, interview with the author, Santa Monica, CA, December 5, 2006.

15. Hal Ashby memorial service, December 30, 1988.

16. Dianne Schroeder Hanks, telephone interview with the author, April 20, 2006.

17. Cook, "Stalking the *Hamster of Happiness*," 27.

18. James William Guercio, telephone interview with the author, July 15, 2006.

19. Champlin, "Robert Blake Shifts Gears," 34.

20. Haskell Wexler, interview with the author, Santa Monica, CA, December 5, 2006.

21. Champlin, "Robert Blake Shifts Gears," 34.

22. Letter from Hal Ashby to Ed Bondy, September 2, 1978.

23. Scott Bowles, "Actor Bert Remsen a Reel Veteran of Films," *Daily Texan*, April 30, 1981, 18.

24. Louise Sweeney, "Jerzy Kosinski and the Nine Million Dollar Glass of Water," *Christian Science Monitor*, March 27, 1979, B15.

25. Young and Bruns, "Hal Ashby: Satisfaction in Being There," 91.

26. Bob Jones, telephone interview with the author, April 14, 2006.

27. Young and Bruns, "Hal Ashby: Satisfaction in Being There," 91.

28. Caleb Deschanel interview, *Millimeter*, July 1980, 91.

29. Powers, "Dialogue on Film: Hal Ashby," 53.

30. John Hartl, "'Being There' a Seven-Year Project for Ashby, Sellers," *Seattle Times*, February 17, 1980, J14.

31. Lee Grant, "Film Clips," *Los Angeles Times*, January 24, 1979, IV-7.

32. Andrew Braunsberg, telephone interview with the author, April 4, 2006.

33. Young and Bruns, "Hal Ashby: Satisfaction in Being There," 97.

34. Mitchell Glazer, "The Strange World of Peter Sellers," *Rolling Stone*, April 17, 1980, 46.

35. "What Peter Sellers Didn't Say," Lorimar press release, 2.

36. Draft of letter from Hal Ashby to Melvyn [Douglas?] and Roger [Ebert?], ca. August/September 1980.

37. Douglas and Arthur, *See You at the Movies*, 226–28.

38. Powers, "Dialogue on Film: Hal Ashby," 53.

39. Robert Downey Sr., interview with the author, New York, January 3, 2006.

40. Michael Dare, "How the 'Walking on Water' Shot in *Being There* Actually Got Made," http://www.dareland.com/lastshot.htm.

41. Rebello, "A Mild and Wild Maverick," 97.

42. Hal Ashby memorial service, December 30, 1988.

43. Powers, "Dialogue on Film: Hal Ashby," 60.

44. Letter from Hal Ashby to Leonard Hirshan, March 5, 1979.

45. Letter from Bo Smith to Hal Ashby, February 15, 1979.

46. Caleb Deschanel, telephone interview with the author, January 8, 2007.

47. Caleb Deschanel interview (*Millimeter*), 93.

48. Powers, "Dialogue on Film: Hal Ashby," 54.

18. *Being There*

Epigraph: Letter from Hal Ashby to Merv Adelson, August 12, 1980.

1. Rex Reed, "Shirley: Suffering a Fool Gladly," *Daily News*, March 25, 1979, 10.

2. Jack and Beth Ashby, telephone interview with the author, December 18, 2003.

3. Wiley and Bona, *Inside Oscar*, 565.

4. William Overend, "An Oscar Comes Home," *Los Angeles Times*, April 11, 1979.

5. Note from Haskell Wexler to Hal Ashby, April 10, 1979.

6. Glazer, "The Strange World of Peter Sellers," 43.

7. Charles Clapsaddle, telephone interview with the author, July 30, 2006.

8. Letter from Hal Ashby to Merv Adelson, February 27, 1979.

9. Ibid.

10. Adrian Hodges, "Flying Start for Ashby," *Screen International*, May 18, 1980, 44.

11. Letter from Terry Southern to Hal Ashby, September 10, 1979.

12. Memo from Hal Ashby to Jeff Berg, Bert Fields, Michael Sherman, Lawrence Iser, and J. Hornstein, January 17, 1986.

13. Ibid.

14. Aljean Harmetz, "Book by Kosinski, Film by Ashby," *New York Times*, December 23, 1979, 2-19.

15. Fischer, "Peter Sellers' Chance of a Lifetime," 63–64.

16. David Alexander, "But Who Really Played Peter Sellers," *New West*, April 21, 1980, 7.

17. Pollock, "Whatever Happened to Hal Ashby?" 23–24.

18. Letter from Gerry Ayres to Hal Ashby, March 10, 1980.

19. Pollock, "Whatever Happened to Hal Ashby?" 24.

20. Letter from Mike Kaplan to Hal Ashby, October 21, 1980.

21. Letter from Hal Ashby to Merv Adelson, August 12, 1980.

22. Young and Bruns, "Hal Ashby: Satisfaction in Being There," 96.

23. Andrew Braunsberg, telephone interview with the author, April 4, 2006.

24. Young and Bruns, "Hal Ashby: Satisfaction in Being There," 95.

25. Alexander Walker, *Peter Sellers: The Authorized Biography* (London: Weidenfeld & Nicolson, 1981), 213.

26. Letter from Terry Southern to Hal Ashby, September 8, 1980.

19. *Lookin' to Get Out*

Epigraphs: Pauline Kael, "Why Are Movies So Bad? or, The Numbers," *New Yorker*, June 23, 1980; letter from Hal Ashby to Merv Adelson, August 12, 1980.

1. Charles Schreger, "A Script Jon Can Live With," *Los Angeles Times*, April 14, 1980.

2. *Lookin' to Get Out* Paramount press notes, 13.

3. Jon Voight interview, interviewer unknown, ca. 1981.

4. Letter from Hal Ashby to Merv Adelson, August 12, 1980.

5. Ibid.

6. Memo from Hal Ashby to Jeff Berg, Bert Fields, Michael Sherman, Lawrence Iser, and J. Hornstein, January 17, 1986.

7. Young and Bruns, "Hal Ashby: Satisfaction in Being There," 97.
8. Hal Ashby, draft scene for *Lookin' to Get Out,* 1980.
9. Memo from Hal Ashby to Jeff Berg, Bert Fields, Michael Sherman, Lawrence Iser, and J. Hornstein, January 17, 1986.
10. Ibid.
11. Letter from Hal Ashby to Merv Adelson, May 5, 1980.
12. Letter from Hal Ashby to Merv Adelson, August 12, 1980.
13. Jon Voight, interview with the author, Santa Monica, CA, December 5, 2006.
14. Jeff Wexler, interview with the author, Venice, CA, November 6, 2004.
15. Biskind, *Easy Riders, Raging Bulls,* 353.
16. Chuck Mulvehill, telephone interview with the author, April 12, 2006.
17. Jon Voight interview, interviewer unknown, ca. 1981.
18. Jon Voight, interview with the author, Santa Monica, CA, December 5, 2006.
19. Eva Gardos, telephone interview with the author, January 20, 2007.
20. Memo from Hal Ashby to Jeff Berg, Bert Fields, Michael Sherman, Lawrence Iser, and J. Hornstein, January 17, 1986.
21. Letter from Hal Ashby to Merv Adelson, August 12, 1980.
22. Lee Grant, telephone interview with the author, July 22, 2006.
23. Jon Voight interview, interviewer unknown, ca. 1981.
24. Ibid.
25. Ibid.
26. *Lookin' to Get Out* Northstar production notes.
27. Al Schwartz, interview with the author, Los Angeles, December 5, 2006.
28. Biskind, *Easy Riders, Raging Bulls,* 353.
29. Jon Voight, telephone interview with the author, October 20, 2006.
30. Haskell Wexler, interview with the author, Santa Monica, CA, December 5, 2006.
31. Memo from Hal Ashby to Jeff Berg, Bert Fields, Michael Sherman, Lawrence Iser, and J. Hornstein, January 17, 1986.
32. "Oral History with Robert F. Boyle," 256.
33. Memo from Hal Ashby to Ed Rubin, September 25, 1980.
34. Memo from Hal Ashby to Jeff Berg, Bert Fields, Michael Sherman, Lawrence Iser, and J. Hornstein, January 17, 1986.
35. Pollock, "Whatever Happened to Hal Ashby?" 23.
36. Rick Padilla, telephone interview with the author, October 13, 2006.
37. Pollock, "Whatever Happened to Hal Ashby?" 23.
38. Charles Clapsaddle, telephone interview with the author, July 30, 2006.
39. Pollock, "Whatever Happened to Hal Ashby?" 24.
40. Mike Kaplan, interview with the author, London, March 17, 2004.
41. Mailgram from Hal Ashby to Gordon Weaver, Paramount, NY, April 30, 1981.
42. Archer Winsten, review of *Second Hand Hearts, New York Post,* May 8, 1981, 41.

43. Bill Kenly, press screening report, April 28, 1981.

44. C.B., "*Second Hand Hearts*," *Motion Picture Product Digest,* June 3, 1981, 98.

45. Vincent Canby, "Calling All Hamsters," *New York Times,* May 8, 1981, C11.

46. Charles Eastman, interview with the author, Venice, CA, November 6, 2004.

20. Like a Rolling Stone

Epigraphs: Peter Bart, "The Players: The Men Who Fell to Earth," *GQ,* August 1995, 65; Hundley, "The Ultimate Hollywood Outlaw," 90–91.

1. Memo from Hal Ashby to Jeff Berg, Bert Fields, Michael Sherman, Lawrence Iser, and J. Hornstein, January 17, 1986.

2. Biskind, *Easy Riders, Raging Bulls,* 353.

3. Ibid., 354.

4. Eva Gardos, telephone interview with the author, January 20, 2007.

5. Prince Rupert Loewenstein, interview with the author, London, March 15, 2004.

6. Andrew Braunsberg, telephone interview with the author, April 4, 2006.

7. Letter from Andrew Braunsberg to Hal Ashby, June 10, 1981.

8. Robert Downey Sr., interview with the author, New York, January 3, 2006.

9. Andrew Braunsberg, telephone interview with the author, April 4, 2006.

10. Ibid.

11. Mike Kaplan, telephone interview with the author, May 15, 2004.

12. Jeff Wexler, interview with the author, Venice, CA, November 6, 2004.

13. Jack and Beth Ashby, telephone interview with the author, December 18, 2003.

14. Letter from Jack Schwartzman to Hal Ashby, February 20, 1979.

15. Ray Loynd, "Ashby's Future with 'Tootsie' on Hold at Columbia," *Hollywood Reporter,* October 20, 1981, 10.

16. Kenneth Kleinberg, telephone interview with the author, June 28, 2005.

17. Robert Palmer, "They Filmed as the Stones Rolled," *New York Times,* February 6, 1983, 15.

18. Ibid.

19. Memo from Hal Ashby to Jeff Berg, Bert Fields, Michael Sherman, Lawrence Iser, and J. Hornstein, January 17, 1986.

20. Ibid.

21. Palmer, "They Filmed as the Stones Rolled," 15.

22. Prince Rupert Loewenstein, interview with the author, London, March 15, 2004.

23. Jeff Wexler, interview with the author, Venice, CA, November 6, 2004.

24. Prince Rupert Loewenstein, interview with the author, London, March 15, 2004.

25. Carlos Clarens, "Mick Jagger," *Moviegoer*, September 1982, 16.
26. Palmer, "They Filmed as the Stones Rolled," 20.
27. From draft script of pay-per-view show.

21. Getting Out

Epigraph: "Directors of the 9th Era," 69.
1. Letter from Merv Adelson to Hal Ashby, January 27, 1982.
2. Agreement between Lorimar and Ashby, February 8, 1982, quoted in letter from Brian C. Lysaght to Joseph A. Eisenberg, June 1, 1984.
3. Letter from Hal Ashby to Kenneth Kleinberg, April 29, 1982.
4. Martin A. Grove, "'Get Out' May Be Last Film for Lorimar," *Los Angeles Herald Examiner*, April 29, 1982.
5. Lisa Day, telephone interview with the author, December 16, 2006.
6. Sonya Sones, telephone interview with the author, April 22, 2004.
7. Carl Arrington, "Mr. Rolling Stone Finds Sweet Satisfaction with Rock's Richest Tour Ever," *People*, ca. January 1982.
8. Letter from Mike Kaplan to Phil Smith, April 29, 1982.
9. Leslie Shatz, "Robert 'Buzz' Knudson," *Editors' Guild Newsletter*, May/June 2000.
10. Mailgram from Hal Ashby to Mick Jagger, May 18, 1982.
11. Mike Kaplan, interview with the author, London, March 17, 2004.
12. Biskind, *Easy Riders, Raging Bulls*, 354.
13. Jon Voight, telephone interview with the author, October 20, 2006.
14. Pollock, "Whatever Happened to Hal Ashby?" 24.
15. Mailgram from Ashby to Frank Mancuso of Paramount, Buffy Shutt, Shelly Hochran, and Gordon Weaver, September 24, 1982.
16. Lor., "*Lookin' to Get Out*," *Variety*, October 6, 1982.
17. Robert Osborne, "*Lookin' to Get Out*," *Hollywood Reporter*, October 4, 1982, 3, 9.
18. Charles Champlin, "Critic at Large," *Los Angeles Times*, October 15, 1982, VI-8.
19. Fischer, "Peter Sellers' Chance of a Lifetime," 64.
20. Robert Schaffel, interview with the author, Los Angeles, January 26, 2007.
21. "Oral History with Robert F. Boyle," 257.
22. Kenneth Kleinberg, telephone interview with the author, June 28, 2005.
23. Pollock, "Whatever Happened to Hal Ashby?" 24.
24. Mike Kaplan, interview with the author, London, March 17, 2004.
25. Steve Barnett, "'Let's Spend the Night Together': Multitrack Music Editing, Post-Production and Re-Recording Stages," *Recording Engineer/Producer*, February 1983, 60, 75.
26. Cart., "Time Is on Our Side," *Variety*, August 25, 1982; Tina Daniell, "Let's Spend the Night Together," *Hollywood Reporter*, August 19, 1982, 22.

27. Janet Maslin, "Rock Glamour," *New York Times*, February 11, 1983, C8.
28. *Let's Spend the Night Together* Embassy Pictures draft press notes.
29. *Let's Spend the Night Together* Embassy Pictures production notes.
30. Palmer, "They Filmed as the Stones Rolled," 20.
31. John Blake, "Mick and Keith in Big Film Flare-Up," *London Sun*, April 22, 1983, 15.
32. Prince Rupert Loewenstein, interview with the author, London, March 15, 2004.

22. Old Man

1. Pollock, "Whatever Happened to Hal Ashby?" 1.
2. Letter from Mike Kaplan to Hal Ashby, October 5, 1982.
3. Pollock, "Whatever Happened to Hal Ashby?" 1, 23.
4. Ibid., 1, 23.
5. Ibid., 23, 1.
6. Mike Kaplan, "Ashby Story—a Biased Viewpoint?" (letter), *Los Angeles Times*, October 24, 1982, Calendar section, 20.
7. Chuck Mulvehill, telephone interview with the author, July 8, 2008.
8. Transcript of Deposition of Hal Ashby, January 21, 1986.
9. Letter from Hal Ashby to Eileen Ashby, July 9, 1963. Courtesy Jack Ashby.
10. Scott Young, *Neil and Me* (London: Rogan, 1997), 243.

23. *The Slugger's Wife*

Epigraph: Letter from Hal Ashby to Merv Adelson, August 12, 1980.
1. Note from Ray Stark to Hal Ashby, December 18, 1973.
2. Letter from Ray Stark to Hal Ashby, January 17, 1980.
3. Andrew Yule, *Enigma: David Puttnam, the Story So Far* (Edinburgh: Mainstream, 1988), 312.
4. Warren Beatty, telephone interview with the author, January 18, 2007.
5. Email from Michael O'Keefe to the author, February 2, 2004.
6. Caleb Deschanel, telephone interview with the author, January 8, 2007.
7. Thomas Wiener, "Rebecca De Mornay on Deck," *American Film*, April 1985, 38.
8. Memo from Ray Stark to Hal Ashby, January 27, 1984.
9. Card from Ray Stark to Hal Ashby, March 6, 1984.
10. Inscription from Neil Simon to Hal Ashby, February 19, 1984.
11. Email from Michael O'Keefe to the author, October 9, 2006.
12. Jeff Wexler, interview with the author, Venice, CA, November 6, 2004.
13. Rebello, "A Mild and Wild Maverick," 109.
14. Ibid.
15. Letter from Ray Stark to Hal Ashby, April 14, 1984.

16. Caleb Deschanel, telephone interview with the author, January 8, 2007.
17. Letter from Ray Stark to Hal Ashby, April 14, 1984.
18. Caleb Deschanel, telephone interview with the author, January 8, 2007.
19. *The Slugger's Wife* Columbia Pictures production notes.
20. Email from Michael O'Keefe to the author, January 27, 2004.
21. Email from Michael O'Keefe to the author, February 2, 2004.
22. Jeff Wexler, interview with the author, Venice, CA, November 6, 2004.
23. Rudy Wurlitzer, telephone interview with the author, April 17, 2006.
24. Email from Guy D'Alema to the author, February 27, 2004.
25. Note from Dianne Schroeder to Hal Ashby, March 2, 1984.
26. Letter from Carleigh [Hoff?] to Hal Ashby, April 13, 1984.
27. Email from Michael O'Keefe to the author, February 2, 2004.
28. Letter from Neil Simon to Ray Stark, May 30, 1984.
29. Memo from Ray Stark to Hal Ashby, June 1, 1984.
30. Memo from Ray Stark to Hal Ashby, June 9, 1984.
31. Memo from Hal Ashby to Ray Stark, June 9, 1984.
32. Jeff Wexler, interview with the author, Venice, CA, November 6, 2004.
33. Memo from Hal Ashby to Jeff Berg, Bert Fields, Michael Sherman, Lawrence Iser, and J. Hornstein, January 17, 1986.
34. Letter from Robert L. Robinson to Hal Ashby, August 3, 1984.
35. Memo from Hal Ashby to Jeff Berg, Bert Fields, Michael Sherman, Lawrence Iser, and J. Hornstein, January 17, 1986.
36. Ibid.
37. "Trouble Brews over Final Cut on Columbia's 'Slugger's Wife,'" *Daily Variety*, December 20, 1984, 1.
38. Hal Ashby, interview by Catherine Wyler, February 12, 1985.
39. Email from Michael O'Keefe to the author, October 9, 2006.
40. Janet Maslin, "Foul Ball," *New York Times*, March 29, 1985, C10.
41. Rex Reed, "'Slugger' Strikes Out," *New York Post*, March 29, 1985, 23.
42. Merrill Shindler, "*The Slugger's Wife* Strikes Out," *Los Angeles Magazine*, April 1985, 34.
43. David Ansen, "Matrimonial Slump," *Newsweek*, April 1, 1985.
44. Jagr., review of *The Slugger's Wife*, *Variety*, March 20, 1985.
45. John Horn, "Simon Takes Swing at 'Slugger's Wife,'" *Los Angeles Times*, April 15, 1985.
46. Transcript of Deposition of Hal Ashby, January 21, 1986.
47. Duane Byrge, "*The Slugger's Wife*," *Hollywood Reporter*, March 28, 1985, 21.

24. *8 Million Ways to Die*

Epigraphs: Chuck Mulvehill, interview with the author, Los Angeles, December 5, 2004; memo from Hal Ashby to Chuck Mulvehill, July 19, 1985.
1. Transcript of Deposition of Hal Ashby, January 21, 1986.
2. Letter from Mark Damon to Hal Ashby, January 24, 1985.

3. Gregg Kilday, "Many Bridges to Cross," *Los Angeles Herald Examiner*, April 11, 1985.

4. Steve Burum, interview with the author, Santa Monica, CA, November 17, 2004.

5. Transcript of Deposition of Hal Ashby, January 21, 1986.

6. Kilday, "Many Bridges to Cross."

7. Michael Dare, "How to Kill a Movie," *LA Weekly*, May 16, 1986, 32.

8. Chuck Mulvehill, telephone interview with the author, April 12, 2006.

9. Letter from Lance Hill to Hal Ashby, June 29, 1985.

10. Draft memo (unsent) from Hal Ashby to John Hyde, July 25, 1985.

11. Transcript of Deposition of Hal Ashby, January 21, 1986.

12. Draft memo (unsent) from Hal Ashby to John Hyde, July 25, 1985.

13. Transcript of script conference with Robert Towne, Hal Ashby, and Bart [?], July 3, 1985.

14. Memo from Hal Ashby to Chuck Mulvehill, July 19, 1985.

15. Memo from Hal Ashby to John Hyde of PSO, July 24, 1985.

16. Transcript of Deposition of Hal Ashby, January 21, 1986.

17. Steve Burum, interview with the author, Santa Monica, CA, November 17, 2004.

18. "Hal Ashby" by Jeff Bridges, statement sent to author via e-mail, August 10, 2004.

19. Dare, "How to Kill a Movie," 32.

20. Steve Burum, interview with the author, Santa Monica, CA, November 17, 2004.

21. Dare, "How to Kill a Movie," 32.

22. Alexandra Paul, telephone interview with the author, February 12, 2004.

23. Steve Burum, interview with the author, Santa Monica, CA, November 17, 2004.

24. Dare, "How to Kill a Movie," 33.

25. Biskind, *Easy Riders, Raging Bulls*, 428–29.

26. Transcript of Deposition of Hal Ashby, January 21, 1986.

27. James Riordan, *Stone: The Controversies, Excesses and Exploits of a Radical Filmmaker* (London: Aurum, 1996), 142.

28. Rochelle O'Gorman, "Interview with Lawrence Block," *Audiobook Café*, December 3, 2003, http://web.archive.org/web/20050503054706/http:/www.audiobookcafe.com/FtrLst.cfm?FtrCatCod=1&Code=578.

29. Regina Hackett, "Mystery Writer's Killer Insight Is, Well, a Secret," *Seattle Post-Intelligencer*, February 15, 1997.

30. Lawrence Y. Iser, Arbitration Brief of Case Put by Hal Ashby to DGA, February 19, 1986.

31. Steve Burum, interview with the author, Santa Monica, CA, November 17, 2004.

32. Dare, "How to Kill a Movie," 32.

33. Alexandra Paul, telephone interview with the author, February 12, 2004.

34. Transcript of Deposition of Hal Ashby, January 21, 1986.
35. Ibid.
36. Letter from Kevin Koloff to Jeff Berg, February 6, 1985.
37. Letter from L. Andrew Stone to Hal Ashby, November 27, 1985.
38. Note from Bob Lawrence to Hal Ashby, ca. December 5, 1985.
39. Letter from Hal Ashby to Michael Sherman, December 13, 1985.

25. The Last Movie

Epigraphs: Andy Garcia, telephone interview with the author, January 10, 2007; Dare, "How to Kill a Movie," 32.

1. Chuck Mulvehill, interview with the author, Los Angeles, December 5, 2004.
2. Dare, "How to Kill a Movie," 33.
3. Letter from Hal Ashby to Mark Damon, December 19, 1985.
4. Dare, "How to Kill a Movie," 32.
5. Ibid.
6. Transcript of Deposition of Hal Ashby, January 21, 1986.
7. Biskind, *Easy Riders, Raging Bulls,* 436.
8. Chuck Mulvehill, interview with the author, Los Angeles, December 5, 2004.
9. Dare, "How to Kill a Movie," 33.
10. Mike Kaplan, interview with the author, London, March 17, 2004.
11. Alexandra Paul, telephone interview with the author, February 12, 2004.
12. Ronald Bergan, *Dustin Hoffman* (London: Virgin, 1991), 220.
13. Dare, "How to Kill a Movie," 33.
14. Brit., review of *8 Million Ways to Die, Variety,* April 23, 1986.
15. Duane Byrge, "*Eight Million Ways to Die,*" *Hollywood Reporter,* April 21, 1986, 9.
16. Walter Goodman, "Stone Cold," *New York Times,* April 25, 1986, C17.
17. Pauline Kael, "*8 Million Ways to Die,*" *New Yorker,* May 19, 1986, 102.
18. Dare, "How to Kill a Movie," 32.
19. Mike Figgis, "Rosanna Arquette," in *Projections 10,* ed. Mike Figgis (London: Faber & Faber, 1999), 80.
20. Dare, "How to Kill a Movie," 32.
21. Ibid., 33.
22. Steve Burum, interview with the author, Santa Monica, CA, November 17, 2004.
23. Andy Garcia, telephone interview with the author, January 10, 2007.
24. Dare, "How to Kill a Movie," 31.
25. Ibid., 33.
26. Luke Ford, "Mark Damon Interview," http://www.lukeford.net/profiles/profiles/mark_damon.htm.
27. "Hal Ashby" by Jeff Bridges.

26. Starting Over

Epigraph: Penn quoted in Hundley, "The Ultimate Hollywood Outlaw," 89.

1. Bob Jones, telephone interview with the author, April 14, 2006.
2. Rudy Wurlitzer, telephone interview with the author, April 17, 2006.
3. Jim Harrison, *Off to the Side: A Memoir* (New York: Atlantic Monthly Press, 2002), 272–73.
4. Rudy Wurlitzer, telephone interview with the author, April 17, 2006.
5. Lee Grant, "Vietnam Milieu for Ashby Movie," *Los Angeles Times,* November 20, 1976.
6. AFI Seminar with Hal Ashby, interview by James Powers, January 30, 1980.
7. Rick Padilla, telephone interview with the author, October 13, 2006.
8. Rudy Wurlitzer, telephone interview with the author, April 17, 2006.
9. Bart, "The Players," 68.
10. Rebello, "A Mild and Wild Maverick," 110.
11. Rick Padilla, telephone interview with the author, October 13, 2006.
12. Ibid.
13. Email from John Teton to the author, March 26, 2005.
14. Rick Padilla, telephone interview with the author, October 13, 2006.
15. John Mandel, telephone interview with the author, March 18, 2006.
16. Jeff Jarvis, "Beverly Hills Buntz," *People Weekly,* November 30, 1987.
17. Bok., "Beverly Hills Buntz," *Variety,* November 18, 1987.
18. Richard Hack, "TeleVisions," *Hollywood Reporter,* November 9, 1987, 7.
19. Richard T. Kelly, *Sean Penn: His Life and Times* (London: Faber & Faber, 2004), 210.
20. Hal Ashby memorial service, December 30, 1988.
21. Kelly, *Sean Penn,* 209, 210.
22. Ibid., 210.
23. Jim Yoakum, "Graham Chapman's Journey," *Rolling Stone,* November 17, 1988, 47.
24. Joyce Gallie, interview with the author, March 19, 2004.
25. Kim "Howard" Johnson, *Life Before and After Monty Python: The Solo Flights of the Flying Circus* (London: Plexus, 1993), 226.
26. Celia Imrie, telephone interview with the author, July 29, 2004.
27. Chris Young, telephone interview with the author, January 4, 2007.
28. Ibid.
29. Johnson, *Life Before and After Monty Python,* 227.
30. Hal Ashby memorial service, December 30, 1988.
31. Ibid.
32. Jerry Hellman, telephone interview with the author, August 2, 2006.
33. Biskind, *Easy Riders, Raging Bulls,* 436.
34. Warren Beatty, telephone interview with the author, January 18, 2007.
35. Rick Padilla, telephone interview with the author, October 13, 2006.

27. Do Not Go Gentle

1. Biskind, *Easy Riders, Raging Bulls,* 436.
2. Rick Padilla, telephone interview with the author, October 13, 2006.
3. Email from Lynn Griffis to the author, November 5, 2006.
4. Biskind, *Easy Riders, Raging Bulls,* 437.
5. Email from Lynn Griffis to the author, November 5, 2006.
6. Dustin Hoffman, interview with the author, New York, February 15, 2007.
7. Hundley, "The Ultimate Hollywood Outlaw," 91.
8. Dustin Hoffman, interview with the author, New York, February 15, 2007.
9. Al Schwartz, telephone interview with the author, October 23, 2006.
10. Kelly, *Sean Penn,* 224.
11. Email from John Teton to the author, March 26, 2005.
12. Robert Downey Sr., interview with the author, New York, January 3, 2006.
13. Hal Ashby memorial service, December 30, 1988.
14. Ibid.
15. Hundley, "The Ultimate Hollywood Outlaw," 91.
16. "Hal Ashby: A Man Out of Time" documentary, on *Coming Home* DVD.
17. Rick Padilla, telephone interview with the author, October 13, 2006.
18. Jon Voight, telephone interview with the author, October 20, 2006.
19. Norman Jewison, telephone interview with the author, April 25, 2006.
20. Biskind, *Easy Riders, Raging Bulls,* 437.
21. Gordon Weeks, "Woman Reflects on Life of Hollywood Director Brother," *Ogden Standard Examiner,* December 30, 1988.
22. Al Schwartz, telephone interview with the author, October 23, 2006.
23. Kelly, *Sean Penn,* 245.
24. Rick Padilla, telephone interview with the author, October 13, 2006.
25. Biskind, *Easy Riders, Raging Bulls,* 437–38.
26. Al Schwartz, interview with the author, Los Angeles, December 5, 2006.
27. Bob Jones, telephone interview with the author, April 14, 2006.
28. Jerry Hellman, telephone interview with the author, August 2, 2006.
29. Robert Downey Sr., interview with the author, New York, January 3, 2006.
30. Young and Bruns, "Hal Ashby: Satisfaction in Being There," 96–97.
31. "Morning Report," *Los Angeles Times,* December 30, 1988.
32. Hal Ashby memorial service, December 30, 1988.
33. Ibid.
34. Ibid.
35. Ibid.

Index

Made in the USA
Columbia, SC
04 May 2024

35277759R00262